HEALTH BEHAVIOR CHANGE: THEORIES, METHODS AND INTERVENTIONS

We live in an era where people live longer but also suffer from more chronic illnesses. Yet these two issues present not only significant challenges to healthcare professionals, but also governments seeking cost-effective ways to manage their health and social care budgets. Encouraging people to live healthier lifestyles is, therefore, a fundamental issue for both those at risk as well as for society as a whole.

This is the first textbook to present not only the theoretical foundations that explain health behavior change but also the methods by which change can be assessed and the practical contexts where theory and method can be applied. Covering behavior change aimed at improving health as well as preventing disease, it places these issues firmly in context with the social and demographic changes which make it so important, from the rise in levels of obesity to an aging population. The book considers the role of individuals but also other important influences on health behavior, such as the environment in which people live, public policy and technological changes.

Fostering a critical perspective, and including case studies in each chapter with key issues highlighted throughout, the book provides a complete understanding of health behavior change, from its theoretical building blocks to the practical challenges of developing and testing an intervention. It will be essential reading for students and researchers of health psychology, public health and social work, as well as any professional working in this important area.

Andrew Prestwich is Senior Lecturer in Health & Social Psychology at the University of Leeds, UK. His research examines the impact of theory-based interventions on health behavior. He has previously held posts at the University of Oxford, University of Essex and University College London.

Jared Kenworthy is Associate Professor of Psychology at the University of Texas at Arlington, USA. His research concerns social categorization and social influence in group processes, as well as intergroup relations and prejudice reduction. Before his post at the University of Texas at Arlington, he held a post-doctoral research position at the University of Oxford, and studied the development of inter-community trust in Northern Ireland.

Mark Conner is Professor of Applied Social Psychology at the University of Leeds, UK. His research focuses on understanding and changing health behaviors with a focus on the role of affect, attitudes and intentions. He has published over 200 papers and edited a number of books in this area.

HEALTH BEHAVIOR CHANGE

THEORIES, METHODS AND INTERVENTIONS

ANDREW PRESTWICH, JARED KENWORTHY
AND MARK CONNER

Routledge
Taylor & Francis Group

LONDON AND NEW YORK

First published 2018
by Routledge
2 Park Square, Milton Park, Abingdon, Oxon OX14 4RN

and by Routledge
711 Third Avenue, New York, NY 10017

Routledge is an imprint of the Taylor & Francis Group, an informa business

British Library Cataloguing in Publication Data
A catalogue record for this book is available from the British Library

Library of Congress Cataloging in Publication Data
Names: Prestwich, Andrew, 1978- author. | Kenworthy, Jared, 1973- author. |
Conner, Mark, 1962- author.
Title: Health behavior change : theories, methods and interventions /
Andrew Prestwich, Jared Kenworthy, and Mark Conner.
Description: Abingdon, Oxon ; New York, NY : Routledge, 2018. | Includes
bibliographical references.
Identifiers: LCCN 2017033220 (print) | LCCN 2017035336 (ebook) |
ISBN 9781315527215 (master ebook) | ISBN 9781315527208 (web pdf) |
ISBN 9781315527192 (epub) | ISBN 9781315527185 (mobipocket) |
ISBN 9781138694811 (hbk) | ISBN 9781138694828 (pbk)
Subjects: | MESH: Health Behavior
Classification: LCC RA776 (ebook) | LCC RA776 (print) | NLM W 85 |
DDC 613—dc23
LC record available at https://lccn.loc.gov/2017033220

ISBN: 978-1-138-69481-1 (hbk)
ISBN: 978-1-138-69482-8 (pbk)
ISBN: 978-1-315-52721-5 (ebk)

Typeset in Bembo
by Keystroke, Neville Lodge, Tettenhall, Wolverhampton

DEDICATION

This book is written in memory of Colin John Maher who always wanted to write a book but never had the opportunity to do so, and is also dedicated to our partners Karen, Mary Kate and Sarah.

CONTENTS

1

CHAPTER 1
INTRODUCTION

> Behavior is strong or weak because of many different variables, which it is the task of a science of behavior to identify and classify.
>
> (Skinner, 1953, p. 71)

The idea that the behaviors we engage in might influence our health is not a new one. Over 40 years ago the Alameda County study followed nearly 7,000 people for a period of over 10 years and found that seven key behaviors were associated with increased levels of illness and shorter life expectancy (or morbidity and mortality as they are referred to in the research literature). The behaviors were smoking, high levels of alcohol intake, lack of exercise, being overweight, snacking, not eating breakfast and sleeping less than 7 to 8 hours per night (Belloc & Breslow, 1972; Breslow & Enstrom, 1980). These behaviors (like smoking) and outcomes (like being overweight) are therefore, literally, a matter of illness and death.

Since the Alameda study a large number of studies have confirmed these sorts of associations for various health promoting and health risking behaviors. Most of these studies are conducted by epidemiologists or public health specialists and involve large numbers of people who are followed over a number of years and relate earlier behavior with later health outcomes like illness and death. So, for example, studies might look at the relationship between consumption of dietary fiber as reported by study participants at the beginning of the study with incidence of bowel cancer in the same individuals many years later. These studies, in order to achieve a clearer view of the relationship between dietary fiber and bowel cancer, will take into account, statistically, various other known influences on bowel cancer. The role of behavioral science has usually been in terms of understanding why individuals do or do not engage in these behaviors and how we might change these behaviors.

To foster the understanding of these behaviors, including the factors that can influence them, several **theories** have emerged. These theories specify the relationships between **constructs** (variables influencing behavior). In doing so, they provide suggestions about which targets (i.e., constructs) to try to change through intervention in order to change health behavior. In a recent book, Michie, West, Campbell, Brown and Gainforth (2014) identified 83 theories – many of which overlap in some way by specifying some of the same or similar constructs. In Chapter 2, we overview and evaluate several of the most commonly used theories related to health behavior change.

Theories can be useful not just because they indicate constructs that should be targeted for intervention but because some theories also specify *how* these constructs should be changed. For instance, Bandura (1977) outlines different ways in which **self-efficacy** for a particular behavior can be enhanced and these have been integrated within Social Cognitive Theory – a popular theory which we introduce and evaluate in Chapter 2. In Chapter 3, we describe different **behavior change techniques (BCTs)** that can be used to change health behavior. Behavior change techniques are important aspects of interventions that represent what is done to the target participants or groups in order to facilitate behavior change. We also highlight **behavior change taxonomies** which define and standardize behavior change techniques. These are important because they provide a common language helping researchers to apply the same technique and describe them in the same way in scientific papers. This makes it easier for researchers to combine the results of equivalent studies together to provide new insights regarding which behavior change techniques work and when, as well as identifying techniques that often do not work.

Theories also provide useful frameworks within which to accumulate evidence regarding health behavior change. Like taxonomies of behavior change techniques, theories provide a common language to describe different constructs and their impact on health behavior. Studies that test a particular theory can, in principle, be combined with other studies that do likewise in order to identify which theories are particularly useful and when. To do this, however, researchers need to ensure that their interventions are sufficiently theory-based so that the theory is applied and tested appropriately. Chapter 4 describes and discusses theory-based interventions and illustrates how a theory-based intervention can be designed and evaluated.

On the topic of research design and evaluation, in Chapter 5 we cover research methods and in Chapter 6 we cover statistical analyses that are used to evaluate health behavior change interventions. Different methodologies have various strengths and weaknesses that have an impact on the overall quality of the evidence provided by any particular study. While there is no such thing as a perfect study, applying rigorous methods and appropriate statistics serve to minimize bias, enhance the quality of evidence and are fundamental aspects of a scientific approach to health behavior change. The scientific approach to health behavior change and how it is considered within this book are illustrated in Figure 1.1. In this diagrammatic representation, the cyclical nature of the scientific process to health behavior change is emphasized given the need to continuously use the best available evidence to refine and improve the better theories and to discard the theories that are of little use.

All sorts of behaviors are now known to influence health. These can usefully be split into **health promotion** and **health risk behaviors**, as well as **health checking behaviors**. Health promotion behaviors include things such as exercise, healthy eating, vaccination against disease, condom use in response to the threat of HIV/AIDS and compliance with medical regimens. Health risk behaviors include smoking and excessive alcohol consumption. Health checking behaviors include attending for health screening (e.g., for various types of cancer like cervical cancer and bowel cancer) and self-examination behaviors like breast or testicular self-examination.

A unifying theme across these different health behaviors is that each of them has immediate or longer-term effects upon the individual's health and are at least partially within the individual's control (see Burning Issue Box 1.1). Mark, one of the authors of this book, loves to exercise and is careful that he eats healthy foods. However, he is partial to the odd alcoholic beverage. So Mark's health may benefit from his exercise and eating behaviors and also be harmed by his drinking, but in each case he has control over whether he performs each of these behaviors. Given the large amount of research on

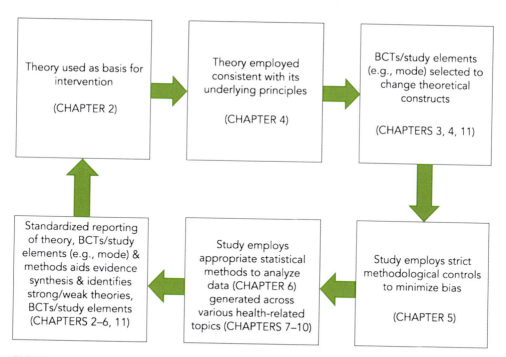

FIGURE 1.1 Scientific approach to health behavior change (and its coverage by chapter) Note: BCTs = Behavior change techniques.

health behaviors, we devote Chapter 7 to examining health promoting behaviors (and health check behaviors) and Chapter 8 to health risk behaviors. Most of this research focuses on individual occasions of performing a behavior like healthy eating. However, we should remember that the health consequences of healthy eating are usually based on performing the same behavior (e.g., choosing an apple over chocolate for a snack) over many occasions and over prolonged periods of time.

Various features of the environment such as the size of a plate or drinking glass, menus in restaurants, positioning of food and drink products in supermarkets, displays next to steps or elevators can influence our behavior in relatively automatic ways. In addition, policymakers can influence our behavior for instance through mandating warning labels on the front of cigarette packets, by banning smoking in public places or by taxing heavily unhealthy foods or sugary drinks. These environmental and policy-relevant influences on health behavior are covered in Chapter 9.

As well as an increased awareness around the role of the environment and the impact of different policies on health behaviors and outcomes, the last few years have also seen rapid technological developments that can be used to measure or track health behaviors, as well as to change them. As such, it is only right and proper that our penultimate chapter (Chapter 10) considers the role of technology in health behavior change interventions. Chapter 11 draws the book to a close by highlighting three broad themes that represent key challenges for future research: identifying and characterizing factors that influence intervention success; achieving health behavior change at a population level to address significant challenges to global health; accelerating the progress made by the science of health behavior change.

BURNING ISSUE BOX 1.1

HOW HEALTH BEHAVIORS INFLUENCE HEALTH OUTCOMES

All sorts of behaviors influence health. These range from health-enhancing behaviors such as exercise participation and healthy eating, to health-protective behaviors such as vaccination against disease and condom use in response to the threat of HIV/AIDS. They also include health-detection behaviors such as health screening clinic attendance and breast/testicular self-examination, and avoidance of health-harming behaviors such as smoking and excessive alcohol consumption. Finally they include sick-role behaviors such as compliance with medical regimens. A key question is how these behaviors influence health but to answer that question we also need to define health behaviors.

Several definitions of health behaviors have been suggested, including:

- 'any activity undertaken by a person believing himself to be healthy for the purpose of preventing disease or detecting it at an asymptomatic stage' (Kasl & Cobb, 1966, p. 246);
- 'any activity undertaken for the purpose of preventing or detecting disease or for improving health and well-being' (Conner & Norman, 2015, p. 2).

Behaviors encompassed in these definitions include medical service usage (e.g., physician visits, vaccination, screening), compliance with medical regimens (e.g., dietary, diabetic, anti-hypertensive regimens) and self-directed health behaviors (e.g., diet, exercise, breast or testicular self-examination, brushing and flossing teeth, smoking, alcohol consumption and contraceptive use).

These different health behaviors influence our health (morbidity and mortality) through three major pathways (Baum & Posluszny, 1999):

- generating direct biological changes such as when smoking cigarettes damages the lungs;
- changing exposure to health risks, as when the use of a sunscreen protects against skin cancer;
- ensuring early detection and treatment of disease, as when attending screening appointments leads to early detection of a cancer that can more easily be treated.

BOOK FEATURES

The book is separated into two parts. In the first part, we introduce the reader to the scientific approach underpinning health behavior change research. This involves the application of theory (Chapter 2) and behavior change techniques (Chapter 3) in the form of theory-based interventions (Chapter 4); adopting a strong methodological approach that minimizes the risk of bias that can unduly influence the findings of the study (Chapter 5) and applying appropriate statistical methods to evaluate the data (Chapter 6). The second part of the book focuses on the application of this scientific approach to different types of behaviors and contexts: health promotion behaviors (Chapter 7); health risk behaviors (Chapter 8); the environment and policy (Chapter 9) and technology (Chapter 10).

In this book, we use three core features: the Critical Skills Toolkit; Science of Health Behavior Change: In Action; and Burning Issue Boxes. The Critical Skills Toolkit is applied in the first part of the text, while the Science of Health Behavior Change: In Action feature is used in the second part of the text. The other features are applied across the book.

CRITICAL SKILLS TOOLKIT

Being critical is not a bad thing. In fact, it is a really good thing when done constructively because it challenges the status quo and can lead to refinements, improvements and innovation. Health behavior change needs to be underpinned by good science and good science needs criticism (as well as a rigorous, systematic approach). In our experience, being critical is something that people can find difficult, not necessarily because of politeness but more because they are unsure where to start. In this book, our aim is to arm the reader with a set of generic critical thinking skills that can be applied systematically to evaluate studies testing health behavior change interventions. As such, the reader can develop the ability to evaluate the strength of the evidence provided by any particular study.

SCIENCE OF HEALTH BEHAVIOR CHANGE: IN ACTION

This feature illustrates how the scientific approach overviewed in the first part of the text, as well as the critical thinking skills developed via the Critical Skills Toolkit, can be applied to evaluate specific studies. As such, it is designed to illustrate how the reader can apply a systematic and rigorous approach to evaluating research concerning health behavior change.

BURNING ISSUE BOXES

In this feature we introduce important issues that are critical to the discipline, being addressed by recent research or need to be examined more in the future. In some instances, this feature complements the main text by examining an issue in more detail; in other instances, the feature supplements the main text by covering a distinct topic.

OTHER FEATURES

In addition to the features already described, plus chapter overviews and summaries, each chapter directs the reader to further readings which expand on some of the issues that we introduce in the text. Moreover, key terms are emphasized in bold and defined within a glossary section.

_____

FURTHER READING

The rest of this book! In Chapter 1, we couldn't really recommend anything else. But maybe we're biased.

_____

GLOSSARY

Behavior change taxonomy: a classification system that represents and defines a set of behavior change techniques.

Behavior change technique (BCT): a systematic strategy used in an attempt to change behavior (e.g., providing information on consequences; prompting specific goal setting; prompting barrier identification; modeling the behavior; planning social support).

Construct: a key concept or building block within a theory/model.

Health promotion behaviors: behaviors that help protect or maintain health when engaged in. These include things such as exercise, healthy eating, vaccination against disease, condom use in response to the threat of HIV/AIDS and compliance with medical regimens. **Health checking**

behaviors also serve to protect or maintain health by looking for signs of ill health. These include attending for health screenings (e.g., for various types of cancer such as bowel cancer or cervical cancer) and self-examinations (e.g., breast or testicular self-examinations). These behaviors are normally distinguished from **health risk behaviors** where performance is associated with damage or risk to health (e. g., smoking, drinking alcohol).

Self-efficacy: belief in one's capability to successfully execute the recommended courses of action/behaviors.

Theory: 'a set of interrelated concepts, definitions and propositions that present a *systematic* view of events or situations by specifying relations among variables, in order to *explain* or *predict* the events or situations' (Glanz, Rimer & Viswanath, 2015, p. 26).

_____

REFERENCES

Bandura, A. (1977). Self-efficacy: toward a unifying theory of behavioral change. *Psychological Review, 84,* 191–215.

Baum, A. & Posluszny, D.M. (1999). Health psychology: mapping biobehavioral contributions to health and illness, *Annual Review of Psychology, 50,* 137–163.

Belloc, N.B. & Breslow, L. (1972). Relationship of physical health status and health practices. *Preventive Medicine, 9,* 409–421.

Breslow, L. & Enstrom, J.E. (1980). Persistence of health habits and their relationship to mortality. *Preventive Medicine, 9,* 469–483.

Conner, M. & Norman, P. (2015). *Predicting and Changing Health Behaviour: Research and Practice with Social Cognition Models* (3rd edn). Maidenhead, UK: Open University Press.

Glanz, K., Rimer, B.K. & Viswanath, K. (2015). Theory, research and practice in health behavior. In K. Glanz, B.K. Rimer & K. Viswanath (Eds.), *Health Behavior: Theory Research & Practice* (5th edn; pp. 24–40). San Francisco: Jossey-Bass.

Kasl, S.V. & Cobb, S. (1966) Health behavior, illness behavior and sick role behavior. *Archives of Environmental Health, 12,* 246–266.

Michie, S., West, R., Campbell, R., Brown, J. & Gainforth, H. (2014). *ABC of Behaviour Change Theories.* London: Silverback Publishing.

Skinner, B.F. (1953). *Science and Human Behavior.* New York: The Free Press.

2

CHAPTER 2
THEORY

OVERVIEW

Think of **theory** as the 'General.' Essentially it chooses its soldiers (**constructs** – or components of theory) and demands how these soldiers are organized. Specifically, the General will decide the rank of the soldier (its proximity to the key **outcome** – in health behavior change, this really is health behavior but could be improved health) as well as how the different soldiers should communicate with, or relate to, other soldiers under the General's control. If you don't want to talk about Generals and soldiers, perhaps you could draw upon a more formal definition of theory such as this: 'A theory presents a systematic way of understanding events or situations. It is a set of concepts, definitions, and propositions that explain or predict these events or situations by illustrating the relationships between variables' (Glanz & Rimer, 2005, p. 4).

Over time, theories should be developed, tested and, on the basis of the results, refined into a better theory (or a more informed, efficient and practical General . . .). This is how the science of health behavior change, and science in general, progresses. As Clarke (1987) expresses, applying theory leads both to 'a steadily richer and more potent picture of how things work' (p. 35) and to the refinement of the theory in question.

In Chapter 4, we will examine how theory can be used to develop interventions to change behavior. However, what are these theories? Which theories are the most popular in health behavior change? What are their strengths and weaknesses? After overviewing some of the more classic theories, we describe and evaluate more recent theories relevant to health behavior change. Towards the end of the chapter, we consider the issue of behavior change maintenance, as well as looking at dual-process models that bring automatic processes more strongly to the forefront of health behavior change. We focus our attention on more general theories that can be applied across several health behaviors (and indeed outside the domain of health) rather than models that have been designed for one specific type of behavior (such as drinking or smoking). Although such models exist, they have typically been researched much less often than the theories that we do highlight in this chapter.

CLASSIC THEORIES OF BEHAVIOR CHANGE

OPERANT LEARNING THEORY (SKINNER, 1953)

According to this theory, the likelihood or frequency at which a behavior is performed in the future is strongly influenced by the consequences of the behavior. If the consequences are positive then the behavior is more likely to be repeated in the future; if the consequences are negative then the behavior is less likely to be repeated. These positive and negative consequences can be manipulated by the addition or removal of reinforcers (to increase behaviors) or punishment (intended to reduce behaviors).

Positive reinforcers involve the pairing of something desirable or rewarding with the behavior. For instance, Andrew (one of the authors of this book) uses a sticker chart to reinforce good behavior by his young daughter Milla. If Milla behaves well (e.g., helps to tidy the house or walks to the shops instead of insisting that she's too tired and wants to be carried – both behaviors linked to being more physically active) she receives a sticker to add to her chart (see Figure 2.1a). These reinforcers do not need to delivered by a person – they can occur through other aspects of the environment. For instance, Andrew's youngest child, Sonny, has recently started to use a 'Jumperoo' (see Figure 2.1b) which encourages jumping by eliciting sounds, music and lights after he jumps! Negative reinforcers involve the removal of something aversive (such as Milla tidying her room to prevent Andrew from nagging her). Positive punishment involves the introduction of a new stimulus to reduce the undesired behavior (such as Milla being told off if she is grumbling too much), while negative punishment reduces the undesired behavior by removing a desired stimulus. Returning to the sticker chart, if Milla is naughty then a sticker is removed from her chart!

a. Milla's sticker chart

b. Sonny and his Jumperoo

FIGURE 2.1 Operant Learning Theory in practice. Milla's sticker chart (Figure 2.1a): a tried and tested example of positive reinforcement (and negative punishment . . .). Sonny's Jumperoo uses sounds, music and lights as positive reinforcers to encourage jumping (Figure 2.1b)

Over time, when reinforcers are no longer provided for a particular behavior, the frequency at which the behavior occurs should reduce through a process termed operant extinction. If the behavior had been reinforced a lot prior to extinction then the process of extinction may be slow; if the behavior had only been reinforced a few times prior then extinction will occur much more rapidly.

The reinforcement can be delivered for every instance of the desired behavior or intermittently. Generally, intermittent reinforcement leads to more persistent responding than rewarding every instance of desired behavior; intermittent reinforcement also leads to slower rates of extinction. Thus, Milla does not receive stickers for every instance of good behavior!

According to Skinner (1953), punishment is generally less effective than reinforcement; punishment – even when severe and sustained – is argued to lead only to a temporary suppression of the undesired behavior. It can also generate negative emotions including fear, anxiety, rage or frustration that can lead to illness. As such, alternatives to punishment are recommended. These include a) do nothing (e.g., if a child going through a developmental phase then they should grow out of it); b) avoid situations which can elicit the undesired behavior (e.g., if a person smokes cigarettes only in bars then the person should avoid bars if they want to quit smoking); c) undergo extinction (e.g., Milla's undesired behaviors could be ignored if the attention paid by Andrew is encouraging the behavior, so that Milla is no longer reinforced by the attention); d) condition incompatible behaviors using positive reinforcement (e.g., reward instances in which Milla is calm when otherwise she may have become frustrated or upset).

SOCIAL LEARNING THEORY (BANDURA, 1971)

Behaviorism, which incorporates operant conditioning, sees behavior as being determined by the environment and, in particular, one's own direct experiences with the consequences of responses. Social Learning Theory differs from Operant Learning Theory by describing a reciprocal determinism between the environment and a person's behavior such that they influence each other. Moreover, it differs because the theory notes that, as well as learning by direct experience, behavior can be learned vicariously by observing others and seeing the consequences of these actions. As an example, Milla used to be scared of going down large slides before observing her dad go down a few times first (without injury and enjoying himself! See Figure 2.2a). As illustrated by this example, the consequences can be behavioral or emotional. She has also learned more complex climbing behaviors by observing older children engaging in such behaviors over a period of time (see Figures 2.2b and 2.2c).

Key elements of the theory include: attention (exposing people to models [people] to help guide their behavior is only useful if the individual pays attention to the model and people pay more attention to certain models than others such as those with desirable qualities); retention (the individual needs to have some memory of observing others to be influenced by their behavior in the future and such memories can be strengthened by rehearsing the sequence of behavior either mentally or behaviorally); motor responses (the individual

a. Milla observes dad

b. Younger Milla

FIGURE 2.2 Social Learning Theory in practice. Milla observes her dad go down a big slide in the local park (Figure 2.2a) and masters climbing after observing older children (Figures 2.2b and 2.2c)

c. Older Milla

must possess the sub-skills needed to put together the behavioral sequence; if not then the sub-skills need to be developed first through modeling and practice); and reinforcement/ motivation. The consequences for other people can serve to increase the behavior for the observer when the consequences are positive (vicarious rewards) or reduce the likelihood of behavior for the observer when the consequences are negative (vicarious punishment). Thus, the same behavior that is observed in others may not be performed by the observer; if they paid insufficient attention to the actions, failed to retain the information, they do not possess the relevant skills or there is insufficient reinforcement or motivation.

Social Learning Theory also acknowledges that people can make use of their cognitive abilities – for instance they can foresee the probable consequences (good or bad) of different actions and use this to guide their behavior. They can also learn about behavioral consequences through verbal or other types of communication so they do not need to try everything for themselves first! Furthermore, people can self-regulate their behavior. They can do this, in keeping with Social Learning Theory, by trying to change or alter the stimuli or cues preceding behavior and/or the consequences of their behavior.

Together Operant Learning Theory and Social Learning Theory have influenced many of the theories considered in the next section of this chapter, as well as a number of **behavior change techniques (BCTs)** considered in Chapter 3 such as the use of financial incentives. In the next section, we consider more recent theories related to health behavior change. While we are unable to cover all theories, we have tried to describe and evaluate many of the most popular and often-used theories used within the field.

MODELS OF SOCIAL/HEALTH COGNITION

These more recent theories of behavior each comprise a number of constructs which are interrelated with one another and are linked either directly, or indirectly (via other constructs), with behavior. They are essentially models of prediction having been built predominantly upon correlational research (see Chapters 5 and 6 for more information about correlational research).

In this type of research, participants typically complete questionnaires assessing each of the constructs, or components, of the model. For example, to test the Theory of Planned Behavior, participants would complete questionnaire items assessing an individual's attitudes towards the behavior (e.g., 'My using condoms is: good-bad, beneficial-harmful' etc.), subjective norms (e.g., 'My friends would approve of my using condoms': strongly agree-strongly disagree), perceived behavioral control (e.g., 'If I wanted to, I am capable of using condoms'), intentions (e.g., 'I will use condoms') and behavior (e.g., 'I use condoms'). Responses on these questionnaires are subsequently analyzed such that the correlations, or relationships, between them can be assessed. If the correlations between the constructs are such that they explain lots of variance in behavior (see Critical Skills Toolkit 2.1) then the model is said to be useful in understanding behavior and that it has a good level of predictive validity (see Chapter 5 for overview of predictive validity).

Across the theories, there are several instances where the same (or similar) constructs appear in several theories (e.g., intention/motivation, perceived behavioral control/self-efficacy) suggesting that these are important constructs. However, each model has some element that makes it unique from the other theories. Each theory in this section is a model of social/health cognition containing constructs that underlie one's motivation to perform a particular behavior. They can be used to differentiate between those individuals that perform the behavior in question and those that do not.

Is one theory better than another? This is an interesting question for which there is no definitive answer. Each model has its own strengths and weaknesses which are highlighted in the following section. One way in which models can be compared is on the amount of variance that the model explains in behavior (see Critical Skills Toolkit 2.1).

CRITICAL SKILLS TOOLKIT 2.1

THE CONCEPT OF EXPLAINING VARIANCE AND THE TRADE-OFF BETWEEN PARSIMONY AND EXPLAINING MORE VARIANCE

Imagine a box representing all the reasons why people exceed the driving speed limit. The more reasons you put into the box, the more the box fills up (in other words, the more variables in your model of behavior, the more variance in speeding you explain).

The more variance your model explains, the more you might understand why somebody exceeds the driving speed limit, or at least the factors associated with their speeding (meaning your model gets better and so you can use it to make better [more reliable/accurate] predictions). If your model explained 100% of variance in speeding, then you'd be able to use your model to perfectly predict how much any individual speeds.

In model 1 (comprising only what a person intends to do [i.e., intentions]), intentions explain 15% of the variance in speeding – so your box becomes 15% full (see below).

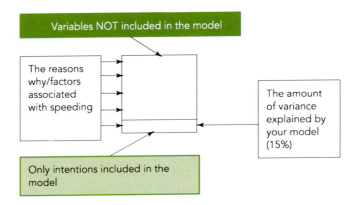

MODEL 1 Intentions as a predictor of speeding

In model 2 (comprising what a person intends to do [i.e., intentions] and their perceived behavioral control [PBC; the extent to which the individual feels that they have the capabilities to enact the behavior], 35% of the variance in speeding is explained – so your box becomes 35% full (see below). Obviously, you can never explain more than 100% variance in your outcome variable, so variance explained will always be in the range 0–100%.

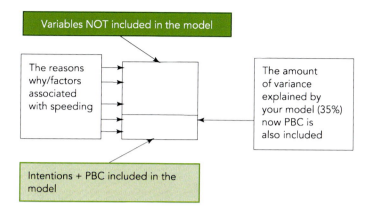

MODEL 2 Intentions and PBC as predictors of speeding

Please note that this doesn't necessarily mean that intentions explain 15% of variance in speeding in total, and PBC explains 20% in total – remember intentions and PBC will correlate with each other to some extent – thus, they *share some variance*. You know that intention and PBC together explain 35% of variance and that PBC explains 20% of *unique* variance (i.e., the variance that isn't explained by intentions). The aim of developing models, conceptually speaking, is to fill up this box by explaining more and more *unique* variance (i.e., the proportion of variance in speeding that is unexplained by the other predictors in the model) because by doing so, we can predict with more accuracy the amount that an individual speeds when they drive.

However, there is a trade-off. If we measure more and more variables then we'd explain more variance in speeding (which is good). However, measuring lots of variables (or manipulating lots of variables) is cumbersome and time consuming, and makes our model of prediction really complex (which is bad). Ideally, your model of prediction would explain most of the variance in the outcome (dependent) variable using as few variables as possible (i.e., it has parsimony).

So, to critique models or theories, ask yourself the following questions:

1. Does the model explain large portions of variance in key outcomes such as behavior?
2. Is the model parsimonious (i.e., it explains lots of variance in key outcomes using few variables) or does it contain variables that relate only weakly to key outcomes and other variables in the model?
3. Are any important variables missing such as those which would explain large portions of variance in key outcomes?

THEORY OF PLANNED BEHAVIOR (TPB; AJZEN, 1991)

The TPB, considered also in Chapters 4 and 7–9, is a model that can be used to predict an individual's behavior. According to the TPB, the direct precursor to behavior is one's underlying behavioral intentions (the degree to which an individual is ready and willing to try to perform the behavior). One's behavioral intentions are jointly determined by one's attitudes towards the behavior (whether the individual views their own performance of the behavior as positive or negative), subjective norms (whether the individual perceives other people – who are important to the individual such as friends and family – would approve of their engaging in the behavior) and PBC. As well as predicting one's intentions, PBC also moderates the link between intentions and behavior such that intentions are more likely to lead to behavior when an individual possesses high (rather than low) levels of PBC. This model is outlined in Figure 2.3. It originates from the Theory of Reasoned Action (TRA; Ajzen & Fishbein, 1980). The key difference between the two models is the inclusion of PBC in the TPB.

The TPB has been widely tested and successfully applied to the understanding of a variety of behaviors (for reviews see Ajzen, 1991; Armitage & Conner, 2001). For example, in a meta-analysis of the TPB (Armitage & Conner, 2001) intentions emerged as the strongest predictors of behavior, while attitudes were the strongest predictors of intentions. In a recent review of experimental studies, Steinmetz, Knappstein, Ajzen, Schmidt and Kabst (2016) reported that behavior change interventions based on the TPB generate medium sized effects ($d = .50$, see Chapter 6 for an explanation of effect sizes).

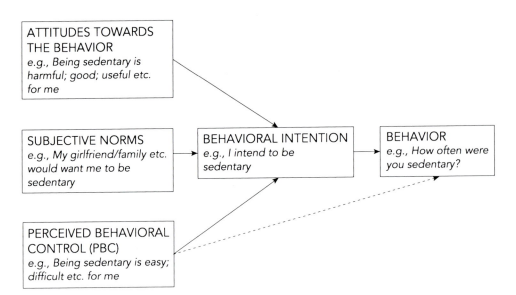

FIGURE 2.3 Theory of Planned Behavior applied to being sedentary (dashed line denotes that PBC directly predicts behavior when it reflects actual behavioral control)

BURNING ISSUE BOX 2.1

ADVANTAGES AND DISADVANTAGES OF THE THEORY OF PLANNED BEHAVIOR

Advantages

1. Many studies support the model (however, these studies are primarily correlational providing evidence for the model as a model of *predicting* behavior).
2. Clear definitions of constructs.
3. Standardized measures (i.e., clear direction regarding how to measure constructs – see www.midss.org/content/theory-planned-bahaviour-questionnaire).
4. Viewed as a parsimonious model. In other words, it explains relatively high proportions of variance in intentions and behavior with few constructs (see Critical Skills Toolkit 2.1).

Disadvantages

1. It was not designed as a model of behavior *change*. Although an increasing number of studies have tested TPB-based interventions (see review by Steinmetz et al., 2016) it is not clear how many of these interventions target all of the constructs within the TPB.
2. It assumes the influences of many other predictor variables are subsumed by the constructs specified in this model (attitudes, subjective norms, PBC). Recent work suggests that a range of predictors can influence one's underlying intentions and behavior over and above the constructs specified in the TPB (e.g., moral norms, goals etc.). Consequently, other key variables are not specified in the model. Thus, on the flipside of Advantage 4, the model has been argued by Sniehotta, Presseau and Araújo-Soares (2014) and others to be *too* parsimonious.

MODEL OF GOAL-DIRECTED BEHAVIOR (MGB; PERUGINI & BAGOZZI, 2001) AND EXTENDED MODEL OF GOAL-DIRECTED BEHAVIOR (EMGB; PERUGINI & CONNER, 2000)

Many social/health cognition models such as the TPB are not explicit about the role of goals – the reasons why an individual would perform a particular behavior. Instead these models implicitly assume that the effects of goals on behavioral intentions and behavior are subsumed by more proximal **determinants** such as one's perceived behavioral control and attitudes. However, there are more recent models that do not present this single-level view of information processing from goals to behavioral intentions.

Within the EMGB (see Figures 2.4a and 2.4b), in particular, the interplay between goal and behavioral levels is brought into the forefront by considering behaviors in terms of the goals for which they are functional. The EMGB maintains the TPB constructs with attitudes, subjective norms and PBC determining one's behavioral intentions which, in turn, directly predict behavior. However due to the insufficiency of these constructs to

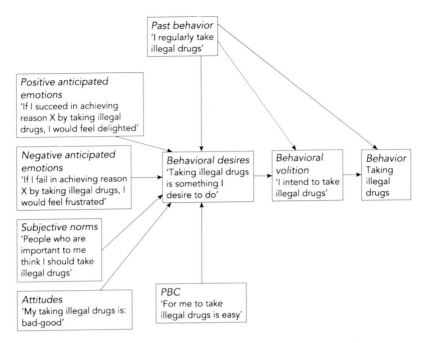

FIGURE 2.4A Model of Goal-Directed Behavior applied to taking illegal drugs

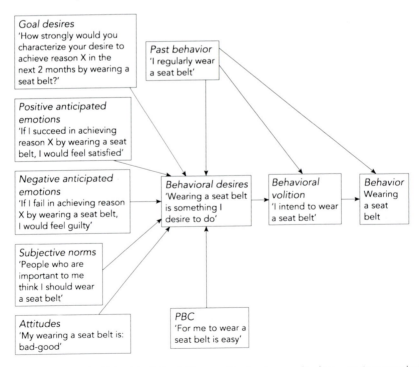

FIGURE 2.4B Extended Model of Goal-Directed Behavior applied to wearing seat belts when travelling by car

fully understand and explain one's intentions (Armitage & Conner, 2001), the EMGB incorporates additional areas of motivation (behavioral desires, goal desires), affect (positive and negative anticipated emotions) and habit (past behavior).

The EMGB and its more succinct version, the MGB (see also Chapter 7), have been successfully applied to the prediction of a range of behaviors such as weight control, studying and learning of statistical software (Leone, Perugini & Ercolani, 2004; Perugini & Bagozzi, 2001; Perugini & Conner, 2000). The constructs within this model typically explain around 30% more variance in intentions than the TPB. In part, this is attributable to having more constructs in the EMGB than the TPB (more constructs mean that it is likely more variance will be explained).

Goal desires provide a link between one's goals and intentions (e.g., 'I desire to achieve goal Y by performing behavior X'), and represent one factor that explains the additional variance. Moreover, in a series of studies by Prestwich, Perugini and Hurling (2008) it was shown that goal desires moderate the relationship between intentions and behavior (see Chapter 6 for an explanation of moderation). This means that depending on whether an individual has a strong desire to achieve a particular goal (e.g., to be healthy) by performing the target behavior (e.g., exercise) or weak desire will influence the relationship between intentions and behavior. Specifically, if an individual has a strong goal desire then they are likely to act on their intentions (thus there will be correspondence between intentions and behavior). If the underlying goal desire is weak, it is less likely that having strong intentions will lead to an individual performing the behavior. Here are a couple of examples:

1. Many female smokers intend to quit smoking but find it very difficult. Rates of quitting smoking increase when women become pregnant – in other words they become more likely to act on their intentions. This is, in no small part, due to having the goal desire to protect the unborn baby by stopping smoking.

2. If you live in the UK, you'll know that travelling by train in the UK can be very expensive if you buy your ticket on the day of travel. It can, however, be reasonably priced if you book your ticket in advance. The risk of buying your ticket in advance is that the pre-booked ticket is only valid on that particular service. If you miss the train then you have to buy an expensive on-the-day ticket. Recently Andrew had booked, in advance, a seat on a train from Leeds to London. To catch the train he had to catch a bus from his home to the city center and then walk across the city center to the train station. However, on this particular occasion his bus was late and if he then walked across the city, as opposed to run fast, he would miss his train. He intended to catch that particular train. After getting off the bus he began to run across the city towards the station. He was carrying a (very!) heavy bag and started to feel tired. As a result, he was tempted to stop running and give up on catching the train. At that moment, he remembered his goal of saving money and felt more energized and fulfilled his intention of catching the train. Here is a clear example of how having strong goal desires can help people act on their intentions.

Given this moderating effect of goal desires on intention-behavior relations, the more distal role of goal desires articulated in the EMGB seems to underplay their role. Consequently, the EMGB might be further extended in the future.

BURNING ISSUE BOX 2.2

ADVANTAGES AND DISADVANTAGES OF THE MODEL OF GOAL-DIRECTED BEHAVIOR AND EXTENDED MODEL OF GOAL-DIRECTED BEHAVIOR

Advantages

1. The models give an insight into the process through which attitudes, PBC and other constructs influence intentions. Specifically, the model and its supportive body of literature illustrate that attitudes and other constructs within the model influence intentions by increasing the extent to which the individual wants (desires) to perform the behavior.
2. The MGB/EMGB explain more variance in intentions and behavior than other models such as the TPB.
3. They bring other important constructs, that have been overlooked by other models, to the fore such as goal desires.
4. They provide a useful integration of the influences of motivation, affect and habit on behavior.

Disadvantages

1. The model has fewer (correlational) studies that have tested the model than other models.
2. It was not designed as a model of behavior *change*. Like other models such as the TPB, it is primarily a model of prediction.
3. There have been no experimental tests of the MGB or EMGB and it lacks studies that have tested how it might inform interventions.
4. While it highlights the role of goal desires, it seems that the goal desires can have a more proximal effect on behavior.
5. Given the number of constructs incorporated in the EMGB, in particular, developing behavior change interventions that are faithful to the model as a whole would be complex.

PROTECTION MOTIVATION THEORY (PMT; ROGERS, 1983)

At a basic level this theory suggests that people engage in two types of appraisal: threat appraisal (how severe a negative outcome is and how vulnerable one is to this negative outcome) and coping appraisal (how effective and easy it is to perform a behavior that will reduce the negative threat). These two appraisals interact to determine one's level of protection motivation (how motivated one is to engage in a behavior that will help to minimize their risk).

This theory has been applied within interventions designed to change behavior. According to this theory, to change behavior, people need to be threatened by feeling vulnerable (perceived vulnerability) to a severe consequence (perceived severity) and then identify a new behavior that one is capable of (self-efficacy), has little cost (response

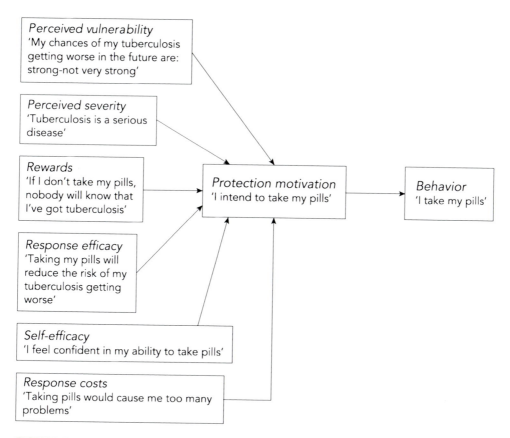

FIGURE 2.5 Protection Motivation Theory

BURNING ISSUE BOX 2.3

ADVANTAGES AND DISADVANTAGES OF THE PROTECTION MOTIVATION THEORY

Advantages

1. Compared to other models, such as the Theory of Planned Behavior (TPB) and the Health Belief Model (HBM), the PMT has been more consistently subjected to experimental (rather than correlational) tests. These tests are useful in helping to determine which constructs cause change (rather than which constructs are related to one another).
2. All threat and coping variables (except response costs), according to Milne, Sheeran and Orbell's (2000) review of PMT, can be manipulated or changed fairly easily through written communications.

Disadvantages

1. Although there have been a number of experimental tests of the PMT, there is little evidence that changing the constructs within the PMT (i.e., threat and coping appraisals) leads to behavior change (the focus has been on identifying which constructs cause change in protection motivation).
2. While the PMT seems to be quite good in predicting ongoing behavior, it does less well when trying to predict how people will act in the future (see Milne et al., 2000).
3. Threat appraisals are not always good predictors of intentions and behavior (coping appraisals tend to be better predictors of intentions and behavior; see Milne et al., 2000). Threat appraisals might be linked to processes that hinder behavior change such as avoidance, feelings of hopelessness or denial. As a consequence, trying to instill a sense of threat, for certain individuals at least, may be a poor behavior change approach.

costs) and is something that is effective at reducing the threat (response efficacy). Interventionists take note: according to this theory, to make people change their health behavior (e.g., start exercising) we need to make people worry about a gruesome illness (e.g., their risk of heart disease) and then present the healthy behavior (e.g., exercise) as an easy to perform, effective means, with little cost, to reduce their risk of the illness.

PMT has been successfully applied to the prediction of a number of behaviors (see Norman, Boer, Seydel & Mullan, 2015). Meta-analytic reviews of PMT (e.g., Milne et al., 2000) indicate intentions and self-efficacy to be the most powerful predictors of behavior, while self-efficacy and response costs were most strongly associated with intentions (see Chapter 6 for more detail about the model).

HEALTH BELIEF MODEL (HBM)

The HBM (see Figure 2.6) is based on a set of core beliefs relating to threat (perceived susceptibility and perceived severity) and perceived benefits (one's belief in the efficacy of the recommended action to reduce the risk or seriousness of the consequence). Sound familiar? In these respects, it is very similar to the PMT. In addition, it has a perceived barriers construct, cues to action (e.g., a close relative dying of a particular illness) and self-efficacy (which was added by Rosenstock, Strecher & Becker, 1988). Chapter 7 provides a further illustration of the model.

In Janz and Becker's (1984) review of 18 prospective studies, of the four core beliefs (perceived severity, perceived vulnerability, benefits, barriers), perceived severity was the least consistent predictor and barriers the most consistent. There is some experimental support for the model. For example, in a review of studies by Jones, Smith and Llewellyn (2014) that used the HBM to develop an intervention to promote adherence behaviors such as adherence to antibiotics or uptake of vaccinations, 14 out of 18 studies demonstrated a significant effect of the intervention; and seven studies produced medium or large effect sizes. However, as is the case for many experimental tests of theory, few studies (only six) targeted all constructs in the HBM (excluding the self-efficacy component added in 1988), and the HBM-based interventions were typically compared against no-intervention or usual care control groups rather than against other theory-based interventions. Thus, whether the interventions benefited from being based on the HBM rather than on any particular theory is not clear.

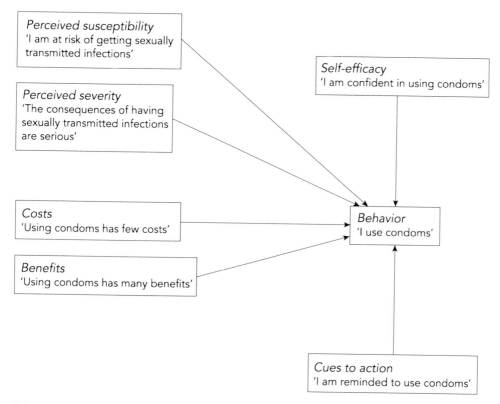

FIGURE 2.6 Health Belief Model

Disadvantages

1. Threat-based models have been criticized as threat is not a consistent determinant of behavior (e.g., Albarracin et al., 2005).
2. Suffers from a lack of clear operational definitions of the constructs within the model (Abraham & Sheeran, 2015).
3. While there are a number of studies showing that the model predicts behavior, the effects tend only to be small (Abraham & Sheeran, 2015).
4. Comparisons across studies are difficult as when the model has been tested, there have been inconsistencies in which constructs have been tested and which have not been tested (Abraham & Sheeran, 2015). Relatedly, not all of the HBM constructs are typically targeted within interventions (Jones et al., 2014).
5. Within analyses, rather than test the individual effects of each construct, authors have sometimes combined constructs (e.g., by adding or multiplying them; Quine, Rutter & Arnold, 1998). These different analytic approaches make it difficult to compare across studies.

SOCIAL COGNITIVE THEORY (SCT; BANDURA, 1997)

The key construct within SCT is self-efficacy which reflects a person's confidence in performing a particular behavior and is linked with one's behavioral capability – the knowledge and skill that an individual has to perform a given behavior. Bandura (1977) has outlined four sources of information that can be used to change self-efficacy:

- *mastery experiences* – having the opportunity to practice a behavior (or sub-set of skills necessary to perform the behavior) and then master them;

- *modeling (vicarious experience)* – observing others successfully perform the behavior;

- *social/verbal persuasion* – others expressing confidence in your ability to perform a particular behavior; remembering positive comments from somebody;

- *physiological experience* – correcting potentially harmful emotional beliefs such as butterflies in the stomach which should be seen as normal/useful.

In a meta-analysis (see Chapter 6 for a detailed look at meta-analyses) examining the best means to change self-efficacy (Ashford, Edmunds & French, 2010), feedback on one's past behavior or the behavior of others, as well as modeling/vicarious experience, were the most effective. Persuasion, mastery experiences and barrier identification were less successful.

The second major construct within the theory are action-outcome expectancies (the outcomes anticipated from the behavior and the extent that one's actions help one to achieve the outcomes). The outcomes could be physical (e.g., get healthier), social (e.g., approval from others) or self-evaluative (e.g., feeling good about oneself), and thus they represent a mixture of attitudinal and subjective norm beliefs.

The third key construct within the model are barriers (including changes to the environment, emotional barriers or perceptions of them). Other variables such as self-control (how well an individual can personally regulate their behavior) and goals have been linked to the theory. Bandura has more recently added socio-structural factors (such as living conditions and health, political, economic and environmental systems) which can impede or facilitate behavior (see Chapter 7 for a more detailed description).

SCT has been successfully applied to predicting various health behaviors, although as yet there is no systematic review of its application to predicting behavior (see Luszczynska & Schwarzer, 2015, for one non-systematic review).

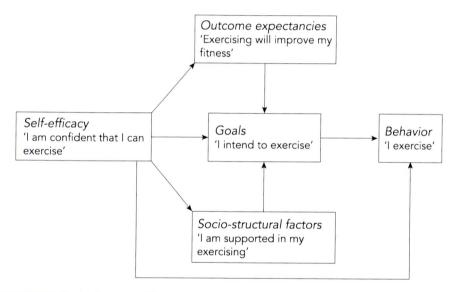

FIGURE 2.7 Social Cognitive Theory

Disadvantages

1. As a number of constructs have been linked to the theory and not all of the constructs within the model are specifically well-defined, this has led to inconsistencies in the testing of the model.
2. This lack of consistency in the implementation of the theory makes it difficult to pool evidence/generalize across studies.
3. Measures of self-efficacy (phrased as whether an individual 'can do' the behavior) have been argued to strongly overlap with or even reflect motivation rather than somebody's perceived capability. As such, authors such as Williams and Rhodes (2016) have argued that self-efficacy may reflect motivation rather than be a factor that determines motivation.

HEALTH ACTION PROCESS APPROACH (HAPA; SCHWARZER, 1992)

There are three key features of the HAPA model that mark it out from many other theories of behavior or behavior change. First, it incorporates (coping and action) planning which helps to bridge the 'intention-behavior gap' (a gap considered in detail later in this chapter). Second, it is a hybrid model between stage- and non-stage-based models. Third, it incorporates three different types of self-efficacy (task, coping and recovery) that predominate at different stages of the behavior change process.

1. Incorporation of planning to reduce the intention-behavior gap

While many other theories of behavior or behavior change specify intention as being a direct predictor of behavior, the HAPA model inserts planning between intention and behavior (see Figure 2.8) to overcome, to some extent, the intention-behavior gap (predominately the problem that people who intend to perform a specific action do not always do it).

According to the model, people who intend to perform an action are more likely to plan how they will act either in the form of action plans or coping plans. It is forming these plans that help an individual to do what they intend to do (in other words, these plans mediate the relationship between intentions and behavior – see Chapter 6, 'Mediation and Moderation').

Within the model, there are two types of plans. When forming action plans, individuals decide the situation (when and where) they will perform a specific behavior (e.g., 'When I'm in my local supermarket, I will buy vegetables'). Coping plans are similar but link specific coping responses to situations that threaten to disrupt one's goal achievement (e.g., 'If I'm shopping and tempted to buy a food high in calories, I will tell myself that I want to stay slim!'). Action plans and coping plans are analogous to implementation intentions considered in Chapters 3 and 7.

The HAPA model (along with other models such as the Model of Action Phases described later in this chapter) posits that forming an intention is not necessarily sufficient to lead to behavior – other (planning) processes are often required. Thus, according to the HAPA, there are distinct phases to achieving one's goal – a goal-setting/motivational phase and a goal-striving/volitional phase.

2. A hybrid model

As well as being described as a two-stage/process model, the HAPA has also been dissected into a three-phase model representing non-intenders, intenders and actors. The constructs relevant to non-intenders are the constructs to the left-hand side of the model (i.e., risk perceptions, outcome expectancies, task self-efficacy and intention – see Figure 2.8). The constructs relevant to intenders are the constructs in the middle of the model (planning, coping self-efficacy, plus task self-efficacy-again!). The constructs relevant to actors are action, recovery self-efficacy, plus coping self-efficacy again! By incorporating such features (see Lippke, Ziegelmann & Schwarzer, 2005), the model flexibly shifts between a non-stage-based model (like the TPB, HBM, PMT etc.) to a stage-based model (like the Transtheoretical Model [TTM] considered later in this chapter).

3. Three types of self-efficacy

As outlined above (and also in Figure 2.8), the model explicitly differentiates between various types of self-efficacy unlike other models that incorporate self-efficacy (such as TTM) or related constructs such as PBC (like the TPB).

• Task (motivational) self-efficacy: one's confidence in being able to start to engage in the behavior even when one doesn't feel like doing the behavior (e.g., lacking in some form of motivation).

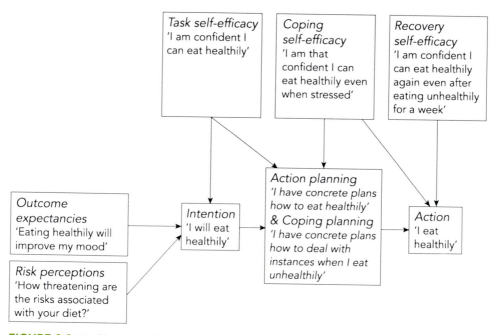

FIGURE 2.8 Health Action Process Approach

- Coping (volitional) self-efficacy: one's confidence in continuing to perform the behavior in instances when time is needed (e.g., when one does not see immediate benefits; or when the behavior takes a while to become routine).

- Recovery self-efficacy: one's confidence in re-engaging in the behavior after setbacks.

BURNING ISSUE BOX 2.6

ADVANTAGES AND DISADVANTAGES OF THE HEALTH ACTION PROCESS APPROACH

Advantages

1. Actively addresses the intention-behavior gap through the inclusion of planning and various forms of self-efficacy.
2. There is some experimental evidence demonstrating that manipulating motivation and planning leads to stronger changes in behavior than manipulating only motivation or only planning components (see review by Prestwich & Kellar, 2014). This supports the premise that there are distinct motivational and volitional components to goal-striving.
3. The maintenance of behavior (change) is often neglected by behavioral scientists who like to focus on promoting behavior (change) – in fairness, it is much more expensive to run studies (particularly experimental studies) targeting behavior change in the long term. However, there is evidence that components of the model not explicitly featured in other models – coping self-efficacy and recovery self-efficacy – are useful in understanding behavior maintenance (Scholz, Sniehotta & Schwarzer, 2005).
4. The stage-based version (more so than the continuum-version) could be seen as good for behavior change interventions. The continuum (non-stage-based) version could be seen as better for predicting behavior.

Disadvantages

1. More experimental tests needed (a lot of the research testing the model has been correlational) to examine whether changes in one construct causes changes in a related construct.
2. To support the stage-based element of the theory, more experimental evidence is needed to show that stage-matched interventions are more effective than stage-mismatched interventions.

RUBICON MODEL/MODEL OF ACTION PHASES (MAP; GOLLWITZER, 1990)

This model shares the stage-based features of other models (e.g., HAPA, Transtheoretical Model [TTM]). The MAP specifies that goal striving has four phases. The *predecisional phase* is represented by a sea of competing wishes and desires. We like to do a lot of different things – sometimes at the same time – but even the best multi-taskers cannot do it all! Conflicting wishes (e.g., wanting to eat tasty food versus wanting a healthy diet) is one thing, lack of time is another. As a friend of Andrew's likes to say, 'There are not enough hours in the day.' Given this, at the predecisional stage, people evaluate the various behavioral options in terms of their feasibility (how easily one can perform the behavior) and desirability (do you want to perform the behavior, or do you really want to perform the behavior). One can only do so much so these evaluations can be useful in helping us to prioritize one goal over another.

After making a decision to act, whereby an individual translates their wishes and desires into a goal intention, an individual 'crosses the Rubicon' and moves into the *preactional phase*. Planning when, where, how to perform the behavior and for how long is important in this phase but only when a smooth transition into the next (actional) phase is not possible due to the presence of various obstacles. One would not need to spend time planning a simple unobstructed behavior.

When the action/behavior is initiated, the individual moves into the *actional phase*. Goal intentions are thought to lead to action initiation when there is a good degree of 'volitional strength' (whether the person is sufficiently committed to the action). However, sometimes things do not go in our favor and no matter how committed we are, the situation may be particularly unfavorable for action (e.g., we may be fully committed to having a break from work but unforeseen work deadlines have a tendency of 'rearing their ugly heads' and make it difficult to take a break). Thus, whether an intention is translated to an action is dependent on commitment and the favorability of the situation. Planning can help when situations are unfavorable or difficult to manage.

In the fourth phase (*postactional phase*), one evaluates whether the goal striving was successful or not. This may be done by judging whether the intended outcome was achieved (though sometimes this can be difficult when there is no objective marker of achievement such as when revising for an exam – 'have I revised sufficiently?'). Moreover, in light of achieving a goal, a process can occur where an individual compares the actual outcomes of the goal against the value that one expected at the onset. If the actual outcome is negatively evaluated then this could reduce the likelihood that the individual continues to work towards the goal.

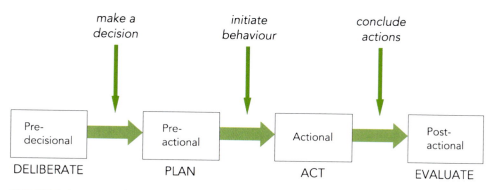

FIGURE 2.9 Model of Action Phases

It is not always necessary to pass through all four stages each time one acts. For instance, when an individual has performed the behavior regularly in the past (or is being resumed from an earlier occasion), they do not need to figure out whether the behavior is feasible or desirable.

BURNING ISSUE BOX 2.7

ADVANTAGES AND DISADVANTAGES OF THE MODEL OF ACTION PHASES

Advantages

1. Incorporates planning elements which can be useful in explaining the intention-behavior gap.
2. By including a postactional phase it can help explain why some behaviors are repeated and others are not.
3. Like the HAPA model, there is evidence suggesting that combining behavior change techniques targeted at motivation and planning are more effective than targeting either motivation or planning constructs.

Disadvantages

1. The stage-based nature of the model leaves it open to similar criticisms as the TTM (see below) such as the arbitrariness of the stages.
2. More experimental tests needed to inform its use for behavior change interventions and to examine the underlying constructs and processes.
3. To support the stage-based element of the theory, more experimental evidence is needed to show that stage-matched interventions are more effective than stage-mismatched interventions.

TRANSTHEORETICAL MODEL (TTM; PROCHASKA & DICLEMENTE, 1983)

The most popular stage-based model, the TTM, proposes five qualitatively distinct stages of behavior change: pre-contemplation (where an individual has not considered performing the behavior), contemplation (where the individual considers the pros and cons of the behavior but has not made formal plans to do so), preparation (where an individual plans and makes preparations for the behavior), action (where an individual has started to perform the behavior, not performing the behavior regularly) and maintenance (this reflects individuals who have sustained behavior change).

Ten processes of change (e.g., rewarding oneself, finding out more about the behavior) have been described as useful techniques to change behavior/move people from one stage to another. Different processes are thought to be useful at different stages. For example, finding out more about the behavior (consciousness raising) should be particularly useful for those in the pre-contemplation stage while rewards (contingency management) should be more useful for those in the action or maintenance phases.

Changes in self-efficacy and decisional balance (one's evaluation of the positive and negative aspects of performing the behavior) underlie the effects of these processes of change and translation from one stage to another. Increasing levels of self-efficacy and an increasingly favorable decisional balance promote positive changes in stages.

BURNING ISSUE BOX 2.8

ADVANTAGES AND DISADVANTAGES OF THE TRANSTHEORETICAL MODEL

Advantages

1. By specifying processes of change, it gives some reasonable guidance regarding how to change behavior.
2. If there are distinct qualitative differences between people at the different stages, it could be used to effectively tailor behavior change interventions to the needs of the individual.

Disadvantages (see West, 2005; West, 2006)

Robert West has argued that the theory does not provide a particularly complete or accurate description of behavior change. So unimpressed with the model, West (2005) has stated 'reverting back to the common sense approach that was used prior to the Transtheoretical Model would [be] better than staying with the model' (p. 1036).

1. It has been argued that there are no stages of change. Instead, by devising stages of behavior change, the theory has taken continuous variables of motivation (desire and ability to change) and chopped it up into separate, arbitrary stages. As a result these stages are unstable and there is a continuous cycle of change.
2. TTM constructs have been argued to be no better than desire or intention as predictors of behavior.
3. The model needs to explain how people can 'change' with sudden, minimal triggers. There is only a small body of evidence looking at the transitions between stages and the factors that underlie them (Armitage, 2006; Armitage, Sheeran, Conner & Arden, 2004).
4. It falsely makes the assumption that people always make formal plans and by focusing on conscious decision-making processes, it neglects more automatic (less conscious) determinants of behavior such as habits.
5. By categorizing people in arbitrary, unstable stages, it gives a false sense of diagnosis. By presenting such a 'diagnosis' the model has been seen by some people as an appealing theory.
6. By describing people as being within a particular stage, it gives the impression that progressing by one step is 'good.' We need to go the 'whole hog,' do the 'Full Monty' and strive for sustained behavior change.

7. It is not clear that basing an intervention on the TTM leads to larger degrees of behavior change. In a review of 37 studies, Bridle et al. (2005) demonstrated that there was little evidence that interventions based on TTM were particularly effective in changing health behaviors. Specifically, of the 37 studies, 35 compared how effective an intervention based on the TTM was in changing health behavior against a non-stage-based intervention or no-intervention control group. In these 35 studies, there were 42 comparisons: 11 comparisons showed a benefit of using the TTM; 20 showed no difference between the intervention based on the TTM and the control; 11 were inconclusive as they showed mixed effects. In addition, according to a review by Conn, Hafdahl, Brown and Brown (2008) interventions based on the TTM were less effective than interventions that were not based on the TTM. A more recent review has shown that interventions based on the TTM (or the SCT) were no more effective than interventions not reporting a theory base (Prestwich et al., 2014).

CRITICAL SKILLS TOOLKIT 2.2

GENERAL CRITICISMS OF THESE HEALTH/SOCIAL COGNITION MODELS

1. They have typically been designed as models of predicting behavior rather than models of behavior change. For example, in their meta-analysis of longitudinal studies concerning the TPB, Sutton and Sheeran (2003, cited in Sheeran, Milne, Webb & Gollwitzer, 2005) reported past behavior explained 26% of variance in future behavior, while intentions explained an additional 7% of variance over and above past behavior. In other words, intentions explain little variance in behavior change.
2. They have been developed with the aim of predicting as much variance in behavior as possible and as such have been built upon correlational rather than experimental evidence. Due to the correlational nature of the data it is not possible to infer causation (see Chapter 5).
3. Few studies have demonstrated *how* these models can be used to inform behavior change *interventions*.
4. The models are not specific about which behavior change techniques should be used to change the theoretical constructs (but see TTM and Bandura, 1977).
5. These models tend to view intentions as the direct precursor of behavior (see 'intention-behavior gap' in the next section of this chapter).
6. None of these models are comprehensive – other constructs can always be added to the model to explain additional variance.
7. Many of the models are difficult to refute (Noar & Zimmerman, 2005). As they are built on correlational evidence, at what point are the intercorrelations between the constructs too weak?
8. These models primarily treat individuals as rational actors in which we consider and subsequently use our explicit cognitions (e.g., PBC, response costs) to direct our behavior which overlooks many of the more automatic processes influencing behavior (see Dual Process Models later in this chapter for an alternative approach).

A COMMON PROBLEM FOR MANY OF THESE THEORIES: THE INTENTION-BEHAVIOR GAP

WHAT IS IT?

According to many of the theories described above, intentions are seen as the main, immediate determinant of behavior and thus there should be a strong relationship between intentions and behavior. In other words, if a person intends to eat healthily then they should eat healthily. Similarly, if a person does not intend to speed while driving then they should not speed.

However, this does not always happen. Sometimes people who do not intend to speed actually do it and sometimes people who intend to eat healthily do not do it. This latter group in particular represent the most common scenario underlying what is called the intention-behavior gap (Orbell & Sheeran, 1998). The intention-behavior gap is a term used to reflect the fact that, sometimes, people do not always do what they intend to do.

WHY DO PEOPLE FAIL TO ACT ON THEIR INTENTIONS?

According to Sheeran et al. (2005) two main factors can influence the likelihood that intentions are translated into behavior. If one's intentions are difficult to activate or they have not been elaborated upon then one is less likely to act on their intentions. *Intention activation* relates to the ease with which contextual demands can change the direction or intensity of the focal intention. If one's intentions are difficult to activate then they may be forgotten or re-prioritized. There is some meta-analytic support for this. Cooke and Sheeran (2004) presented evidence that intentions more strongly predict behavior when intentions are more highly accessible. The second factor, intention elaboration, relates to the degree to which an individual has decided how and when they will realize their intentions. The notion that greater intention elaboration is associated with stronger intention-behavior relations is supported by evidence concerning the efficacy of implementation intentions (see Chapter 3 for a description of implementation intentions and an evaluation of their efficacy) and evidence for their moderating role in intention-behavior relations. For example, Prestwich, Lawton and Conner (2003) demonstrated that participants given an implementation intention intervention combined with an intervention designed to boost their intentions to exercise actually exercised more than those asked only to form implementation intentions, those exposed only to the intervention designed to boost intentions and those allocated to a control group who were not exposed to an intervention.

Cooke and Sheeran (2004) provide a useful review that covers, amongst other things, the moderators that influence the relationship between intentions and behavior. Moderators are variables that influence the strength of the relationship between two other variables (see Chapter 6 for more details). In addition to those noted earlier in this section (e.g., intention accessibility; implementation intentions), moderators of intention-behavior relations include:

- *Intention certainty* – refers to being unbudgeable on an issue (Bassili, 1996).

- *Intention stability* – the extent to which intentions do not change over time – intentions are more strongly associated with behavior when intentions remain stable across time (e.g., Conner, Sheeran, Norman & Armitage, 2000).

- *Anticipated regret* – reflects beliefs regarding whether or not feelings of regret will arise when one fails to act. If one anticipates that they will regret not performing a specific behavior then they are more likely to perform their intended behavior. There are at least three possible reasons for this (Sheeran & Orbell, 1999). First, anticipated regret might increase the accessibility of intentions thus increasing the likelihood that these intentions are activated and subsequently acted upon. Second, anticipated regret could encourage people to plan more how they will act thus influencing intention elaboration, or, third, by associating inactivity with negative affect anticipated regret might bind people to their intentions (see also Abraham & Sheeran, 2003).

- *Goal prioritization* – when the behavior is prioritized over other competing behaviors then intentions are more likely to be predictive of behavior. For example, Conner et al. (2016) demonstrated that a measure of goal priority (e.g., 'I would be prepared to give up many other goals and priorities to exercise vigorously at least three times per week over the next two weeks') influenced the extent to which intentions to exercise vigorously predicted levels of vigorous exercise. Specifically, those individuals who prioritized vigorous exercise over other goals were more likely to follow-through on their intentions to do vigorous exercise.

- *Habits* – when behaviors are performed consistently in the same (non-changing) context then they become habitual and are guided not by conscious decision-making but by automatic processes (Ouellette & Wood, 1998). Consequently, intentions correspond with behavior more strongly when habits are weak than when habits are strong (e.g., Verplanken, Aarts, van Knippenberg & Moonen, 1998).

MODERN APPROACHES

THEORY INTEGRATION

As you can see, there are a large number of theories of behavior – only some of which have been outlined above. A problem one faces when trying to understand, predict or change behavior is which theory should I choose? One way of getting around this problem is to try to integrate these key theories into one 'super-theory.'

There have been two independent attempts, based on expert consensus, that have identified the most important determinants of behavior (Fishbein et al., 2001; Michie et al., 2005). Looking through the overviews of the theories above, you'll notice that a number of constructs (elements within a theory), or very similar constructs (e.g., PBC and self-efficacy; attitudes and outcome expectancies), appear in more than one theory.

This overlap between the theories provides the basis for attempting to combine, or integrate, the theories.

A leading team of psychologists, led by Martin Fishbein, first attempted to identify the key determinants of behavior from the leading theories of health/social behavior (see Figure 2.10). They concluded there were eight key determinants of any behavior:

1. *Intentions*: how committed individuals are to performing the behavior;
2. *Environmental constraints* preventing behavior (e.g., not having sports facilities near to where one lives might be viewed as an environmental constraint hindering exercise);
3. *Skills*: whether the person has the *actual* ability or skills to perform the behavior;
4. *Self-efficacy*: whether the person *thinks* they have the ability to perform the behavior in a variety of situations;
5. *Emotional reactions* to the behavior and whether these are positive or negative;
6. *Self-standards and sanctions*: whether the person sees their performing the behavior as being consistent or inconsistent with how they see themselves;
7. *Perceived normative pressure*: whether individuals feel that people important to them, want them to perform the behavior or not – peer pressure could be seen as a fairly strong example of this;
8. *Anticipated outcomes*: attitude towards performing the behavior.

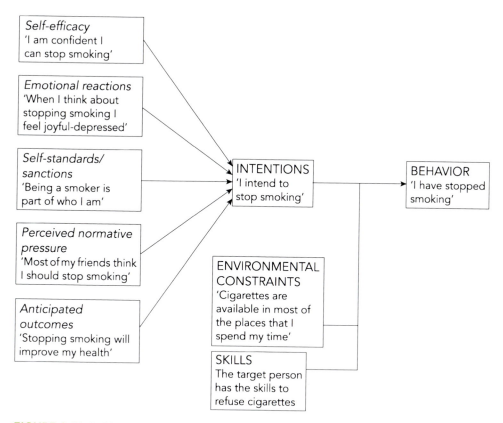

FIGURE 2.10 Fishbein et al.'s (2001) Theoretical Integration of Key Behavioral Determinants

These determinants should help explain why some people perform a given behavior while others do not. The first three determinants are viewed as necessary (i.e., if a person does not have positive intentions *or* there are environmental constraints *or* the person does not have the skills needed to perform the behavior then the behavior will not be performed) and sufficient (i.e., if an individual has the intention to ask for a pay rise, there are no environmental constraints [e.g., a poor financial climate] and has the skills to ask for a pay rise, the individual is very likely to ask for a pay rise). Determinants 4–8 are seen as influencing intention.

A second attempt (Michie et al., 2005) used a similar consensus approach to identify key determinants of changing the behavior of health professionals such that they act in line with the best practice. The final list of determinants overlapped significantly with the determinants of Fishbein et al. which, as the work was conducted independently, provides some level of confidence that there are key determinants of behavior. In addition to the eight determinants identified by Fishbein et al. (2001), four additional determinants were identified by Michie et al.: knowledge (e.g., regarding particular illnesses/risks associated with performing/not performing the behavior; knowing how to perform the behavior); memory, attention and decision processes (e.g., will an individual remember to perform the behavior or be distracted by features of the environment); behavioral regulation (largely related to tackling the intention-behavior gap through strategies such as planning and self-monitoring); and nature of the behaviors (e.g., whether it has become part of one's routine or whether it is a behavior that the individual has not performed before).

DUAL PROCESS MODELS

While the models above have tended to focus predominately on explicit cognition that one is consciously aware of and requires effort to process relevant information (i.e., thoughts and feelings about a behavior), more recent theories have also sought to incorporate implicit cognition – that which occurs quickly, efficiently, with little or no effort and happens outside of one's conscious awareness. Models that take into account both explicit and implicit processes have been labeled dual process models.

There are a fairly large number of dual process models that have been referred to within the psychological literature (predominately in the sub-disciplines of social psychology and cognitive psychology; see Smith & DeCoster, 2000, for a review). Probably the most popular dual process model at the moment is Strack and Deutsch's (2004) Reflective-Impulsive Model (RIM).

The RIM (see also Chapters 8 and 9) describes behavior as being influenced by two distinct systems of processing – a reflective system and an impulsive system. The reflective system is analogous to the type of systems and processes outlined in many of the theories that we have considered in this chapter in that there is a decision process that results in intending. For example, once an individual sees an object such as a piece of fruit, classifies it as a piece of fruit, draws on factual (e.g., it is an apple) and evaluative (e.g., I like apples) information, they come to the point of forming an intention relating to whether they will buy/approach or not buy/avoid this particular piece of fruit. The impulsive system operates through a process of spreading activation whereby activation of particular concepts (e.g., apples) following perceptual input (e.g., seeing the apple) leads to the quick-fire activation of associated concepts (e.g., love, tasty). These two systems can interact and jointly activate behavioral schemata that directly precede action. Consequently, both impulsive and reflective systems can jointly influence action and their relative contributions can vary as a function of different factors.

Hofmann, Friese and Wiers (2008) classified three groups of factors that influence the extent to which implicit attitudes relate to behavior: 1) availability of control resources, 2) reliance on impulses and 3) motivation to control one's behavior (see also Friese, Hofmann & Schmitt, 2009). Implicit attitudes are argued to be more strongly predictive of behavior when control resources are not available and/or one is not motivated to control their behavior (e.g., when doing so is too effortful, there are few costs in relation to performing the behavior) or when one relies on impulses.

Implicit attitude research is currently an emerging topic in health behavior change having received much attention in social psychology and applied areas such as consumer psychology. As well as correlational evidence that implicit attitudes can predict product choice (e.g., Friese, Hofmann & Wänke, 2008; Friese, Wänke & Plessner, 2006; Gibson, 2008; Perugini, 2005; Richetin, Perugini, Prestwich & O'Gorman, 2007; Scarabis, Florack & Gosejohann, 2006), there is some experimental evidence supportive of the role of implicit attitudes in determining consumer behavior. In a study by Strick, van Baaren, Holland and van Knippenberg (2009) those participants that were exposed to humorous cartoons related to a novel energy drink or household products were more likely to choose these products when given the choice. Changes in implicit attitudes explained (mediated, see Chapter 6) the effect of these cartoons on product choice suggesting that implicit attitudes can be important in determining behavior. Hollands, Prestwich and Marteau (2011) have also shown, in the context of health behavior change, that exposing individuals to images illustrating the adverse consequences of an unhealthy diet can promote healthier implicit attitudes and healthier food choices.

THEORIES OF MAINTENANCE OF BEHAVIOR CHANGE

While health benefits can be achieved by changing some health behaviors once (e.g., promoting attendance at a sexual health clinic), for many health behaviors such as healthy eating, physical activity and smoking cessation, initial changes do not lead to significant or indeed any benefit unless these changes are maintained over an extended period of time. A recent review by Kwasnicka, Dombrowski, White and Sniehotta (2016) identified 100 theories that included hypotheses about behavior change maintenance. Of these, 43 theories suggested distinctions in the processes underlying initiation and maintenance. In reviewing these 43 theories, Kwasnicka et al. identified five themes that appear pivotal for maintenance:

1. Specific *motives* including undertaking the behavior because a) they enjoy the behavior or are satisfied with the outcomes arising from initial behavior changes;

   b) the behavior is consistent with their identity and how they see themselves;
   c) they are self-determined (e.g., an individual does something because they feel
   pressured either by others or by themselves [extrinsic motivation] may be useful for
   initial change but doing it because they want to do it [intrinsic motivation] is critical
   for maintenance);
2. *Self-regulation* which involves controlling behavior by replacing unwanted behaviors
   triggered through more automatic processes with goal-directed behaviors;
3. *Habits* (see description of habits earlier in the chapter);
4. *Resources.* Both physical and psychological resources need to remain high for
   maintenance;
5. *Environment and social influences* which can provide incentives or cues which derail
   initial changes in health behaviors.

Of the theories that we overviewed earlier in the chapter, only the MGB/EMGB and
Michie et al.'s (2005) integrative model were not included within the 100 theories
relevant to maintenance identified by Kwasnicka et al. (2016). However, given these
two theories incorporate constructs included in other maintenance-relevant theories
(e.g., the EMGB contains all of the TPB constructs and additionally considers, amongst
other variables, past behavior or habit), these theories can also be considered as being
relevant for maintenance.

Based on responses from 40 experts in theory who were consulted by Kwasnicka et al.,
the most commonly identified theories relevant to maintenance were the TTM, HAPA,
SCT (all described earlier in this chapter), plus the Relapse Prevention Model and
Self-Determination Theory which we briefly overview next.

RELAPSE PREVENTION MODEL (MARLATT & GEORGE, 1984; MARLATT & GORDON, 1985)

This model has been typically applied to the maintenance of abstinence from unhealthy
or addictive behaviors but could, in principle, also be applied to the maintenance of
healthy behaviors. According to the Relapse Prevention Model, an individual is at risk
of relapse when they have weak self-efficacy (whereby the individual feels they have an
inability to cope) combined with positive expectancies about engaging in the unhealthy
behavior (e.g., thinking that having a cigarette will make them feel better). Relapse is
most likely when an individual experiences negative emotions (such as feeling depressed,
stressed or anxious), interpersonal conflict (such as difficulties with their partner or
friends) or social pressure from others to engage in the unhealthy behavior.

To encourage maintenance, an individual should view a 'relapse' as a transitional process
rather than an all-or-nothing process. As such, a smoker who has quit cigarettes who
smokes a cigarette again should view this instance as a lapse or a slip that has been
triggered in a high-risk situation rather than a full-blown relapse. To maintain change,
an individual should 1) undergo skills training to identify and cope with triggers for lapse
(e.g., by using coping plans, along the lines of implementation intentions [see Chapter 3],
to identify triggers and plan how to deal with them); 2) use cognitive re-framing to deal
with lapse (e.g., framing lapses as attributable to external, environmental factors that are

avoidable rather than internal factors to do with the individual, in order to boost their self-efficacy in maintaining behavior change); 3) develop broader lifestyle changes in order to enhance an individual's general coping capacity. Adopting such techniques strengthens their ability/perceived ability to maintain positive changes in health behavior.

SELF-DETERMINATION THEORY (SDT; DECI & RYAN, 1985)

SDT distinguishes between different types of motivation that can influence behavior. According to this theory, there are three main types of motivation: intrinsic motivation (whereby an individual performs the behavior for its own sake: e.g., Dave exercises because he finds it enjoyable), extrinsic motivation (whereby an individual performs the behavior because of more external reasons: e.g., Maeve exercises to please Dave) and amotivation (whereby an individual has no motivation to do the behavior). Extrinsic motivation can be sub-divided into integrated regulation (whereby an individual does the behavior because it aligns with their values or identity), identified (the individual does the behavior because it leads to outcomes that they value), introjected (the individual does the behavior to avoid negative emotions such as guilt or to obtain approval) and external (to avoid punishment or to get a reward). These types of motivation lie on a continuum from the most autonomous or internalized forms of motivation, where the reasons for performing the behavior originate from oneself, to the least autonomous forms, where the reasons for performing the behavior are more pressured by external forces (see Figure 2.11). The more autonomous, or internalized, the motivation underlying the behavior, the greater effort and persistence the individual will put in to drive behavior change and maintenance.

The process of internalization can be facilitated by fulfilling three basic psychological needs: autonomy (when the person feels like they have a sense of choice and undertakes a behavior under their own volition or free will), competence (when the person feels

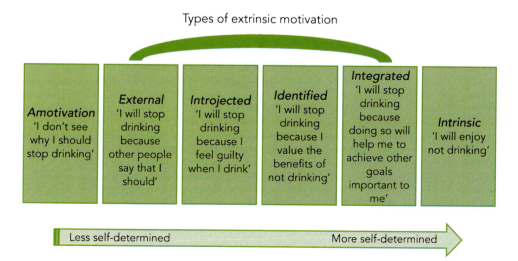

FIGURE 2.11 Self-Determination Theory: the continuum of motivation types

capable of being able to perform the behavior) and relatedness (when the person feels connected to and understood by important others). The basic needs can be boosted by various behavior change techniques. For example, autonomy can be boosted by exploring values and offering choice; competence can be enhanced by skills-building and problem solving; relatedness can be improved via techniques such as developing empathy and interpersonal relationships. When these three needs are met in a particular context (e.g., in an exercise class) then the behaviors relevant to that context (i.e., exercising within the class) will be more likely to be autonomously driven and thus more likely to be maintained in the future.

BURNING ISSUE BOX 2.9

PROSPECT THEORY AND GAINS AND LOSSES

In simple expectancy-value models we might expect gains and losses to be given similar weights in deciding how we act. Prospect Theory (Tversky & Kahneman, 1981) suggests that losses are actually more painful than gains are pleasurable (i.e., they are not simple opposites). For example, people are more upset by a loss of £100 than they are pleased by a gain of £100. Indeed individuals want approximately one and a half times as much gain to balance a loss (e.g., to be prepared to bet and lose £10 on a coin toss they want to be able to potentially win £15 to think it is a worthwhile bet).

As well as showing that a loss is more significant than the equivalent gain, Prospect Theory also shows that a sure gain is favored over a probabilistic gain, and that a probabilistic loss is preferred to a definite loss. This difference between gains and losses also shows up in framing studies. The framing effect is an example of a cognitive bias, in which people react differently to a particular choice depending on whether it is presented as a loss or as a gain. People tend to avoid risk when a positive frame is presented but seek risks when a negative frame is presented. The classic example is one where people were asked to imagine that they are responsible for deciding between two policies in the face of a flu epidemic that was expected to kill 600 people. In the positive frame presented below, 72% choose option A and 28% choose option B. In the negative frame presented below, 78% choose option B and 22% choose option A. Clearly the differing options present the same net outcome but the framing drives the choices made.

	Option A	Option B
Positive frame:	200 lives saved	One-third chance 600 lives saved, two-thirds chance 0 lives saved
Negative frame:	400 lives lost	One-third chance 0 lives lost, two-thirds chance 600 lives lost

Such framing effects can be used to influence how decisions are made and are one example of the fact that we do not always act as rational decision makers but show systematic biases in the way we use information.

SUMMARY

In this chapter we covered a range of different theories that have been influential in the field of health behavior change. Many of these theories overlap and researchers have used this as a basis to form more integrative theories. Many of the theories covered in this chapter focus primarily on fairly slow, reflective processes and on the initiation of health behaviors. However, dual process models take into account automatic processes and other modern theories are useful when explaining maintenance of health behaviors. These types of theories include constructs that play important roles in behavior maintenance including habits, satisfaction with the outcomes of behavior and supportive environments.

FURTHER READING

Kwasnicka, D., Dombrowski, S. U., White, M. & Sniehotta, F. (2016). Theoretical explanations for maintenance of behavior change: a systematic review of behavior theories. *Health Psychology Review, 10,* 277–296. A useful, recent review of the theories and common processes underlying health behavior maintenance.

Sniehotta, F.F., Presseau, J. & Araújo-Soares, V. (2014). Time to retire the theory of planned behavior. *Health Psychology Review, 8,* 1–7. An editorial providing strong criticism against the Theory of Planned Behavior and the need to identify better theories.

Steinmetz, H., Knappstein, M., Ajzen, I., Schmidt, P. & Kabst, R. (2016). How effective are behavior change interventions based on the Theory of Planned Behavior? A three-level meta-analysis. *Zeitschrift für Psychologie, 224,* 216–233. A recent review of the experimental evidence relating to a highly popular health/social cognition model.

Strack, F. & Deutsch, R. (2004). Reflective and impulsive determinants of social behavior. *Personality and Social Psychology Review, 8,* 220–247. An introduction to the Reflective-Impulsive Model that provides an alternative approach to theories focusing purely on reflective processes.

GLOSSARY

Behavior change technique (BCT): a systematic strategy used in an attempt to change behavior (e.g., providing information on consequences; prompting specific goal setting; prompting barrier identification; modeling the behavior; planning social support).

Theories, theory (or model): 'a set of interrelated concepts, definitions and propositions that present a *systematic* view of events or situations by specifying relations among variables, in order to *explain* or *predict* the events or situations' (Glanz, Rimer & Viswanath, 2015, p. 26).

Theory-relevant construct: a key concept or building block within a theory/model upon which the intervention is based. Example constructs in the Theory of Planned Behavior are attitudes towards the behavior, perceived behavioral control, subjective norms etc. Constructs can be further broken down into **determinants** (the predictors such as attitudes, subjective norms, PBC) or **outcomes** (such as behavior).

REFERENCES

Abraham, C. & Sheeran, P. (2003). Acting on intentions: the role of anticipated regret. *British Journal of Social Psychology, 42,* 495–511.

Abraham, C. & Sheeran P. (2015). The health belief model. In Conner, M. and Norman, P. (Eds.), *Predicting and Changing Health Behaviour: Research and Practice with Social Cognition Models* (3rd edn; pp. 30–69). Buckingham, UK: Open University Press.

Ajzen, I. (1991). The theory of planned behavior. *Organizational Behavior and Human Decision Processes, 50,* 179–211.

Ajzen, I. & Fishbein, M. (1980). *Understanding Attitudes and Predicting Social Behavior.* Englewood Cliffs, NJ: Prentice-Hall.

Albarracin, D., Gillette, J.C., Earl, A.N., Glasman, L.R., Durantini, M.R. & Ho, M.H. (2005). A test of major assumptions about behavior change: a comprehensive look at the effects of passive and active HIV-prevention interventions since the beginning of the epidemic. *Psychological Bulletin, 131,* 856–897.

Armitage, C.J. (2006). Evidence that implementation intentions promote transitions through the stages of change. *Journal of Consulting and Clinical Psychology, 74,* 141–151.

Armitage, C.J. & Conner, M. (2001). Efficacy of the theory of planned behaviour: a meta-analytic review. *British Journal of Social Psychology, 40,* 471–499.

Armitage, C.J., Sheeran, P., Conner, M. & Arden, M.A. (2004). Stages of change or changes of stage? Predicting transitions in transtheoretical model stages in relation to healthy food choice. *Journal of Consulting and Clinical Psychology, 72,* 491–499.

Ashford, S., Edmunds, J. & French, D.P. (2010). What is the best way to change self-efficacy to promote lifestyle and recreational physical activity? A systematic review with meta-analysis. *British Journal of Health Psychology, 15,* 265–288.

Bandura, A. (1971). *Social Learning Theory.* New York: General Learning Press.

Bandura, A. (1977). Self-efficacy: toward a unifying theory of behavioral change. *Psychological Review, 84,* 191–215.

Bandura, A. (1997). *Self-Efficacy: The Exercise of Control.* New York: W.H. Freeman and Company.

Bassili, J.N. (1996). Meta-judgmental versus operative indexes of psychological attributes: the case of measures of attitude strength. *Journal of Personality and Social Psychology, 71,* 637–653.

Bridle, C., Riemsma, R.P., Pattenden, J., Sowden, J.A., Mather, L., Watt, I.S. & Walker, A. (2005). Systematic review of the effectiveness of health behavior interventions based on the transtheoretical model. *Psychology & Health, 20,* 283–301.

Clarke, D.D. (1987). Fundamental problems with fundamental research: a meta-theory for social psychology. *Philosophica, 40,* 23–61.

Conn, V.S., Hafdahl, A.R., Brown, S.A. & Brown, L.M. (2008). Meta-analysis of patient education interventions to increase physical activity among chronically ill adults. *Patient Education and Counseling, 70,* 157–172.

Conner, M., Abraham, C., Prestwich, A., Hutter, R., Hallam, J., Sykes-Muskett, B., Morris, B. & Hurling, R. (2016). Impact of goal priority and goal conflict on the intention-health-behavior relationship: tests on physical activity and other health behaviors. *Health Psychology, 35,* 1017–1026.

Conner, M., Sheeran, P., Norman, P. & Armitage, C. J. (2000). Temporal stability as a moderator of relationships in the theory of planned behaviour. *British Journal of Social Psychology, 39*, 469–493.

Cooke, R. & Sheeran, P. (2004). Moderation of cognition-intention and cognition-behaviour relations: a meta-analysis of properties of variables from the theory of planned behaviour. *British Journal of Social Psychology, 43*, 159–186.

Deci, E.L. & Ryan, R.M. (1985). Intrinsic motivation and self-determination in human behavior. New York: Plenum.

Fishbein, M., Triandis, H.C., Kanfer, F.H., Becker, M., Middlestadt, S.E. & Eichler, A. (2001). Factors influencing behaviour and behaviour change. In A. Baum, T.A. Revenson & J.E. Singer (Eds.), *Handbook of Health Psychology* (pp. 3–17). Mahwah, NJ: Lawrence Erlbaum Associates.

Friese, M., Hofmann, W. & Wänke, M. (2008). When impulses takes over: moderated predictive validity of explicit and implicit attitude measures in predicting food choice and consumption behaviour. *British Journal of Social Psychology, 47*, 397–419.

Friese, M., Hofmann, W. & Schmitt, M. (2009). When and why do implicit measures predict behavior? Empirical evidence for the role of opportunity, motivation, and process reliance. *European Review of Social Psychology, 19*, 285–338.

Friese, M., Wänke, M. & Plessner, H. (2006). Implicit consumer preferences and their influence on product choice. *Psychology and Marketing, 23*, 727–740.

Gibson, B. (2008). Can evaluative conditioning change attitudes toward mature brands? New evidence from the implicit association test. *Journal of Consumer Research, 35*, 178–188.

Glanz, K. & Rimer, B.K. (2005). *Theory at a Glance: A Guide for Health Promotion Practice* (2nd edn). National Cancer Institute, NIH, Public Health Service. U.S. Government Printing Office.

Glanz, K., Rimer, B.K. & Viswanath, K. (2015). Theory, research and practice in health behavior. In K. Glanz, B.K. Rimer and K. Viswanath (Eds.), *Health Behavior: Theory Research & Practice* (5th edn; pp. 24–40). San Francisco: Jossey-Bass.

Gollwitzer, P.M. (1990). Action phases and mindsets. In E.T. Higgins and J.R. Sorrentino (Eds.), *The Handbook of Motivation and Cognition* (Vol. 2, pp. 53–92). New York: Guilford.

Hofmann, W., Friese, M. & Wiers, R. (2008). Impulsive versus reflective influences on behavior: a theoretical framework and empirical review. *Health Psychology Review, 2*, 111–137.

Hollands, G.J., Prestwich, A. & Marteau, T.M. (2011). Using aversive images to enhance healthy food choices and implicit attitudes: an experimental test of evaluative conditioning. *Health Psychology, 30*, 195–203.

Janz, N.K. & Becker, M.H. (1984). The health belief model: a decade later. *Health Education Quarterly, 11*, 1–47.

Jones, C.J., Smith, H. & Llewellyn, C. (2014). Evaluating the effectiveness of health belief model interventions in improving adherence: a systematic review. *Health Psychology Review, 8*, 253–269.

Kwasnicka, D., Dombrowski, S.U., White, M. & Sniehotta, F. (2016). Theoretical explanations for maintenance of behaviour change: a systematic review of behaviour theories. *Health Psychology Review, 10*, 277–296.

Leone, L., Perugini, M. & Ercolani, A.P. (2004). Studying, practicing, and mastering: a test of the Model of Goal-Directed Behavior (MGB) in the software learning domain. *Journal of Applied Social Psychology, 34*, 1945–1973.

Lippke, S., Ziegelmann, J.P. & Schwarzer, R. (2005). Stage specific adoption and maintenance of physical activity: testing a three-stage model. *Psychology of Sport & Exercise, 6*, 585–603.

Luszczynska, A. & Schwarzer, R. (2015). Social cognitive theory. In M. Conner & P. Norman (Eds.), *Predicting and Changing Health Behaviour: Research and Practice with Social Cognition Models* (3rd edn; pp. 225–251). Buckingham, UK: Open University Press.

Marlatt, G.A. & George, W.H. (1984). Relapse prevention: introduction and overview of the model. *British Journal of Addiction, 79*, 261–273.

Marlatt, G.A. & Gordon, J.R. (1985). *Relapse Prevention: Maintenance Strategies in the Treatment of Addictive Behaviors*. New York: Guilford Press.

Michie, S., Johnston, M., Abraham, C., Lawton, R., Parker, D. & Walker, A. (2005). 'Psychological theory' group. Making psychological theory useful for implementing evidence based practice: a consensus approach. *Quality and Safety in Health Care, 14,* 26–33.

Milne, S., Sheeran, P. & Orbell, S. (2000). Prediction and intervention in health-related behaviour: a meta-analytic review of protection motivation theory. *Journal of Applied Social Psychology, 30,* 106–143.

Noar, S.M. & Zimmerman, R.S. (2005). Health behavior theory and cumulative knowledge regarding health behaviors: are we moving in the right direction? *Health Education Research, 20,* 275–290.

Norman, P., Boer, H., Seydel, E.R. & Mullan, B. (2015). Protection motivation theory. In M. Conner and & P. Norman (Eds.), *Predicting and Changing Health Behaviour: Research and Practice with Social Cognition Models* (3rd edn; pp. 70–106). Buckingham, UK: Open University Press.

Orbell, S. & Sheeran, P. (1998). 'Inclined abstainers': a problem for predicting health-related behaviour. *British Journal of Social Psychology, 37,* 151–165.

Ouellette, J.A. & Wood, W. (1998). Habit and intention in everyday life: the multiple processes by which past behavior predicts future behavior. *Psychological Bulletin, 124,* 54–74.

Perugini, M. (2005). Predictive models of implicit and explicit attitudes. *British Journal of Social Psychology, 44,* 29–45.

Perugini, M. & Bagozzi, R.P. (2001). The role of desires and anticipated emotions in goal-directed behaviours: broadening and deepening the Theory of Planned Behaviour. *British Journal of Social Psychology, 40,* 79–98.

Perugini, M. & Conner, M. (2000). Predicting and understanding behavioral volitions: the interplay between goals and behaviors. *European Journal of Social Psychology, 30,* 705–731.

Prestwich, A. & Kellar, I. (2014). How can the impact of implementation intentions as a behaviour change intervention be improved? *European Review of Applied Psychology, 64,* 35–41.

Prestwich, A.J., Lawton, R.J. & Conner, M.T. (2003). The use of implementation intentions and the decision balance sheet in promoting exercise behaviour. *Psychology & Health, 18,* 707–721.

Prestwich A., Perugini, M. & Hurling, R. (2008). Goal desires moderate intention-behaviour relations. *British Journal of Social Psychology, 47,* 49–71.

Prestwich, A., Sniehotta, F.F., Whittington, C., Dombrowski, S.U., Rogers, L. & Michie, S. (2014). Does theory influence the effectiveness of health behavior interventions? Meta-analysis. *Health Psychology, 33,* 465–474.

Prochaska, J.O. & DiClemente, C.C. (1983). Stages and processes of self-change smoking: toward an integrative model of change. *Journal of Consulting and Clinical Psychology, 51,* 390–395.

Quine, L., Rutter, D.R. & Arnold, L. (1998). Predicting and understanding safety helmet use among schoolboy cyclists: a comparison of the theory of planned behaviour and the health belief model. *Psychology & Health, 13,* 251–269.

Richetin, J., Perugini, M., Prestwich, A. & O'Gorman, R. (2007). The IAT as a predictor of spontaneous food choice: the case of fruits versus snacks. *International Journal of Psychology, 42,* 166–173.

Rogers, R.W. (1983). Cognitive and physiological processes in fear appeals and attitude change: a revised theory of protection motivation. In J. Cacioppo & R. Petty (Eds.), *Social Psychophysiology* (pp. 153–176). New York: Guilford Press.

Rosenstock, I.M., Strecher, V.J. & Becker, M.H. (1988). Social learning theory and the Health Belief Model. *Health Education Quarterly, 15,* 175–183.

Scarabis, M., Florack, A. & Gosejohann, S. (2006). When consumers follow their feelings: the impact of affective or cognitive focus on the basis of consumers' choice. *Psychology & Marketing, 23,* 1005–1036.

Scholz, U., Sniehotta, F.F. & Schwarzer, R. (2005). Predicting physical exercise in cardiac rehabilitation: the role of phase-specific self-efficacy beliefs. *Journal of Sport and Exercise Psychology, 27,* 135–151.

Schwarzer, R. (1992). Self-efficacy in the adoption and maintenance of health behaviors: theoretical approaches and a new model. In R. Schwarzer (Ed.), *Self-Efficacy: Thought Control of Action* (pp. 217–242). Washington, DC: Hemisphere.

Sheeran, P., Milne, S., Webb, T.L. & Gollwitzer, P.M. (2005). Implementation intentions and health behaviour. In M. Conner & P. Norman (Eds.), *Predicting Health Behaviour* (2nd edn; pp. 276–323). Maidenhead, UK: Open University Press.

Sheeran, P. & Orbell, S. (1999). Augmenting the theory of planned behavior: roles for anticipated regret and descriptive norms. *Journal of Applied Social Psychology, 29*, 2107–2142.

Skinner, B.F. (1953). *Science and Human Behavior.* New York: Macmillan.

Smith, E.R. & DeCoster, J. (2000). Dual process models in social and cognitive psychology: conceptual integration and links to underlying memory systems. *Personality and Social Psychology Review, 4*, 108–131.

Sniehotta, F.F., Presseau, J. & Araújo-Soares, V. (2014). Time to retire the theory of planned behaviour. *Health Psychology Review, 8*, 1–7.

Steinmetz, H., Knappstein, M., Ajzen, I., Schmidt, P. & Kabst, R. (2016). How effective are behavior change interventions based on the Theory of Planned Behavior? A three-level meta-analysis. *Zeitschrift für Psychologie, 224*, 216–233.

Strack, F. & Deutsch, R. (2004). Reflective and impulsive determinants of social behavior. *Personality and Social Psychology Review, 8*, 220–247.

Strick, M., van Baaren, R.B., Holland, R.W. & van Knippenberg, A. (2009). *Journal of Experimental Psychology: Applied, 15*, 35–45.

Tversky, A. & Kahneman, D. (1981). The framing of decisions and the psychology of choice. *Science, 211*(4481), 453–458.

Verplanken, B., Aarts, H., van Knippenberg, A. & Moonen, A. (1998). Habit versus planned behavior: a field experiment. *British Journal of Social Psychology, 37*, 111–128.

West, R. (2005). Time for a change: putting the Transtheoretical (Stages of Change) Model to rest. *Addiction, 100*, 1036–1039.

West, R. (2006). The Transtheoretical Model of behaviour change and the scientific method. *Addiction, 101*, 774–778.

Williams, D.M. & Rhodes, R.E. (2016). The confounded self-efficacy construct: conceptual analysis and recommendations for future research. *Health Psychology Review, 10*, 113–128.

3

CHAPTER 3
BEHAVIOR CHANGE TECHNIQUES

OVERVIEW

Behavior change techniques (BCTs) are methods employed by behavioral scientists, psychologists, medical staff and others to try to change the behavior of individuals or groups of people and/or the motivations or other factors/constructs that influence behavior. We first look at how behavior change techniques have been classified within taxonomies. We then consider a number of behavior change techniques, all of which have received extensive examination in the literature. Many of these have a good level of evidence to support their use and have been applied across a wide range of health behaviors. A number of these have links with some of the theories considered in Chapter 2 such as **implementation intentions** that are closely aligned with the Health Action Process Approach (HAPA) and the Model of Action Phases (MAP). We then look at behavior change techniques in a variety of settings including the workplace and in healthcare. Different contexts bring with them unique challenges and here we give you a flavor of these as well as an illustration of attempts to change important health behaviors across these varied environments.

BEHAVIOR CHANGE TAXONOMIES

One major goal for the Science of Health Behavior Change is to identify which behavior change techniques are the most effective in changing specific health behaviors. Aside from issues concerning what these specific behaviors might be, an important challenge is to ensure that individuals apply the same definitions of these techniques. Without clearly understood and widely applied definitions, there is a risk that different individuals apply different labels to the same techniques or the same labels to different techniques. The impact of this would be to delay the development of a clear evidence base either supporting or refuting the effectiveness of specific techniques because it is more difficult to identify and synthesize the evidence from studies testing the same behavior change techniques. In recent years, there have been attempts to identify and categorize behavior change techniques and to clearly define them within behavior change taxonomies.

A key feature of science is replication. Findings demonstrated in one study should be replicated if the method (what was done and to whom) is repeated. In order to do this, what was done within an experiment needs to be clearly reported. With this in mind, Abraham and Michie (2008) developed a taxonomy of 26 behavior change techniques that provides a common language to describe the techniques that make up an intervention. In addition to increasing the likelihood of replicating studies, using a common language to describe techniques making up an intervention can be helpful in determining what caused any changes in behavior. If techniques were used within interventions but they are not clearly described then potentially important, but 'hidden' (as they are not clearly conveyed), techniques might have caused changes in behavior. In this situation, it is not possible to accurately identify which technique caused the change in behavior (see also Critical Skills Toolkit 3.1).

CRITICAL SKILLS TOOLKIT 3.1

HOW TO IDENTIFY EFFECTIVE COMPONENTS OF AN INTERVENTION

Interventions often comprise a number of different behavior change techniques. Take this example. Milne, Orbell and Sheeran (2002) conducted a study testing which techniques can increase the likelihood of engaging in at least one 20-minute session of exercise over a week. They randomly allocated their participants to one of three groups:

Group 1 (control group) did not receive any active behavior change techniques (they were simply asked to read three paragraphs of a novel).

Group 2 (experimental group 1) were asked to read a motivational message.

Group 3 (experimental group 2) were asked to read a motivational message and form an implementation intention regarding when and where they would exercise over the following week.

They demonstrated that at follow-up, 38% of participants in group 1 (control group) and 35% of participants in group 2 (experimental group 1) reported exercising. However, in group 3 (experimental group 2) the percentage of participants reporting exercising increased dramatically to 91%.

Based on the above, it is not clear whether forming an implementation intention *by itself* was responsible for increasing exercise or whether it was the *combination* of forming an implementation intention and reading the motivational message that increased exercise (the motivational message *by itself* was not effective in increasing exercise as the percentage of participants reporting exercise in experimental group 1 and the control group was similar).

In summary, when an intervention comprises a number of different behavior change techniques, it is not clear which specific behavior change technique was responsible for specific changes in constructs or behavior unless a **fully-crossed (full factorial) design** is used.

When an intervention comprises two behavior change techniques, it could use a 2 x 2 (4 groups) full factorial design; when it comprises three behavior change techniques, it could use a 2 x 2 x 2 (8 groups) design; four behavior change techniques could use a 2 x 2 x 2 x 2 (16 groups) design, and so on. For the most basic of these (the 2 x 2 design), there will be 4 groups (group 1 receives technique A and technique B, group 2 receives technique A but not technique B, group 3 receives technique B but not technique A and group 4 receives neither technique A nor technique B). This design is illustrated in Table 3.1:

TABLE 3.1 2 x 2 full factorial design that could have been incorporated by Milne et al. (2002) to help identify the active component(s) of their interventions

		Technique B: MOTIVATIONAL MESSAGE?	
		YES	NO
Technique A: IMPLEMENTATION INTENTION?	YES	Implementation intention + Motivational message	Implementation intention only
	NO	Motivational message only	No intervention control group

In the example shown, in order for Milne et al. (2002) to conclude which techniques, or combination of techniques, caused the differences in exercise across conditions, they should have used a 2 x 2 design (implementation intention + motivational message; implementation intention only; motivational message only; no intervention control). By omitting the implementation intention only condition, Milne et al. could not determine whether it was the combination of implementation intentions plus the motivational message that caused the increase in exercise or whether implementation intentions (without the motivational message) would have increased exercise behavior by itself.

Employing these full factorial designs (along with statistical procedures such as ANOVA, see Chapter 6) allows you to identify which specific behavior change technique is responsible for the effects of your intervention and also which behavior change techniques interact (i.e., lead to bigger effects when used in combination rather than using each technique alone).

Abraham and Michie's (2008) taxonomy of 26 different techniques is presented in Burning Issue Box 3.1 to give you an indication of the type of strategies that have often been employed as a means to change the actions of individuals or groups of people. Since 2008, this list has been expanded to incorporate a wider range of techniques (Michie et al., 2011) with the latest version incorporating 93 distinct behavior change techniques (Michie et al., 2013). In addition, lists defining behavior change techniques focused on specific behaviors including alcohol intake (Michie et al., 2012) and smoking (Michie, Hyder, Walia & West, 2011b) have been developed. These lists have been used to systematically review the evidence to determine the most effective behavior change techniques for a variety of behaviors across various contexts using **meta-analyses**

BURNING ISSUE BOX 3.1

HOW CAN WE CHANGE BEHAVIOR? OVERVIEW OF BEHAVIOR CHANGE TECHNIQUES (ABRAHAM & MICHIE, 2008)

According to Abraham and Michie (2008) there are 26 common methods that individuals can use to try to change the behavior of other people. The 26 techniques overviewed within Abraham and Michie's taxonomy were:

1–3. *Provide information.* These techniques rest on the assumption that educating individuals is a vital component of behavior change. Presenting information is likely to be most effective when the behavior (e.g., buying a particular product) or issue (e.g., climate change) is novel or not well understood. Moreover, while providing basic information about a disease may not have much impact on behavior, other types of information (e.g., providing information on the consequences of behavior) may be more useful (see Fishbein, 1995). Abraham and Michie (2008) categorized providing information into three different techniques:

   1. *On behavior-health link.* This can include factual information concerning the risks the individual has of developing illness or educational materials concerning the health benefits or problems concerned with health behaviors.
   2. *On consequences.* This educational technique concerns what happens if the individual performs/does not perform the behavior and the benefits and costs associated with these.
   3. *About others' approval.* Provides information relating to whether others would approve/disapprove of the behavior.

4. *Prompt intention formation.* Encourages people to come to a decision to act (e.g., I will exercise) or to achieve a goal (e.g., I will be healthy). This is distinct from technique 10 (specific goal setting) as the decision is not accompanied with a plan regarding how to act (e.g., when and where to act).
5. *Prompt barrier identification.* The individual is asked to think about the factors (e.g., competing goals/demands/situations) that might disrupt their plans and ways to overcome them.
6. *Provide general encouragement.* This can involve praise or rewards for effort. It can also include attempts to increase confidence in their ability through persuasion. It is distinct from technique 14 (contingent rewards) as the rewards do not depend on achieving their goal/sub-goal. *See 'Incentives' section in this chapter for further details.*
7. *Set graded tasks.* This involves setting the individual a series of tasks to work towards their goals. The tasks in the sequence gradually become more demanding, challenging or difficult.
8. *Provide instruction.* Involves *telling* the person individually or in groups, or by tips, *how* to perform the behavior or preparatory behaviors.
9. *Model/demonstrate the behavior. Showing* the individual (e.g., in classes, videos etc.) how to perform the behavior.

10. *Specific goal setting.* Prompts the individual to plan to perform a specific behavior (e.g., with reference to frequency, intensity or duration of the behavior) in a specific context (e.g., with reference to at least one of the following: where, when, how or with whom the behavior will be performed). *See 'Implementation Intentions' section in this chapter for further details.*

11. *Review of behavioral goals.* The individual is asked to review previous goals or plans. Typically this will follow goal setting (technique 10) and an attempt to act on these goals.

12. *Self-monitoring.* The individual keeps a record (e.g., diary) of their target behaviors. *See 'Self-Monitoring' section in this chapter for further details.*

13. *Feedback.* Receiving information about how the performance of the individual compares to their set goals (building on technique 10) or the behavior of others.

14. *Contingent rewards.* Praise, encouragement or other rewards (e.g., money) are given to reward achievement of their goal or sub-goals. *See 'Incentives' section in this chapter for further details.*

15. *Teach to use prompts/cues.* Teaches the individual to identify cues in the environment (e.g., time of day, places) which can remind them to perform a behavior.

16. *Agree behavioral contract.* Typically involves signing a contract/statement, witnessed by another, which specifies the behavior that the individual will perform.

17. *Prompt practice.* This involves encouraging practice of the behavior.

18. *Use of follow-up prompts.* This technique follows other components of an intervention and often involves sending letters, making telephone calls or visits.

19. *Provide opportunity for social comparison.* This technique places participants in situations in which they can compare their behaviors against those of others (e.g., in group sessions, through video etc.)

20. *Plan social support/social change.* Provides the individual with support from another (e.g., a buddy system) or encourages the individual to think about how others can help them change behavior.

21. *Prompt identification as a role model/position advocate.* Gives an opportunity to the individual to be a good example to others (e.g., giving talks, persuading others).

22. *Prompt self-talk.* Encourages individuals to talk to themselves (silently or out loud) before and during behavior performance to motivate and support action.

23. *Relapse prevention.* Similar to technique 5 (identify barriers) but occurs after initial behavior change has taken place. The individual is asked to identify situations that put them at risk of relapse and/or situations that can help them maintain the initial change in behavior.

24. *Stress management.* Can comprise a range of techniques (e.g., slow breathing) which attempt to reduce anxiety/stress rather than change the behavior directly.

25. *Motivational interviewing.* See 'Motivational Interviewing' section in this chapter for further details.

26. *Time management.* Any technique that helps the individual be able to fit the behavior into their schedule.

TABLE 3.2 Overview of meta-analyses identifying the most effective behavior change techniques to change specific health behaviors

Authors	Year	Behavior(s)	Sample	Taxonomy*	Number of studies (k)	Most effective behavior change techniques
Abraham & Graham-Rowe	2009	Physical activity	Healthy employees	1 (sub-set only)	37	Review of goals; set graded tasks
Avery et al.	2012	Glucose control	Type 2 diabetics	2	17	Prompting generalization of a target behavior; use of follow-up prompts; prompt review of behavioral goals; provide information on where and when to perform physical activity; plan social support/ social change; goal setting (behavior); time management; prompting focus on past success; barrier identification/problem solving; providing information on the consequences specific to the individual
Bartlett et al.	2014	Smoking	Smokers with COPD	6	17	Facilitate action planning/develop treatment plan; prompt self-recording; advise on methods of weight control; advise on/facilitate use of social support
Brannon & Cushing	2015	Physical activity/diet	Children & adolescents	1	74	Physical activity: modeling; providing consequences for behavior; providing information on others' approval; intention formation; self-monitoring; behavioral contract Diet: modeling; practice; social support
Dombrowski et al.	2012	Weight-related	Obese adults with comorbidities	1	44	Provide instruction; self-monitoring; relapse prevention; prompt practice

Author	Year	Behavior	Population	No.	n	Techniques
French et al.	2014	Physical activity	Older adults	2	16	Barrier identification/problem solving; provide rewards contingent on successful behavior; model/demonstrate the behavior
Hartmann-Boyce et al.	2014	Weight management	Overweight/ obese adults	2, 3 (modified)	29	Cluster of techniques concerning comparison of behavior (especially model/demonstrate the behavior)
Henrich et al.	2015	IBS symptoms & well-being	Adult patients with IBS	2 (modified)	48	General empathic support; self-monitoring of symptoms; self-monitoring of cognitions; drawing an explicit link between self-monitored symptoms and cognitions; providing feedback; relapse prevention or coping planning; assertiveness training; prompt practice of new behaviors
Hill et al.	2013	Gestational weight gain	Pregnant women	2	19	Providing information on the consequences of behavior to the individual; provide rewards contingent on successful behavior; prompt self-monitoring of behavior; motivational interviewing
Lara et al.	2014	Healthy eating	Older adults	2	22	Barrier identification/problem solving; plan social support/social change; use of follow-up prompts; goal setting
Michie et al.	2009	Healthy eating/ physical activity	Adults without chronic illness	1	101	None were significant (but self-monitoring was the best)
Michie et al.	2012	Alcohol	Primary care pop.	4	18	Prompt self-recording; prompt commitment from the client there and then
Olander et al.	2013	Physical activity	Obese adults	2	42	Various but especially: teach to use prompts/cues; prompt practice; prompt rewards contingent on effort or progress towards behavior; goal setting (behavior); action planning; provide feedback on performance; barrier identification/problem

TABLE 3.2 continued

Authors	Year	Behavior(s)	Sample	Taxonomy*	Number of studies (k)	Most effective behavior change techniques
						solving; provide instruction; provide normative information about others' behavior; plan social support/social change; provide rewards for behavior; self-monitoring of behavior; provide information on the consequences in general; provide information on the consequences for the individual
Taylor et al.	2011	Physical activity	Healthy employees	1	26	None
Webb et al.	2010	Physical activity	General	1 (modified)	85	Several, especially: stress management; general communication skills training; relapse prevention/ coping planning; goal setting; action planning; provide feedback on performance; barrier identification; provide instruction
West et al.	2010	Smoking	Stop Smoking service attendees	5	43 Stop Smoking services	Strengthen ex-smoker identity; elicit client views; measure carbon monoxide; give options for additional/later support; provide rewards contingent on stopping smoking; advise on changing routine; facilitate relapse prevention and coping; ask about experiences of stop smoking medication; advise on stop smoking medication
Williams & French	2011	Physical activity	Healthy, non-student adults	2	27	Provide information on consequences of the behavior in general; action planning; reinforcing effort or progress towards behavior; provide instruction; facilitate social comparison; time management

* Taxonomy used: 1. Abraham & Michie (2008); 2. Michie et al. (2011) CALO-RE taxonomy; 3. Michie et al. (2013); 4. Michie et al. (2012); 5. Michie et al. (2011b); 6. Michie et al. (2011a)

(see Table 3.2) or less formal, statistical approaches where meta-analyses were not possible (e.g., Arnott et al., 2014; Bhattarai et al., 2013; Bird et al., 2013; Gilinsky et al., 2015; Golley, Hendrie, Slater & Corsini, 2011; Hill, Richardson & Skouteris, 2015; Liu et al., 2013; Lorencatto, West & Michie, 2012; Lyzwinski, 2014; Martin, Chater & Lorencatto, 2013; Pal et al., 2014).

Taxonomies of behavior change techniques are useful for accumulating evidence from different studies within **systematic reviews**/meta-analyses, in that they help to group together studies that have employed the same behavior change techniques. Such studies are then compared against studies that have not used the specific behavior change technique in question. However, taxonomies are only useful if they can be used reliably. Evidence that they can be used reliably is not particularly strong or widespread.

The most detailed taxonomy (i.e., the taxonomy comprising the most behavior change techniques) was produced by Michie et al. (2013). Although it comprises 93 techniques, to help individuals in their coding or use of behavior change techniques, the techniques are grouped into 19 clusters. For instance, a cluster labeled 'social support' comprises three behavior change techniques relating to social support (social support-unspecified; social support-practical; social support-emotional), while another cluster labeled 'self-belief' comprises four techniques designed to increase an individual's belief that they can perform a particular behavior (verbal persuasion about capability, mental rehearsal of successful performance, focus on past success, self-talk). Despite the behavior change techniques being grouped into hierarchies to make the task of identifying the behavior change techniques within study reports easier, there is evidence suggesting that users fail to code many behavior change techniques reliably – even after training (Wood et al., 2015). Further discussion regarding the use of taxonomies can be found in Chapter 11.

POPULAR BEHAVIOR CHANGE TECHNIQUES

There are many reasons for attempting to change health behaviors across many sectors of society such as business, health services, education and general living as well as a number of important questions to address. For example, how might marketing companies encourage consumers to select their healthier product? How might doctors help patients to take the correct amount of medication and continue to do so throughout their treatment period (or even better, how might doctors help the patient to avoid illness in the first place)? How can governments build healthier societies? In an attempt to address these questions, we could employ a range of different behavior change techniques aimed at educating people (see Burning Issue Box 3.1, techniques 1–3); try to encourage individuals to pay closer attention to their actions (see Burning Issue Box 3.1, technique 12); or provide opportunities for different groups of people to find out more information about one another (see Burning Issue Box 3.1, technique 19).

A broad range of behavior change techniques is outlined in Burning Issue Box 3.1. The relative impact of these techniques on behavior, according to Michie, Abraham, Whittington, McAteer & Gupta's (2009) review of healthy eating and physical activity

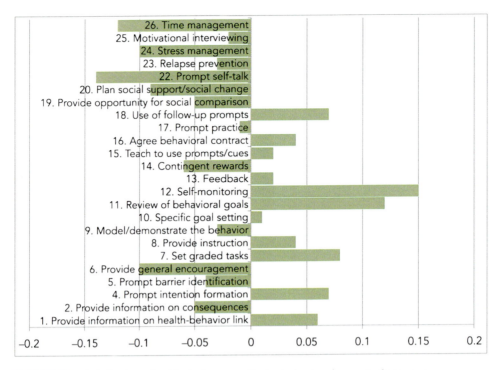

FIGURE 3.1 Relative benefit of including a particular behavior change technique vs.
not including the behavior change technique in an intervention (effect of
interventions including the specific behavior change technique minus effect
of interventions not including the specific behavior change technique) on physical
activity and dietary behaviors. Positive scores indicate that the technique is
beneficial. Negative scores indicate the technique is less beneficial (based on
Michie et al., 2009)

interventions, is shown in Figure 3.1. On the basis of this review, **self-monitoring**
appears to be the most useful behavior change technique for promoting healthy eating/
physical activity, while prompting self-talk appears to be the least useful. Even when we
consider a broader range of systematic reviews that attempt to identify the most effective
behavior change techniques across various behaviors (see Table 3.2), self-monitoring is
often identified as an effective technique. Specifically, self-monitoring has been shown
to be particularly effective for smoking reduction (Bartlett, Sheeran & Hawley, 2014),
alcohol reduction (Michie et al., 2012), improving Irritable Bowel Syndrome symptoms
and well-being (Henrich et al., 2015), as well as promoting physical activity and/or
healthy diets (Brannon & Cushing, 2015; Dombrowski et al., 2012; Hill, Skouteris &
Fuller-Tyszkiewicz, 2013; Olander et al., 2013).

These reviews are useful when we wish to have a general picture of which techniques
are most effective for changing different types of behavior. Reviews that focus on
specific behavior change techniques, however, have the potential to more clearly
establish the overall effect of a specific behavior change technique because they typically
comprise studies that compare interventions that differ only in the presence or absence
of a specific behavior change technique (e.g., self-monitoring). We consider this type

of review in the following section. Of particular use in identifying whether a specific behavior change technique is effective or not is the use of full factorial designs (see Critical Skills Toolkit 3.1).

Throughout the book we will cover a variety of behavior change techniques. For example, message framing is considered in Chapter 8 and choice architecture or 'nudge'-type interventions in Chapter 9. However, as there is such a wide range of techniques available to change behavior (see for example, Michie et al., 2013, who identify 93 techniques), we address some techniques in more depth than others. In the following section we outline a number of techniques commonly used to change health behaviors: self-monitoring, **motivational interviewing**, implementation intentions, and **incentives**. In addition, we overview how effective these techniques appear to be and look at *how* they are thought to change behavior. We focus on these techniques due to the large amount of literature devoted to them as well as their potential use across a wide range of health behaviors. These techniques appeal to healthcare professionals (particularly motivational interviewing) and policymakers (particularly incentives), and have the potential to change behavior at low cost across large populations (implementation intentions and self-monitoring). Given the suggestion from the broad reviews (that look at the effectiveness of a wide range of behavior change techniques) that self-monitoring is a particularly effective strategy to promote a wide range of health behaviors, we consider this strategy first.

SELF-MONITORING

What is it?

Self-monitoring involves an individual keeping a record of their target behaviors. This could take many different forms including an individual keeping a diary, completing a wall-chart or filling in a self-report questionnaire each day or week. For example, in a weight loss study, participants may be required to write down, in a diary, everything they eat and drink each day, perhaps noting down the fat content of each food. In the domain of physical activity, pedometers (i.e., step counters) and accelerometers (i.e., movement measures) can provide an objective measure that an individual can use to self-monitor their level of activity.

How does it work?

The majority of self-monitoring studies have focused on the effects of the technique on behavior change rather than trying to identify how or why this technique changes behavior. There are a number of possible mechanisms: increased awareness of one's level of activity which may, or may not, compare favorably with one's targets or goals; serve as a cue to action; be motivational in nature. Recent evidence suggests one potential mechanism is that self-monitoring boosts self-efficacy so that an individual is more confident in their ability to perform the target behavior (Prestwich et al., 2014).

Sometimes, within diaries, participants may record their mood, or other barriers to behavior change (such as poor weather). As such, they could use this additional information to identify the impact of different factors or barriers on their behavior and to cue the individual to consider how these barriers may be overcome. They could thus provide a useful tool to enhance one's knowledge and understanding of behavior and to aid problem solving.

Is it effective?

On the basis of the set of general reviews of behavior change techniques presented earlier in this chapter, they certainly appear to be effective. For instance, in a comparison of 26 behavior change techniques and their ability in changing physical activity and healthy eating, across a total of 122 tests, Michie et al. (2009) concluded that self-monitoring was the most effective behavior change technique for both behaviors. This conclusion was based on comparing across studies – in other words, the studies that incorporated self-monitoring within their intervention were compared against studies that did not include self-monitoring as part of their intervention. Comparing across studies may be ok when there are a large number of studies upon which to base the analysis. However, as inevitably different studies will pair self-monitoring with various techniques and the studies draw on different samples and test in different contexts there will be some 'noise' (i.e., less precision in your conclusions).

In a recent review that focused on the effect of self-monitoring on goal attainment, Harkin et al. (2016) found that self-monitoring had an effect on goal attainment that was nearly medium in size ($d = .40$). The effects were slightly stronger for certain behaviors/ outcomes (e.g., physical activity, asthma management, blood pressure) than for others (e.g., diet, weight).

A key factor in the success of self-monitoring, in general, is likely to be whether the individual continues to self-monitor by filling in self-report diaries or adhering to other self-monitoring methods. In the long term, this can be a time-consuming behavior change method.

MOTIVATIONAL INTERVIEWING (MI; MILLER & ROLLNICK, 2002)

What is it?

Motivational interviewing (MI) attempts to replace ambivalence (feeling both positive and negative towards behavior change) with stronger intrinsic motivation to change. In other words, rather than feeling indifferent to change, the individual becomes really keen to change their behavior. Moreover, they are keen to change their behavior because it is really important to them rather than simply wanting to change because of some external source (e.g., somebody else wants them to change or there are financial rewards on offer for behavior change). In this way, MI has connections with Self-Determination Theory (see, for example, Markland, Ryan, Tobin & Rollnick, 2005) covered in Chapter 2.

How does it work?

MI can lead to changes in behavior either by the therapist doing something in MI that is not done within the control treatment or by causing particular changes within the client, or both. There are many possible mechanisms that explain how or why MI can cause behavior change and these have been reviewed by Apodaca and Longabaugh (2009) with respect to problem drinking and the use of illegal substances. These include the therapist:

1. showing empathy, acceptance, warmth and genuineness [MI-Spirit];
2. being affirming and reflective listeners [MI-consistent behaviors];
3. *not* confronting, directing or warning [MI-inconsistent behaviors];
4. using specific techniques (e.g., decisional balance and personalized feedback) [specific therapist techniques].

Any of these factors can drive changes in the clients' behavior and these changes might occur via change in clients':

5. intention, commitment or plans to change [change talk/intention];
6. readiness to change (e.g., stage of change);
7. cooperation, engagement or disclosure [client engagement/involvement];
8. resistance to change [client resistance];
9. self-confidence;
10. sense of discrepancy such that they experience discomfort at how the current behavior fits in with their general values or life goals [experience of discrepancy].

Of these 10 categories of mechanisms, Apodaca and Longabaugh (2009) concluded that MI-inconsistent behaviors had the strongest evidence as a mediator of change (see Chapter 6, 'Mediation and Moderation') – in other words, by *not confronting, directing or warning the client* (potential features of minimal interventions, standard care and other treatments such as Cognitive Behavioral Therapy [CBT]), therapists evoke less resistance to change within the client, engage them more and achieve better outcomes. There was some evidence that *specific therapist techniques* (particularly *decisional balance*) were associated with better outcomes. *Client change talk* was viewed by Apodaca and Longabaugh (2009) as a consistent and promising mediator of change and clients in MI groups compared to standard care control groups tended to have more positive *intentions* to change substance use. MI was more engaging than other methods and greater *engagement* was associated with better outcomes – although this was based on only one test. *Experience of discrepancy* appears an important, promising but understudied potential mechanism of the relationship between MI and positive substance abuse outcomes.

MI-Spirit and client confidence did *not* appear to explain the positive effects of MI. Most studies did *not* support the role of readiness to change in explaining the effects of MI on changing substance use. There were insufficient tests of MI-consistent behaviors and client resistance.

Apodaca and Longabaugh (2009) bemoaned the lack of studies that have actually presented some test of the mechanisms of MI (i.e., tested how MI changes behavior). As such, at this stage, there is an insufficient evidence base to either support or refute Miller and Rollnick's (2002) Motivational Interviewing theory.

Is it effective?

The evidence is not wholly consistent (i.e., MI is not always effective). For example, a recent review by Morton et al. (2015) found that MI produced positive changes in health behaviors (diet, physical activity, alcohol intake) in only about half of the studies (18 out of 33). Moreover, according to Vasilaki, Hosier and Cox (2006), MI appears to be more useful in the short term (less than three months) than in the long term (greater than three months). Hettema, Steele and Miller (2005) reach similar conclusions noting that MI produces large behavior change effects in the short term (d = .77) which become small around one year (d = .30). This concurs with the results of a separate review by Cummings, Cooper and Cassie (2009) who concluded that there was conflicting evidence regarding the effectiveness of MI in achieving long-term improvements in lifestyle and health behaviors. They argue that this might be due to differences in the intensity and/or length of treatment (dosage) and the specific type of MI delivered.

IMPLEMENTATION INTENTIONS (GOLLWITZER, 1993)

What are they?

Implementation intention (Gollwitzer, 1993) manipulations often request an individual to think about good (or critical) situations to act and appropriate responses within those situations, then write them down in an IF-THEN form (e.g., in relation to attempting to increase exercise levels: IF it's Monday morning at 9am THEN I will go for a run from my house around the park) and commit themselves to act at this time. For example, if John was subjected to an implementation intention manipulation concerning exercise then he might be asked to consider when and where would be a good time and place for him to exercise and to also think about specific exercises (e.g., playing football, going for a run) that he would be able to do in that situation. Forming such plans has been shown to be useful in promoting desired (e.g., healthy) behaviors and reducing undesired behaviors (e.g., buying unhealthy foods). Implementation intentions (sometimes referred to as action plans) play important roles in bridging the intention-behavior gap in the Rubicon Model and the Health Action Process Approach that were considered in Chapter 2.

How do they work?

Implementation intentions have been argued to be effective through two processes. First, by planning in advance the situation in which an individual will act, the planned situation (and the cues within it) becomes particularly accessible such that an individual is less likely to miss (when encountering the situation) a good opportunity to act (see Aarts, Dijksterhuis & Midden, 1999). Beyond this, by mentally linking together a good situation to act with a suitable action, the association between the situation and response is strengthened meaning the behavior is more likely to be enacted when the planned situation is encountered. In other words, when the planned situation is encountered the individual does not need to then decide what to do and how. Instead, the planned behavior can occur quickly. Some have argued that, following the formation of an implementation intention, the initiation of behavior in a planned situation is more likely to be automatic (i.e., occurring immediately, more efficiently) and can be cued outside of conscious awareness (see Webb & Sheeran, 2007).

Are they effective?

Based on a review that incorporated 94 independent tests of implementation intentions, Gollwitzer and Sheeran (2006) concluded that implementation intentions have a medium-to-large-sized effect on behavior. Beneficial effects of implementation intentions were demonstrated across a range of behavioral domains including pro-social, environmental-related, health and academic behaviors as well as in prejudice reduction.

A recent review by Prestwich and Kellar (2014) suggests that a key factor that determines whether implementation intentions are likely to change behavior is whether an individual is actually motivated to perform the behavior in the first place. If an individual is motivated they will benefit more from forming an implementation intention than somebody who is not motivated. Take somebody who has no intention to try to save money. Forming an implementation intention regarding when, where and how they will save money is unlikely to help them. However, somebody who is keen to become more frugal with their cash should benefit much more from forming a relevant implementation intention. Furthermore, the type of behavior may influence effectiveness. For example, in the domain of healthy eating, Adriaanse, Vinkers, De Ridder, Hox and De Wit (2011) noted stronger effects of implementation intentions for the promotion of healthy eating than for the reduction of unhealthy eating.

INCENTIVES

What are they?

Also referred to as contingency management in the mental health or substance abuse fields (e.g., Pilling, Strang & Gerada, 2007), or as reinforcement therapy, the basic idea is that desired behaviors (e.g., abstinence from cocaine use) is rewarded to reinforce the change. Over time, these reinforcements are removed when the behavior change can be sustained without such reinforcement. The idea of rewarding desired changes in behavior is most consistent with Operant Learning Theory (see Chapter 2).

How do they work?

The approach rests on basic behaviorist principles; if behavior is positively reinforced (rewarded) then it will be repeated and if behavior is punished then it is less likely to be repeated. There are basic variants of this treatment which use different incentives. For example, in voucher-based reinforcement patients earn vouchers that can be exchanged for retail items. There was uproar in the media recently when the UK National Health Service (NHS) announced plans to trial this treatment in Fife, Scotland. In their scheme, smokers who gave up smoking for three months were entered into a prize draw for a helicopter trip or an overnight stay in a luxury hotel and other prizes included iPods. Similar schemes have operated in other parts of the UK. Camden Primary Care Trust has offered Nintendo Wiis and iPods to those who attend chlamydia testing.

Are they effective?

They have been argued to be cost-effective because such schemes a) raise awareness; b) bring individuals into contact with health services allowing earlier screening and treatment of illness; and c) can be effective in changing health and clinical behaviors thus preventing disease and reducing the costs associated with such disease. Pilling et al. (2007) pointed to over 25 studies that consistently show the effectiveness of these positive reinforcers to shape behavior change in the area of illicit drug use. Despite tending to involve monetary-based rewards, Pilling et al. highlight their cost-effectiveness. Voucher-based incentive therapy has been shown to be particularly effective in treating substance abuse (Lussier, Heil, Mongeon, Badger & Higgins, 2006) though evidence from Cahill and Perara (2011) generally questions the long-term effectiveness of such schemes (see also Giles, Robalino, McColl, Sniehotta & Adams, 2014; Mantzari et al., 2015). Interestingly, the positive effects on illicit substance use did not initially appear to translate to licit drug use (smoking: Cahill & Perara, 2011; Johnston, Liberato & Thomas, 2012) though a more recent review by Mantzari et al. (2015) noted small, significant benefits of personal financial incentives for three health behaviors that included smoking (physical activity and diet were also represented). Moreover, in this review, a group of six studies, with follow-ups between 12 and 18 months, indicated financial incentives have a medium-sized effect on smoking outcomes. Effects after 18 months post-baseline, or more than three months after the incentives had been withdrawn, were non-significant. Giles et al. (2014) also reported that financial incentives were useful in helping smoking cessation particularly up to six months with smaller effects beyond six months.

Across reviews of this technique, the evidence is quite mixed though there are some positive findings. It is not especially clear which rewards work best, though there is some evidence that cash incentives may be better than other incentives for longer-term smoking reduction (Giles et al., 2014); it is likely, however, the incentive must be perceived as desirable and rewarding to the user.

CRITICAL SKILLS TOOLKIT 3.2

DON'T TAKE OUR WORD FOR IT: HOW TO QUICKLY LOCATE USEFUL LITERATURE

One of the best ways of effectively critiquing research is to ensure that your topic-related knowledge is up-to-date. However, in this day and age, where papers can often be readily accessed online through your library or search engines such as Google Scholar (http://scholar.google.co.uk/), you can be over-faced with too many potentially relevant health behavior change papers to look for. Often text books (hopefully like this one) can be a good place to start. They should provide a clear summary of the literature. However, there are no guarantees that the studies highlighted in any particular text book are going to be the best, most interesting or relevant for your needs. Importantly, the science of health behavior change is fast moving so what might appear ground-breaking today might appear 'old-hat,' or irrelevant, tomorrow. Here are some tips to help you keep ahead without drowning in a sea of information.

Google Scholar

Google Scholar is a search engine through which you can access health behavior change and other academic journal articles. Clearly this is a good thing – you can often, at the very least, access an abstract of any particular article which summarizes the key findings. Sometimes you can access the full-text paper (even better!). However, the website has another benefit. It gives you an indication of the number of times that the article has been cited by other articles. In other words, you can use this to quickly identify the key papers in any particular area – the key papers will be more likely to have been cited more often.

When looking at the citation count of an article keep in mind that a paper published in 2016 would have had less time to have been cited by others than an article published in 2006. As a general rule of thumb, multiply the number of years that an article has been published by 10 as a benchmark for a good impact on any particular field. This is a rough estimate. Citations of key papers will usually grow exponentially – so a paper that has been cited five times within its first year might be cited 10 times the next year, 20 times the year after that and so on.

Let somebody else do the hard work

Along with text books, a good place to start to identify the most important literature is a review paper or meta-analysis. In other words, instead of trying to summarize the relevant material yourself, try to find review papers (and, if you're keen, update them).

To identify relevant reviews quickly you can use Google Scholar. To efficiently update the review, you could use Google Scholar to see which other papers have cited the review (click the 'Cited by' tab) and then take a look at those papers. If you have the time, you could adopt a more rigorous approach by conducting a systematic review yourself (see Chapter 5).

Journal articles can often take years to be published

From the time that a study is conducted to the time that it is published, a few years might have passed by and so, in some instances, papers might be out-of-date by the time that they are published! So how can you find even more timely research? One option is to 'Google' the top people in any particular area. Academics sometimes have their articles or working papers online – even before they are published. Look for the phrase 'in press' (or 'accepted for publication'). This tells you that the manuscript will definitely be published but it hasn't been published yet. Often academics will let you know which projects they are working on now (which is helpful to see where the field could move to in the future). They might even provide additional resources such as online experiments so that you can get a feeling for the sort of experiments that they conduct. For example, Ralf Schwarzer, a professor at Freie University, Berlin, who has made important contributions to the science of behavior change including the development of theory (particularly the Health Action Process Approach [HAPA] model), measures and interventions, provides academic papers and resources – including, for the adventurous, access to a free meta-analysis program at http://userpage.fu-berlin.de/health/author.htm.

Some journals are viewed as more prestigious than others

Journals are ranked based on the number of times that papers appearing in their journal are cited by others. A proxy measure of the likely importance of an article is to take a look at the impact factor rating of the journal within which it is published. Impact factors are usually published on the website of the journal and change from year to year. As a benchmark, for behavioral science journals related to health, an impact factor rating over 3 is high. Look for the following journals as they are often ranked as the top journals in the field (their impact factor ratings for 2015 are provided in parentheses): *Health Psychology* [3.611], *Annals of Behavioral Medicine* [4.195], *Health Psychology Review* [8.976].

Some high-ranking general journals (within which health behavior change articles often appear) are: *Psychological Bulletin* [15.575] and *Psychological Review* [9.797] (journals which publish reviews).

APPLYING BEHAVIOR CHANGE TECHNIQUES IN VARIOUS CONTEXTS

Behavior can be changed across a variety of different contexts. In this section, we highlight various reviews and empirical studies demonstrating effective strategies to change a range of health behaviors across a number of contexts: schools, the workplace and in healthcare settings.

SCHOOL-BASED INTERVENTIONS

Why?

The school, given the role of compulsory physical education classes, can be a useful way to increase physical activity and fitness. There are a number of ways in which changes to school-based physical education classes can increase physical activity. For example, the number of classes can be increased, the duration of classes can be increased or the type of exercises/sports conducted in class can be altered. Through classes, educational and other behavior change techniques can also be applied directly to pupils to tackle a range of different health behaviors.

Examples

In a systematic review of physical activity interventions, Kahn et al. (2002) concluded there was strong evidence that modifications to physical activity classes can increase aerobic capacity, flexibility and muscular endurance. These improvements seemed to be achieved without adverse consequences to other school work.

As well as promoting physical activity directly, school-based interventions have been used to reduce sedentary behavior. Television and video-game use are important contributors to sedentary lifestyles which, in turn, have been associated with negative health outcomes. On the basis that American children, outside of sleep, spend most of their time watching television and playing video games, Robinson (1999) designed an intervention aimed at reducing the time spent doing these activities. It was anticipated that, by changing this activity, children's body mass index could be reduced because replacement activities would use more energy. One group received lessons from their teachers (who were trained first by the experimenters) concerning self-monitoring of television and video-game use; students were then challenged to go 'cold turkey' by not watching television or playing video games for 10 days before being given a 7-hour per week budget of time they could spend on these activities. This intervention was supported by materials designed to motivate parents to enforce these rules and an electronic monitor that could ration the number of hours the television could be switched on per week. Finally, students were asked to be advocates for reduced media use. Compared to a control group of students who simply reported on their behavior, the students exposed to the school-based intervention appeared to watch significantly less television and play video games less than the control group. The intervention group, relative to the control group, also had significant reductions in body mass index over the course of the study plus additional benefits (e.g., improved waist-to-hip ratios). Consequently, school-based interventions can be used to change health behaviors which may help in the battle against childhood obesity (but see Kahn et al., 2002).

WORKSITE INTERVENTIONS

Why?

The workplace is another important context in which to change health behaviors given many employed adults spend around half of the time that they are awake at work. Improving the health of one's workforce can have important and tangible benefits for companies. In a meta-analysis by Conn, Hafdahl, Cooper, Brown and Lusk (2009), worksite-based interventions, designed to increase physical activity, increased physical activity and had small effects on increasing attendance and reducing job-related stress (see effect sizes in Chapter 6). In addition, obesity in the workplace is linked with absenteeism, sick leave, disability, injuries and healthcare claims (Anderson et al., 2009). Reducing obesity through effective behavior change strategies may be one way, therefore, of reducing staff-related costs. Interventions designed to change health behaviors in the workplace can also benefit the economy more widely by reducing the demands on health services and medical costs. The workplace, therefore, can be seen as a convenient and economically viable environment within which to try to change important health behaviors.

Interestingly, the size of the workplace has been shown *not* to influence the success of behavior change interventions linked to health (Conn et al., 2009). Effective interventions can, in principle therefore, be delivered with similar outcomes in small-, medium- and large-sized companies.

Examples

In a review of worksite-based interventions to promote physical activity, Taylor, Conner and Lawton (2012) concluded that such interventions yield small increases in physical activity, on average. However, the review did not detect any behavior change techniques to be especially effective in this context. Similarly, based on the results of the higher quality studies included in a review of worksite interventions on health outcomes, Heaney and Goetzel (1997) concluded that it is unlikely that simply raising health awareness across the workforce will create substantial change. According to Heaney and Goetzel (1997), a more targeted approach to high-risk individuals involving risk-reduction counseling is likely to be more useful in effecting change.

Anderson et al. (2009) presented an explanatory model highlighting how the worksite can be used to deliver changes in dietary and physical activity-related behaviors and, thus, changes in body size and composition of their employees. According to Anderson et al. (2009), there are three main ways in which an organization can promote exercise and diet. First, an organization can make changes to its policy and environment by, for example, providing free worksite gyms to encourage employees to participate in regular exercise. This would help counter barriers of cost and the inconvenience of finding opportunities to exercise for employees. Second, organizations can raise awareness about the benefits of exercise through, for example, presenting health-related information on the intranet or through posters and leaflets distributed in the workplace. Third, organizations could offer social support or skills training aimed at increasing employees' confidence in their ability to improve diet or increase physical activity.

INTERVENTIONS IN PRIMARY CARE/HEALTHCARE

Why?

In the past, doctors, nurses and other healthcare professionals have focused on treating the sick. In the UK, Lord Darzi's report *NHS Next Stage Review* (Department of Health, 2008) which sets out a strong vision for innovation, quality and personalized care, informed the strategies of many organizations within the National Health Service (NHS). According to this review, a key focus and challenge here is to prevent ill health as well as treating sickness within healthcare settings.

Relative to interventions conducted in the workplace or school-based settings, behavior change in healthcare faces the challenge of lack of time in contact with the person who is the target for behavior change. Previous research has, therefore, focused on screening of people at risk (e.g., using the alcohol use disorders test, AUDIT; Bohn, Barbor & Kranzler, 1995) within primary care (e.g., at the General Practice). There is a need, therefore, to develop effective brief interventions to change key health behaviors.

There are other challenges to developing and delivering effective behavior change interventions in healthcare settings. The interventions need to be seen as feasible and acceptable to the users (those delivering it and those receiving it). For example, there has been concern that doctors (general practitioners, GPs) may not be able to deliver brief interventions designed to change health behaviors due to factors such as worries about damaging the GP-patient relationship, lack of incentive for GPs and lack of training (e.g., O'Donnell, Wallace & Kaner, 2014). Strong evidence for the efficacy (i.e., the ability of the intervention to cause changes in behavior) will be a key factor in how acceptable the intervention is to the users and whether it will be adopted and used over a sustained period of time, even when intervention studies cease. Fortunately, there is some evidence supporting the use of brief interventions designed to change health behaviors within healthcare settings and we consider some examples next.

Examples

In a meta-analysis comprising 17 tests, Stead, Bergson and Lancaster (2008) concluded that doctors giving brief advice concerning smoking cessation could increase quit rates significantly compared to groups receiving no advice, raising quit rates to 4–6% compared to 2–3% without assistance. Brief advice has also been shown to be useful for other health and drug-related behaviors including alcohol use (Bien, Miller & Tonigan, 1993; O'Donnell et al., 2014). Miller and Sanchez (1994) have also advocated the use of a FRAMES approach to change health behaviors in healthcare settings. The FRAMES approach is a brief intervention comprising Feedback (providing information on behavior relative to goals or others), Responsibility (emphasizing the individual is ultimately responsible for their health), Advice (providing verbal or written advice to change behavior), Menu (providing a range of self-help strategies), Empathy (the healthcare practitioner adopting a warm, understanding approach) and Self-Efficacy (enhancing confidence in the individual's ability to change through persuasion).

BURNING ISSUE BOX 3.2

QUESTIONS AND ANSWERS ON BEHAVIOR CHANGE

Question 1: Which behavior change technique is the most effective?

At a general level, it has been demonstrated within a review on HIV intervention strategies (Albarracin et al., 2005) that passive interventions (simply presenting arguments) are less effective than more active interventions (such as behavioral skills training).

At the level of specific techniques, self-monitoring appears to be a particularly effective strategy. In a meta-analysis of patient education to increase physical activity, Conn, Hafdahl, Brown and Brown (2008) reported that interventions that incorporated self-monitoring were more effective than those that did not while other techniques (barriers management, contracting, consequences, exercise prescription, feedback, fitness testing, goal setting, problem solving and stimulus/ cues) were unrelated to effect sizes. This is consistent with results of a review by Michie et al. (2009) that also concluded self-monitoring was the most effective behavior change technique for healthy eating and physical activity, as well as a review examining the impact of self-monitoring across several types of behavior (Harkin et al., 2016).

While different techniques might be more effective for different behaviors, and there is a degree of imprecision in the approach adopted by Conn et al. and Michie et al. (given they consider multiple behavior change techniques), self-monitoring clearly appears to be a powerful behavior change technique. This is supported also by the number of times it emerges as an effective behavior change technique relative to other techniques in other reviews (see Table 3.2).

Question 2: Is it better to change multiple behaviors at the same time?

By changing one behavior successfully, this might increase one's confidence in one's ability to change other behaviors. However, Bull, Dombrowski, McCleary and Johnston (2014), in a review of health behavior interventions for low income groups, reported interventions targeting only physical activity produced larger effects than studies targeting multiple behaviors including physical activity. This finding was consistent with Conn et al.'s (2008) meta-analysis which reported that interventions targeting only physical activity yielded larger effects on physical activity than those targeting physical activity and other behaviors (e.g., diet) together. Attempting to change two behaviors at the same time has been argued to lead to less than twice the change of an intervention targeting one behavior (i.e., sub-additivity), as the more complex intervention is more difficult for the participant to adhere to (e.g., The Trials of Hypertension Collaborative Research Group, 1997). However, even in studies where adherence is high, sub-additivity still occurs (e.g., Sacks et al., 2001). Most recently, a review by Wilson et al. (2015) suggested that making 2–3 recommendations led to stronger behavioral improvements than making 0, 1 or 4 or more recommendations. In sum, targeting multiple behaviors at the same time may lead to greater overall change but sub-additivity is one drawback of this approach along with putting greater demands on participants, those delivering the intervention and total costs.

Question 3: Are interventions that comprise more behavior change techniques more effective?

In their review of internet-based interventions to promote physical activity, Webb, Joseph, Yardley and Michie (2010) reported that interventions with more techniques tended to produce greater increases in physical activity. In a review of workplace-based interventions designed to reduce stress, Murphy (1996) concluded studies that used a combination of techniques reported larger effects on outcome measures than studies that incorporated interventions comprising single techniques. Some recent reviews have provided equivocal support with more techniques leading to larger effects on some outcomes but not others (e.g., Bishop, Fenge-Davies, Kirby & Geraghty, 2015). When assessing the impact of self-regulatory techniques on exercise and dietary behaviors (prompting intention formation; providing feedback on performance; self-monitoring; prompting specific goal setting; prompting review of behavioral goals), Michie et al. (2009) reported that combining three self-regulatory techniques generated a medium effect on behavior; using 2, 4 or 5 self-regulatory techniques resulted in small-to-medium effects; while 0 or 1 self-regulatory techniques generated the smallest effects. Thus, it appears that moderately complex interventions (that combine a small number of techniques) might be the most useful for behavior change.

Question 4: Does tailoring educational materials to the needs of the individual rather than presenting everybody with the same information yield larger changes in behavior?

Tailoring interventions via computers, for example, allows those delivering interventions to provide personalized self-assessment and feedback and respond to the specific beliefs and cognitions of individuals. By providing only information that is relevant to the individual, the amount of irrelevant information is reduced and this may explain why this approach could increase the likelihood that the educational materials are read and the key points recalled (Brug, Campbell & van Assema, 1999). Personalized feedback should seek to compare the individual's behavior against peer averages which highlights to the individual the need to change (e.g., Brug, Steenhuis, van Assema & De Vries, 1996). In a review of 57 studies, however, tailoring was found to have a small benefit on the effectiveness of behavioral interventions (Noar, Benac & Harris, 2007).

Engagement, or involvement in the message, is likely to be a key factor in the influence of tailoring as with any form of educational materials (see Petty & Cacioppo, 1986). Presenting tailored information in an interactive format might be one way to maximize user engagement and subsequent behavior change. For example, Hurling, Fairley and Dias (2006) demonstrated that an interactive version of an internet website was rated as more engaging as indexed by higher user retention, it enhanced exercise expectations, and it increased self-reported exercise more than a less interactive version and no intervention.

Brug et al. (1999) tentatively concluded that computer-tailored information may be more motivating – especially in reducing fat intake – than general information. However, Conn et al. (2008) reported that individually tailored interventions were no more effective than presenting the same content to everybody within their meta-analysis of educational physical activity interventions for patients.

SUMMARY

A large number of behavior change techniques are available and represent different ways to change behavior. These techniques have been defined and categorized within taxonomies enabling consistent use and descriptions of interventions. As these taxonomies become refined over time, and effective training methods developed to ensure such taxonomies can be used reliably, they will become an increasingly important means to organize the evidence base. Of the techniques available, self-monitoring appears to have a lot of promise. The techniques that we have focused on within this chapter tend to produce medium-to-large effects in the short term but their effects become smaller in the longer term.

FURTHER READING

Adams, J., Giles, E.L., McColl, E. & Sniehotta, F.F. (2014). Carrots, sticks and health behaviours: a framework for documenting the complexity of financial incentive interventions to change health behaviours. *Health Psychology Review*, 8, 286–295. Identifies nine different domains across which to describe financial incentive interventions: direction, form, magnitude, certainty, target, frequency, immediacy, schedule and recipient.
The National Centre for Smoking Cessation and Training (NCSCT) website provides access to a variety of resources relevant to behavior change techniques. These include videos and other training resources concerning very brief advice on smoking, as well as a variety of documents designed for smoking cessation practitioners. See: www.ncsct.co.uk/
BCT Taxonomy v1 Online Training website provides online training in how to use Michie et al.'s (2013) classification of 93 behavior change techniques. See: www.bct-taxonomy.com/

GLOSSARY

Behavior change technique (BCT): a systematic strategy used in an attempt to change behavior (e.g., providing information on consequences; prompting specific goal setting; prompting barrier identification; modeling the behavior; planning social support).

Fully-crossed (full factorial) design: a methodological approach in which each behavior change technique is delivered individually and in combination with all other behavior change techniques used within a study across study groups. Useful for identifying which behavior change techniques change behavior and which do not.

Implementation intention: a specific plan an individual makes, in advance, regarding the context (e.g., when/where) they will perform a specific action.

Incentives: typically reflects a reward to encourage behavior change (though a

broader definition may also encompass the removal of punishment or related threat).

Meta-analysis: a statistical procedure used to combine, compare and contrast the findings of studies on a related topic.

Motivational interviewing: 'prompting the person to provide self-motivating statements and evaluations of their own behavior to minimize resistance to change' (Abraham & Michie, 2008, p. 382).

Self-monitoring: 'the person is asked to keep a record of specified behavior(s) (e.g., in a diary)' (Abraham & Michie, 2008, p. 382).

Systematic review: a rigorous and replicable approach to identify, and synthesize evidence from, studies tackling a specific issue.

REFERENCES

Aarts, H., Dijksterhuis, A. & Midden, C. (1999). To plan or not to plan? Goal achievement or interrupting the performance of a mundane behaviours. *European Journal of Social Psychology, 29,* 971–979.

Abraham, C. & Graham-Rowe, E. (2009). Are worksite interventions effective in increasing physical activity? A systematic review and meta-analysis. *Health Psychology Review, 3,* 108–144.

Abraham, C. & Michie, S. (2008). A taxonomy of behavior change techniques used in interventions. *Health Psychology, 27,* 379–387.

Adriaanse, M.A., Vinkers, C.D., De Ridder, D.T., Hox, J.J. & De Wit, J.B. (2011). Do implementation intentions help to eat a healthy diet? A systematic review and meta-analysis of the empirical evidence. *Appetite, 56,* 183–193.

Albarracín, D., Gillette, J.C., Earl, A.N., Glasman, L.R., Durantini, M.R. & Ho, M-H. (2005). A test of major assumptions about behavior change: a comprehensive look at the effects of passive and active HIV-prevention interventions since the beginning of the epidemic. *Psychological Bulletin, 131,* 856–897.

Anderson, L.M., Quinn, T.A., Glanz, K., Ramirez, G., Kahwati, L.C., Johnson, D.B., Buchanan, L.B., Archer, W.R., Chattopadhyay, S., Kalra, G.P., Katz, D.L. & Task Force on Community Preventive Services (2009). The effectiveness of worksite nutrition and physical activity interventions for controlling employee overweight and obesity. *American Journal of Preventive Medicine, 37,* 340–357.

Apodaca, T.R. & Longabaugh, R. (2009). Mechanisms of change in motivational interviewing: a review and preliminary evaluation of evidence. *Addiction, 104,* 705–715.

Arnott, B., Rehackova, L., Errington, L., Sniehotta, F. F., Roberts, J. & Araujo-Soares, V. (2014). Efficacy of behavioural interventions for transport behaviour change: systematic review, meta-analysis and intervention coding. *International Journal of Behavioral Nutrition & Physical Activity, 11,* 133.

Avery, L., Flynn, D., van Wersch, A., Sniehotta, F.F. & Trenell, M.I. (2012). Changing physical activity behavior in type 2 diabetes: a systematic review and meta-analysis of behavioral interventions. *Diabetes Care, 35,* 2681–2689.

Bartlett, Y. K., Sheeran, P. & Hawley, M.S. (2014). Effective behaviour change techniques in smoking cessation interventions for people with chronic obstructive pulmonary disease: a meta-analysis. *British Journal of Health Psychology, 19,* 181–203.

Bhattarai, N., Prevost, A.T., Wright, A.J., Charlton, J., Rudisill, C. & Gulliford, M.C. (2013). Effectiveness of interventions to promote healthy diet in primary care: systematic review and meta-analysis of randomised controlled trials. *BMC Public Health, 13,* 1203.

Bien, T.H., Miller, W.R. & Tonigan, J.S. (1993). Brief interventions for alcohol problems: a review. *Addiction, 88,* 315–336.

Bird, E.L., Baker, G., Mutrie, N., Ogilvie, D., Sahlqvist, S. & Powell, J. (2013). Behaviour change techniques used to promote walking and cycling: a systematic review. *Health Psychology, 32,* 829–838.

Bishop, F.L., Fenge-Davies, A.L., Kirby, S. & Geraghty, A.W.A. (2015). Context effects and behaviour change techniques in randomized trials: a systematic review using the example of trials to increase adherence to physical activity in musculoskeletal pain. *Psychology & Health, 30,* 104–121.

Bohn, M.J., Barbor, T.F. & Kranzler, H.R. (1995). The alcohol use identification test (AUDIT): validation of a screening instrument for use in medical settings. *Journal of Studies on Alcohol, 56,* 423–432.

Brannon, E.E. & Cushing, C.C. (2015). Is there an app for that? Translational science of pediatric behavior change for physical activity and dietary interventions: a systematic review. *Journal of Pediatric Psychology, 40,* 373–384.

Brug, J., Campbell, M. & van Assema, P. (1999). The application and impact of computer-generated personalized nutrition education: a review of the literature. *Patient Education and Counseling*, *36*, 145–156.

Brug, J., Steenhuis, I.H.M., van Assema, P. & De Vries, H. (1996). The impact of a computer-tailored nutrition intervention. *Preventive Medicine*, *25*, 236–242.

Bull, E.R., Dombrowski, S.U., McCleary, N. & Johnston, M. (2014). Are interventions for low-income groups effective in changing healthy eating, physical activity and smoking behaviours? A systematic review and meta-analysis. *BMJ Open*, *4*, e006046.

Cahill, K. & Perara, R. (2011). Competitions and incentives for smoking cessation. *Cochrane Database of Systematic Reviews*, Issue 4. Art. No.: CD004307.

Conn, V. S., Hafdahl, A.R., Brown, S.A. & Brown, L.M. (2008). Meta-analysis of patient education interventions to increase physical activity among chronically ill adults. *Patient Education and Counseling*, *70*, 157–172.

Conn, V.S., Hafdahl, A.R., Cooper, P.S., Brown, L.M. & Lusk, S.L. (2009). Meta-analysis of workplace physical activity interventions. *American Journal of Preventive Medicine*, *37*, 330–339.

Cummings, S.M., Cooper, R.L. & Cassie, K.M. (2009). Motivational interviewing to affect behavioral change in older adults. *Research on Social Work Practice*, *19*, 195–204.

Department of Health (2008). *High Quality Care For All: NHS Next Stage Review Final Report*. London: TSO.

Dombrowski, S.U., Sniehotta, F.F., Avenell, A., Johnston, M., MacLennan, G. & Araújo-Soares, V. (2012). Identifying active ingredients in complex behavioural interventions for obese adults with obesity-related co-morbidities or additional risk factors for co-morbidities: a systematic review. *Health Psychology Review*, *6*, 7–32.

Fishbein, M. (1995). Developing effective behavior change interventions: some lessons learned from behavioral research. In T.E. Becker, S.L. David & G. Saucey (Eds.), *National Institute on Drug Research Monograph Series 155* (pp. 246–261). Rockville, MD: National Institute on Drug Research.

French, D.P., Olander, E.K., Chisholm, A. & McSharry, J. (2014). Which behaviour change techniques are the most effective at increasing older adults' self-efficacy and physical activity behaviour? A systematic review. *Annals of Behavioral Medicine*, *48*, 225–234.

Giles, E.L., Robalino, S., McColl, E., Sniehotta, F.F. & Adams, J. (2014). The effectiveness of financial incentives for health behaviour change: systematic review and meta-analysis. *PLOS ONE*, *9*, e90347.

Gilinsky, A.S., Dale, H., Robinson, C., Hughes, A.R., McInnes, R. & Lavallee, D. (2015). Efficacy of physical activity interventions in post-natal populations: systematic review, meta-analysis and content coding of behaviour change techniques. *Health Psychology Review*, *9*, 244–263.

Golley, R.K., Hendrie, G.A., Slater, A. & Corsini, N. (2011). Interventions that involve parents to improve children's weight-related nutrition intake and activity patterns – what nutrition and activity targets and behaviour change techniques are associated with intervention effectiveness? *Obesity Reviews*, *12*, 114–130.

Gollwitzer, P.M. (1993). Goal achievement: the role of intentions. In W. Stroebe and M. Hewstone (Eds.), *European Review of Social Psychology*, *4*, 141–185. Chichester, UK: Wiley.

Gollwitzer, P.M. & Sheeran, P. (2006). Implementation intentions and goal achievement: a meta-analysis of effects and processes. *Advances in Experimental Social Psychology*, *38*, 249–268.

Harkin, B., Webb, T.L., Chang, B.P.I., Prestwich, A., Conner, M., Kellar, I., Benn, Y. & Sheeran, P. (2016). Does monitoring goal progress promote goal attainment? A meta-analysis of the experimental evidence. *Psychological Bulletin*, *142*(2), 198–229.

Hartmann-Boyce, J., Johns, D.J., Jebb, S. & Aveyard, P. (2014). Effect of behavioural techniques and delivery mode on effectiveness of weight management: systematic review, meta-analysis and meta-regression. *Obesity Reviews*, *15*, 598–609.

Heaney, C.A. & Goetzel, R.Z. (1997). A review of health-related outcomes of multi-component worksite health promotion programs. *American Journal of Health Promotion*, *11*, 290–307.

Henrich, J.F., Knittle, K., De Gucht, V., Warren, S., Dombrowski, S.U. & Maes, S. (2015). Identifying effective techniques within psychological treatments for irritable bowel syndrome: a meta-analysis. *Journal of Psychosomatic Research, 78*, 205–222.

Hettema J., Steele J. & Miller, W.R. (2005). Motivational interviewing. *Annual Review of Clinical Psychology, 1*, 91–111.

Hill, B., Richardson, B. & Skouteris, H. (2015). We know how to design effective health coaching interventions: a systematic review of the state of the literature. *American Journal of Health Promotion, 29*, e158–168.

Hill, B., Skouteris, H. & Fuller-Tyszkiewicz, M. (2013). Interventions designed to limit gestational weight gain: a systematic review of theory and meta-analysis of intervention components. *Obesity Reviews, 14*, 435–450.

Hurling, R., Fairley, B.W. & Dias, M.B. (2006). Internet-based exercise intervention systems: are more interactive designs better? *Psychology & Health, 21*, 757–772.

Johnston, V., Liberato, S. & Thomas, D. (2012). Incentives for preventing smoking in children and adolescents. *Cochrane Database of Systematic Reviews*, Issue 10. Art. No.: CD008645.

Kahn, E.B., Ramsey, L.T., Brownson, R.C., Heath, G.W., Howze, E.H., Powell, K.E., Stone, E.J., Rajab, M.W., Corso, P. & the Task Force on Community Preventive Services (2002). The effectiveness of interventions to increase physical activity: a systematic review. *American Journal of Preventive Medicine, 22*, 73–107.

Lara, J., Evans, E.H., O'Brien, N., Moynihan, P.J., Meyer, T.D., Adamson, A.J., Errington, L., Sniehotta, F.F., White, M. & Mathers, J.C. (2014). Association of behaviour change techniques with effectiveness of dietary interventions among adults of retirement age: a systematic review and meta-analysis of randomised controlled trials. *BMC Medicine, 12*, 177.

Liu, S., Dunford, S.D., Leung, Y.W., Brooks, D., Thomas, S.G., Eysenbach, G. & Nolan, R.P. (2013). Reducing blood pressure with internet-based interventions: a meta-analysis. *Canadian Journal of Cardiology, 29*, 613–621.

Lorencatto, F., West, R. & Michie, S. (2012). Specifying evidence-based behavior change techniques to aid smoking cessation in pregnancy. *Nicotine & Tobacco Research, 14*, 1019–1026.

Lussier, J.P., Heil, S.H., Mongeon, J.A., Badger, G.J. & Higgins, S.T. (2006). A meta-analysis of voucher-based reinforcement therapy for substance use disorders. *Addiction, 101*, 192–203.

Lyzwinski, L.N. (2014). A systematic review and meta-analysis of mobile devices and weight loss with an intervention content analysis. *Journal of Personalized Medicine, 4*, 311–385.

Mantzari, E., Vogt, F., Shemilt, I., Wei, Y., Higgins, J.P.T. & Marteau, T.M. (2015). Personal financial incentives for changing habitual health-related behaviors: a systematic review and meta-analysis. *Preventive Medicine, 75*, 75–85.

Markland, D., Ryan, R.M., Tobin, V.J. & Rollnick, S. (2005). Motivational interviewing and self-determination theory. *Journal of Social and Clinical Psychology, 24*, 811–831.

Martin, J., Chater, A. & Lorencatto, F. (2013). Effective behaviour change techniques in the prevention and management of childhood obesity. *International Journal of Obesity, 37*, 1287–1294.

Michie, S., Abraham, C., Whittington, C., McAteer, J. & Gupta, S. (2009). Effective techniques in healthy eating and physical activity interventions: a meta-regression. *Health Psychology, 28*, 690–701.

Michie, S., Ashford, S., Sniehotta, F.F., Dombrowski, S.U., Bishop, A. & French, D.P. (2011). A refined taxonomy of behaviour change techniques to help people change their physical activity and healthy eating behaviours: the CALO-RE taxonomy. *Psychology & Health, 26*, 1479–1498.

Michie, S., Churchill, S. & West, R. (2011a). Identifying evidence-based competences required to deliver behavioural support for smoking cessation. *Annals of Behavioral Medicine, 41*, 59–70.

Michie, S., Hyder, N., Walia, A. & West, R. (2011b). Development of a taxonomy of behaviour change techniques used in individual behavioural support for smoking cessation. *Addictive Behaviors, 36*, 315–319.

Michie, S., Richardson, M., Johnston, M., Abraham, C., Francis, J., Hardeman, W., Eccles, M.P., Cane, J. & Wood, C.E. (2013). The behavior change technique taxonomy (v1) of 93 hierarchically clustered techniques: building an international consensus for the reporting of behavior change interventions. *Annals of Behavioral Medicine, 46*, 81–95.

Michie, S., Whittington, C., Hamoudi, Z., Zarnani, F., Tober, G. & West, R. (2012). Identification of behaviour change techniques to reduce excessive alcohol consumption. *Addiction, 107*, 1431–1440.

Miller W. R. & Rollnick S. (2002). *Motivational Interviewing: Preparing People for Change* (2nd edn). New York: Guilford Press.

Miller, W.R. & Sanchez, V. C. (1994). Motivating young adults for treatment and lifestyle change: In G. Howard (Ed.), *Issues in Alcohol Use and Misuse by Young Adults* (pp. 55–82). Notre Dame, IN: University of Notre Dame Press.

Milne, S.E., Orbell, S. & Sheeran, P. (2002). Combining motivational and volitional interventions to promote exercise participation: protection motivation theory and implementation intentions. *British Journal of Health Psychology, 7*, 163–184.

Morton, K., Beauchamp, M., Prothero, A., Joyce, L., Saunders, L., Spencer-Bowdage, S., Dancy, B. & Pedlar, C. (2015). The effectiveness of motivational interviewing for health behaviour change in primary care settings: a systematic review. *Health Psychology Review, 9*, 205–223.

Murphy, L.R. (1996). Stress management in work settings: a critical review of health effects. *American Journal of Health Promotion, 11*, 112–135.

Noar, S.M., Benac, C.N. & Harris, M.S. (2007). Does tailoring matter? Meta-analytic review of tailored print health behaviour change interventions. *Psychological Bulletin, 133*, 673–693.

O'Donnell, A., Wallace, P. & Kaner, E. (2014). From efficacy to effectiveness and beyond: what next for brief interventions in primary care? *Frontiers in Psychiatry, 5*, 113.

Olander, E., Fletcher, H., Williams, S., Atkinson, L., Turner, A. & French, D.P. (2013). What are the most effective techniques in changing obese individuals' physical activity self efficacy and behaviour: a systematic review and meta-analysis. *International Journal of Behavioral Nutrition and Physical Activity, 10*, 29.

Pal, K., Eastwood, S.V., Michie, S., Farmer, A., Barnard, M.L., Peacock, R., Wood, B., Edwards, P. & Murray, E. (2014). Computer-based interventions to improve self-management in adults with Type 2 diabetes: a systematic review and meta-analysis. *Diabetes Care, 37*, 1759–1766.

Petty, R.E. & Cacioppo, J.T. (1986). The elaboration likelihood model of persuasion. *Advances in Experimental Social Psychology, 19*, 123–205.

Pilling, S., Strang, J. & Gerada, C. (2007). Psychosocial interventions and opioid detoxification for drug misuse: summary of NICE guidance. *British Medical Journal, 335*, 203–205.

Prestwich, A. & Kellar, I. (2014). How can implementation intentions as a behaviour change intervention be improved? *European Review of Applied Psychology, 64*, 35–41.

Prestwich, A., Kellar, I., Parker, R., MacRae, S., Learmonth, M., Sykes, B., Taylor, N. & Castle, H. (2014). How can self-efficacy be increased? Meta-analysis of dietary interventions. *Health Psychology Review, 8*, 270–285.

Robinson, T.M. (1999). Reducing children's television viewing to prevent obesity: a randomized controlled trial. *Journal of the American Medical Association, 282*, 1561–1567.

Sacks, F.M., Svetkey, L.P., Vollmer, W.M. et al., for the DASH-Sodium Collaborative Research Group (2001). A clinical trial of the effects on blood pressure of reduced dietary sodium and the DASH dietary pattern (the DASH-Sodium Trial). *New England Journal of Medicine, 344*, 3–10.

Stead, L.F., Bergson, G. & Lancaster, T. (2008). Physician advice for smoking cessation. *Cochrane Database of Systematic Reviews*, Issue 2. Art. No.: CD000165.

Taylor, N., Conner, M. & Lawton, R. (2012). The impact of theory on the effectiveness of worksite physical activity interventions: a meta-analysis and meta-regression. *Health Psychology Review, 6*, 33–73.

The Trials of Hypertension Prevention Collaborative Research Group (1997). Effects of weight loss and sodium reduction intervention on blood pressure and hypertension incidence in overweight people with high normal blood pressure: the trials of hypertension prevention, phase II. *Archives of Internal Medicine, 157,* 657–667.

Vasilaki, E.I., Hosier, S.G. & Cox, W.M. (2006). The efficacy of motivational interviewing as a brief intervention for excessive drinking: a meta-analytic review. *Alcohol & Alcoholism, 41,* 328–335.

Webb, T.L., Joseph, J., Yardley, L. & Michie, S. (2010). Using the internet to promote health behavior change: a systematic review and meta-analysis of the impact of theoretical basis, use of behavior change techniques, and mode of delivery on efficacy. *Journal of Medical Internet Research, 12*(1), e4.

Webb, T.L. & Sheeran, P. (2007). How do implementation intentions promote goal attainment? A test of component processes. *Journal of Experimental Social Psychology, 43,* 295–302.

West, R., Walia, A., Hyder, N., Shahab, L. & Michie, S. (2010). Behavior change techniques used by the English Stop Smoking Services and their associations with short-term quit outcomes. *Nicotine & Tobacco Research, 12,* 742–747.

Williams, S. & French, D. (2011). What are the most effective behaviour change techniques for changing physical activity self-efficacy and physical activity behaviour – and are they the same? *Health Education Research, 26,* 308–322.

Wilson, K., Senay, I., Durantini, M., Sánchez, F., Hennessy, M., Spring, B. & Albarracín, D. (2015). When it comes to lifestyle recommendations, more is sometimes less: a meta-analysis of theoretical assumptions underlying the effectiveness of interventions promoting multiple behavior domain change. *Psychological Bulletin, 141,* 474–509.

Wood, C.E., Richardson, M., Johnston, M., Abraham, C., Francis, J., Hardeman, W. & Michie, S. (2015). Applying the behaviour change technique (BCT) taxonomy v1: a study of coder training. *Translational Behavioral Medicine, 5,* 134–148.

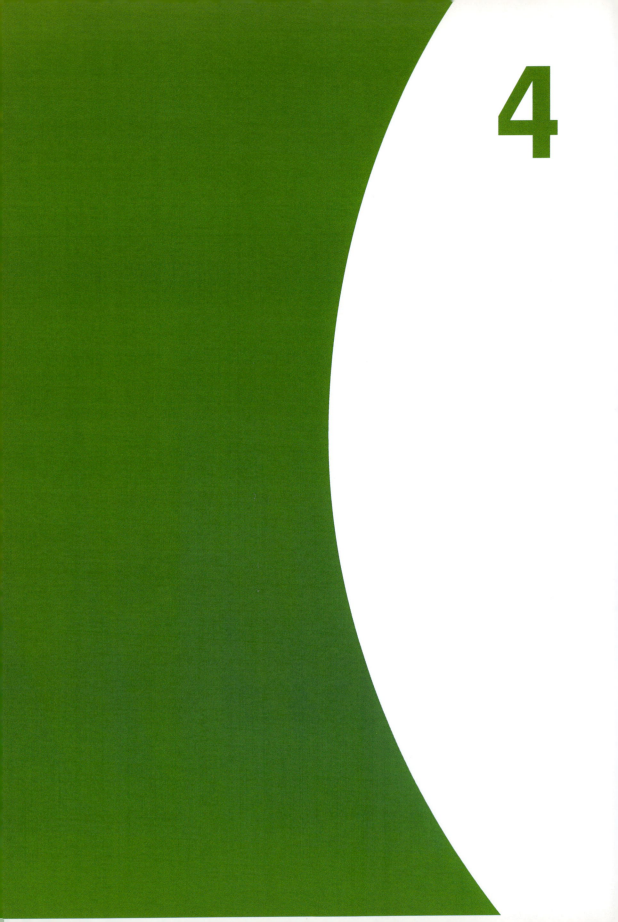

4

CHAPTER 4
THEORY-BASED INTERVENTIONS

OVERVIEW

In the previous chapters you were introduced to a variety of **theories** and **behavior change techniques** that have been used to understand, predict and change behavior. In this chapter, we deal with more challenging issues: what are theory-based interventions and why is it useful for a health-related intervention to be theory-based? As this chapter extends what you have learned in the opening chapters, it is important that you read these first. The issues covered in Chapter 4 are challenging, but hopefully stimulating, and represent key obstacles for the progression of the science of health behavior change.

A great deal of research has been conducted to identify what factors (**determinants**) predict behavior and you would have come across many of these determinants (expressed as theoretical constructs) in Chapter 2. Various studies have highlighted the importance of attitudes (whether a person has a positive or negative evaluation of a particular object or behavior or thinks positive outcomes will follow from performing the behavior), self-efficacy (whether an individual feels they have the ability to perform a particular behavior or are confident they can perform it), threat appraisal (which comprises an individual considering both the likelihood and the severity of the negative consequences (e.g., illness) associated with doing or not doing certain behaviors), intentions (one's willingness to try to perform a particular behavior) and a whole host of other determinants that drive a wide variety of behaviors. By identifying the determinants of health behavior, individuals can then set about changing health behavior. This chapter will reflect on what constitutes a **theory-based intervention** and highlight the potential benefits, and problems, associated with designing and evaluating a theory-based intervention. We then consider how to develop theory-based interventions using a four-step approach and Intervention Mapping.

WHAT IS A THEORY-BASED INTERVENTION?

Behavioral scientists within the field of health behavior change research often refer to their interventions as 'theory-based.' What does this actually mean? In practice, its meaning can vary from an author loosely referring to their intervention in the context of a particular theory within the introduction of a journal article to using theory systematically at the various steps of the research process.

THE THEORY CODING SCHEME (MICHIE & PRESTWICH, 2010)

To measure the extent to which theory is used to develop and test a behavior change intervention, Michie and Prestwich (2010) developed the **Theory Coding Scheme**. The Theory Coding Scheme comprises 19 items. These items cover whether theory is mentioned; whether the constructs within a particular intervention were targeted for change by specific behavior change techniques; whether theory is used to select participants (e.g., only targeting individuals that lack motivation, or hold weak intentions, to stop drink driving) or tailor interventions to the needs of particular interventions (e.g., delivering different behavior change techniques to those who are not motivated to change their behavior but have the skills to do so if they wanted and those who are motivated to change their behavior but lack their skills to do so); whether the theory underlying the intervention is tested by a) measuring the appropriate theoretical constructs before and/or after the delivery of the intervention; b) whether changes in the theoretical constructs explain the effectiveness of the intervention on behavior change (see Chapter 6, 'Mediation and Moderation'); and finally whether theory is refined on the basis of the results of the study in which the intervention was tested.

The Theory Coding Scheme has a number of potential benefits and applications. First, within **systematic reviews** and **meta-analyses** (see Chapters 5 and 6) it can be used to rigorously and systematically examine the use of theory within intervention research. Such reviews in the past have tended to rely on very basic examination of theory (e.g., Albarracin et al., 2005; Baban & Craciun, 2007; Trifiletti, Gielen, Sleet & Hopkins, 2005; Webb & Sheeran, 2006) such as comparing those studies which explicitly state that the interventions described are based on theory against those that are not. As stated above, this is problematic as there is great variation in what researchers have termed theory-based interventions. Moreover, the attempts to compare theory-based behavior change interventions against more **atheoretical interventions** have consistently failed to consider exactly how theory has informed the intervention. The Theory Coding Scheme provides a means to test, in a much more rigorous fashion, whether the use of theory can enhance the effects of interventions and *how* these benefits can be accrued. Second, it might encourage a more systematic approach to describe interventions, and the role that theory has played, within journal articles by providing a framework upon which to do so. Third, the scheme might influence the design of theory-based interventions by encouraging researchers to systematically consider and examine what constitutes a theory-based intervention and the role of theory in informing and evaluating such interventions.

THE LITMUS TEST OF THEORY (NIGG & PAXTON, 2008)

Alternatives to the Theory Coding Scheme exist. For example, Nigg and Paxton's (2008) Litmus Test of Theory incorporates eight items relating to theory use. There is a reasonably large overlap between the Litmus Test and the Theory Coding Scheme. For instance, both consider whether a theory has been mentioned, the relationship between behavior change techniques and theoretical constructs, and the measurement and change in theoretical mediators following intervention. The key differences are that the Litmus Test, but not the Theory Coding Scheme, considers whether the theory has been described by the authors, the fidelity of the intervention and whether the target of the theory-based intervention is consistent with the measure used to assess the intervention. In relation to the latter, an example in which there is inconsistency is when an intervention targets a specific type of physical activity (e.g., walking) but the measure relates to overall physical activity. On the other hand, the Theory Coding Scheme considers the relationship between behavior change techniques and theoretical constructs in more detail (i.e., using five items), as well as considering other factors not present in the Litmus Test such as how theory has been used to tailor interventions, the implications of the results for theory, whether the intervention is based on a single or multiple theories and the reliability and validity of the measures. In addition, the process of development of the Theory Coding Scheme has been made clear along with its ability to be used reliably across multiple coders.

CRITICAL SKILLS TOOLKIT 4.1

'THEORY-BASED' INTERVENTIONS

In health behavior change research, those who design an intervention might describe their intervention as theory-based. By using the term 'theory-based' intervention, their intervention is open to a number of potential criticisms as the term 'theory-based' intervention can take on multiple different meanings and interpretations:

1. *Is the intervention based on one theory or a combination of theories?* Often an intervention might be based on elements of different theories. As such, basing an intervention on multiple theories means that the theories have been combined and synthesized into a new untested theory. Being untested, and by combining elements of different theories together in a non-systematic or evidence-based way, could in effect make their intervention atheoretical (i.e., not theoretical). In Figure 4.1, the underlying constructs specified within the Theory of Planned Behavior (TPB) are targeted by an intervention (comprising three behavior change techniques: BCT1, BCT2, BCT3) but an additional construct (threat) is also targeted. Given this combination of constructs, the rationale would need to be clear (and convincing) why threat was also targeted alongside the constructs within the TPB.

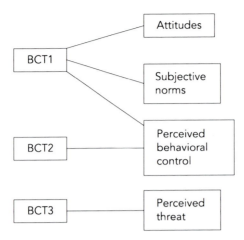

FIGURE 4.1 A diagrammatic representation of an intervention comprising three behavior change techniques (BCT1, BCT2, BCT3) targeting the Theory of Planned Behavior constructs plus perceived threat

2. *Are all constructs specified within a theory (excluding behavior) targeted by the intervention?* If only some elements are targeted then is the intervention faithful to the theory? Maybe not. If only particular constructs were targeted, do the authors provide a clear rationale why they have targeted these constructs rather than others?

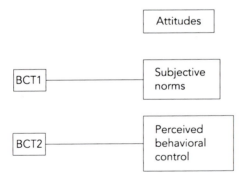

FIGURE 4.2 A diagrammatic representation of an intervention comprising two behavior change techniques (BCT1, BCT2) targeting only two of the Theory of Planned Behavior constructs

3. In any intervention, it should be clear why each behavior change technique has been incorporated within an intervention. In a *theory-based* intervention, it should be clear *which behavior change technique is targeting which specific construct*. Ideally, the authors should present evidence and a reasoned rationale why a specific technique should change a specific construct and how, in turn, changing this construct should change behavior. It is fairly common for an intervention to incorporate multiple behavior change techniques but it is not especially common for the inclusion of each behavior change technique to be

clearly justified and linked to a specific theoretical construct (see Prestwich et al., 2014b). Figure 4.3a provides a diagrammatic representation where all three behavior change techniques (BCT1, BCT2, BCT3) used within an intervention are linked to two constructs within a theory (C1, C2). Figure 4.3b provides a diagrammatic representation where only two of the behavior change techniques (BCT1, BCT2 but not BCT3) are linked to a construct within a theory.

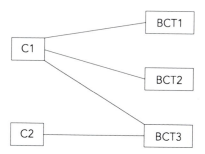

FIGURE 4.3A A diagrammatic representation where all behavior change techniques (BCT1, BCT2, BCT3) are linked to at least one construct (C1 and/or C2)

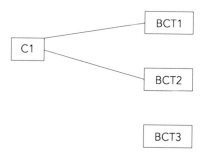

FIGURE 4.3B A diagrammatic representation where some, but not all, of the behavior change techniques (BCT1, BCT2 but not BCT3) are linked to at least one construct (C1)

4. *Identifying why an intervention is effective or ineffective*. The authors might describe their intervention as theory-based but not test its theoretical basis. The theory-based intervention could be appropriately tested by measuring participants' levels on each construct after (and preferably before) the intervention and testing statistically whether these changes mediate (i.e., explain) the effect of the intervention on behavior change (see Chapter 6, 'Mediation and Moderation'). Sometimes authors do take steps to measure theoretical constructs within their study or randomized controlled trial. However, even when they do this and present evidence that their intervention changes behavior and changes at least one theoretical construct, they might fail to test whether changes in the theoretical construct explain the effect of the intervention on behavior (i.e., conduct mediation analysis). As such, it is not clear why their intervention was effective in changing behavior and it does not provide sufficient evidence to validate and support the theory upon which the intervention was based.

FOR BEHAVIOR CHANGE, DOES THEORY ACTUALLY MATTER?

Many scientists like to label themselves as either 'theoretical' or 'applied' in perspective. Theoretical scientists develop theories and may look to test them. Applied scientists are more focused on solving problems. However, the two perspectives go hand-in-hand. Applied scientists can use theory to guide and develop their behavior change interventions. In turn, the **outcomes** from theory-based interventions can inform the refinement of current theories and inspire the generation of 'better' theories that are more effective in real-life settings. The benefits of using theory to develop and test health behavior interventions are as follows.

(I) IDENTIFY KEY CONSTRUCTS (DETERMINANTS) TO TARGET

If there is evidence that a construct (e.g., attitudes; threat; self-efficacy) is associated with (or, even better, *causes*) health behavior, changing these constructs should change health behavior. However, if a particular theory or **model** specifies a number of constructs, which construct is the most important to target? Constructs might be selected by considering the following three factors:

1. Whether your sample scores high or low on a particular theoretical construct (see Burning Issue Box 4.1).
2. The amount of variance in health behavior that is explained by the construct (see Critical Skills Toolkit 2.1) or, put more simply, the extent to which health behavior is associated with a determinant (see Critical Skills Toolkit 4.1). In the absence of a measure of health behavior, researchers could focus on targeting constructs which are strongly related to (explain a lot of variance in) behavior such as behavioral intentions.
3. The variability in the measure assessing a particular construct (see Critical Skills Toolkit 4.2).

BURNING ISSUE BOX 4.1

IF YOU HAD TO CHOOSE, HOW WOULD YOU DECIDE WHICH THEORETICAL DETERMINANT TO TARGET IN YOUR INTERVENTION?

You're tasked with changing the eating patterns of a group of overweight people. You may decide to target the theoretical construct which has the highest correlation with unhealthy eating patterns. However, assume for a minute that the theoretical construct that correlates most strongly with unhealthy eating patterns is attitudes towards dieting and that most, or all, of your target sample already have positive attitudes towards dieting. In this sense, there might be better determinants to tackle.

If you are using the Theory of Planned Behavior (see Chapter 2) as a basis for your intervention then the other candidates for behavior change would be to alter subjective norms and/or perceived behavioral control (PBC). Of these constructs, subjective norms might already be positive – many people within the target group might already perceive their friends, family and/or important others to want them to diet. This leaves PBC – the degree to which an individual feels they have the skills to diet. In a sample of overweight people, PBC might be low and thus targeted for intervention.

CRITICAL SKILLS TOOLKIT 4.2

LACK OF VARIABILITY AND ITS IMPACT ON CORRELATION. SHOULD YOU TARGET ONLY THE CONSTRUCTS THAT EXPLAIN SIGNIFICANT PORTIONS OF VARIANCE IN BEHAVIOR (OR MORE PROXIMAL DETERMINANTS)?

Imagine you've run a pilot study where you've measured Theory of Planned Behavior (TPB) constructs (attitudes, subjective norms [SN], PBC, intentions and behavior) in a sample of students. The study attempts to identify the constructs that most strongly relate to/predict the number of days per week that students exercise for 30 minutes.

After measuring these constructs, you've assessed the correlations (relationships) between them (for more information on correlations, see Chapter 6). The average level of each construct (Mean), the spread/variability of the scores in your sample (standard deviation, SD) and the intercorrelations between the variables are presented in Table 4.1.

TABLE 4.1 Descriptives and intercorrelations between variables from a fictitious study

	Scale	Mean	SD	Attitude	SN	PBC	Intention	Exercise
Attitudes	1–7	2.25	0.25	–	.08	.02	.05	–.02
SN	1–7	4.50	1.30		–	.11	.12	.09
PBC	1–7	3.25	1.25			–	.42	.33
Intention	1–7	4.45	1.23				–	.35
Exercise	0–7	1.50	1.50					–

All of the mean scores are comfortably below their maximum possible score (7) and thus there is room for an intervention to try to increase the levels of any of the constructs. On this basis, all of the constructs (attitudes, SN, PBC) could be targeted for intervention as a means to make students' intentions to exercise more positive (and, in turn, to increase their exercise participation). So what else could we use to determine which construct to target with our intervention?

We can look at the size of the correlations between the variables to identify which variables most strongly relate to intentions and/or behavior. In this example, PBC looks like the best candidate as it more strongly correlates with intention ($r = .42$) and exercise behavior ($r = .33$) than the other candidates (SN and attitudes). As it is the most strongly related, changing PBC (rather than attitudes or SN) should lead to the biggest/most reliable changes in intentions and ultimately behavior. However, this isn't the full story ...

Look at the standard deviation of scores for attitudes – it is very low. This means that nearly all of your participants have the same level of attitudes towards exercising. When a construct (in this case, attitudes) has very little variability then it is almost impossible that it will correlate with anything (and looking at the correlations between attitudes and the other variables, the correlations are near zero reflecting very weak relationships). This weak correlation might arise from poor reliability and/or validity of your attitude measure (see Chapter 5). In this instance, attitudes might still be an important determinant of intentions and behavior. Targeting attitudes in an attempt to make them more positive towards exercising might still be an effective method to change behavior.

Looking at SN, although its mean score is rather low (suggesting that there is room for an intervention to make SN more positive), it does not correlate highly with intentions or behavior nor is it hindered by low levels of variability. As such, there would be less benefit in your intervention targeting SN compared to the other constructs. On the basis of the TPB (which informs your initial list of candidate target constructs – attitudes, SN, PBC) and the data above, your intervention should target PBC. You should also consider trying to change attitudes.

(II) HELP TO SELECT APPROPRIATE INTERVENTION TECHNIQUES

Theory can be used as a guide to select the most appropriate combination of behavior change techniques to incorporate within a behavior change intervention (see step 2 of the 'Four-Step Cycle of Theory-Based Behavior Change' outlined later in this chapter).

(III) REFINE OR TAILOR INTERVENTION TECHNIQUES AND THEORIES

a) Attitudes and PBC, according to certain theories, are two key determinants of behaviors such as exercising. Take Barry and Jeremy – two individuals who have difficulty in exercising frequently. On the basis of the theories highlighting the importance of attitudes and PBC, Barry and Jeremy should complete measures of attitudes and PBC. After completing such measures, it turns out Barry has a positive attitude towards exercising but low PBC and Jeremy has a negative attitude towards exercising but high PBC. On this basis, Barry should be exposed to an intervention designed to enhance PBC and Jeremy should receive an intervention to make his attitudes towards exercising more positive. This example illustrates how theory can be used to tailor interventions to the specific needs of the individual.

b) By designing and implementing studies that have a theoretical framework then we can continuously test the theory and identify in which contexts and for which populations and behaviors it is most effective. This can lead to the refinement of theory and helps to build up the generalizability of the theory (by identifying various situations that the theory can be usefully applied; see step 4 of the 'Four-Step Cycle of Theory-Based Behavior Change' outlined later).

(IV) INFORM INTERVENTIONS THAT MORE EFFECTIVELY CHANGE HEALTH BEHAVIOR

There is some evidence that basing an intervention on theory can lead to larger effects on behavior. For example, in a meta-analysis, Albarracin et al. (2005) indicated that studies that reported using theory as a basis for their intervention yielded stronger changes in HIV-related behaviors than studies that did not do this. While there are other reviews also suggesting that interventions based on theory may be more effective than those that are not, many of these reviews do not examine the extent to which an intervention has been based on theory using measures such as the Theory Coding Scheme. Moreover, there are also some reviews suggesting that theory-based interventions do not produce stronger changes in health behaviors than those interventions that are not based on theory. So, all in all, the evidence is mixed regarding whether using theory to develop health behavior interventions leads to stronger changes in behavior. We consider these issues in detail elsewhere (see Prestwich, Webb & Conner, 2015).

(V) INDICATE WHY AN INTERVENTION WAS EFFECTIVE, OR INEFFECTIVE, IN CHANGING BEHAVIOR

By measuring key determinants (constructs) in your participants after they have been exposed to an intervention one can gain an understanding of why an intervention was effective (or ineffective) in changing behavior. By taking this approach, the following outcomes are possible.

a) Successfully change theoretical constructs and behavior

Here, there is a possibility that you can identify why your intervention was effective. Essentially if your intervention changes a determinant (e.g., attitudes) and behavior (e.g., exercise) then you could conclude that your intervention successfully changed exercise by changing attitudes. This conclusion would be stronger on the basis of mediation analysis (see Chapter 6, 'Mediation and Moderation').

b) Does not change theoretical construct but does change behavior

If this outcome is achieved then one might gain an understanding of how the intervention was effective by ruling out (or minimizing) the role of the theoretical constructs not affected by the intervention.

c) Successfully change theoretical constructs but behavior does not change

In this instance either: a) the change in the theoretical constructs was not sufficient to change behavior (e.g., your intervention might have made your sample's attitudes towards exercising more positive, but not positive enough, to promote exercise; or you might have changed attitudes but not other determinants that are necessary to change behavior); or b) the theoretical determinant/construct does not cause behavior. In the latter case, the theory might be refined by removing this 'determinant' from the theory. This illustrates an additional benefit of using theory to inform behavior change interventions – *theory-based interventions can be used to refine and improve theories*. Theory-based interventions are only as good as the theories upon which the intervention is based. If an intervention is based on a theory which identifies inappropriate determinants then the intervention is unlikely to change behavior and the theory needs to be improved. In this way, there is a 'synergistic cycle' where theory informs intervention development and evaluation and this evaluation informs (refines or supports) the theory upon which the intervention was based.

d) Does not change the theoretical construct and does not change behavior

Here, the theory might be appropriate but the intervention technique was inappropriate (as it didn't change a key behavioral determinant or behavior). One might conclude here that the intervention was ineffective because it did not change the underlying behavioral determinant (although this is not fully testable - if the intervention had changed the behavioral determinant in question then it might not necessarily have changed behavior).

DEVELOPING AND TESTING THEORY-BASED INTERVENTIONS 1: FOUR-STEP CYCLE

After identifying the health behavior to change, changing behavior essentially incorporates (up to) four steps (see Figure 4.4). Step 1 involves using the best theories to identify the most likely determinants of behavior from the **theory-relevant constructs**. Step 2 then requires the identification of behavior change techniques that are most likely to change the key determinants of behavior and consequently the behavior of interest. Step 3 requires the adoption of the stringent methods and statistics that we overview in Chapters 5 and 6 to evaluate the effect of the intervention. The final step is to use the evaluation to refine the intervention and/or underlying theory. Given the results of the study should be used to refine the underlying theory, the process should be seen as a cycle that continually refines and improves the underlying theory in order to develop better theories that lead to the development of more effective behavior change interventions.

Many individuals and organizations interested in health behavior change, such as the UK National Health Service (NHS) or multinational businesses, might argue that step 1 is

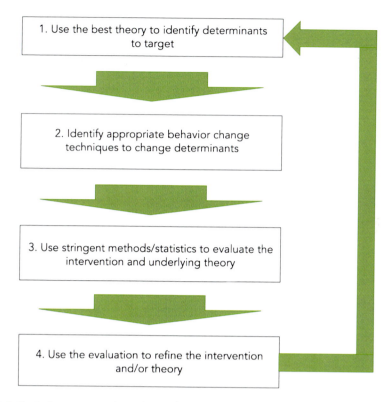

FIGURE 4.4 Basic four-step cycle to theory-based behavior change

unnecessary and that step 2 simply involves the identification of a technique that changes health behavior directly (without changing, necessarily, the determinants specified within any particular theory). They might view the ultimate aim as changing health behavior (e.g., increasing attendance for cervical cancer screenings; increasing physical activity; reducing alcohol intake etc.) and as long as a particular strategy changes behavior (more women attend cervical cancer screenings; more people increase their physical activity levels and people drink less alcohol) then they are happy (particularly if they meet their targets. . .). However, omitting step 1 and passing quickly over step 2 eliminates the role of theory and the potential benefits that it might bring. We now consider the four steps in more detail.

STEP 1: USE THE BEST THEORY TO IDENTIFY DETERMINANTS TO TARGET

At the very least, there should be some evidence to support the theory; this could be correlational evidence showing that determinants within the theory correlate with behavior. Preferably, however, there would be experimental evidence that changes in theoretical determinants cause changes in behavior. Ideally, there will be lots of studies providing consistent experimental evidence demonstrating that the theory is supported and outperforms other theories that could be used as a starting point to develop your intervention. A rigorous systematic review and meta-analysis (an approach that statistically combines the findings from lots of relevant studies – see Chapters 5 and 6) supporting a particular theory would be useful at this first step, should such a review exist.

Over time, it will become clearer which theories are the best theories upon which to base your intervention (see Burning Issue Box 4.3 for more detailed consideration of this issue). Once you've identified an appropriate theory upon which to develop and evaluate your intervention, you can identify the theory-relevant constructs to target as the theory suggests that they determine behavior (see Burning Issue Box 4.1 for further information about which determinants/theory-relevant constructs to target).

STEP 2: IDENTIFY APPROPRIATE BEHAVIOR CHANGE TECHNIQUES TO CHANGE DETERMINANTS

By identifying theoretical constructs (determinants) to target, theory provides a means for selecting one behavior change technique over another. According to Bandura (1977), for instance, self-efficacy (your belief that you are capable of performing a particular task or behavior) can be promoted by persuasion, successfully performing the task/behavior yourself or seeing somebody else complete the task. However, most health/social cognition models, highlighted in Chapter 2, only specify which constructs predict behavior and do not specify which intervention techniques change these constructs. In such instances, researchers have three options.

Option 1: preferably conduct or identify relevant reviews that have attempted to find which techniques are the most useful methods to change the determinant of interest (e.g., Prestwich et al., 2014a). When these reviews do not exist, however, researchers could follow option 2 or 3.

Option 2: apply (educated) guesswork based on their assumptions or previous experiences with changing constructs or using particular behavior change techniques. To help with this, behavior change experts have, using consensus methods, tried to agree which techniques should and should not change specific determinants of health behavior (e.g., Michie, Johnston, Francis, Hardeman & Eccles, 2008).

Option 3: alternatively, apply the techniques theorized within Intervention Mapping to change specific determinants (see the supplementary materials provided by Kok et al., 2016).

STEP 3: USE STRINGENT METHODS/STATISTICS TO EVALUATE THE INTERVENTION AND UNDERLYING THEORY

It is important to use an appropriate methodological and statistical approach to evaluate the effect of the intervention on the theoretical constructs and its subsequent impact on health behaviors. We consider appropriate methodological approaches throughout the book including, in particular, this chapter and Chapter 5. A useful statistical analysis, called mediation analysis (see Chapter 6), helps identify whether the changes in behavior can be attributed to changes in the theoretical constructs stipulated in the underlying theory used to inform the intervention. If the changes in behavior can be attributed to changes in the relevant theoretical constructs then there is evidence to support the theory.

STEP 4: USE THE EVALUATION TO REFINE THE INTERVENTION AND/OR THEORY

If the changes in behavior are not explained by changes in the relevant theoretical constructs that the theory stipulates (and assuming the study is sufficiently methodologically strong with a sufficient number of participants) then there is evidence to suggest that the theory is inadequate. While you may not want to change a theory on the basis of one null finding, over time, if such null results accumulate within several studies then the theory should be refined in line with the evidence. Based on a review by Prestwich et al. (2014b) which explored how theory is used in relation to developing and evaluating physical activity and dietary interventions, there appears to be a real reluctance by authors to do this. In fact, on the basis of this review, fewer than 3% of experimental studies that test theory-based interventions involve the authors suggesting refinements to the theory through the addition or removal of new constructs to the theory or by identifying which relationships between theoretical constructs should be changed. Relatedly only 1 in 10 studies provided adequate support (or refutation) of a theory based on appropriate mediation analyses. These low rates of theory-based inferences and suggested refinements serve to slow down the progress of the science of behavior change as poor theories will continue to be used and newer, better theories will develop more slowly (see Prestwich et al., 2015).

DEVELOPING AND TESTING THEORY-BASED INTERVENTIONS 2: INTERVENTION MAPPING

Intervention Mapping (IM) is a process, outlined by Bartholomew, Parcel and Kok (1998) and more recently by Kok et al. (2016), to design, develop and evaluate behavior change interventions. Central to the process is the need for the intervention to be theory-based and evidence-based. IM provides guidance regarding the steps that (IM recommends) should be taken when developing an intervention. In essence it takes a problem (e.g., obesity), identifies the key behaviors (e.g., diet, physical activity) that should be changed to address the problem, attempts to identify the factors that determine these key behaviors (e.g., high availability of energy dense foods; poor self-efficacy) and the methods that change these determinants (e.g., changes to the environment; modeling) which are then tweaked so that they can be adopted by the users (the people delivering the intervention and the people that receive it) before the intervention is evaluated in the final step (see Figure 4.5).

The IM procedure is outlined below in more detail. Reference to Kwak et al.'s (2007) development of a worksite intervention to prevent weight gain using IM (The NHF-NRG In Balance-Project) is presented within brackets.

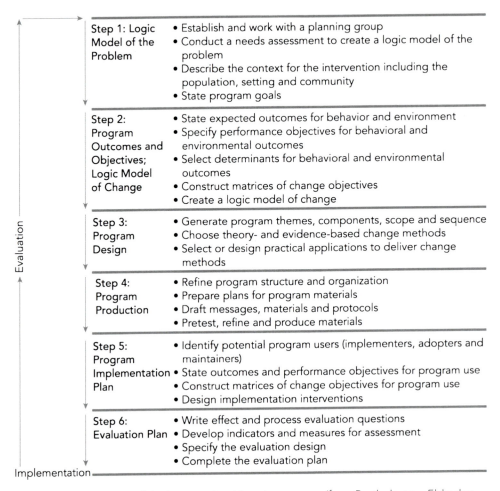

Evaluation →	Step 1: Logic Model of the Problem	• Establish and work with a planning group • Conduct a needs assessment to create a logic model of the problem • Describe the context for the intervention including the population, setting and community • State program goals
	Step 2: Program Outcomes and Objectives; Logic Model of Change	• State expected outcomes for behavior and environment • Specify performance objectives for behavioral and environmental outcomes • Select determinants for behavioral and environmental outcomes • Construct matrices of change objectives • Create a logic model of change
	Step 3: Program Design	• Generate program themes, components, scope and sequence • Choose theory- and evidence-based change methods • Select or design practical applications to deliver change methods
	Step 4: Program Production	• Refine program structure and organization • Prepare plans for program materials • Draft messages, materials and protocols • Pretest, refine and produce materials
	Step 5: Program Implementation Plan	• Identify potential program users (implementers, adopters and maintainers) • State outcomes and performance objectives for program use • Construct matrices of change objectives for program use • Design implementation interventions
	Step 6: Evaluation Plan	• Write effect and process evaluation questions • Develop indicators and measures for assessment • Specify the evaluation design • Complete the evaluation plan

Implementation

FIGURE 4.5 Overview of the Intervention Mapping process (from Bartholomew Eldredge, Markham, Ruiter, Fernández, Kok & Parcel, 2016)

1. *Logic model of the problem.* The nature of the problem [weight gain], the underlying behaviors [reduction in routine, daily physical activities; eating larger portions of food and energy dense foods], the key associated environmental contexts in which the underlying behaviors take place [workplace] are each identified. The stage culminates in the specification of program objectives [decrease energy intake through diet and/or increase physical activity within 25–40 year olds in the workplace].

2. *Program outcomes and objectives; logic model of change.* The program objectives identified in the first step are broken down into behaviors that can be targeted for change [increase walking/cycling as mode of transport; increase physical activity at work; decrease food portion sizes; replace high fat foods with low fat foods; replace low fiber foods with high fiber foods; replace saturated fats with unsaturated fats]. These are then broken down into *performance objectives* which tend to involve writing down the step-by-step changes that you wish to make [e.g., for replacing low

fiber foods with high fiber foods, the target population: a) need to know what fiber-rich foods are; b) self-assess their fiber intake; c) have a negative attitude towards foods low in fiber; d) indicate the importance of consuming fiber-rich foods; e) choose to consume fiber-rich foods; f) set achievable goals; g) form plans to reach these goals...]. These changes can occur at multiple levels (e.g., changes to the individual or environment).

The performance objectives are then linked to the *key determinants* [at the level of the individual: knowledge; awareness; taste preference; attitude; self-efficacy; habit. At the level of the environment: availability; management commitment/support; social support; company policy; cost] often through focus groups and/or systematic literature reviews. A matrix of behavior change objectives is formed by mapping the *performance objectives* to *key determinants*, at various levels (individual, interpersonal, organizational, community, societal).

3. *Program design.* The general techniques for changing determinants (theory-based methods) are identified (by reviewing empirical evidence and theories) [prompts; social support etc.] and then translated into practical strategies that can be deployed within the population/environment in question [e.g., placing prompts at elevators=prompts; setting up lunchtime walking groups=support].

4. *Program production.* The practical strategies identified in step 3 are then put together in a plan where the sequence of strategies and their scope are determined. The program materials are put together at this stage. It is often useful to check that the materials are pretested and that the materials match the performance objectives [brainstorm with experts to identify useful materials that already exist; tweak existing materials, where necessary; develop new materials where needed].

5. *Program implementation plan.* This step follows the procedures outlined in step 2 but the end-point is the formation of a detailed plan regarding program adoption and implementation by influencing the behavior of the people that will use the intervention. This stage needs to take into account the environment in which the intervention will be delivered (and those delivering it) and modified, where necessary, to ensure adoption. Pretesting of the materials in the environment can be useful to identify, at an early stage, any potential problems regarding adoption and implementation.

6. *Evaluation plan.* This stage is useful to identify whether the assumed linkages (e.g., between key determinants and performance objectives) were supported. This stage should attempt to assess changes in quality of life and health, behaviors, performance objectives, change determinants and level of implementation. Of course in order to assess these factors, they need to be considered during the earlier stages of IM and reliable and valid measures should be used or developed.

BURNING ISSUE BOX 4.2

WHAT ARE THE LIMITATIONS OF INTERVENTION MAPPING?

- Can require significant time and cost.
- The evidence base required for various linkages (e.g., determinants to techniques) could be lacking.
- The process of linking determinants to techniques (e.g., by conducting systematic reviews) is often not clearly articulated. More generally, IM does not give detailed guidance regarding *how* to use theory to design interventions, nor how theory can be tested and improved through appropriate modifications (Michie, Sheeran & Rothman, 2007).
- The generation of determinants encourages the integration of various theories within a single intervention. By combining theories, does the intervention remain theory-based?

BURNING ISSUE BOX 4.3

QUESTIONS AND ANSWERS ON THEORY-BASED INTERVENTIONS

Question 1: Which theory should I base my intervention upon?

At the moment, it is unclear which theory is the most useful for basing interventions. It is likely that some theories might be more appropriate in different situations and for different behaviors. For instance, a key factor might be whether the intervention is concerned with the initiation of behavior change or with the maintenance of the behavior (for the former, many of the theories outlined in Chapter 2 would be helpful; for the latter, theories such as the Relapse Prevention Model (Marlatt & George, 1984) might be useful). However, the selection of the most appropriate theory remains a complex issue. This is partly as a result of the variation in what comprises a theory-based intervention (i.e., even with two interventions described as being based on the Theory of Planned Behavior (TPB), there is likely to be some variation in the number of TPB constructs targeted, the selection of different behavior change techniques, variation in measures used to evaluate the effectiveness of the intervention etc.). Consequently, an adequate answer to this question is some way off – the evidence base is insufficient.

Question 2: Should my intervention always be theory-based?

From a pragmatic viewpoint, where you want to change behavior and you are not interested in why your intervention is effective or ineffective then there is less need for an intervention to be theory-based. Instead, your intervention should be selected on the criterion that it is *evidence-based* (i.e., previous studies have shown that a particular intervention is effective in changing your target behavior in a population that is representative of your population). If, however, you wish to understand the mechanisms underlying the effects of your intervention (for example, if you want to improve your intervention in the future or you wish to test a particular theory) then your intervention should be theory-based and you should test it accordingly.

Question 3: How should I test my theory-based intervention?

At the most basic level, you might choose to a) design an intervention which comprises a number of different behavior change techniques that targets each of the constructs within a theory, b) randomly allocate participants to the intervention group or a no-intervention control group, c) measure each of the constructs after (and preferably before) the intervention in both groups, and d) then compare the effectiveness of the intervention relative to a no-intervention control group in changing the theoretical constructs and behavior. This approach would give you an indication of:

a) whether an intervention based on all constructs of a theory is effective in changing behavior,
b) which constructs were changed by the intervention and
c) which construct changes (if any) explained the changes in behavior.

However, there are limitations. If there are multiple behavior change techniques within the intervention then additional experimental conditions are required to identify which components (behavior change techniques within the intervention) were effective in changing a theoretical construct or behavior (see Critical Skills Toolkit 3.1). In addition, simply measuring constructs, such as intentions, has been shown to be able to change behavior itself and thus can be viewed as an intervention in itself. This is known as the *mere-measurement or Question-Behavior effect*. As well as potentially reducing the size of the benefit of the intervention over the control (or even eliminating it), it is unclear whether the intervention would have been effective over the control condition *without* measuring the constructs. A Solomon four-group design is an approach to combat this problem whereby exposure to the intervention is crossed with exposure to measures of key determinants before completing the follow-up measure (i.e., resulting in four study conditions: intervention + measures; measures only; intervention only; control (neither intervention nor measures)).

Question 4: How many constructs should my intervention target?

One viewpoint would be that, if you're basing your intervention on a particular theory, your intervention should target all of the constructs underlying or predicting behavior. However, doing so leads to the problems described in response to Question 3 – either you have two groups (one intervention and one control) and consequently you struggle to find one technique that can change each of the theoretical constructs, or you use a number of different behavior change techniques and you consequently do not know which behavior change techniques underlies your study effects (to do so, you would need to adopt a full factorial design).

An alternative might be to target only certain (key) constructs allowing you to use fewer behavior change techniques and more basic designs (which comprise fewer intervention groups). The drawback here is that you are not being fully faithful to the theory as a whole. To complicate matters, some constructs appear in more than one theory (thus a TPB-based intervention that targets only PBC/self-efficacy could be described as a social cognitive theory-based intervention, for example).

Question 5: Is it OK to target constructs from different theories at the same time?

Yes, you might choose to target constructs that most strongly correlate with behavior regardless of the theory from which it is derived (see Critical Skills Toolkit 4.1). However, a consequence is that by putting together constructs from different theories, you are essentially developing and testing a new theory.

Question 6: Is there anything else I should bear in mind when designing a theory-based intervention?

One thing to keep in mind with theory-based interventions, as with any intervention, is that it should be consistently delivered to your participants in the way it is intended – in other words, it should have high fidelity. For example, you could design a brilliant intervention on paper but if only part of this intervention is delivered then your intervention might be ineffective in changing behavior. It is often useful, particularly when you are relying on others to deliver your intervention (and where time and funds permit), to run a process analysis where you check that participants receive the intervention as intended.

SUMMARY

In this chapter we considered the degree of variation that exists in claims regarding whether particular health behavior change interventions are theory-based, as well as different approaches that can be used to assess the extent of theory use. In addition, we considered the various benefits of using theory and critically evaluated whether the use of theory leads to stronger effects than interventions not based on theory. We conclude that the evidence is rather mixed but that theory use still has several benefits. On that basis, we ended the chapter by considering different ways in which theory-based interventions can be developed and tested including using the Intervention Mapping approach.

FURTHER READING

Kok, G., Gottlieb, N.H., Peters, G.Y., Mullen, P.D., Parcel, G.S., Ruiter, R.A.C., Fernández, M.E., Markham, C. & Bartholomew, L.K. (2016). A taxonomy of behaviour change methods: an Intervention Mapping approach. *Health Psychology Review, 10*, 297–312. A recent paper highlighting the Intervention Mapping approach and which provides tables overviewing methods to change different determinants of health behavior.

Michie, S. & Abraham, C. (2004). Interventions to change health behaviours: evidence-based or evidence-inspired? *Psychology & Health, 19*, 29–49. This paper lays the groundwork for subsequent work on behavior change taxonomies and theory-based interventions.

Michie, S. & Prestwich, A. (2010). Are interventions theory-based? Development of a theory coding scheme. *Health Psychology, 29*, 1–8. A 19-item coding scheme that can be used to assess how, and to what extent, any particular health behavior intervention is theory-based.

Prestwich, A., Webb, T.L. & Conner, M. (2015). Using theory to develop and test interventions to promote changes in health behaviour: evidence, issues, and recommendations. *Current Opinion in Psychology, 5*, 1–5. A paper challenging the assumption that using theory to inform health behavior interventions leads to larger changes in behavior.

GLOSSARY

Atheoretical intervention: an attempt using one or more behavior change techniques to change behavior or related outcomes without reference to, or use of, theory.

Behavior change technique: a systematic strategy used in an attempt to change behavior (e.g., providing information on consequences; prompting specific goal setting; prompting barrier identification; modeling the behavior; planning social support).

Meta-analysis: a statistical procedure used to combine, compare and contrast the findings of studies on a related topic.

Systematic review: a rigorous and replicable approach to identify, and synthesize evidence from, studies tackling a specific issue.

Theories, theory (or model): 'a set of interrelated concepts, definitions and propositions that present a *systematic* view of events or situations by specifying relations among variables, in order to

explain or *predict* the events or situations' (Glanz, Rimer & Viswanath, 2015, p. 26).

Theory-based intervention: an approach to change behavior or other outcomes (such as those related to health) that draws on one or more underlying theories to identify which determinants of behavior/ outcomes to target, which behavior change techniques to employ and for whom.

Theory Coding Scheme: an approach to assess how, and the extent to which, theory has been used to inform the development and evaluation of an intervention.

Theory-relevant construct: a key concept or building block within a theory/model upon which the intervention is based. Example constructs in the Theory of Planned Behavior are attitudes towards the behavior, perceived behavioral control, subjective norms etc. Constructs can be further broken down into **determinants** (the predictors such as attitudes, subjective norms, PBC) or **outcomes** (such as behavior).

REFERENCES

Albarracin, D., Gillette, J.C., Earl, A.N., Glasman, L.R., Durantini, M.R. & Ho, M.H. (2005). A test of major assumptions about behavior change: a comprehensive look at the effects of passive and active HIV-prevention interventions since the beginning of the epidemic. *Psychological Bulletin*, *131*, 856–897.

Baban, A. & Craciun, C. (2007). Changing health-risk behaviors: a review of theory and evidence-based interventions in health psychology. *Journal of Cognitive and Behavioral Psychotherapies*, 7, 45–67.

Bandura, A. (1977). Self-efficacy: toward a unifying theory of behavioral change. *Psychological Review*, *84*, 191–215.

Bartholomew, L.K., Parcel, G.S. & Kok, G. (1998). Intervention mapping: a process for developing theory- and evidence-based health education programs. *Health Education and Behavior*, *25*, 545–563.

Bartholomew Eldredge, L.K., Markham, C.M., Ruiter, R.A.C., Fernández, M.E., Kok, G. & Parcel, G.S. (2016). *Planning Health Promotion Programs: An Intervention Mapping Approach* (4th edn). San Francisco: Jossey-Bass.

Glanz, K., Rimer, B.K. & Viswanath, K. (2015). Theory, research and practice in health behavior. In K. Glanz, B.K. Rimer and K. Viswanath (Eds.), *Health Behavior: Theory Research & Practice* (5th edn; pp. 24–40). San Francisco: Jossey-Bass.

Kok, G., Gottlieb, N.H., Peters, G.Y., Mullen, P.D., Parcel, G.S., Ruiter, R.A.C., Fernández, M.E., Markham, C. & Bartholomew, L.K. (2016). A taxonomy of behaviour change methods: an Intervention Mapping approach. *Health Psychology Review*, *10*, 297–312.

Kwak, L., Kremers, S.P.J., Werkman, A., Visscher, T.L.S., van Baak, M.A. & Brug, J. (2007). The NHF-NRG In Balance-Project: the application of intervention mapping in the development, implementation and evaluation of weight gain prevention at the worksite. *Obesity Reviews*, *8*, 347–361.

Marlatt, G.A. & George, W.H. (1984). Relapse prevention – introduction and overview of the model. *British Journal of Addiction*, *79*, 261–273.

Michie, S., Johnston, M., Francis, J., Hardeman, W. & Eccles, M. (2008). From theory to intervention: mapping theoretically derived behavioural determinants to behaviour change techniques. *Applied Psychology: An International Review*, *57*, 660–680.

Michie, S. & Prestwich, A. (2010). Are interventions theory-based? Development of a theory coding scheme. *Health Psychology*, *29*, 1–8.

Michie, S., Sheeran, P. & Rothman, A. (2007). Advancing the science of behaviour change. Invited editorial. *Psychology and Health*, *22*, 249–253.

Nigg, C.R. & Paxton, R.J. (2008). Conceptual perspectives used to understand youth physical activity and inactivity. In A.L. Smith & S.J.H. Biddle (Eds.), *Youth Physical Activity and Inactivity: Challenges and Solutions* (pp. 79–113). Champaign, IL: Human Kinetics.

Prestwich, A., Kellar, I., Parker, R., MacRae, S., Learmonth, M., Sykes, B., Taylor, N. & Castle, H. (2014a). How can self-efficacy be increased? Meta-analysis of dietary interventions. *Health Psychology Review*, *8*, 270–285.

Prestwich, A., Sniehotta, F.F., Whittington, C., Dombrowski, S.U., Rogers, L. & Michie, S. (2014b). Does theory influence the effectiveness of health behavior interventions? Meta-analysis. *Health Psychology*, *33*, 465–474.

Prestwich, A., Webb, T.L. & Conner, M. (2015). Using theory to develop and test interventions to promote changes in health behaviour: evidence, issues, and recommendations. *Current Opinion in Psychology*, *5*, 1–5.

Trifiletti, L.B., Gielen, A.C., Sleet, D.A. & Hopkins, K. (2005). Behavioural and social sciences theories and models: are they being used in unintentional injury prevention research? *Health Educational Research*, *20*, 298–307.

Webb, T.L. & Sheeran, P. (2006). Does changing behavioral intentions engender behavior change? A meta-analysis of experimental evidence. *Psychological Bulletin*, *132*, 249–268.

5

CHAPTER 5
THE METHODOLOGY OF HEALTH BEHAVIOR CHANGE

OVERVIEW

Love it or hate it, research methods (and their best friend, statistics) represent a vital element of health behavior change. What are the most effective behavior change techniques to tackle obesity? How can we prevent medical errors? What are the barriers that prevent people, particularly those from lower socio-economic groups, from eating healthily? While we can try to answer such questions without scientific investigation – for example, in relation to the last question, we could suppose cost is a crucial barrier preventing people from eating healthily – what evidence supports this and how strong is this evidence? In this chapter, as well as introducing various methods of data collection, we highlight their pros and cons, and overview means to evaluate the quality of data.

SURVEY/QUESTIONNAIRE METHODS

Within surveys or questionnaires, behavioral scientists can look to identify the relationships between a whole range of different factors including those that are societal (e.g., socio-economic status) and individual (e.g., attitudes towards exercising).

CRITICAL SKILLS TOOLKIT 5.1

**ADVANTAGES AND DISADVANTAGES OF SURVEYS/
QUESTIONNAIRES USING RATING SCALES**
The following advantages and disadvantages refer specifically to surveys and questionnaires that use rating scales rather than open-ended questions.

To illustrate the advantages and disadvantages of surveys/questionnaires, the examples below have been applied within the context of assessing attitudes towards exercising.

Rating scales assessing attitudes towards exercising could look like this:

	Strongly disagree			Strongly agree
I really like exercising	1	2	3	4
Exercising is fun	1	2	3	4

Or

Exercising is:	Boring	1	2	3	4	5	Exciting
	Harmful	1	2	3	4	5	Beneficial
	Bad	1	2	3	4	5	Good

Advantages

1. Rating scales quickly assess people's attitudes. For example, a random sample of school children could respond to questions like those above to give an indication of the attitudes of school children to exercising.
2. They can be relatively cheap to develop.
3. When applied in correlational studies (see Chapter 6), they can indicate which variables correlate (i.e., are related) with each other. For example, questionnaire measures of attitudes towards exercising may correlate with questionnaire measures of the number of times that people exercise per week. By identifying which variables correlate with one another, behavioral scientists can generate hypotheses that can be tested using experimental designs. For example, one could hypothesize that exposing school children to an intervention designed to promote more favorable attitudes towards exercising will result in these school children exercising more in the future compared to a second group of school children not exposed to this intervention.

Disadvantages

1. Their potential utility is dependent on their design. To be of use, the questionnaire/survey should have strong evidence of **reliability** (e.g., **internal reliability**; **test-retest reliability**) and **validity** (e.g., **convergent validity**; **divergent validity**).
2. If the questionnaire is not reliable then you have an inaccurate representation of whatever it is you're trying to measure (e.g., school children's attitudes towards exercising). In turn, it would have limited use in *predicting* behavior (e.g., how often school children exercise).
3. When used in correlational (rather than experimental) designs they tell us little about causation. For example, measuring attitudes towards exercising and the number of times people exercise per week does not determine whether positive attitudes towards exercising encourages more frequent exercise (attitudes cause behavior), or whether frequently exercising promotes positive attitudes towards exercising (behavior causes attitudes). Experimental designs provide stronger evidence than correlational designs regarding causation.

To maximize the likelihood that any particular survey or questionnaire provides a good snapshot of current opinions, rather than just a snapshot, and to increase the likelihood that it accurately, rather than inaccurately, predicts future outcomes (such as the number of times people exercise) one must ensure that the survey/questionnaire is well-designed. In other words, it should have good evidence of reliability and validity (see Critical Skills Toolkit 5.2).

TABLE 5.1 Different types of questionnaire items

Type	Description	Sample items
Categorical	Participants are asked to select a specific category that best fits them or their opinion (the response options may or may not be provided)	'Are you male or female?' Male Female 'How much money do you earn per year?' Less than £20,000 £20,000 to £40,000 More than £40,000
Ranking	Require participants to rank order several response options	'Rank the following food types in order of preference from 1 = most preferred to 4 = least preferred:' Fruit Confectionary Savoury snacks Vegetables
Likert	Require individuals to rate their level of agreement with a statement along a scale	'I enjoy playing football.' Strongly Strongly disagree agree 1 2 3 4
Semantic differential	Similar to Likert scales but use opposing adjective pairs as anchors	'I find playing football is:' Fun 1 2 3 4 5 Boring Good 1 2 3 4 5 Bad Healthy 1 2 3 4 5 Unhealthy
Open-ended	Participants are not constrained in their response options (unlike the other types of questionnaire items)	'Why do you exercise as often as you do?' 'Tell me about your feelings towards exercising.' 'What factors influence the foods that you buy?'

CRITICAL SKILLS TOOLKIT 5.2

DESIGNING A RELIABLE AND VALID RATING SCALE QUESTIONNAIRE

Designing a reliable and valid questionnaire can take time and benefits from careful development. When you are evaluating questionnaires, you should look for evidence of scale development plus reliability and validity. A reliable measure produces consistent responses. A valid measure assesses what it claims to measure. If a measure is said to assess attitudes towards exercise but actually assesses emotions concerning food then the measure would be said to be invalid.

Ensuring a measure has reliability and validity helps reduce measurement error (the difference between what the individual responds on the measure and their actual 'true' score). If behavioral scientists use measures that do not have evidence of reliability and/or validity, the conclusions that arise from their studies are more likely to be inaccurate and the findings are less likely to be replicated by others in the future.

Developing a reliable/valid scale requires careful development via the following steps.

1. Generate a large pool of items

You might think attitudes, and other psychological constructs, may be accurately measured through a single item within a questionnaire. A single item measure is less likely than a measure with multiple items, however, to accurately represent a person's attitude. Think of a person (Jimmy) asked to try to hit the bulls-eye on a dartboard with a single dart. Think of another person (Ted) asked to try to hit the bulls-eye on a dartboard with 20 darts. You want to use these scenarios to measure the dart-playing ability of Jimmy and Ted by measuring the distance of the (average) dart from the bulls-eye. Your estimate of Ted's ability is likely to be more accurate (Jimmy may have one particularly good or bad dart which greatly influences your assessment of his darting ability). The same principle applies to developing a reliable questionnaire – more items (questions) on your questionnaire should enhance its reliability.

2. Take care when writing the specific items

a) The set of items should accurately and comprehensively represent the diversity and complexity of the psychological construct (e.g., attitudes towards healthy eating; self-esteem) that is being assessed. This will help ensure **content validity** of the measure.

b) Some of the items should be reversed to avoid acquiescence bias (the tendency to agree with statements). For example when measuring attitudes towards exercise, somebody with a very favorable attitude towards exercise would likely respond '5' to item 'i' and '1' to item 'ii'.

i. Doing physical active is fantastic

Strongly disagree				Strongly agree
1	2	3	4	⑤

ii. Doing physical activity is dull

Strongly disagree				Strongly agree
①	2	3	4	5

c) Reliability and validity of the questionnaire can also be enhanced by constructing specific items carefully. Here is a list of common problems that could apply to items within a questionnaire:

i. The items should be answerable on the scale provided. For example, somebody would struggle to answer the question: 'How much money do you earn?' on a 'strongly agree' to 'strongly disagree' rating scale.

ii. Items should avoid acronyms as the participant may not understand them. For example: 'The BPS is a worthwhile organization' may be difficult to answer for somebody who doesn't know that the BPS stands for the British Psychological Society.

iii. Ambiguous language should be avoided: 'I like rock' could refer to a specific type of music, rocks on the ground or rock that you eat by the seaside.

iv. Loaded questions that make assumptions or assess only one part of the issue should be avoided. For example, 'Are you still exercising?' assumes the individual used to exercise.

v. It is important that a question helps to differentiate between people and this wouldn't happen when everybody agrees or disagrees with a particular statement. Thus, statements that everybody would agree (or disagree) with such as 'Murder is a bad thing' should not be used.

vi. Leading questions are problematic: 'Everybody should exercise, shouldn't they?'

vii. Double-barreled questions or statements should be avoided as people may not feel the same to each element (e.g., 'Skin self-examinations are boring and unpleasant') – somebody may find them unpleasant but not boring...

viii. Double negatives can be difficult to understand (e.g., instead of saying 'not unpleasant' use 'pleasant' as the simpler language is easier to follow).

ix. Items should be brief, jargon-free, simple to understand and not intellectualized.

3. Pilot the measure

Once a set of items has been generated, it is useful for the measure to be trialed by handing the questionnaire to participants and asking them to complete it. This pilot step can be used to identify any weak items.

a) *Remove items that elicit responses that are inconsistent with responses on other related items*

In a scale assessing individuals' intentions to exercise all items should attempt to measure intentions towards exercising. As the items should all be striving to measure the same thing (i.e., intentions towards exercising) then participants should respond to the items in a consistent way. See responses to item set A and responses to item set B. Responses to item set A are consistent, while responses to item set B are inconsistent.

Set A: Consistent responses indicative of a reliable scale (responses suggest strong intentions to exercise)

		Strongly disagree				Strongly agree
		1	2	3	4	5
1	I intend to exercise	1	2	3	4	⑤
2	I am keen to exercise	1	2	3	4	⑤
3	My desire to exercise is weak	①	2	3	4	5
4	I want to exercise	1	2	3	4	⑤

Set B: Inconsistent responses indicative of an unreliable scale (it is unclear from the set of responses whether the individuals has strong, moderate or weak intentions to exercise)

		Strongly disagree				Strongly agree
		1	2	3	4	5
1	I intend to exercise	1	2	3	4	⑤
2	I am keen to exercise	①	2	3	4	5
3	My desire to exercise is weak	1	2	③	4	5
4	I want to exercise	①	2	3	4	5

A measure that elicits consistent responses across items is said to have high **internal reliability**. Internal reliability is assessed by Cronbach's alpha and should be between 0.7 and 1 in a reliable measure. If it falls below 0.7 then the level of internal reliability is typically judged to be unacceptable (the lower the number, the less internally reliable the measure). In statistical packages (such as SPSS), when requesting Cronbach's alpha, the output will typically also show the impact on the Cronbach's alpha score should any specific item be deleted. This is a helpful way to identify any items that seem to elicit responses that are inconsistent with responses on other items. Another way is to assess the correlation between responses on each specific item with the total (summed) score across all items. To generate a more reliable scale, researchers would remove from their questionnaire any item that has a low item-total correlation.

b) *Remove items that are unlikely to discriminate among individuals*

If the measure is to be of use, it should be able to discriminate accurately between different groups of people. Take the measure of intentions to exercise above; you might expect that people who exercise a lot would have stronger intentions to exercise than people who do little exercise. If the measure is trialed on a sample where half of the participants exercise a lot and the other half exercise little or not at all (more sedentary individuals) then you may expect the standard deviation of responses would not be too low and thus has some discriminatory value. One strategy to enhance validity of the scale is to remove items that have very low standard deviations. Alternatively, or in addition, items that do not seem to differentiate between your two groups of participants (high exercisers and more sedentary people) in the expected manner could be removed in the pilot phase of scale development. This strategy will help maximize the **criterion-related validity** of your scale: the extent that your measure is related to distinct criteria in the real world (in this case, the extent that it can differentiate between high exercisers and more sedentary people).

4. Further test the reliability and validity of your measure

The **dimensionality** of the scale should be examined to help make clear whether the scale is measuring one thing (thus making it unidimensional) or several things (thus making it multidimensional). This can be achieved through factor analysis.

Test-retest reliability should be assessed by giving participants the same questionnaire twice on two separate occasions. If the measure has high test-retest reliability then responses should be very similar across both time-points.

When looking through the items of a scale, judge the **face validity** – do all of the items look like they assess what they are supposed to assess? This is a pretty straightforward but subjective, non-standardized way of assessing validity. Other types of validity can be assessed more formally.

The **predictive validity** of a scale can be measured by testing whether responses on the questionnaire predict future events that you would expect it should predict. For example, does the measure of intentions to exercise predict how much exercise people do in the future? If it does then you could argue the measure has predictive validity.

The convergent validity of the measure can be determined by assessing the correlation between the measure and a related measure that has been previously validated. For example, when developing a new measure of intentions to exercise then the responses that participants give on the new measure should be similar to (correlate with) responses on a measure of exercise intentions that has been previously validated.

The discriminant (divergent) validity of the scale can be established by checking that responses on the scale are unrelated to responses on scales that it should be unrelated to. In the example of developing a measure of intentions to exercise, you would expect it would be unrelated to responses on a measure of attitudes towards washing up, for instance.

BURNING ISSUE BOX 5.1

HEALTH RISK BEHAVIORS AND ALTERED STATES

Studies that use models like the Theory of Planned Behavior (TPB) or the Prototype Willingness Model require participants to complete questionnaires reporting their thoughts and feelings about a behavior in a 'cold' state (e.g., in a carefully controlled laboratory situation). These self-reports are then used to predict later decisions to perform a behavior taken in a 'hot' state (e.g., when under the influence of alcohol or when sexually aroused or when really hungry). The problem is that these cold cognitions measured in the laboratory may not show a good match with the real world hot cognitions that drive behavior in the real world. George Loewenstein (1996) describes this difference as the 'empathy gap' suggesting we are not good at predicting how we will feel in altered states. A number of studies have shown this effect in relation to craving for cigarettes (Sayette, Loewenstein, Griffin & Black, 2008), hunger and food choice (Read & Leeuwen, 1998) and sexual arousal (Loewenstein, Nagin & Paternoster, 1997). Conner et al. (2008) had respondents complete measures based on the TPB in relation to having sex without a condom among samples of students who were or were not intoxicated with alcohol. Being intoxicated increased men's but not women's intention to have unprotected sex. Interestingly intoxication also changed the relationship between thoughts and feelings about unprotected sex (i.e., a moderation effect). In women intoxication significantly increased the importance of affective attitudes on intentions to have unprotected sex. In other words being intoxicated made the women place more emphasis on how they thought the behavior would make them feel in deciding whether to have unprotected sex.

The importance of altered states needs to be considered in developing interventions to change behavior (see MacDonald, MacDonald, Zanna & Fong, 2000, for an example in relation to promoting condom use in young people).

OBSERVATIONAL METHODS

Sometimes we can't ask people questions – babies, for instance, can't complete questionnaires or surveys but we can observe them. In these cases, observational methods, whereby behavior is observed within its natural environment, could be a useful option. Using this method, all variables are typically free to vary with little interference. This lack

FIGURE 5.1 Researchers sometimes observe and examine physical activity levels in green spaces, such as this one in London

of interference helps maximize **ecological validity** – the extent to which the findings can be generalized to other real world settings. Just as with survey methods, behavioral scientists can use observational methods to identify co-occurring events which can provide an insight into the factors underlying behavior. For example, they can attempt to identify features of green space that influence levels of physical activity (see Figure 5.1).

In addition, observational methods can be combined with other approaches. For example, experimental methods (see next section) can be used with observational methods to examine the impact of adding signs encouraging people to use steps instead of escalators at train stations, or to assess the influence of other environmental influences on health behavior (e.g., music played in a supermarket; discounting healthy foods etc.).

There are different types of naturalistic observation: undisclosed and disclosed. **Undisclosed observation** prevents the right to informed consent but has the advantage that people should behave naturally. Under **disclosed observation**, observed individuals are informed beforehand, running the risk that their thoughts and actions are affected.

CRITICAL SKILLS TOOLKIT 5.3

ADVANTAGES AND DISADVANTAGES OF OBSERVATIONAL METHODS

Advantages

1. High ecological validity.
2. If the experimenter isn't detected then many biases can be overcome such as:

   a) demand effects: participants behaving in a way that they feel the experimenter wants them to act;
   b) experimenter bias: an experimenter acting in a way that may encourage the participant to act in line with the hypothesis;
   c) bias associated with the participant being worried about being observed.

3. Can provide an accurate account of spontaneous behavior.
4. If conducted purely through undisclosed methods, observational methods can be conducted quickly and at low cost.
5. It can be used with young children where other methods might be unreliable.

Disadvantages

1. Can be prone to observer bias in which the observer sees what they want to see to support their chosen hypothesis.
2. Different observers may see different things. A good strategy when using observational methods is to use at least two observers and then compare their rates of agreement (to assess the inter-rater reliability).
3. On the flipside of enhanced ecological validity is a possible reduction in experimental control which may reduce **internal validity** (where you can confidently deduce that one variable causes a specific outcome).
4. Disclosed observation may cause an individual to act unnaturally thus off-setting many of the potential benefits of observational methods.

EXPERIMENTAL METHODS

While survey/questionnaire and observational methods help identify co-occurring factors, experimental methods help to identify the causes of behavior as well as the effects of various manipulations to the environment, individuals or related factors such as social groups (see, for example, Chapter 7 for applications to health promotion behaviors; Chapter 8 for applications to health risk behaviors).

There are three common types of experimental design: **between-subjects, within-subjects, mixed**. The advantages and disadvantages of these different types of experimental designs are reported in the next chapter (see Critical Skills Toolkit 6.1). Examples of the three types of design are provided below in relation to assessing the effect of a complex intervention comprising self-monitoring and implementation intentions (see Chapter 3) designed to promote exercising against a basic intervention comprising a leaflet noting the benefits of exercising:

a) Between-subjects (independent groups) design: *different* participants are allocated to different experimental groups (e.g., one group of participants receives the complex intervention designed to promote exercise and one group of participants receives the basic intervention before completing a measure of how much they exercise, say, one month later).

b) Within-subjects (repeated measures) design: where the *same* participants take part on multiple occasions (e.g., all participants receive the basic intervention and then complete a measure of how much they exercise one month later before being exposed to the complex intervention. Another month later they complete the measure of how much they exercise for a second time).

c) Mixed design: this uses both between-subjects and within-subjects elements. For example, half of the participants receive the basic intervention and half of the participants receive the complex intervention. Exercise behavior is measured twice (once before being exposed to either of the interventions and for a second time one month after receiving the intervention). As one group of participants receives the basic intervention while a different group of participants receives the complex intervention, there is a between-subjects element. As participants complete the **dependent variable (DV)** measure (of exercise) more than once (twice in total – once after each type of intervention), there is a within-subjects element. Putting these together results in a mixed design.

CRITICAL SKILLS TOOLKIT 5.4

ADVANTAGES AND DISADVANTAGES OF EXPERIMENTAL METHODS

Advantages

1. Allows behavioral scientists to identify causal relationships (high internal validity).
2. Laboratory-based experiments present a high degree of control that helps minimize the impact of **extraneous variables** (background variables that can influence the outcome of the study).

3. Tightly controlled experiments should be replicable. Many effects in health behavior change can be relatively small thus replicating significant effects can be more difficult compared to studies that yield large effects. To increase the likelihood of replication, the exact same procedures should be used across studies, similar participants should be sampled and the researchers should ensure there is a large sample size (larger sample sizes, everything else being equal, should increase the precision of the estimated experimental effect sizes).

4. Experimental methods can be used inside and outside of the laboratory. Conducting experiments outside the laboratory should increase ecological validity (the extent to which the results reflect real life) although it can reduce internal validity (the degree to which we can conclude the experimental effect was caused by the independent variable).

Disadvantages

1. Due to the sampling of specific participants and testing within specific, controlled environments (e.g., laboratories), ecological validity/**external validity** (the extent to which results can be generalized) can be limited. Field experiments can partially reduce this.

2. Conducting certain types of experiments can introduce participants to scenarios or stressors that they may not typically encounter (or want to encounter!).

3. Informed consent and minimizing deception can be important to protect the participants. However, letting participants know what they will do and the purpose of the experiment can introduce demand effects – whereby participants behave in the way that they feel the experimenter wants them to act.

4. If the experimenter knows which experimental condition the participant is in when they interact with them before or during the study, this can lead to experimenter effects. These effects can be minimized through **blinding** the experimenter to condition (so that the experimenter does not know which study condition the participant is in). When blinding is done successfully, the experimenter is unable to consciously or unconsciously affect the behavior of the participant in line with the experimental hypothesis.

5. If used alongside other methods (survey/questionnaire or observation), the accompanying methods need to demonstrate high levels of reliability and validity (see Critical Skills Toolkit 5.2).

When using experimental methods, behavioral scientists deliberately try to produce a change in one variable (the independent variable) and record the effect this change has on other variables (the dependent variables). To ensure that conclusions relating to these causal effects are valid, the researchers should be sure that they manipulate only the **independent variable (IV)** of interest, thus ruling out the effects of extraneous variables. This is just one risk of bias in experimental studies (see Critical Skills Toolkit 5.5 for other risks). When the risk of bias is reduced, the accuracy of the results should increase.

RISK OF BIAS

The Cochrane Collaboration has put forward a tool to assess the risk of bias in randomized controlled trials (RCTs). In RCTs, participants are randomly allocated to an experimental group receiving an intervention or to a control group that does not receive this intervention. The Cochrane Collaboration Risk of Bias tool can be used to judge whether adequate steps have been taken to minimize various risks of bias (yes/no/unclear) such as those outlined in the Critical Skills Toolkit 5.5.

CRITICAL SKILLS TOOLKIT 5.5

IDENTIFYING RISK OF BIAS IN EXPERIMENTAL TRIALS

1. Non-random allocation to conditions

Random allocation of participants to experimental conditions should increase the likelihood that the participants in each group are similar to one another (which helps to ensure that any comparisons between the two groups, after manipulating the independent variable, are fair). Studies in which participants choose which experimental condition they wish to be in can introduce **self-selection bias** because the type of person who chooses group A may be different to the type of person who chooses group B.

2. Incomplete outcome data should be adequately addressed

Often, particularly in studies that follow up participants at a later date, participants can drop out of your study. The percentage of participants that drop out is known as your **attrition rate** and can introduce bias into your study. Attrition rates should ideally be low and be similar across experimental conditions. Higher attrition rates within an experimental group versus a control group could suggest that the manipulation employed in the experimental group is not acceptable or is harmful in some way. Moreover, the type of person who drops out should be similar to the type of person who remains in the study to permit wider generalizations of your study findings.

One way to address incomplete outcome data is to employ **intention-to-treat (ITT) analysis** (see Chapter 6 for more details). In ITT analysis, participants who drop out of the study are treated as if they did not drop out by carrying across their scores from baseline to follow-up (i.e., treating them as if they did not change from baseline to follow-up) or using other forms of ITT analysis (such as multiple imputation in which missing scores are replaced with plausible, estimated scores).

3. Blinding research staff and participants

Blinding those individuals who screen participants entering the study is important. If a researcher can see the **allocation sequence** which determines the order which participants entering the study are allocated to experimental or control groups, the allocation sequence is not concealed. Lack of **allocation concealment** can bias the likelihood that the researcher accepts or rejects the individual for the trial. For example, if the researcher, upon meeting a potential participant, feels they may not be influenced by the experimental manipulation/intervention, they may be more likely to reject the participant if they know the next person accepted onto the trial will be allocated to the experimental condition (or increase the likelihood of accepting the person onto the trial if they are to be allocated to the control condition). Similarly, blinding the researcher delivering the intervention or interacting with the participant can minimize the risk of experimenter effects; blinding to condition the statistician analyzing the data can reduce bias in the selection of statistical tests; blinding observers can minimize observational bias; blinding participants to condition can reduce demand effects. However, it may not always be possible to blind researchers and/or participants to condition.

4. Selective outcome reporting

Researchers may be more inclined to report outcomes on which there were significant differences between the experimental and control groups. The primary and all secondary outcomes taken in the study and the results for each of these should be reported (i.e., reporting of results should not be selective). Pre-published trial protocols in which all of the measures to be taken in the study are specified prior to the study being conducted can be particularly helpful. This practice is becoming increasingly more common in studies of health behavior change.

5. Could you be manipulating other variables beyond your identified independent variable?

When variables are similar to one another (e.g., the respect we have for our local doctor (GP) may be related to how much we like them), conclusions are stronger (i.e., more valid) if you are able to demonstrate that you have only manipulated the independent variable (e.g., respect) and not related variables (e.g., liking). These can be done by a series of manipulation checks whereby the researcher tests for changes in the independent variable and lack of changes in related variables shortly after the attempt to manipulate the specific independent variable.

6. Dependent variables should be measured reliably and validly

See Critical Skills Toolkit 5.2.

CONSORT, TREND and TIDieR guidelines

Take a journal article reporting the results of a randomized controlled trial (RCT). Give it a cursory read. Probably everything, at first glance, looks in order. Take a closer look, especially if it is an article that was published several years ago and/or is located in a journal that does not require authors to adhere to the CONSORT (CONsolidated Standards Of Reporting Trials; Schulz, Altman & Moher, 2010) guidelines. Key details that would allow you to fairly and accurately assess the methodological quality of the trial could be missing. For example, were research staff dealing with participants aware of which condition (intervention or control group) the participant was allocated to when they dealt with them (i.e., were the research staff blinded to condition)? The

CONSORT group, by providing their guidelines, strive for transparency in the reporting of RCTs. As a result, readers should be able to more accurately judge the reliability of the trial taking into account methodological limitations that could lead to bias.

More and more journals (particularly those related to health) require researchers conducting RCTs to adhere to these guidelines when writing up the results of their study in a journal article. By requiring behavioral scientists to clearly report information linked to the risk of bias/study quality, it is likely that behavioral scientists will more often employ the types of procedures that minimize bias (such as concealing the allocation sequence and blinding researchers to experimental conditions). A similar reporting guideline for nonrandomized designs is also available (TREND: Transparent Reporting of Evaluations with Nonrandomized Designs).

To better address the issue of poor reporting regarding the content of interventions, an extension of one of the CONSORT items (item 5) was made in the form of the Template for Intervention Description and Replication (TIDieR; Hoffmann et al., 2014). This 12-item checklist attempts to ensure that authors consistently report more detailed information regarding the content of interventions to help ensure that the intervention can be implemented by others (e.g., clinicians) and researchers can replicate or build on the reported interventions. The checklist includes items relating to what content was delivered (including any physical or informational materials used with electronic links to the full set of materials), as well as who provided it, how, where, when, how much and why (including reference to any underlying theory). In addition, the TIDieR checklist includes items relating to tailoring (i.e., whether the materials were personalized in any way), any modifications made and intervention adherence/fidelity (the extent to which the intervention was delivered as planned).

SYSTEMATIC REVIEWS AND META-ANALYSES

Systematic reviews identify a set of studies tackling a specific issue (e.g., ways to prevent young adults from exceeding the speed limit while driving) and then attempt to synthesize evidence from these studies. A systematic review follows various stages.

First, researchers think about the topic they wish to review as well as the type of studies (e.g., RCTs, qualitative studies etc.) and populations that they wish to investigate. In accordance with these, the reviewer will produce a set of search terms that they will enter into database search engines (such as PsycINFO, Embase or Medline) to identify a set of studies that are potentially of interest.

Next, screening the potential papers identified by the search terms against inclusion/exclusion criteria allows the systematic reviewer to decide which studies should be included in their review and which studies should be excluded (e.g., because they do not address the topic of interest, do not include the relevant population of people or do not employ the desired methods). Once the reviewer has identified the studies that meet the desired criteria, information (data) from each study can be taken.

In a systematic review, the same types of information should be consistently taken (extracted) from each paper. To help reviewers to do this, a data extraction sheet (listing various items relating to the conduct of the study, the population tested, how the manipulation was delivered, the methodological quality of the study, the study findings etc.) is typically used. The data extracted as part of this process will then be brought together (synthesized) to draw overall conclusions on the basis of the studies included in the review. When this synthesis is statistical, the review becomes a **meta-analysis**. Meta-analyses are statistical versions of systematic reviews in which the results (effect sizes) across various studies are combined and contrasted (see Chapter 6 for further details).

Similar to the CONSORT guidelines which encourage the standard reporting of key methodological details from RCTs, the PRISMA (Preferred Reporting Items for

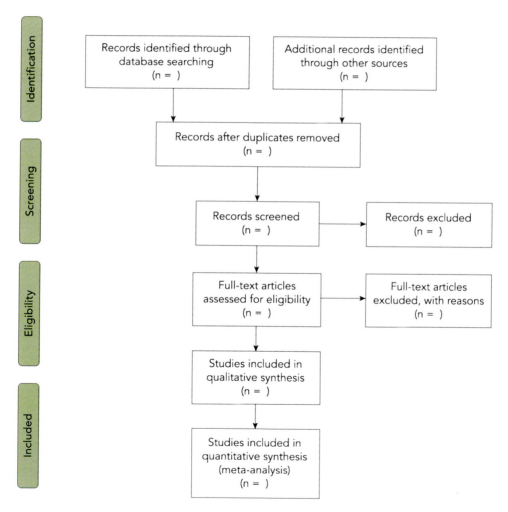

FIGURE 5.2 Flow diagram for study selection in, 'Preferred Reporting Items for Systematic Reviews and Meta-Analyses' (PRISMA) (from Moher, Liberati, Tetzlaff, Altman & The PRISMA Group, 2009)

Systematic Reviews and Meta-Analyses) statement encourages the standard reporting of key methodological details for systematic reviews and meta-analyses such as how the studies were selected, how the results from the studies were synthesized and the risk of bias of the studies.

INTERVENTION SYNTHESIS

Once a systematic review or meta-analysis has been completed, how should its results be used? This is an important question to address to ensure that the evidence gathered from the review/meta-analysis is appropriately used to develop or implement evidence-based health behavior change interventions. Typically, in this field, a systematic review or meta-analysis is based on poorly reported descriptions of health behavior change interventions (problem 1) and different studies have closely related but rarely identical interventions which may differ in various ways such as intensity of intervention (how often and how frequently an individual is exposed to a particular intervention component), setting (e.g., hospital, school, community) or mode of delivery (e.g., leaflet, mobile app) (problem 2). As a result, people (clinicians, researchers etc.) who would like to develop and deliver a specific health behavior change intervention on the basis of the findings of the review/meta-analyses have a difficult task in deciding what to implement. **Intervention synthesis**, described by Glasziou and colleagues (Glasziou, Chalmers, Green & Michie, 2014) is a process to help translate the results from systematic reviews into practical treatments. Glasziou et al. (2014) highlight three basic approaches to intervention synthesis.

1. SINGLE TRIAL-BASED CHOICE

An intervention is developed based on only one study included in the review. The intervention selected has the best trade-off between factors such as likely effectiveness, acceptability, feasibility and cost. The selection criteria regarding which intervention to choose should be made explicit and it should also be established who will rank the trial interventions and how consensus will be achieved. When considering the effect sizes from single trials, one should also take into account the sample size from the trial and, where possible, try to avoid basing decisions on a single trial with a small sample size (larger sample sizes will provide a more precise estimate of the effect size). Relative to the other approaches (Common Components Hybrid and Model-Guided Synthesis), the Single Trial-Based Choice approach requires the least effort.

2. COMMON COMPONENTS HYBRID

Rather than selecting a complete intervention as used in a previous study, this approach leads to a 'new' intervention based on various components (e.g., specific behavior change techniques [see Chapter 3], mode, intensity etc.), picked and mixed from various studies included in the systematic review. One way to do this is to specify the requisite information using relevant taxonomies (e.g., BCTv1, Michie et al., 2013) and then use statistical approaches (e.g., meta-regression) to identify the effective ingredients that could be combined in the 'new' intervention. For this approach to work, there needs to be a sufficient number of studies with the relevant information regarding components clearly reported.

3. MODEL-GUIDED SYNTHESIS

This approach is a variant of the Common Components Hybrid approach but draws on theory to determine which components should be combined and how. Like the Common Components Hybrid approach, it requires a sufficient number of studies to be included in the review that clearly reports the components of the intervention. In addition, across the studies included in the review, there should be tests of all of the relevant elements of the theory/model so that the studies in the review can be used to test the theory. If supported, the theory can then be used to guide the selection of the intervention components.

QUALITATIVE METHODS

Qualitative methods allow behavioral scientists to go beyond numbers. Behavioral scientists can collect qualitative data using open-ended questions through methods such as interviews or focus groups. Whereby more quantitative methods attempt to minimize the impact of the researcher, qualitative methods embrace more the role of the researcher. The focus of qualitative work tends to be broader and more process oriented, exploring the experiences of participants in a non-judgmental fashion and from this generate theories, whereas quantitative methods are narrower in scope, focused on testing hypotheses and controlling extraneous variables in an attempt to provide concrete answers. In the context of health behavior change, qualitative methods can be particularly helpful in identifying issues with implementing behavior change interventions. For example, they can help to figure out whether health behavior interventions were unsuccessful because they were not implemented correctly and help to understand why such difficulties emerged.

Just as quantitative (numerical) data can be analyzed in different ways, qualitative (more descriptive) data can also be analyzed in various ways. For example, thematic analysis involves the researcher presenting, or categorizing, the qualitative material into themes often based around the general research questions. Alternatively, grounded theory involves the researcher coding elements of the text before grouping similar codes together into categories in an attempt to generate a theory which is consistent with the content of the text.

CRITICAL SKILLS TOOLKIT 5.6

ADVANTAGES AND DISADVANTAGES OF QUALITATIVE METHODS

Advantages

1. Qualitative-based studies tend to be based on fewer people than quantitative studies so could be more straightforward in terms of recruiting participants and running studies.
2. Despite being based on fewer people, qualitative methods can lead to 'rich' (in-depth) datasets in which you can uncover more about people and their experiences.
3. On the basis of uncovering such experiences, qualitative methods can be used to generate hypotheses (that could be tested through other methods such as experimental approaches).
4. They may offer unique insights and theories and thus can be complementary to quantitative methods.

Disadvantages

1. A drawback of being based on fewer participants is that it can be more difficult to make generalizations about how your data applies to other people.
2. Can be difficult to analyze and can rely on differing levels of subjectivity – different analyzers may draw different interpretations from the data (this can also be true of quantitative methods).
3. Questions can be leading and this can threaten validity.
4. People who participate in qualitative-based studies (such as interviews or focus groups), and are particularly vocal in such studies, may not be very representative of other groups of people. This reflects potential risks of sampling bias.
5. How people respond in qualitative studies can be influenced by the social context – while this can be seen as advantageous, social desirability (responding in a way that they feel they should) can be a problem causing people to be reluctant to give their true, personal opinion.

SUMMARY

In this chapter we introduced a range of different methods and evaluated their strengths and weaknesses. There is no perfect method – each approach has some form of weakness. Methodological quality, when poor, hinders the development of the science of health behavior change. Researchers need to minimize the risks posed by different sources of bias when conducting their research and need to follow relevant guidelines such as CONSORT and PRISMA when reporting the results.

FURTHER READING

Hoffmann, T., Glasziou, P., Boutron, I., Milne, R., Perera, R., Moher, D., Altman, D., Barbour, V., Macdonald, H., Johnston, M., Lamb, S., Dixon-Woods, M., McCulloch, P., Wyatt, J., Chan, A. & Michie, S. (2014). Better reporting of interventions: template for intervention description and replication (TIDieR) checklist and guide. *BMJ, 348*, g1687. Explains the key elements that should be consistently and clearly reported for studies testing behavioral interventions.

Weinstein, N. (2007). Misleading tests of health behaviour theories. *Annals of Behavioral Medicine, 33*, 1–10. This paper clearly highlights the issue of using correlational designs to test health behavior theories.

The EQUATOR Network strives to improve the transparency of reporting in health/medical-related fields: www.equator-network.org/

For issues relating to the incorporation of randomized controlled trials to inform government policy see: http://onthinktanks.org/2012/03/08/making-policy-better-the-randomisation-revolution-how-far-can-experiments-lead-to-better-policy/

GLOSSARY

Allocation concealment: a list of which experimental condition participants will be assigned to (following a review of whether the participant is eligible or ineligible for the study) is known as the **allocation sequence**. Allocation concealment refers to whether this sequence is hidden from the researchers deciding whether a particular participant should enter the study or not.

Attrition: whether a participant drops out of the study or not. The proportion of participants who drop out during a study reflects the **attrition rate**.

Between-subjects design: a type of design where different groups of participants do different things depending on the experimental condition/group to which they have been assigned.

Blinding: whether the participant/member of the research team is aware of the condition to which the participant has been assigned.

Content validity: the extent to which the measure covers all aspects of the construct that it aims to assess.

Convergent validity: the extent that a measure correlates with other related measures that have been previously validated.

Criterion-related validity: the extent to which the measure can differentiate between different groups of people who should differ on the measure.

Dependent variable (DV): the outcome measure and reflects what is observed following changes in the independent variable.

Dimensionality: whether the scale measures one underlying construct (unidimensional) or several related (but distinct) constructs (multidimensional).

Disclosed observation: observed individuals are informed beforehand.

Discriminant (divergent) validity: extent that responses on the to-be-validated scale are unrelated to responses on other scales that should be unrelated to the to-be-validated scale.

Ecological validity: extent to which the study reflects real life.

Face validity: whether the scale, on the surface, appears to appropriately assess what it is supposed to assess.

External validity: extent to which results can be generalized to different settings, populations, times etc.

Extraneous variable: a third type of variable (after the IV and DV); these variables can potentially influence the DV. Unless controlled, these variables can confound the experiment such that it becomes more difficult to establish whether changes in the IV alone cause changes in the DV.

Independent variable (IV): the variable that is manipulated (changed) by the experimenter in a study. Changes in the dependent variable are observed consequently to establish whether the IV causes changes in the DV.

Intention-to-treat (ITT) analysis: different researchers can mean different things when using this term. First, ITT analysis could mean that data from participants are analyzed on the basis of which treatment group the participants were allocated to (rather than the treatment that the participants received – which could differ, particularly in large, complex experiments). Second, ITT analysis could reflect an approach taken so that participants who drop out are still included in the analysis. ITT analysis could mean either or both of these things.

Internal reliability: the extent to which a measure yields similar responses to related items.

Internal validity: extent to which one can confidently deduce that one variable causes a specific outcome.

Intervention synthesis: a process to help translate the results from systematic reviews into practical treatments.

Meta-analysis: a statistical procedure used to combine, compare and contrast the findings of studies on a related topic.

Mixed design: a type of experimental design that contains at least two independent variables (IV) one of which is a between-subjects IV and the other of which is a within-subjects IV.

Predictive validity: whether the response on a measure predicts future events that one would expect it should predict.

Reliability: the extent to which a measure yields consistent responses.

Self-selection bias: a bias that arises when participants can choose which group to join (or a study compares two groups that differ on an existing variable). This bias is problematic as participants who choose to join one group/condition may differ on many (unmeasured) variables to participants who choose to join another group/condition.

Systematic review: a rigorous and replicable approach to identify, and synthesize evidence from, studies tackling a specific issue.

Test-retest reliability: extent to which responses are similar across time-points.

Undisclosed observation: a form of observational method in which participants are unaware that they are being observed.

Validity: extent to which a measure assesses what it is supposed to measure.

Within-subjects design: a type of design in which the same participants complete different conditions/manipulations.

REFERENCES

Conner, M., Sutherland, E., Thorn, K., Kennedy, F., Grearly, C. & Berry, C. (2008). Impact of alcohol on sexual decision making: differential effects for men and women. *Psychology & Health, 23,* 909–934.

Glasziou, P.P., Chalmers, I., Green, S. & Michie, S. (2014). Intervention synthesis: a missing link between a systematic review and practical treatment(s). *Plos Medicine, 11,* e1001690.

Hoffmann, T., Glasziou, P., Boutron, I., Milne, R., Perera, R., Moher, D., Altman, D., Barbour, V., Macdonald, H., Johnston, M., Lamb, S., Dixon-Woods, M., McCulloch, P., Wyatt, J., Chan, A. & Michie, S. (2014). Better reporting of interventions: template for intervention description and replication (TIDieR) checklist and guide. *BMJ, 348,* g1687.

Loewenstein, G. (1996). Out of control: visceral influences on behavior. *Organizational Behavior and Human Decision Processes, 65,* 272–292.

Loewenstein, G., Nagin, D. & Paternoster, R. (1997). The effect of sexual arousal on expectations of sexual forcefulness. *Journal of Research in Crime and Delinquency, 34,* 443–473.

MacDonald, T.K., MacDonald, G., Zanna, M.P. & Fong, G.T. (2000). Alcohol, arousal, and intentions to use condoms in young men: applying the alcohol myopia theory to risky sexual behavior. *Health Psychology, 19,* 290–298.

Michie, S., Richardson, M., Johnston, M., Abraham, C., Francis, J., Hardeman, W., Eccles, M.P., Cane, J. & Wood, C.E. (2013). The behavior change technique taxonomy (v1) of 93 hierarchically clustered techniques: building an international consensus for the reporting of behavior change interventions. *Annals of Behavioral Medicine, 46,* 81–95.

Moher, D., Liberati, A., Tetzlaff, J., Altman, D.G. & The PRISMA Group. (2009). Prefered Reporting Items for Systematic Reviews and Meta-Analyses: the PRISMA statement. *BMJ, 339,* b2535.

Read, D. & Leeuwen, B. (1998). Predicting hunger: the effects of appetite and delay on choice. *Organizational Behavior and Human Decision Making, 76,* 189–205.

Sayette, M.A., Loewenstein, G., Griffin, K.M. & Black, J.J. (2008). Exploring the cold-to-hot empathy gap in smokers. *Psychological Science, 19,* 926–932.

Schulz, K.F., Altman, D.G. & Moher, D., for the CONSORT Group. (2010). CONSORT 2010 Statement: updated guidelines for reporting parallel group randomised trials. *Annals of Internal Medicine, 152*(11), 726–732.

6

CHAPTER 6
ANALYZING HEALTH BEHAVIOR CHANGE DATA

OVERVIEW

Following on from Chapter 5, this chapter covers statistical tests often used on data from studies concerning health behavior change and illustrates a number of key statistical issues. Regarding statistical tests, we provide a flow diagram to help identify which statistical test to use and when. The chapter also covers reasonably advanced – but important – tests such as **mediation** and **moderation**. These tests really lie at the heart of health behavior change because mediation helps to identify *why* certain interventions affect outcomes (or why variables are related with one another) and moderation identifies *when* interventions affect outcomes and when they do not (or when variables are related with one another and when they are not related). Regarding statistical issues, we consider different types of design, sample sizes and non-linear relationships – all of which will help you expand your critical skills toolkit!

THE RESEARCH AND ANALYTICAL PROCESS

Just as in other areas of science, when considering health behavior change, we formulate predictions (hypotheses) on the basis of previous research. We may predict that what somebody *intends* to do will be associated with what they *actually* do (see Ajzen, 1991) or that individuals exposed to a particular intervention will change their behavior more than those who were not. Such predictions, where we predict an association between variables or a difference between groups, represent **experimental hypotheses**. Where we predict there will be no association or no differences, these are known as **null hypotheses**.

After formulating a prediction, we next design a study to test the prediction. The study may require the experimenter to only *measure* variables (e.g., what somebody intends to do [intentions] and what they actually do [behavior]), in which case we adopt a **correlational design**, or we need to *manipulate* variables (e.g., whether somebody is allocated to a behavior change intervention condition or to a control condition that is not exposed to behavior change content), in which case we adopt an **experimental design**. In an experimental design, we may formulate independent groups (such as exposing participants either to a behavior change intervention or not before measuring their behavior at a later point in the future). In this instance, we have used a between-subjects design (see Chapter 5; also known as an independent groups design or an unrelated design). Alternatively, we may have a single group of participants but measure their behavior when they are exposed to multiple conditions (e.g., during a period in which they are not exposed to behavior change content and, at a later period of time, after they have been exposed to behavior change content). This is known as a within-subjects design (see Chapter 5; also known as a repeated measures design or, for good measure, a related design). We may also have a more complex design that incorporates both between-subjects and within-subjects elements known as a mixed design (see Chapter 5). For example, we may manipulate participants into two independent groups, one that is exposed to behavior change content and another group which is not (this is the between-subjects/independent groups/unrelated aspect of our design). In addition, all of the participants are required to complete a measure assessing their behavior twice – once at the beginning of the study (before any behavior change content is delivered) and once at the end (after some of the participants have been exposed to the behavior change content; this is the within-subjects/repeated measures/related aspect of our design). Each of these designs has their own advantages and disadvantages (see Critical Skills Toolkit 6.1).

CRITICAL SKILLS TOOLKIT 6.1

ADVANTAGES AND DISADVANTAGES OF WITHIN-SUBJECTS, BETWEEN-SUBJECTS AND MIXED DESIGNS

Within-subjects designs tend to be more powerful than between-subjects designs. Having more **power** means they are more likely to detect significant effects with the equivalent number of participants than between-subjects designs. This is because within-subjects designs involve the same participants minimizing individual differences across conditions (whereas between-subjects designs involve different participants) and each individual provides multiple data under different conditions.

Within-subjects designs are at risk of learning, carry-over and order effects. **Learning effects** (what participants learn on the first task can be used to assist them in the second task), **carry-over effects** (where performance on one task has an impact that is still persistent on a second task) or **order effects** (the order in which the tasks are completed is important: e.g., task A influences task B but task B doesn't influence task A) are potential problems for within-subjects designs. For example, assessing participants' behavior, in a single group design, after they have been exposed to behavior change content and then again at a later date could bias the results (people may still have changed their behavior as a result of their earlier exposure to the behavior change content – i.e., there is a carry-over effect). If you are worried about learning, carry-over or order effects, you can do a number of things to minimize these risks of bias: a) adopt a between-subjects design; b) increase the amount of time between completion of the tasks; c) include a distracter task between the critical tasks that can help people to unlearn, forget, disrupt the influence of one critical task on another; d) counterbalance the order of the tasks (so half of your participants complete task A before task B, and the other half of your participants first complete task B then task A). Counterbalancing the order of the tasks introduces a between-subjects element thus creating a mixed design. *Mixed* *designs therefore allow the experimenter to assess the impact of order effects.* As the same participants provide data under multiple conditions rather than under a single condition (as in a between-subjects design), *mixed designs are more powerful than between-subjects designs* (assuming there are no strong over-riding biases such as learning effects, order effects etc.).

Between-subjects designs deal with various types of bias such as learning effects as participants complete only one task in a single condition (other participants in a different experimental group will either complete a different task or the same task but under a different condition). The drawback is that relative to within-subjects designs, where participants complete measures under multiple conditions, these designs require more participants (due to having less power to detect significant effects). With between-subjects designs, there is a risk that the independent groups are not equivalent on some unmeasured, but important, characteristic that impacts on your study in some unknown way.

After collecting data consistent with our design we then need to analyze the data. The design that we've adopted will determine the statistical test that we should use (see Figure 6.1). For instance, if we measure attitudes towards eating healthily (what people think and feel about eating healthily) and healthy eating behavior because we are interested in whether these variables are related, we would adopt a correlational design. If we fail to meet relevant (parametric) assumptions, then we should conduct a Spearman's Rho test. If we have a correlational design, we meet parametric assumptions, we have three or more variables (attitudes towards eating healthily, intentions to eat healthily, healthy eating behavior) and we think one variable (intentions to eat healthily) helps explain why two other variables (attitudes towards eating healthily and healthy eating behavior) are related, we would conduct a mediation analysis (see Chapter 6, 'Mediation and Moderation').

Based on our analysis, we will either find evidence to support our prediction (supporting our experimental hypothesis) or not (supporting our null hypothesis) – a process called null hypothesis significance testing (NHST). In this process, the statistical test that we conduct (e.g., a t-test, ANOVA, chi-square – see Figure 6.1) will produce a test statistic. Next, this test statistic is compared against a known distribution of values of this statistic. From this, we can determine the likelihood of getting a test-statistic of the size that we have if there were no effect in the population. If this probability is less than 0.05 then we conclude that the effect that we have found is 'statistically significant' thus accepting our experimental hypothesis and rejecting our null hypothesis. If the probability is greater than 0.05 then we describe the result as non-significant and accept our null hypothesis and reject our experimental hypothesis.

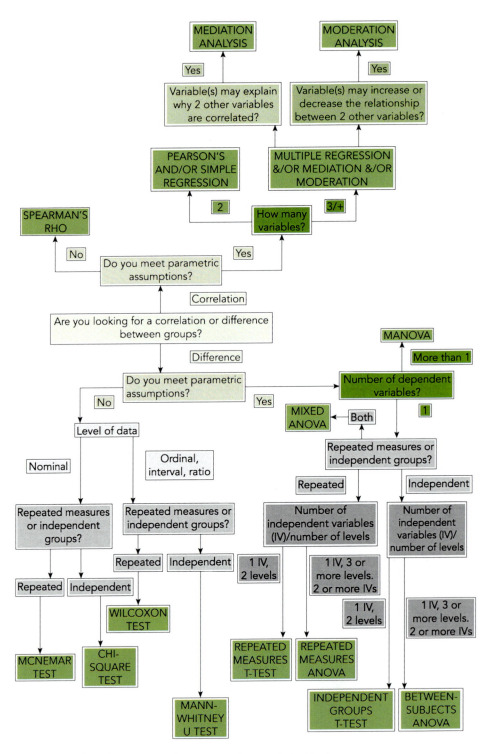

FIGURE 6.1 Flow diagram to select appropriate statistical test

PROBLEMS WITH NULL HYPOTHESIS SIGNIFICANCE TESTING (NHST)

A major problem with NHST is that it is influenced by the number of people included in the analysis (i.e., sample size biases conclusions). For example, when the difference in scores between two groups of participants is the same across two studies, the study with more people included in the analysis will be more likely to achieve a significant result (i.e., $p < 0.05$) – meaning that you will accept the experimental hypothesis and reject the null hypothesis. The opposite is also true; when you have a particularly small sample size, it is difficult to achieve a significant result – meaning that you are more likely to reject the experimental hypothesis and accept the null hypothesis. So, in a nutshell, a very large sample size (e.g., 500,000 participants) is problematic because even a tiny, or trivial, difference between groups will be concluded as being significant; a small sample size (e.g., 10 participants) is problematic because a large, or important, difference between groups is likely to be concluded as being non-significant: sample size bias conclusions drawn from NHST.

A second problem is the obsession within the scientific community (including those interested in health behavior change) for the critical p-value of 0.05. If a statistical test generates a p-value of less than 0.05 (such as 0.04) then we conclude the effect is significant (accepting the experimental hypothesis and rejecting the null hypothesis); if the p-value is greater than 0.05 (such as 0.06) then we conclude the effect is non-significant (rejecting the experimental hypothesis and accepting the null hypothesis). There are two things to note here: 1) The fine lines: p-values of 0.04 and 0.06 are very similar but are associated with very different conclusions; 2) The p-value of 0.05 is somewhat arbitrary – for example, one may argue that the cut-off point for judging whether the effect is significant or not should be $p = .10$ or $p = .01$, or some other p-value!

So, what is the major alternative to NHST? The main option is to calculate and report an effect size.

EFFECT SIZES

Effect sizes are a useful way of reflecting the standardized treatment effect. There are many different types of effect sizes – each calculated in different ways. Two of the most common effect sizes are Cohen's d (representing the standardized difference between two means) and Pearson's r (representing the correlation between the independent and dependent variables). For both of these measures, a larger number represents a larger effect. Moreover, both Cohen's d and Pearson's r can be negative (representing a negative effect – control group produces a larger change than the intervention group) or positive (representing a positive effect – intervention group produces a larger change than the control group). Cohen's d can be of any size (with $d = .2$ reflecting a small effect size; $d = .5$ reflecting a medium effect; and $d = .8$ reflecting a large effect); while Pearson's *r* varies between -1 and +1 (with *r* = .1 reflecting a small effect; *r* = .3 a moderate effect; *r* = .5 a large effect).

Effect sizes are independent of sample size: they can stay the same regardless of whether the sample size becomes larger or smaller. They are useful in making direct comparisons across studies while it is difficult to make such comparisons using *p*-values (because studies tend to have different sample sizes and sample sizes influence *p*-values). Given they are useful for making comparisons across studies, effect sizes represent the building blocks of meta-analyses.

META-ANALYSIS

Meta-analysis is a useful means to combine the findings of studies on a related topic (producing an overall average effect size). Meta-analyses have been conducted widely within health behavior change (see, for example, Table 3.2). Meta-analyses are based on effect sizes. Given studies will produce different effect sizes (reflecting **statistical heterogeneity**), meta-analyses can also compare and contrast findings across studies tackling the same topic, identifying factors that explain why some studies produce larger effects than others. Statistical heterogeneity may occur because studies use different participants, interventions or outcomes (**clinical heterogeneity**) or because they have used different designs or carry different levels or types of risk of bias (**methodological heterogeneity**). The sources of statistical heterogeneity can be investigated through **sub-group analyses** or **meta-regression**. Sub-group analyses are typically used where studies fall into categories (such as studies with young participants and studies with old participants). They compare the effect sizes of studies falling into each category to examine whether the effect sizes of studies falling into one category (e.g., studies recruiting participants under the age of 18) differ to the effect sizes of studies falling into another category (e.g., studies recruiting only participants over the age of 60). Meta-regressions can be used when studies measure a variable on a scale (such as mean age of participants in a study) and also when variables comprise groups (e.g., comparing studies that blinded experimenters to condition versus studies that did not blind experimenters to condition). In meta-regressions, these scale or categorical (group) variables are used to predict study effect sizes.

When investigating statistical heterogeneity, it is important to specify in advance what sub-group analyses and/or meta-regressions were planned prior to conducting the meta-analysis. Given a very large number of sub-group or meta-regressions could be conducted, there is a high-risk of making **Type 1 errors** (incorrectly concluding that a particular moderator or sub-group is influential/significant when it is not). Thus, specifying in advance the analyses to be conducted encourages the researcher only to test moderators that are theoretically or methodologically important which minimizes the number of tests to be conducted and, in turn, minimizes the risk of Type 1 errors.

CRITICAL SKILLS TOOLKIT 6.2

POWER CALCULATIONS – WHAT IS THE RIGHT SAMPLE SIZE?

To avoid problems of under-sampling (recruiting too few participants and inflating the likelihood of making a **Type 2 error** [incorrectly accepting the null hypothesis]) and over-sampling (recruiting too many participants and inflating the likelihood of making a Type 1 error [incorrectly accepting the experimental hypothesis]), it is useful to conduct an a-priori sample size calculation to determine how many participants you should recruit into your study. Recruiting too many participants is potentially a waste of time, effort and money – so a-priori sample sizes really are useful (see Farrokhyar, Reddy, Poolman & Bhandari, 2013)!

Conducting a-priori sample size calculations involves the following concepts:

1. Type 2 or β error – reflects the probability of accepting the null hypothesis when it is false. β = .20 is commonly used in sample size calculations (see concept 2. power).
2. Power – ability to detect a significant effect within the sample of participants used in a study when a significant effect truly exists (i.e., within the entire population). Power = $1 - \beta$. For sample size calculations, this is typically set at .80 (reflecting 80% power).
3. Type 1 or α error – the probability of rejecting the null hypothesis when it is true/accepting the experimental hypothesis when it is false. For sample size calculations, this is typically set at 0.05 for health behavior change studies as with many other areas of science. For issues that are of critical importance (e.g., testing the effects of specific drugs on health-related outcomes) a more stringent value may be set (such as 0.001) to minimize the likelihood that a study incorrectly supports the drug when the drug is in fact not useful.
4. 1-tailed vs. 2-tailed. Using 1-tailed testing (where the direction of the effect is specified: e.g., treatment A will be better than treatment B) produces greater power than 2-tailed testing (where the direction of the effect is not specified: e.g., treatment A will be worse or better than treatment B). Thus, 1-tailed tests require fewer participants than 2-tailed tests.
5. Effect size — the standardized difference between groups. For sample size calculations, the effect size can estimated based on a) effect sizes generated in similar studies or b) conducting a pilot study or c) deciding what would be the minimum meaningful effect size for the planned study.
6. The number of participants allocated to the experimental and control groups – the more these differ, the less power the study has (i.e., for the same total sample size, power is greatest when the number of participants in each group is the same).
7. Type of design – within-subjects (repeated measures or related) designs are more powerful than between-subjects (independent groups or unrelated) designs.

So, when conducting a sample size calculation, the researcher will need to decide 1) power (linked to Type 2 or β error), 2) Type 1 or α error, 3) whether they will use a 1-tailed or 2-tailed test, 4) estimate of the likely (or desired) effect size, 5) the proportion of people allocated to each group, 6) study design. As long as these decisions are all justified then the *planned* sample size calculation is justified. The next step is to ensure that the *planned* sample size matches the *actual* sample size and, if not, the sample size is open to criticism!

MEDIATION AND MODERATION

Both mediation and moderation involve (at least) three variables: a predictor variable, a mediator or moderator and an outcome variable.

MEDIATION

What is mediation?

Mediation assesses *how* two variables (the predictor and outcome) are related. Specifically it tests whether these two variables are related through a third variable (the mediator) that is related to both the predictor and outcome. Running mediation analysis allows us to understand the processes through which the predictor may influence the outcome. For example, in a large randomized trial, Bricker et al. (2010) tested whether an intervention encouraged smoking cessation in adolescents relative to a control group and tried to identify why the intervention was effective in promoting smoking abstinence. They found that self-efficacy to resist smoking in social and stressful situations mediated the effect of the intervention on smoking abstinence. In particular, being in the intervention increased participants' self-efficacy in resisting smoking in social and stressful situations and, in turn, increased the likelihood of abstaining from smoking. So, the increase in self-efficacy helps explain why the intervention increased smoking abstinence. In sum, think of mediated relationships as involving (at least) three variables that flow from the predictor to the outcome via the mediator (see Figure 6.2).

As well as identifying factors that help explain how, for example, a smoking cessation intervention promotes abstinence, mediation analysis (by identifying non-significant mediators) can also be used to rule out potential explanations regarding how the smoking cessation intervention works.

How to test for mediation

Analyses can be conducted in statistical programs (e.g., SPSS) to test for mediation. To identify whether you have a significant mediated relationship there are various different approaches that you can take. A particularly common approach, and the one outlined in

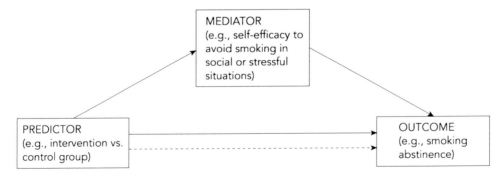

FIGURE 6.2 Mediation (based on Bricker et al., 2010)

detail here, is the method suggested by Baron and Kenny (1986). To establish mediation, according to Baron and Kenny (1986), the following conditions should be met:

1. The predictor (e.g., the intervention vs. control group) should significantly predict the outcome (e.g., smoking abstinence).

    *   To test this condition, the predictor (e.g., the intervention vs. control group) should be entered as the predictor variable and the outcome (e.g., smoking abstinence) should be entered as the outcome variable in a simple linear regression.

2. The predictor (e.g., the intervention vs. control group) should significantly predict the mediator (e.g., self-efficacy).

    *   To test this condition, the predictor (e.g., the intervention vs. control group) should be entered as the predictor variable and the mediator (e.g., self-efficacy) should be entered as the outcome variable in a simple linear regression.

3. The mediator (e.g., self-efficacy) should significantly predict the outcome (e.g., smoking abstinence) while controlling for the predictor (e.g., the intervention vs. control group).

    *   To test this condition, the predictor (e.g., the intervention vs. control group) and the mediator (e.g., self-efficacy) should both be entered as predictor variables and the outcome (e.g., smoking abstinence) should be entered as the outcome variable in a multiple regression.

4. The predictor (e.g., the intervention vs. control group) should *no longer* significantly predict the outcome (e.g., smoking abstinence) when controlling for the mediator (e.g., self-efficacy).

    *   To test this condition, the same multiple regression used to test condition 3 can be used.

If all four conditions are met then this is consistent with the conclusion that the mediator (e.g., self-efficacy) *fully mediates* the relationship between the predictor (e.g., the intervention vs. control group) and the outcome (e.g., smoking abstinence).

If the first three conditions are met, but not condition 4, then this is consistent with the conclusion that the mediator (e.g., self-efficacy) *partially mediates* the relationship between the predictor (e.g., the intervention vs. control group) and the outcome (e.g., smoking abstinence).

If any of conditions 1, 2 or 3 are not met then you should conclude that the mediator (e.g., self-efficacy) *does not mediate* the relationship between the predictor (e.g., the intervention vs. control group) and the outcome (e.g., smoking abstinence). An alternative approach to mediation is bootstrapping which is a non-parametric procedure (thus the assumption of normality does not need to be met) and is useful for testing for mediation in smaller sample sizes.

matter whether your predictor or moderator variables are significant, what is required for a significant moderation is for the interaction term to be significant).

That isn't the end of the story, however. At this stage, you do not know the exact nature of the moderated relationship. For instance, having weaker baseline intentions to do physical activity may increase the effect of the intervention on physical activity or having weaker baseline intentions may decrease the effect of the intervention on physical activity. It may be that the intervention *always* significantly increases physical activity (and strengthening [or weakening] intentions only makes the effect of the intervention on physical activity even more significant) or it may be that the intervention *only* significantly increases physical activity levels when intentions are strong (or weak). To examine the exact nature of the relationship you need to conduct simple slopes analysis; conducting this analysis will answer all of the questions relating to the nature of the moderation in your dataset. Simple slopes analysis can be conducted through various programs (see Further Reading section for details regarding an online calculator and Andrew Hayes's PROCESS approach; Hayes, 2013).

CRITICAL SKILLS TOOLKIT 6.3

VARIABLES MAY BE RELATED BUT NOT LINEARLY

Simple correlations/regressions work on the assumption that two variables may be linearly related (i.e., for each unit increase in one variable, there is a corresponding increase in a second variable [see Figure 6.3a] or a corresponding decrease in a second variable [see Figure 6.3b]).

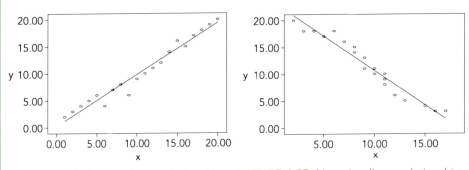

FIGURE 6.3A Positive, linear relationship   **FIGURE 6.3B** Negative, linear relationship

Variable X and Y may be unrelated (e.g., $r = 0$) based on Pearson's correlation but may be related non-linearly. For example, in a study looking at the relationship between task conflict (sample item: 'How often do the members of your team disagree about how things should be done?') and team creativity (sample item: 'Indicate the extent to which the team output was original and practical'), Farh, Lee and Farh (2010) revealed that the two measures demonstrated a non-significant linear relationship but that there was a significant quadratic relationship. This indicated that as task conflict increased, team creativity also increased up to a turning point whereby further increases in task conflict were associated with reduced team creativity (see Figure 6.3c).

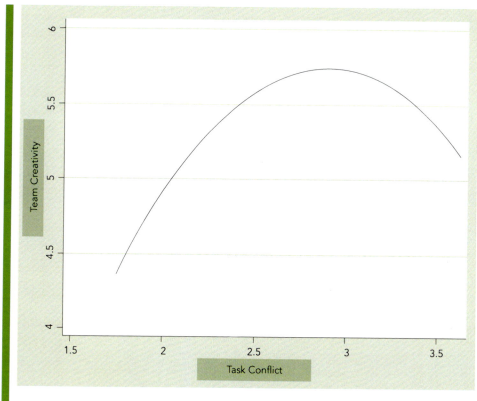

FIGURE 6.3C Curvilinear relationship between task conflict and team creativity (from Farh et al., 2010)

COMMON STATISTICAL ANALYSES IN HEALTH BEHAVIOR CHANGE INTERVENTION STUDIES

In this section, we highlight statistical analyses and statistical issues that are regularly encountered when conducting studies relating to health behavior change. In particular, we focus on analyses and issues that relate to randomized controlled trials of health behavior interventions.

RANDOMIZATION CHECKS

It is hoped that by randomizing participants to conditions, the type of person in condition A is similar to the type of person in condition B. However, this is not guaranteed. A set of analyses are regularly conducted to identify whether the participants in condition A differ to the participants in condition B on any measured variable. A chi-square test, for instance, could examine whether the proportion of men and women differ across intervention and control groups. A MANOVA analysis can be used to check whether participants in two or more conditions differ on a group of different measures that are measured along a scale such as age, intentions, self-efficacy, past behavior etc. Where baseline differences are detected, these variables are often statistically controlled in the main study analyses that compare the study conditions (e.g., intervention versus the control) on the main study outcome variables.

However, this practice of testing for baseline differences and later statistically controlling variables for which there are baseline differences has been criticized on a number of grounds including that some baseline differences could be achieved by chance; for instance, if you use $p < .05$ as a benchmark of significance, and compare two groups on 20 baseline measures, you'd expect one difference, on average. Moreover, controlling for baseline differences can increase the risk that unimportant covariates (i.e., those that are not associated with the outcome) are considered (when there are baseline differences on these measures), and important covariates (i.e., those that are related to the outcome) are not considered (when there are no significant baseline differences on these measures) in the main analyses (see de Boer, Waterlander, Kuijper, Steenhuis and Twisk, 2015, for further discussion).

RECRUITMENT AND ATTRITION ANALYSES

Being able to calculate recruitment and attrition rates are useful in feasibility type studies to give an indication of the time and cost required to run a larger study that is better equipped to more clearly determine the impact of an intervention on health-related outcomes (i.e., a fully powered trial).

The number of people approached, the number meeting eligibility criteria and the number of people agreeing to participate within a particular timeframe can be recorded to infer recruitment rates. Similarly, considering the attrition rate (the proportion of participants who withdraw once accepted onto a trial) and whether this varies across condition is useful. The rate of recruitment should be equivalent across groups. If not, especially if the dropout rates are higher in the intervention/treatment condition than in the control condition, then it is possible that there are issues relating to the acceptability of the intervention – in other words, for whatever reason, participants are at increased risk of not liking or engaging with the intervention. Such results would suggest that your intervention may not be viable to deliver in the 'real world' without some form of modification to address the issues. The rate of attrition and whether it varies across conditions can be determined through chi-square analyses (or equivalent).

The type of participants who complete the study should be similar to those who do not complete the study. If there are detectable differences such that, for example, the people who complete a physical activity study are more likely to have strong intentions to do physical activity, then the generalizability of the findings are compromised and may not relate to specific groups of people (such as those with weaker intentions to do physical activity). MANOVA can be conducted to test whether those who completed the study differ in any measured variables (measured on a scale) compared to those who did not complete the study. Chi-square can be used to compare dropouts against completers on categorical variables (such as sex of the participants, educational qualifications etc.).

MAIN ANALYSES

The main analyses will test the main hypotheses. In health behavior change research, common scenarios include examining whether specific variables correlate with or predict health-related behaviors (which require correlational analyses – see the top segment of Figure 6.1) or whether interventions change the behavior of individuals (which require tests of difference as indicated in the bottom segment of Figure 6.1). If individuals are clustered into groups – for instance in cluster randomized trials in which groups such as whole schools, classes within schools, hospital wards etc. are randomized into conditions – then more sophisticated analyses are required (e.g., multi-level modeling). Multi-level modeling is one way of taking account of such clustering of data. For example, Conner and Higgins (2010) used multi-level modeling to analyze data from a cluster randomized controlled trial of an intervention to reduce smoking initiation. The multi-level modeling allowed the analysis to assess the impact of the intervention on rates of smoking initiation and control for the fact that adolescents were clustered within different schools in different conditions. Another example is that of O'Connor, Jones, Conner, McMillan and Ferguson (2008) who were interested in the relationship between stress and between-meal snacking. They took measures of stress and snacking behavior on a number of consecutive days within the same individuals. They then used multi-level modeling to assess the relationship between stress and eating after controlling for the fact that each individual provided multiple days of data. In effect this analysis answered the question of whether individuals tended to eat more snacks on days when they were more stressed compared to days on which they were less stressed.

HANDLING MISSING DATA

When running a study related to health behavior change, you will more than likely encounter several instances of missing data. This could be as a result of participants intentionally, or unintentionally, not completing a particular measure or because a participant withdraws from a study part way through. Missing data can be handled in two main ways: 1) live with it and analyze your data only on the basis of the responses provided; 2) conduct **intention-to-treat (ITT) analyses** in which the missing data are replaced with estimated values. The advantages and disadvantages of ITT analyses are considered in Critical Skills Toolkit 6.4. A couple of common approaches to ITT analysis are: a) last observation carried forward in which data from a previous timepoint is carried across to the timepoint in which data are missing; b) multiple imputation that is designed to replace missing values with plausible estimates.

CRITICAL SKILLS TOOLKIT 6.4

INTENTION-TO-TREAT (ITT) ANALYSES

Intention-to-treat analyses, in which all participants who have been randomized to condition are analyzed regardless of whether they deviated from the protocol or withdrew from the study, have a number of advantages and disadvantages. Being aware of these is useful when thinking about the strengths and weaknesses of the analytical approach taken within a particular study:

Advantages

1. By analyzing data from all participants, ITT analyses can reduce the risk of generating overly optimistic results that may be produced when only conducting analyses on those who completed the study (reducing the risk of making a Type 1 error; concluding that an intervention is effective when it is not).
2. Linked to the above, people may withdraw from a study because of something adverse about the treatment. The impact of this would be detected through ITT analyses but not through non-ITT analyses in which only study completers are considered.
3. By including all participants in the analyses, statistical power is maintained.
4. May provide a better estimation of how effective the intervention is in the real world/clinical type settings (and have greater generalizability of results) where participants/patients may not always receive the correct intervention, receive only part of the intervention or, in some other way, deviate from what was intended.

Disadvantages

1. ITT analyses can 'muddy the waters' by putting together data from participants who followed the protocol and completed the study; participants who followed the protocol and withdrew; participants who did not follow the protocol (possibly receiving the materials intended for those assigned to a different study condition) and completed the study; and possibly even participants who did not follow the protocol and did not complete the study. As a result, particularly by including data from individuals or groups who did not receive the intervention, it is difficult to accurately estimate the effect of the intended intervention on the outcome.
2. Linked to the above, there is an increased risk of making a Type 2 error. In this context, this would mean that there is an increased risk of concluding that a particular health behavior change intervention was ineffective when it actually is effective.

IDENTIFYING AND HANDLING OUTLIERS

Statistical **outliers** are data points that lie particularly far from other data points. Sometimes they can occur through data-entry error and can thus be corrected by the data analyst or person entering the data in the dataset. However, in practice, it is more likely that the data point(s) represent genuine responses (accurately or inaccurately) provided by, or related to, the participant.

In correlational/regression-based analyses, approaches such as Mahalanobis's distance and Cook's distance can be used to identify the impact of specific cases on the dataset. In experimental analyses, an outlier can be identified by standardizing the scores on the dependent variable (e.g., through z-scores).

Once identified, outliers can be eliminated (or Winsorized to the nearest non-outlier score) when any scores are judged to be too high or low (e.g., often researchers classify standardized scores greater than 3.5 or less than -3.5 as outliers). The impact of eliminating or Winsorizing outliers can be examined by comparing the results from these approaches against the results produced when the outliers are not removed or Winsorized. For transparency, any similarities or differences in the conclusions drawn from these two basic approaches (remove/treat vs. keep in) should be reported in academic papers.

PROCESS EVALUATION

As well as evaluating how effective a health behavior intervention is, it is also important for behavioral scientists to use process evaluations. Process evaluations provide additional useful information regarding: implementation (what is delivered and how), mechanisms of action and the identification of contextual factors that influence the size of the intervention effects. These key features are overviewed in Figure 6.4.

Process evaluations of feasibility/pilot studies are useful in helping to understand how feasibly the intervention can be implemented and tested, its acceptability and identifying how the design and evaluation can be strengthened. At the full trial stage, a process evaluation is useful to strengthen confidence in the effectiveness of the intervention (by taking account of the quality and quantity of what was delivered within the intervention) and its generalizability (by taking account of context).

RE-AIM

RE-AIM (standing for Reach Effectiveness Adoption Implementation Maintenance) is a framework that can be used to consider the extent to which an intervention has the potential to lead to public health benefits (Glasgow, Vogt & Boles, 1999). Interventions may appear to be effective in changing behavior but if they are not widely adopted, for example, then they are unlikely to achieve widespread public health benefits. Interventions with high reach (high proportion of the target population are exposed to the intervention), effectiveness (the intervention is successful), adoption (high proportion of eligible settings, target staff or organizations take up and use the intervention), implementation (the intervention is implemented as intended) and maintenance (the intervention becomes integrated within the routine practice of the organization and the effects of the intervention are maintained over time) represent the interventions most likely to generate public health impact.

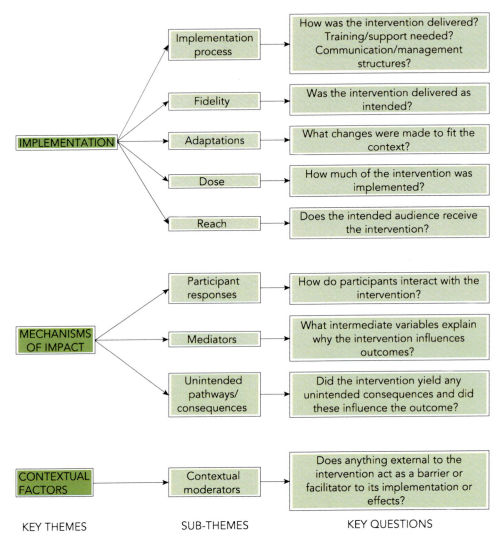

FIGURE 6.4 Overview of the key elements of process evaluation of complex evaluations (based on Moore et al., 2015)

SUMMARY

Analyzing the results of studies related to health behavior change is important to understand the potential for health benefits, to explain why relationships between variables such as exposure to health behavior interventions and health behaviors emerge (via mediation) and when such relationships are stronger or weaker (via moderation). Behavioral scientists have a variety of statistical approaches that they can use to analyze data and it is essential that an appropriate statistical approach is selected. While the most common approaches were overviewed in Figure 6.1, other statistical approaches are required in some instances such as in cluster trials/group randomized trials when approaches such as multi-level modeling are more suitable. A number of hurdles need to be cleared in the statistical analysis procedures such as how best to handle missing data and outliers and we have highlighted key issues in relation to these. As well as considering the effectiveness of health behavior interventions, process evaluations provide additional information relating to how well the intervention is implemented, potential mechanisms and context that can influence, positively or negatively, the effectiveness of the intervention. RE-AIM is a potentially useful framework to consider effectiveness and process-related factors in order to estimate the potential public health benefits that may accrue from a particular health behavior intervention.

FURTHER READING

Hayes, A.F. (2013). *Introduction to Mediation, Moderation, and Conditional Process Analysis*. New York: Guilford Press. Overviews and describes mediation, moderation and their integration plus introduces a macro called PROCESS that can be used within SPSS and SAS to conduct basic and more complex mediation and moderation analyses containing multiple mediators and moderators.

Kristopher Preacher has an excellent website that explains moderation analysis (including simple slopes analyses) in more detail and provides online calculators that you can use to run simple slopes analyses: www.quantpsy.org/interact/

Lee Becker provides a simple-to-use effect size calculator: www.uccs.edu/~lbecker/

G★Power, a program that is useful to help calculate a-priori sample sizes and statistical power, can be downloaded for free: www.psycho.uni-duesseldorf.de/abteilungen/aap/gpower3/download-and-register

More about RE-AIM here: www.re-aim.org/

GLOSSARY

Carry-over effects: a bias linked with within-subject designs where performance on one task has an impact that is still persistent on a second task.

Clinical heterogeneity: reflects differences in studies through use of different participants, interventions or outcomes.

Correlational design: a design in which there is no manipulation of variables – i.e., the experimenter is required only to *measure* variables.

Effect sizes: standardized treatment effect useful for comparing the impact of manipulations (or size of relationships) across studies.

Experimental design: a design in which the experimenter *manipulates* variables to identify whether changes in one variable (the independent variable, IV) cause changes in an outcome variable.

Experimental hypothesis: a prediction in which a significant difference across groups or significant relationship between variables is anticipated.

Intention-to-treat (ITT) analysis: a statistical approach in which data from all participants are analyzed irrespective of whether they chose not to comply, deviated from the protocol or dropped out/withdrew from the study.

Learning effects: a bias linked with within-subject designs where participants' learning on the first task can be used to assist them in subsequent tasks.

Mediation: a statistical approach examining *why* two variables are related.

Meta-analysis: a statistical procedure used to combine, compare and contrast the findings of studies on a related topic.

Meta-regression: a statistical procedure in which measures are used to predict study effect sizes.

Methodological heterogeneity: reflects differences in studies due to using different designs or having different risks of bias.

Moderation: a statistical approach that attempts to identify *when* two variables are related.

Null hypothesis: a prediction in which groups are anticipated not to differ or measures are anticipated to be unrelated.

Order effects: a bias linked with within-subjects design; the order in which the tasks are completed can influence the findings: e.g., task A influences task B but task B doesn't influence task A.

Outliers: data points that differ from the general trend of the dataset and consequently exert a potentially undue effect on the statistical findings.

Power: ability to detect a significant effect within the sample of participants used in a study when a significant effect truly exists (i.e., within the entire population).

Statistical heterogeneity: reflects differences in effect sizes across studies.

Sub-group analysis: statistical procedure where the statistical test is conducted separately for different groups of participants or conditions to identify whether the findings differ across participants/conditions.

Type 1 error: an instance in which an experimental hypothesis is accepted but should have been rejected.

Type 2 error: an instance in which an experimental hypothesis is rejected but should have been accepted.

REFERENCES

Ajzen, I. (1991). The theory of planned behavior. *Organizational Behavior and Human Decision Processes, 50*, 179–211.

Baron, R.M. & Kenny, D.A. (1986). The moderator-mediator variable distinction in social psychological research: conceptual, strategic and statistical considerations. *Journal of Personality and Social Psychology, 51*, 1173–1182.

Bricker, J.B., Liu, J., Comstock, B.A., Peterson, A.V., Kealey, K.A. & Marek, P.M. (2010). Social cognitive mediators of adolescent smoking cessation: results from a large randomized intervention trial. *Psychology of Addictive Behaviors, 24*, 436–445.

Conner, M. & Higgins, A. (2010). Long-term effects of implementation intentions on prevention of smoking uptake among adolescents: a cluster randomized controlled trial. *Health Psychology, 29*, 529–538.

de Boer, M.R., Waterlander, W.E., Kuijper, L.D.J., Steenhuis, I.H.M. & Twisk, J.W.R. (2015). Testing for baseline differences in randomized controlled trials: an unhealthy research behavior that is hard to eradicate. *International Journal of Behavioral Nutrition and Physical Activity, 12*, 4.

de Vet, E., Oenema, A., Sheeran, P. & Brug, J. (2009). Should implementation intentions interventions be implemented in obesity prevention: the impact of if-then plans on daily physical activity in Dutch adults. *International Journal of Behavioral Nutrition and Physical Activity, 6*, 11.

Farh, J-L., Lee C., & Farh, C.I.C. (2010). Task conflict and team creativity: a question of how much and when. *Journal of Applied Psychology, 95*, 1173–1180.

Farrokhyar, F., Reddy, D., Poolman, R.W. & Bhandari, M. (2013). Why perform a priori sample size calculation? *Canadian Journal of Surgery, 56*, 207–213.

Glasgow, R.E., Vogt, T.M. & Boles, S.M. (1999) Evaluating the public health impact of health promotion interventions: the RE-AIM framework. *American Journal of Public Health, 89*, 1322–1327.

Grant, A.M., & Hofmann, D.A. (2011). It's not all about me: motivating hand hygiene among health care professionals by focusing on patients. *Psychological Science, 22*, 1494–1499.

Hayes, A.F. (2013). *Introduction to Mediation, Moderation, and Conditional Process Analysis*. New York: Guilford Press.

Moore, G.F., Audrey, S., Barker, M., Bond, L., Bonell, C., Hardeman, W., Moore, L., O'Cathain, A., Tinati, T., Wight, D. & Baird, J. (2015). Process evaluation of complex interventions: UK Medical Research Council (MRC) guidance. *BMJ, 350*, h1258.

O'Connor, D.B., Jones, F., Conner, M., McMillan, B. & Ferguson, E. (2008). Effects of daily hassles and eating style on eating behavior. *Health Psychology, 27*, S20–S31.

Prestwich, A., Conner, M., Hurling, R., Ayres, K. & Morris, B. (2016). An experimental test of control theory-based interventions for physical activity. *British Journal of Health Psychology, 21*, 812–826.

Sigall, H. & Mills, J. (1998). Measures of independent variables and mediators are useful in social psychology experiments: but are they necessary? *Personality and Social Psychology Review, 2*, 218–226.

7

CHAPTER 7
HEALTH PROMOTION BEHAVIORS

OVERVIEW

Health promotion behaviors, including physical activity, healthy eating, donating blood, safe driving and screening behaviors, positively influence health and are the focus of this chapter. In Chapter 8 we go on to examine health risk behaviors such as smoking and unhealthy food consumption. A key distinction between these types of behaviors is that we are usually trying to make people approach or increase health promotion behaviors and avoid or decrease health risk behaviors. Nevertheless the ways used to understand and change these two types of health behaviors show some degree of overlap. In this chapter, we take a look at the research that has examined the **determinants** (predictors) of these behaviors taken largely from the health/social cognition models that we introduced in Chapter 2. In relation to behavior change the assumption is that identified predictors can be targeted and changed by interventions as a way to change behavior. In the second part of the chapter we examine research that has attempted to encourage performance of health promotion behaviors in order to promote health outcomes based on three promising approaches. In particular we look at how research targeting changes in attitudes or self-efficacy can change health promotion behavior; at how simply asking questions about an individual's plans to perform these behaviors can have an impact; and at how forming more specific plans can help promote performance of these behaviors. In the final section of the chapter, we introduce the Science of Health Behavior Change: In Action feature which is used to evaluate a study testing a behavior change intervention to promote health behavior. This feature illustrates how the scientific, critical approach that we introduced in the first six chapters can be applied in the context of health promotion behaviors.

USING SOCIAL/HEALTH COGNITION MODELS TO PREDICT HEALTH PROMOTION BEHAVIORS

The prevalence of health behaviors varies across different social groups defined by sex, age or social class. For example, in the Western world smoking is generally more prevalent among those from economically disadvantaged backgrounds. This finding would suggest socio-demographic factors as a focus of interventions to change health behaviors. However, socio-demographic factors are often impossible to change or require political intervention at national or international levels (e.g., change in income distribution). This is one reason why research has tended to focus on more modifiable factors assumed to mediate or explain the relationship between socio-demographic factors and health-related behaviors. One important set of factors are the thoughts and feelings the individual associates with performing a particular health behavior. These are commonly referred to as health or social cognitions. Take Mark, one of the authors of this book; he says he really enjoys exercising and thinks it is healthy, but does not perceive his friends to be interested in his exercise behavior. Each of these different health cognitions could be key in making Mark exercise. A group of **social/health cognition models** (SCMs; Conner & Norman, 2015) have been developed to assess the main health cognitions for people in general across a range of behaviors. These SCMs specify the **theory-relevant constructs** or health cognitions and how they interrelate in determining behavior. We broadly covered and critiqued these models in Chapter 2. Here, we focus more deeply on the most popular models: the Health Belief Model (HBM; e.g., Janz & Becker, 1984), Protection Motivation Theory (PMT; Maddux & Rogers, 1983), Theory of Reasoned Action/Theory of Planned Behavior (TRA/TPB; Ajzen, 1991) and Social Cognitive Theory (SCT; Bandura, 2000). As we will see, each model suggests different health cognitions that should be central to making Mark (or anyone else) exercise.

BURNING ISSUE BOX 7.1

ARE DIFFERENCES IN HEALTH BEHAVIORS ACROSS SOCIO-ECONOMIC STATUS GROUPS REFLECTED IN STUDIES TESTING SOCIAL/HEALTH COGNITION MODELS?

Demographic differences (e.g., age, gender, socio-economic status) between individuals have been found to significantly moderate the intention-behavior relationship. Effects for socio-economic status are particularly interesting here because of differences in performance of health behaviors across socio-economic status groups. A variety of studies have found higher levels of engagement with health protective behaviors such as physical activity and healthy eating in higher socio-economic status groups. This could be because of weaker intentions to engage in such behaviors in lower socio-economic status groups, although there is not strong evidence to support this view. A more interesting possibility is that lack of resources available to lower socio-economic status individuals interferes with their ability to translate healthy intentions into healthy behaviors.

Such a moderating effect of socio-economic status on the intention-behavior relationship has been shown for health promotion behaviors such as breastfeeding and physical activity (Conner et al., 2013). In each case the relationship between intentions and behavior was weaker in lower compared to higher socio-economic status groups. This finding could help explain why those from lower socio-economic status groups engage in fewer health promotion behaviors.

HEALTH BELIEF MODEL

The Health Belief Model (HBM) is the oldest and most widely used SCM (see Abraham & Sheeran, 2015). In an early study in this area Hochbaum (1958) reported that perceived susceptibility to tuberculosis and the belief that people with the disease could be asymptomatic (so that screening would be beneficial) distinguished between attendees and non-attendees for chest X-rays. Later, Haefner and Kirscht (1970) extended this research by demonstrating that an intervention designed to increase participants' perceived susceptibility, perceived severity and anticipated benefits resulted in a greater number of check-up visits to the doctor over an eight-month period compared to a control condition.

A brief description of the HBM is provided in Chapter 2 but, to re-iterate, the HBM suggests that health behavior is determined by two sets of cognitions: perceptions of illness threat and evaluation of behaviors to counteract this threat (see Figure 2.6). Threat perceptions are themselves based on two beliefs: first, the perceived susceptibility of the individual to the illness ('How likely am I to get ill?'); and second, the perceived severity of the consequences of the illness for the individual ('How serious would the illness be?'). Similarly, evaluation of behaviors to counteract the threat involves consideration of: first, the potential benefits of performing the behavior; and second, consideration of the barriers or costs to performing the behavior. Together these four beliefs are believed to determine the likelihood of the individual performing a health behavior. So the HBM suggests that individuals are most likely to follow a particular health action if they believe themselves to be susceptible to a particular condition which they also consider to be serious, and believe that the benefits outweigh the costs of the behavior engaged in to counteract the health threat. Many applications of the HBM also include the individual's overall motivation to protect their health (i.e., health motivation) and any cues that might prompt action (i.e., cues to action) and some later revisions added the concept of self-efficacy.

A main strength of the HBM is the common-sense operationalization it uses in including key beliefs related to decisions about health behaviors. A significant weakness has been the omission of important cognitions such as intentions and self-efficacy that subsequent research has shown to be influential in predicting health behaviors (for a more detailed critique, see Chapter 2). A range of studies have applied the HBM to various different health behaviors. For example, Zhao et al. (2012) used the HBM to look at condom use in female Chinese sex workers. Barriers, self-efficacy and benefits were each significant independent predictors of condom use with the strongest effects being associated with perceived barriers. Moreover, Ar-yuwat, Clark, Hunter and James

(2013) used the HBM to predict physical activity in Thai primary school students. Only barriers (self-efficacy was not assessed) were significantly related to physical activity levels. Across studies of the HBM it is susceptibility and barriers (plus self-efficacy when it is measured) that emerge as the strongest predictors of subsequent behavior (Abraham & Sheeran, 2015). This would suggest that interventions to change behavior should focus on changing these constructs.

PROTECTION MOTIVATION THEORY

Protection Motivation Theory (PMT; Maddux & Rodgers, 1983; see Norman, Boer, Seydel and Mulle, 2015, for a review) is overviewed in Chapter 2 but, in summary, it is a revision and extension of the HBM incorporating various improvements. In PMT, the primary determinant of performing a health behavior is the intention to perform a health behavior (labeled protection motivation here; see Figure 2.5). Intention is determined by six health cognitions. Several are familiar from the HBM. The six health cognitions are: perceptions of vulnerability to the illness (labeled susceptibility in the HBM); perceived severity of the health threat; fear about the health threat; expectancy that carrying out a behavior can remove the threat (response efficacy); belief in one's capability to successfully execute the recommended courses of action (self-efficacy); and the perceived costs of adopting the behavior (response costs).

PMT has been used to predict a range of health promoting (e.g., physical activity and diet) and health risking (e.g., smoking and alcohol consumption) behaviors. As with the HBM, some studies have highlighted certain PMT constructs to be important determinants of behavior, while other studies suggest different PMT constructs are more important. For example, Plotnikoff and Higginbotham (1998) applied PMT to the prediction of exercise and dietary intentions and behavior among a group of patients who had recently experienced a myocardial infarction or angina. Self-efficacy emerged as the only PMT variable with a significant effect on exercise intentions and intentions were the only significant predictor of exercise behavior. For eating a low fat diet, self-efficacy was the only significant predictor of intentions, while intentions, perceived vulnerability and fear were significant predictors of behavior. However, Abraham, Sheeran, Abrams and Spears (1994) found that self-efficacy and response costs were predictive of condom use intentions among a sample of male and female adolescents. Moreover, sometimes none of the PMT constructs predict health promoting behaviors. For example, Boer and Seydel (1996) used PMT variables to predict attendance at breast cancer screening by mammography. Response efficacy and self-efficacy were predictive of screening intentions but none of the PMT measures predicted attendance at screening at two-year follow-up.

SOCIAL COGNITIVE THEORY

Social Cognitive Theory (SCT; Bandura, 1982; see Luszczynska & Schwarzer, 2015, for a review) was described and evaluated in Chapter 2. As a reminder, in SCT, behavior is determined by three factors: goals, outcome expectancies and self-efficacy (see Figure 2.7). Goals are plans to act and are very similar to intentions to perform the behavior (see Luszczynska & Schwarzer, 2015). Outcome expectancies are beliefs about the perceived likelihood of different outcomes of performing the behavior and are split into physical, social and self-evaluative depending on the nature of the outcomes considered. Self-efficacy is the belief that a behavior is or is not within an individual's control and is usually assessed as the degree of confidence the individual has that they could still perform the behavior in the face of various obstacles (e.g., 'I am confident I can eat healthily even when out with friends'). Bandura (2000) also includes socio-structural factors to his theory. These are factors assumed to facilitate or inhibit the performance of a behavior and affect behavior via changing goals. Socio-structural factors refer to the impediments or opportunities associated with particular living conditions, health systems, political, economic or environmental systems. They are assumed to inform goal setting and be influenced by self-efficacy. The latter relationship arises because self-efficacy influences the degree to which an individual pays attention to opportunities or impediments in their life circumstances. This component of the model incorporates perceptions of the environment as an important influence on health behaviors.

SCT has also been applied to a range of health promoting behaviors, although in many applications not all components of the SCT are examined. For example, Williams and Bond (2002) showed that among diabetics self-efficacy and outcome expectancies were associated with patients' compliance with blood glucose testing. Similarly, Dilorio, Dudley, Lehr and Soet (2000) showed condom use in sexually active college students was predicted by self-efficacy and outcome expectancies. Studies using objective measures of physical activity, such as motion detectors, have shown that self-efficacy is related to a high level of physical activity among 10- to 16-year-old adolescents (Strauss, Rodzilsky, Burack and Colin, 2001).

THEORY OF PLANNED BEHAVIOR

The Theory of Planned Behavior (TPB; Ajzen, 1991) was developed to explain a range of social behaviors but has been particularly widely applied in relation to health behaviors (see Conner & Sparks, 2015, for a review). It was outlined in Chapter 2 and spells out the cognitions that determine that individual's decision to perform a particular behavior (see Figure 2.3). Importantly this theory added 'perceived behavioral control' to the earlier Theory of Reasoned Action (TRA; Ajzen & Fishbein, 1980). The TPB proposes that the key determinants of behavior are intention to engage in that behavior and perceived behavioral control over that behavior (which influences the relationship between intention and behavior). As in the PMT, intentions in the TPB represent a person's motivation or conscious plan or decision to exert effort to perform the behavior. Perceived behavioral control (PBC) is a person's expectancy that performance of the behavior is within their control and confidence that they can perform the behavior and is similar to Bandura's (1982) concept of self-efficacy (as in the PMT).

In the TPB, intention is assumed to be determined by three factors: attitudes, subjective norms and PBC. Attitudes are the overall evaluations of the behavior by the individual as positive or negative. Subjective norms are a person's beliefs about whether significant others think they should engage in the behavior. PBC is assumed to influence both intentions and behavior because we rarely intend to do things we know we cannot do and because believing that we can succeed enhances effort and persistence and so makes successful performance more likely. In turn, attitudes are based on behavioral beliefs (or outcome expectancies), that is, beliefs about the perceived outcomes of a behavior. In particular, they are a function of the likelihood of the outcome occurring as a result of performing the behavior (e.g., 'How likely is this outcome?') and the evaluation of that outcome (e.g., 'How good or bad will this outcome be for me?'). It is assumed that an individual will have a limited number of consequences in mind when considering performing a behavior or not (i.e., only a few outcomes will be salient). This expectancy-value framework is based on Fishbein's (1967) earlier summative model of attitudes. Subjective norm is based on beliefs about salient others' approval or disapproval of whether one should engage in a behavior (e.g., 'Would my best friend want me to do this?') weighted by the *motivation to comply* with each salient other on this issue (e.g., 'Do I want to do what my best friend wants me to do?'). Again it is assumed that an individual will only have a limited number of individuals or groups (often referred to as referents) in mind when considering performing a behavior. PBC is based on control beliefs concerning whether an individual has access to the necessary resources and opportunities to perform the behavior successfully (e.g., 'How often does this facilitator/inhibitor occur?'), weighted by the perceived power, or importance, of each factor to facilitate or inhibit the action (e.g., 'How much does this facilitator/inhibitor make it easier or more difficult to perform this behavior?'). These factors include both internal control factors (information, personal deficiencies, skills, abilities, emotions) and external control factors (opportunities, dependence on others, barriers). As for the other types of beliefs it is assumed that an individual will only consider a limited number of control factors when considering performing a behavior (see Chapter 2 for a more concise description).

In a review of the TPB as applied to health behaviors McEachan, Conner, Taylor and Lawton (2011) reported the results across 237 prospective tests of the TPB (i.e., when the components of the TPB are measured at one time point and behavior is measured at a later time point preserving the presumed causal ordering of variables). Interestingly the type of behavior moderated the effectiveness of the model. In particular, the TPB did well at predicting physical activity and dietary behaviors (23.9% and 21.2% variance explained respectively; see Chapter 2, Critical Skills Toolkit 2.1, to see an account of the concept of explaining variance) but less well at predicting risk, detection, safer sex and drug abstinence behaviors (between 13.8% to 15.3% variance explained). Of greater interest, this meta-analysis showed that the cognitions most strongly associated with intentions also varied as a function of behavior (Table 7.1). In particular, subjective norms were strong predictors of intentions to engage in sex, dietary behaviors and risk behaviors, but weaker predictors of detection behaviors, abstinence behaviors and physical activity. This would suggest the value of targeting subjective norms when trying to change sex, dietary or risk behaviors and also that such a focus would be less useful when trying to change detection, abstinence or physical activity behaviors. There was also some variation in the cognitions most strongly associated with behavior although this was less pronounced (Table 7.2). For example, intentions were strong predictors of physical activity but weaker predictors of safe sex. It is worth thinking about the value of targeting different components of the TPB when trying to change different behaviors.

TABLE 7.1 Relationship between intentions and predictors in TPB (from McEachan et al., 2011)

Predictor	Type of health behavior	N	k	r
Attitude	A. Risk	14673	29	0.46
	B. Detection	8370	17	0.45
	C. Physical activity	23905	101	0.51
	D. Dietary	9823	30	0.52
	E. Safer sex	4958	15	0.51
	F. Abstinence	6351	13	0.47
Subjective norms	A. Risk	14673	29	0.40
	B. Detection	8370	17	0.33
	C. Physical activity	23499	100	0.32
	D. Dietary	9823	30	0.35
	E. Safer sex	4958	15	0.45
	F. Abstinence	6351	13	0.33
PBC	A. Risk	14673	29	0.43
	B. Detection	8370	17	0.45
	C. Physical activity	23996	102	0.47
	D. Dietary	9823	30	0.44
	E. Safer sex	4958	15	0.44
	F. Abstinence	6351	13	0.43

Note: N is number of participants; k is number of studies and r is the average correlation. These effect sizes are in the medium to large range (Cohen, 1992, suggests that r = 0.1 equates to a small effect size, r = 0.3 to a medium effect size and r = 0.5 to a large effect size).

TABLE 7.2 Relationship between behavior and predictors in TPB (from McEachan et al., 2011)

Predictor	Type of health behavior	N	k	r
Intentions	A. Risk	13710	29	0.37
	B. Detection	8370	17	0.37
	C. Physical activity	23376	103	0.45
	D. Dietary	9047	30	0.38
	E. Safe sex	2605	15	0.34
	F. Abstinence	4406	13	0.35
PBC	A. Risk	13713	29	0.22
	B. Detection	8370	17	0.20
	C. Physical activity	23385	103	0.31
	D. Dietary	9047	30	0.30

TABLE 7.2 continued

Predictor	Type of health behavior	N	k	r
	E. Safe sex	3674	19	0.21
	F. Abstinence	4406	13	0.26
Attitude	A. Risk	13713	29	0.27
	B. Detection	8370	17	0.22
	C. Physical activity	23141	101	0.30
	D. Dietary	9046	30	0.29
	E. Safe sex	2234	14	0.23
	F. Abstinence	4406	13	0.26
Subjective norms	A. Risk	13189	29	0.26
	B. Detection	8370	17	0.19
	C. Physical activity	22849	100	0.18
	D. Dietary	9049	30	0.15
	E. Safe sex	2235	14	0.21
	F. Abstinence	4406	13	0.21

Note: N is number of participants; k is number of studies and r is the average correlation (Cohen, 1992, suggests that $r = 0.1$ equates to a small effect size, $r = 0.3$ to a medium effect size and $r = 0.5$ to a large effect size).

INTEGRATING CONSTRUCTS FROM DIFFERENT THEORIES

As we noted in Chapter 2 there are overlaps between the constructs in different theories. This opens up the possibility of producing an integrated theory such as those attempted by Fishbein et al. (2001) and Michie et al. (2005) overviewed in Chapter 2. Fishbein and Ajzen (2010) have also produced an integrated model that they call the Reasoned Action Approach (RAA; see Conner & Sparks, 2015). This is mainly based on the TRA and the TPB but is intended to integrate various influences on the performance of a behavior.

In the TPB, intention is the main predictor of behavior and intentions are determined by three variables as noted earlier in this chapter: attitudes, subjective norms and PBC. In the RAA, attitude, subjective norms and PBC each break down into two components (see Figure 7.1). Attitudes are replaced with affective (e.g., the extent the behavior is rated as pleasant–unpleasant; interesting–boring) and instrumental attitudes (e.g., the extent the behavior is rated as valuable–worthless), subjective norms are replaced with injunctive norms (concerning the social approval of others) and descriptive norms (perceptions of what others do), while PBC is replaced with (perceived) self-efficacy (the perceived ease/difficulty of performing the behavior and people's confidence in performing the behavior should they wish) and perceived control (people's belief that they have control over the behavior and its performance is up to them). Each of the six components is treated as an independent predictor of intentions (Conner & Sparks, 2015).

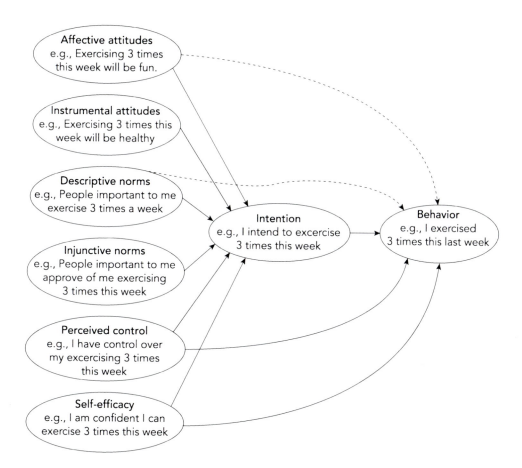

FIGURE 7.1 The Reasoned Action Approach

Recent research has supported the RAA as a powerful predictor of health behaviors. For example, a meta-analysis by McEachan et al. (2016) reported the RAA to explain 58.7% of the variance in intentions and 30.9% of the variance in behavior across a range of health behaviors. Interestingly, in addition to intentions and self-efficacy, affective attitudes and descriptive norms emerged as direct predictors of behavior (independent of intentions) suggesting directions for future research. Moreover, studies have also found affective measures of attitudes to be more closely linked to intentions and behavior than instrumental attitudes (Lawton, Conner & McEachan, 2009).

BURNING ISSUE BOX 7.2

HOW CAN BEING CONSCIENTIOUS IMPROVE HEALTH?
It pays to be conscientious! Conscientiousness refers to the ability to control one's behavior and to complete tasks. Highly conscientious individuals are more organized, careful, dependable, self-disciplined and achievement-oriented

than those low in conscientiousness (McCrae & Costa, 1987). Individuals high in conscientiousness are more likely to report statements such as 'Am always prepared' and 'Am exacting in my work' as good self-descriptors (International Personality Item Pool: http://ipip.ori.org/).

A growing body of research shows the personality trait conscientiousness to have impacts on health behaviors, health outcomes and even longevity. For example, Friedman et al. (1993) showed that those high in conscientiousness at age 11 were likely to live longer (by about two years) compared to those low in conscientiousness.

An important mechanism by which conscientiousness may influence health is through health behaviors. Friedman et al. (1995) showed that the impact of conscientiousness on longevity was partly accounted for by its effect on reducing smoking and alcohol use. A review of work on the relationship between conscientiousness and behavior (Bogg & Roberts, 2004) showed conscientiousness to be positively related to a range of protective health behaviors (e.g., exercise) considered in this chapter but negatively related to a range of risky health behaviors (e.g., smoking) considered in the next chapter. Other studies have shown this effect of conscientiousness on health behaviors such as physical activity to be explained by impacts on intentions. In some studies intentions have been shown to mediate the impact of conscientiousness on behavior. For example, Conner and Abraham (2001) showed that those with higher levels of conscientiousness also had stronger intentions to exercise and this helped explain the effects of conscientiousness on exercise behavior. Other studies have shown moderation effects. For example, Conner, Rodgers and Murray (2007) showed that intentions were better predictors of exercise behavior among those with high compared to low levels of conscientiousness suggesting highly conscientious individuals are more likely to fulfill their intentions.

CHANGING HEALTH PROMOTION BEHAVIORS

The work on social/health cognition models reviewed in the previous section provides the basis for a better understanding of the determinants of health promotion behaviors. A major assumption underlying behavior change, according to these SCMs, is that changing these determinants (predictors) is a key route to change behavior. For example, promoting intentions and self-efficacy to exercise could help promote exercise behavior and so contribute to improving individuals' health outcomes. In this section we review research on changing health behaviors through changing attitudes or self-efficacy.

CHANGING ATTITUDES

Attitude change in response to a persuasive message is something we are all familiar with. But what factors influence the amount of attitude change? In general, research focusing on changing health behaviors through changing attitudes has tended to focus on developing strong messages to change behavior. Petty and Cacioppo (1986) define strong messages as those that produce mainly favorable thoughts about the message. So, if after reading a message about the benefits of eating five portions of fruit and vegetables a day you have mainly positive thoughts, then your attitude towards eating five portions of fruit and vegetables a day is likely to become more positive. If your reactions are negative or quite mixed little or no attitude change will occur.

Changing attitudes via systematic processing and heuristics

Models of attitude change suggest there are two distinct routes to attitude change. In one route, the information in the persuasive message is systematically and carefully considered and attitude change is determined by the extent to which the message produces mainly favorable thoughts about the message. This route to persuasion is called the **central or systematic route**. It is what we traditionally think of as persuasion and requires quite a bit of mental effort. The second route to persuasion does not require careful scrutiny of the message or detailed thought and is labeled the **peripheral or heuristic route**. Here, persuasion depends on the presence of peripheral cues that prompt the use of heuristics. For example, one heuristic is that messages from an expert are more likely to be believed and lead to positive reactions to the message and subsequent attitude change independent of the message content. So if a message is known to come from an expert (e.g., the Chief Medical Officer) it will generally produce more attitude change than the same message from a non-expert. Figure 7.2 sets out the two routes, the factors influencing which route dominates and the consequences of each route for attitude change.

Petty and Cacioppo (1986) argue that because we receive so many messages each day we do not have the motivation or ability to carefully process each one. Petty and Cacioppo refer to the amount of systematic processing devoted to a message as 'cognitive elaboration' and, consequently, their model is known as the Elaboration Likelihood Model (ELM) (see Figure 7.2). High elaboration is associated with central route (effortful) processing of messages while low elaboration is associated with peripheral route (effortless) processing. The ELM suggests that both central processing and peripheral processing occur simultaneously for all messages but that usually one or other will dominate. Likelihood of elaboration is determined by both motivation and ability to think about persuasive messages.

When we are highly motivated because the message is about an issue of interest to us we are more likely to elaborate and so engage in central route processing (Petty & Cacioppo, 1986). Ability to think about a message is determined by factors like not having time pressure or distraction. Central route processing involves greater cognitive elaboration and the strength of the arguments in the message is critical to the amount of persuasion that occurs (via making us think positive thoughts about the message). This is consistent with traditional views of how persuasion works: strong arguments will persuade us to change our views; weak arguments will be dismissed and have little impact on attitude change.

When motivation or ability is low (e.g., when messages are presented quickly amid distractions as is the case in many television or radio advertisements), then elaboration

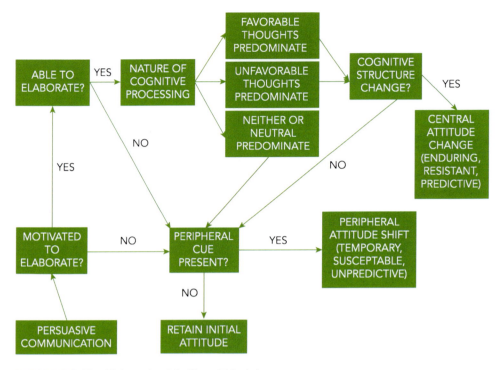

FIGURE 7.2 The Elaboration Likelihood Model

will be less likely and persuasion can occur only through the peripheral route. This route involves little systematic processing (low cognitive elaboration) and other characteristics of the message are more likely to determine whether or not it is persuasive. For example, people use simple rules or decision-making heuristics to evaluate messages (Chaiken, 1980). These include 'expertise = accuracy', that is, they are an expert so what they say must be right, or 'consensus = correctness', that is, if so many people agree they must be right and 'length = strength', that is, there are lots of arguments so it must be true.

Individual differences mean that some people are more or less likely than others to engage in systematic processing. For example, Chaiken (1980) identified people who agreed or disagreed with the 'length = strength' heuristic (using agreement with questionnaire items such as, 'the more reasons a person has for some point of view the more likely they are correct'). These people were then presented with a message containing six arguments in favor of cross-course, end-of-year examinations for students. However, the message was described to participants as either containing ten or two arguments (although it always contained the same six arguments). The results showed that those who endorsed the 'length = strength' heuristic were more likely to be persuaded when the message was described as having ten arguments than were those who did not endorse the heuristic.

In general, research using the ELM has focused on both developing strong messages to change behavior and using peripheral cues to change behavior. Attitude change resulting from systematic (central route) processing is generally more likely to be stable and more likely to influence subsequent behavior. However, as a persuader if you do *not* have strong arguments then you are better discouraging systematic processing and relying instead on peripheral cues like numerous arguments, consensus and perceived expertise. So, if your health product or service has a number of features that are likely to be valued by consumers that are different from similar products then developing a strong message about those features may be the best way to win new customers. This sort of persuasive message is common in paper adverts for high cost items like cars and computers where customers have the motivation and opportunity to carefully consider arguments. In contrast, if your product is very similar to other products then using peripheral cues may be a better approach. This sort of persuasive message is common in television adverts for low cost items like washing powder or food products where customers do not have the motivation or opportunity to carefully consider the product. Peripheral cues like associating the product with a happy tune or getting celebrity endorsements are more common here.

The impact of changing affective attitudes

One example of an attempt to change a health promoting behavior through use of persuasive messages is the study by Conner, Rhodes, Morris, McEachan and Lawton (2011b) focusing on exercise behavior. A sample of university students read a definition of exercise and then self-reported their levels of physical activity. Students were then randomized to one of three conditions: control, cognitive message, affective message. In the control condition participants received no further information. In the cognitive message condition participants read messages focusing on the many benefits of exercising for health and well-being. To emphasize that the evidence supporting these claims were strong, citations to scientific articles supporting these findings were provided (see Figure 7.3). In the affective condition participants read messages focusing on the many affective benefits of exercising including making you feel good and being enjoyable. Again all claims were supported by citations to scientific articles supporting expert sources behind these messages (see Figure 7.3). Participants in all three conditions then reported their cognitive and affective attitudes towards exercising along with a number of other measures. Three weeks later respondents reported their levels of exercise in the intervening three-week period. Figure 7.4 shows the pattern of results found. In the control condition participants' levels of exercise showed a modest decrease from baseline to follow-up. In the cognitive message condition participants' levels of exercise showed a modest increase from baseline to follow-up. In contrast the participants in the affective message condition showed a significant increase in exercise from baseline to follow-up and were reporting several more exercise sessions per week at follow-up compared to the other two conditions. Importantly, additional analyses showed that changes in behavior were explained or mediated by changes in affective attitudes. The authors argue that the data show the value of targeting affective attitudes as one means to achieve behavior change. It may also be the case that the affective messages were more novel to respondents compared to the cognitive messages that should have been more familiar to respondents through general health messages about the benefits of exercising. This greater novelty might have led to more systematic (i.e., careful) processing of the affective messages resulting in more positive affective attitudes and greater impacts on behavior.

AFFECTIVE CONDITION:

It is well-known that regular physical activity can have a tremendous effect on your immediate well-being. Experts say that adults should engage in approximately 30-60 minutes of accumulated physical activity per day (where each separate bout is a minimum of ten minutes)[1]. Another position stand is Activity for adults is defined as a daily energy expenditure of 1.5 kilocalories/kilogram of body weight/day or more; roughly equivalent to brisk walking one half hour every day or more)[2]. Read on for some of the ways physical activity can improve your daily life:

- ⦿ Regular physical activity has been shown to reduce anxiety, depression, and stress which can improve how you feel, your mood, and increase your sense of wellbeing.
- ⦿ Research has shown that regular activity improves general reports of quality of life.
- ⦿ Physical activity can be associated with increased energy levels and reduced fatigue, giving you more energy and vitality to enjoy your day.
- ⦿ Physical activity is an outlet for socializing with friends and creating new social connections for many people through sports, fitness clubs, as well as with exercise partners and groups.
- ⦿ Many types of physical activity provide a fun, enjoyable activity to do in your leisure time.
- ⦿ Physical activity often improves the way one feels about their body/appearance, through more positive body image and self-esteem.

Some Specifics From the Research:

- ⦿ 85% of studies looking at the acute affects of physical activity on mood showed some degree of improved mood following exercise.[3]
- ⦿ Some studies suggest that physical activity can raise endorphin levels, thus decreasing feelings of depression, and elevating mood.[4]
- ⦿ After only 20 minutes of moderate to vigorous physical activity, anxiety symptoms have been shown to decrease.[5]
- ⦿ 60% of studies report a positive association between physical activity and self-esteem. [6]

1. Public Health Agency of Canada. *Physical Activity Unit*, retrieved October 31, 2006 from: http://www.phac-aspc.gc.ca/pau-uap/paguide/why.html
2. World Health Organization. *Physical Activity*, retrieved October 31, 2006 from : http://www.who.int/dietphysicalactivity/publications/facts/pa/en/index.html
3. Yeung, R. (1996). The acute affects of exercise on mood state. *Journal of Psychosomatic Research*, *40*, 123-141.
4. O'Neal, H., Dunn, A., & Martinsen, E. (2000). Depression and exercise. *Journal of Sport Psychology*, *31*, 110-135.
5. O'Connor, P., Raglin, J., & Martinsen, E. (2000). Physical activity, anxiety, and anxiety disorders. *Journal of Sport Psychology*, *31*, 136-155.

FIGURE 7.3A Affective physical activity messages used in Conner et al. (2011b) to promote physical activity

INSTRUMENTAL CONDITION:

It is well-known that regular physical activity can have a tremendous effect on your health. Experts say that adults should engage in approximately 30-60 minutes of accumulated physical activity per day (where each separate bout is a minimum of ten minutes)[1]. Another position stand is for adults is defined as a daily energy expenditure of 1.5 kilocalories/kilogram of body weight/day or more; roughly equivalent to brisk walking one half hour every day or more[2,4]. Research has shown that regular moderate-vigorous physical activity is associated with the following health benefits: [1,2,3,4,5]

- ⦿ Weight control and decreased risk of obesity.
- ⦿ Reduces the risk of dying prematurely.
- ⦿ Reduces the risk of heart disease.
- ⦿ Reduces the risk of developing diabetes.
- ⦿ Reduces the risk of developing high blood pressure.
- ⦿ Helps reduce blood pressure in people who already have high blood pressure.
- ⦿ Reduces the risk of developing colon and breast cancer.
- ⦿ Helps build and maintain healthy bones, muscles, and joints.
- ⦿ There is a linear relationship between increased activity and health benefits (↑PA = ↑benefits).

Some Statistics[4]:

- ⦿ Globally, there are more than 1 billion overweight adults, at least 300 million of them obese.
- ⦿ An estimated 16.7 million - or 29.2% of total global deaths - result from the various forms of cardiovascular disease (CVD), many of which are preventable by action on the major primary risk factors: unhealthy diet, physical inactivity, and smoking. Inactivity greatly contributes to medical costs - by an estimated $75 billion in the USA in 2000 alone.
- ⦿ At least 60% of the global population fails to achieve the minimum recommendation of 30 minutes moderate intensity physical activity daily.
- ⦿ Physical inactivity is estimated to cause 2 million deaths worldwide annually. Globally, it is estimated to cause about 10-16% of cases each of breast cancer, colon cancers, and diabetes, and about 22% of ischaemic heart disease.
- ⦿ The risk of getting a cardiovascular disease increases by 1.5 times in people who do not follow minimum physical activity recommendations.
- ⦿ In Canada, physical inactivity accounts for about 6% of total health care costs.

1. Public Health Agency of Canada. *Physical Activity Unit*, retrieved October 31, 2006 from: http://www.phac-aspc.gc.ca/pau-uap/paguide/why.html
2. CFLRI. Surveys Statistics Summaries, retrieved October 31, 2006 from: http://cflri.ca/eng/statistics/index.php
3. Centers for Disease Control and Prevention. *Physical Activity and Health*, retrieved October 31, 2006 from: http://www.cdc.gov/nccdphp/sgr/contents.htm
4. World Health Organization. *Physical Activity*, retrieved October 31, 2006 from: http://www.who.int/dietphysicalactivity/publications/facts/pa/en/index.html
5. Warburton, D., Nicol, C., & Bredin, S. (2006). Health benefits of physical activity: the evidence. *Canadian Medical Association Journal, 174,* 801-809.

FIGURE 7.3B Instrumental physical activity messages used in Conner et al. (2011b) to promote physical activity

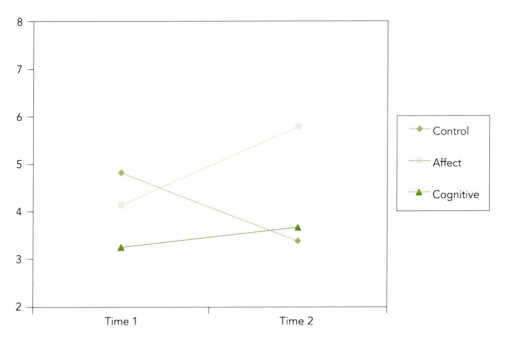

FIGURE 7.4 Frequency of moderate/vigorous exercise of at least 30 minutes duration by condition (from Conner et al., 2011b)

CHANGING SELF-EFFICACY

Bandura (1997) has shown that self-efficacy over performing a behavior can be enhanced in four distinct ways: through mastery experiences, vicarious experience, verbal persuasion or changing perception of physiological and affective states (see Chapter 2). Mastery experiences (i.e., experience of successfully performing the behavior) give people confidence that they can tackle new tasks because they know they have previously succeeded with similar challenges. This finding would suggest the value of graded tasks which involves identifying manageable tasks and only increasing difficulty as confidence and skill grow. Self-efficacy can also be enhanced through observing others' success (i.e., vicarious experience), especially when we see others successfully performing the behavior as being like us. For example, Bandura (1997) showed that observing a model judged to have less skill than ourselves fail had little or no impact on self-efficacy, while observing a model judged to have similar skills to us fail resulted in reduced self-efficacy. When direct experience or modeling are not possible, self-efficacy can be enhanced through verbal persuasion. People can be persuaded by arguments demonstrating that others (like them) are successful in meeting challenges similar to their own as well as persuasion highlighting individuals' own skills, and past success. Finally, changing our own perception of physiological reactions and our interpretations of these reactions can be used to change self-efficacy. Mood, stress and anxiety during performance of a behavior can bolster or undermine self-efficacy. For example, although arousal is normal during demanding performances, it can be interpreted as a sign of panic or incompetence. Such interpretations are likely to disrupt and undermine performance. By contrast, acknowledging arousal as a natural response to performance demands may add to excitement and commitment. Thus interventions designed to reduce negative moods and anxiety and to re-interpret destructive interpretations of arousal can be used to enhance self-efficacy and facilitate skilled performance.

Studies using these techniques either pick on particular techniques or attempt to use all the techniques. For example, Baranowski et al. (2003) targeted vicarious and mastery experiences in relation to children asking for healthy foods inside and outside the home by means of computerized interventions. Using a multimedia game this approach increased mastery in asking for healthy foods at home and when eating out and resulted in increased fruit and vegetable consumption. Based on using all these different means of promoting self-efficacy, Lawrence and colleagues (1997) developed an intervention that included HIV/AIDS education, teaching and rehearsing skills targeting social competence (negotiations with a partner, refusal), mastery of self-protective skills (condom application and increasing sterility of intravenous drug application), technical competence, generating a supportive climate amongst participants and normalizing self-protective behaviors. The intervention targeted a high-risk population of women in prison. After the intervention the women reported higher self-efficacy and frequency of communication with their partners about condom use. They also exhibited more knowledge about HIV/AIDS and improved their ability to apply condoms.

TARGETING INTENTIONS TO CHANGE HEALTH PROMOTION BEHAVIORS

In this section we focus on research that draws on simple techniques to help promote behavior change in those individuals who are generally positively disposed (i.e., motivated) towards performing the behavior but do not seem to get round to doing it. This contrasts with the techniques considered in the previous section that are more useful in getting individuals more motivated to perform a behavior. We consider two such techniques: the question-behavior effect and **implementation intentions**. A range of other behavior change techniques (motivational interviewing; self-monitoring; incentives), as well as implementation intentions, are overviewed and evaluated in Chapter 3.

Question-behavior effect

Research has indicated that merely asking questions about a behavior may be sufficient to produce changes in that or related behaviors (for reviews see Wilding et al., 2016; Wood et al., 2016). This has come to be known as the **question–behavior effect** (QBE). Use of the QBE in relation to changing health behavior is illustrated by Godin, Sheeran, Conner and Germain (2008). This study showed that receiving a questionnaire containing questions about intentions to donate blood (along with a range of other questions from the TPB) resulted in increased blood donation at 6 months (donation rates of 54% vs. 49% respectively) and 12 months (70% vs. 65% respectively) compared to a group not receiving a questionnaire. The QBE has subsequently been tested across a range of health behaviors including physical activity (e.g., Sandberg & Conner, 2011), screening attendance (Sandberg & Conner, 2009) and influenza vaccination (Conner, Godin, Norman & Sheeran, 2011a, Study 2).

The most common explanation of the QBE is that asking behavioral intention questions heightens the accessibility of the person's attitude towards that behavior (**attitude accessibility**) which in turn increases the likelihood that attitude-consistent behavior will be performed. For example, Morwitz and Fitzsimons (2004) showed that completing purchase intention questions increased the activation level of pre-existing brand attitudes. When the brand attitude was both highly accessible and positively valenced participants were more likely to choose that brand, whereas when the activated attitude was both highly accessible and negatively valenced participants were less likely to choose that brand. Wood, Conner, Sandberg, Godin and Sheeran (2014) showed that changes in the accessibility of attitudes mediated, or explained, the effects of asking intention questions on behavior. An interesting consequence of this suggested mechanism is that the QBE can decrease performance of the behavior among those with negative reactions to the behavior. For example, Conner et al. (2011a) showed that screening attendance and influenza vaccination rates among those with negative attitudes and intentions to these behaviors were actually lower for those who completed a questionnaire about these behaviors compared to those who did not receive a questionnaire. Putting these findings together (i.e., QBE increases behavior when the underlying cognitions are positive and the QBE decreases behavior when the underlying cognitions are negative), Ayres et al. (2013) showed that measuring intentions compared to not measuring intentions only resulted in an increase in the behavior (requesting a personalized health plan) when motivation to protect their health was also high (based on receiving feedback or not on their risk factors).

The findings from these and other QBE studies suggest that a relatively simple and cost effective way to promote various health protection behaviors and health detection behaviors is to get individuals to complete intention questions focused on that behavior. However, such effects are only likely to be effective if the underlying cognitions are positive; this makes sense in that it seems unlikely that by simply asking questions we can make someone do something they do not want to do.

Implementation intentions

Another way in which we can increase the performance of health promotion behaviors is through the use of implementation intentions or simple if-then plans. Prestwich, Sheeran, Webb and Gollwitzer (2015, p. 324) note that:

> to form an implementation intention, the person must first identify a response that will lead to goal attainment and, second, anticipate a suitable opportunity to initiate that response. For example, in order to enact the goal intention to exercise, the person might specify the behavior 'go jogging for 20 minutes' and specify a suitable opportunity as 'tomorrow morning before work.'

Mark uses implementation intentions to try and help him exercise at least once per week. Mark's implementation intention is that if it is 5pm on a Wednesday he will get ready to do some exercise. Usually this involves putting his sports gear in a bag to play squash, going to the gym or the climbing wall, although if he is at home it might mean putting his gear on to go out on his mountain bike. Gollwitzer (1993) argues that by forming implementation intentions individuals pass control of intention enactment to the environment. The specified environmental cue prompts the action so that the person does not have to remember the goal intention or decide when to act.

An increasing number of studies have shown the power of implementation intentions to promote both health detection and health promotion behaviors. In relation to the former, Orbell, Hodgkins and Sheeran (1997) was one of the first studies to demonstrate an effect of implementation intentions for a health detection behavior. This study looked at breast self-examination in young women to ensure early detection of abnormalities that might indicate early signs of breast cancer. The young women in the study were randomly allocated to one of two conditions, one where no implementation intention was formed and one where an implementation intention was formed (e.g., 'I will perform breast self-examination when I take my bath on a Friday night'). At follow-up, self-reported rates of breast self-examination were dramatically different: 16% in the control condition and 64% in the implementation intention condition. Studies have shown similar effects in relation to health protection behaviors. For example, Prestwich, Lawton and Conner (2003) showed implementation intentions could be used to promote exercise and increased both self-reported exercise and objectively assessed fitness. Importantly this study showed that forming implementation intentions was most effective when combined with a motivational manipulation. This makes sense as we might expect an implementation intention to be mainly useful in changing behavior among those who want to change this behavior. Implementation intentions have been shown to increase the performance of a range of health behaviors with, on average, a medium effect size (see Gollwitzer and Sheeran, 2006, for a meta-analysis; for a more detailed evaluation of their impact on behavior, see Chapter 2).

Prestwich et al. (2015) provide an in-depth review of both basic and applied research with implementation intentions along with a taxonomy of implementation intentions to change behavior (see Figure 7.5). It is interesting to note that the application of implementation intentions to changing health protection behaviors usually requires the individual to identify appropriate opportunities to perform the behavior. In contrast, the application of implementation intentions to changing health risk behaviors usually requires the individual to identify appropriate alternative ways to act or other strategies when faced with the temptation to perform the health risk behavior (see Figure 7.5).

An interesting recent development has been the idea of collaborative implementation intentions. This is where a pair of individuals form an implementation intention to perform the behavior together. Prestwich et al. (2012) showed such collaborative implementation intentions to be more effective than individual implementation intentions, partner support or a control condition in promoting physical activity over 1-, 3- and 6-month periods. Studies have also shown such collaborative implementation intentions to be effective for promoting breast self-examination (Prestwich et al., 2005), though effects on healthy eating are less clear cut (Prestwich et al., 2014).

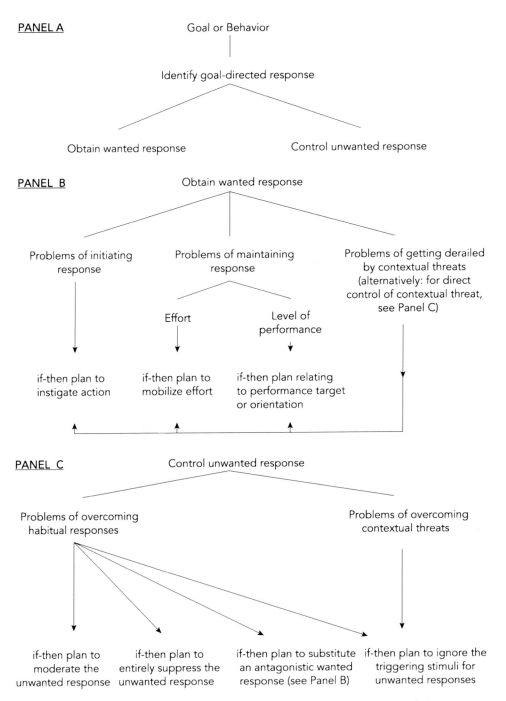

FIGURE 7.5 A framework for operationalizing implementation intentions in relation to particular volitional problems (redrawn from Prestwich et al., 2015). Note panel B applies to using implementation intentions to increase health promotion behaviors (Chapter 7) and panel C applies to using implementation intentions to reduce health risk behaviors (Chapter 8)

BURNING ISSUE BOX 7.3

QUESTIONS AND ANSWERS ON CHANGING HEALTH PROMOTION BEHAVIORS

Question 1: Are particular health promotion behaviors easier to predict than others?

The most common way to measure how easy it is to predict behaviors is in terms of how much variance in behavior key predictors account for. So, for example, McEachan et al. (2011) reviewed the use of the Theory of Planned Behavior (TPB) to predict various health behaviors. They found that the TPB explained the most variance in physical activity and the least variance in safer sex behaviors. That would suggest that physical activity is easier to predict than safer sex! However, we must remember that studies will vary in other ways than just the behavior they measure. For example, many physical activity studies now report objective measures of behavior while safer sex studies are usually reliant on self-reported behavior.

Question 2: Could particular theories work better for certain health behaviors?

The social/health cognition models we have examined were developed to work for a broad range of health behaviors rather than being specific to particular behaviors. As such it could be that particular theories work better for some types of health behavior and other theories work better for other types of health behaviors. However, directly comparing theories in this way can be difficult because different numbers and types of predictors are involved. It is easier to compare particular components of theories across different behaviors. For example, McEachan et al. (2011) showed that intentions were stronger predictors of physical activity than abstinence behaviors like reducing drinking.

Question 3: How can intentions be made more stable?

To increase the performance of health promotion behaviors getting individuals to have positive and stable intentions to perform them may lead to long-term performance. For example, Conner, Norman and Bell (2002) showed that stable intentions to eat healthily were associated with healthy eating six years later. However, to date we know relatively little about what promotes stable intentions. Conner et al. (2016) suggest that if we can get individuals to prioritize their intentions to perform health promotion behaviors this may lead to more stable intentions. They also showed that simple messages suggesting the importance of such prioritization could be effective. Nevertheless future studies identifying effective interventions to promote stable intentions would be a useful development in this area.

Question 4: What's more important in predicting behavior: an individual's personality or their cognitions?

Personality traits like conscientiousness show only small- to medium-sized effects on health behaviors while cognitions like intentions show medium- to large-sized effects. So cognitions are the more important predictors (see Conner & Abraham, 2001).

Question 5: Given the effects of the QBE on behavior change tend to be small, is it an important behavior change technique?

In selecting a behavior change technique to apply the associated effect size is a key consideration. However, cost of implementing the intervention is often another consideration. While the QBE is associated with a small effect size it would be a cheap intervention to implement. It may well therefore be a useful intervention in certain circumstances. For example, various screening programs that require individuals to be sent invitations could very cheaply add a questionnaire about the screening behavior to produce a valuable increase in participation rates.

SCIENCE OF HEALTH BEHAVIOR CHANGE: IN ACTION

In the first section of the book, you learned about how to take a scientific approach to health behavior change (broadly overviewed in Chapter 1). In particular, you learned about different theories (Chapter 2) and behavior change techniques (Chapter 3) and how to apply them to develop theory-based interventions (Chapter 4). In addition, you learned about how to design studies adopting different methodological approaches (Chapter 5) and to statistically test whether a particular intervention was effective in changing behavior (Chapter 6). Along the way, you encountered examples of different critical thinking skills to help you to evaluate the quality of health behavior change studies. Below, we present the first of our Science of Health Behavior Change: In Action boxes. These boxes take a published individual study that attempted to change a health behavior and critically evaluate it against what we have learnt. Chapters 8, 9 and 10 similarly provide In Action boxes in relation to the types of health behaviors considered in those chapters.

In Action Box 7.1 considers the study of Milne, Orbell and Sheeran (2002) who tested the impact of implementation intentions on exercise participation. In particular, they aimed to assess the effects of an implementation intention plus a motivational intervention compared to a motivational intervention alone or a control condition. Theory would suggest that implementation intentions are particularly effective when individuals are motivated to perform the behavior. Therefore it was expected that the combined implementation intention plus motivational intervention would be particularly effective in increasing exercise participation.

SCIENCE OF HEALTH BEHAVIOR CHANGE

In Action Box 7.1

Study: Milne et al. (2002). *Combining motivational and volitional interventions to promote exercise participation: Protection motivation theory and implementation intentions*	
Aim: To increase exercise in undergraduate students.	
Method: Participants were randomized to one of three conditions: a combined motivational and volitional intervention (based on Protection Motivation Theory (PMT) and implementation intentions), a motivational intervention only (the same PMT-based intervention) or a control.	
Results: The PMT-manipulation changed PMT constructs related to threat and appraisal but it did not influence exercise behavior. Those in the combined group increased their exercise significantly more than those in the motivational intervention group or control group.	
Authors' conclusion: Both motivation and volition are needed for goal attainment.	

THEORY AND TECHNIQUES OF HEALTH BEHAVIOR CHANGE		
BCTs	INTERVENTION: Based on Michie et al.'s (2013) taxonomy:	
	Combined intervention: 1.1 Goal setting (behavior); 1.4 Action planning; 5.1 Information about health consequences; 5.2 Salience of consequences; 15.1 Persuasion of ability; 15.2 Mental rehearsal of successful performance.	
	Motivational intervention only: 5.1 Information about health consequences; 5.2 Salience of consequences; 15.1 Persuasion of ability; 15.2 Mental rehearsal of successful performance.	
	CONTROL: None	
Critical Skills Toolkit		
3.1	Does the design enable the identification of which BCTs are effective?	*No – adding an implementation intention-only condition would ensure a 2 (implementation intention: yes/no) x 2 (PMT: yes/no) full-factorial design. Without this condition, it is unclear whether both implementation intentions and the motivational intervention are needed or whether implementation intentions only are sufficient for behavior change.*
4.1	Is the intervention based on one theory or a combination of theories (if any at all)?	*Combined intervention: Protection Motivation Theory (PMT) with implementation intentions (a BCT rather than a theory) added to it. While adding implementation intentions to PMT risks undermining the established theory (by modifying PMT), the modification is in keeping with the Model of Action Phases which specifies behavior is determined through a combination of motivational and volitional elements.* *PMT-only intervention: based only on PMT.*

	Are all constructs specified within a theory targeted by the intervention?	The main determinants of protection motivation: threat appraisal (via perceived severity and perceived vulnerability) and coping appraisal (via self-efficacy, response efficacy and response costs) were targeted by specific BCTs in the PMT conditions. The only element of the theory that was not explicitly targeted by the PMT-interventions was rewards (intrinsic and extrinsic) that increase the likelihood of a maladaptive response.
	Are all behavior change techniques explicitly targeting at least one theory-relevant construct?	Yes – 1.1 Goal setting (behavior) and 1.4 Action planning targeted implementation intentions; 5.1 Information about health consequences targeted perceived severity, perceived vulnerability and response efficacy; 5.2 Salience of consequences targeted perceived vulnerability; 15.1 Persuasion of ability and 15.2 Mental rehearsal of successful performance targeted self-efficacy.
	Do the authors test why the intervention was effective or ineffective (consistent with the underlying theory)?	No – mediation analyses were not conducted. Although the PMT variables changed as a result of the PMT manipulation, it is not clear whether changes in the PMT variables mediated the effect of the PMT-based messages on intentions.
4.2	Does the study tailor the intervention based on the underlying theory?	No – all participants within a study condition received the same materials. However, given the brevity and likely low cost of the intervention, the lack of tailoring is unlikely to represent a major issue.
2.1, 2.2	What are the strengths/ limitations of the underlying theory?	See Burning Issue Box 2.3 for strengths and limitations of Protection Motivation Theory.
THE METHODOLOGY OF HEALTH BEHAVIOR CHANGE		
5.1, 5.3, 5.4, 5.6	Methodological approach	The study adopted an experimental design (see Critical Skills Toolkit 5.4).
6.1	For experimental designs: is the study between-subjects, within-subjects or mixed?	Mixed design because participants were allocated to one of three conditions (between-subjects) and completed measures at multiple time-points (within-subjects). For advantages and disadvantages of this design, see Critical Skills Toolkit 6.1.
5.2, 5.5	Are the measures reliable and valid?	The main outcome variable – exercise – was measured by a single item with no known reliability or validity. The measures of PMT variables were, in some cases, not internally reliable (though these were appropriately analyzed as single items) and these measures had not been previously validated.

5.5	May other variables have been manipulated other than the independent variable?	*Low risk of bias. The manipulations appeared appropriate. Thus, the internal validity of the experiment was not threatened by the risk of confounds.*
	Non-random allocation of participants to condition	*Unclear risk. Participants were randomized to condition but it is not clear how this randomization took place (hence, an inappropriate method of randomization could have been used). Although there were no reported differences across the groups at baseline (suggesting randomization was successful), differences between the groups (arising from potentially inappropriate randomization methods) could be present on unmeasured variables.*
	Blinding and allocation concealment	*Unclear risk. The authors note that the 'participants were anonymous to the experimenter' but this does not necessarily mean that the experimenter was blinded to condition. There was no other evidence of blinding or allocation concealment and this may be more problematic given exercise was measured by self-report rather than objectively.* *There was also risk of demand effects given the text used in the implementation intention condition may have led participants to believe that their behavior should change: 'It has been found that if you form a definite plan of exactly when and where you will carry out an intended behavior you are more likely to actually do so' (p. 170).*
ANALYZING HEALTH BEHAVIOR CHANGE DATA		
6.2	Was the sample size calculated a-priori?	*The sample size was not calculated a-priori. However, given the effects of the combined intervention was large, this is unlikely to be a major issue.*
Fig. 6.1	Was the hypothesis tested with an appropriate statistical test?	*Yes.*
5.5, 6.4	Incomplete outcome data	*It is unclear whether attrition rates differed across the three study conditions. It is a possibility, therefore, that attrition may have been higher in the experimental groups which would suggest an issue with acceptability. Moreover, the analyses were not conducted on an intention-to-treat basis. However, the attrition rates were reasonably low (of the 273 participants who completed the questionnaire at baseline, 250 participants completed the questionnaires at both follow-ups). Moreover, given the effects of the combined intervention were large, it is unlikely that the results would suggest different conclusions if they were analyzed on an intention-to-treat basis. The participants who dropped out were similar on the measured variables compared to those who completed the study, suggesting that the results are generalizable to the types of participants recruited (i.e., other undergraduate students).*

5.5	Selective outcome reporting	*Unclear given the trial protocol was not pre-published – however, all of the measures reported in the Method section were analyzed and reported in the Results section.*
4.2	Lack of variability (non-sig. effects only)	*Not applicable – the participants in the combined intervention exercised more during the follow-up period compared to those in the PMT-only and control groups. Those in the PMT-based conditions increased their PMT-relevant cognitions as predicted.*
6.3	Non-linear relationship (non-sig. effects only)	*Not applicable – effects significant.*

SUMMARY

This chapter examined health promotion behaviors. A series of key social/health cognition models (health belief model; protection motivation theory; social cognitive theory; theory of planned behavior; reasoned action approach) were reviewed and examples of their application to health promotion behaviors described. Approaches to changing health promotion behaviors were examined including changing attitudes, self-efficacy and targeting intentions. In relation to attitudes we described the elaboration likelihood model as one way of understanding attitude change. In relation to self-efficacy we noted the different means of changing this construct, while in relation to intentions we described work on the question-behavior effect and on implementation intentions as ways to change behavior.

FURTHER READING

Bogg, T. & Roberts, B.W. (2004). Conscientiousness and health-related behaviors: a meta-analysis of the leading behavioral contributors to mortality. *Psychological Bulletin, 130*, 887–919. An interesting overview of how conscientiousness relates to a variety of health behaviors.

Conner, M.A. & Norman, P. (2015). Predicting and changing health behavior: a social cognition approach. In M. Conner and P. Norman (Eds.), *Predicting and Changing Health Behavior: Research and Practice with Social Cognition Models* (3rd edn; pp. 1–29). Maidenhead, UK: Open University Press. This chapter provides a useful overview of work on social cognition models and health behaviors.

Gollwitzer, P.M. & Sheeran, P. (2006). Implementation intentions and goal achievement: a meta-analysis of effects and processes. *Advances in Experimental Social Psychology, 38*, 69–119. A review and meta-analysis of the use of implementation intentions to change behavior.

Norman, P. & Conner, M. (2015). Predicting and changing health behavior: future directions. In M. Conner and P. Norman (Eds.), *Predicting and Changing Health Behavior: Research and Practice with Social Cognition Models* (3rd edn; pp. 390–430). Maidenhead, UK: Open University Press. This chapter looks at future directions for research on social cognition models and health behaviors.

McEachan, R., Taylor, N., Harrison, R., Lawton, R., Gardner, P. & Conner, M (2016). Meta-analysis of the Reasoned Action Approach (RAA) to understanding health behaviors. *Annals of Behavioral Medicine, 50,* 592–612. A recent review and meta-analysis of the Reasoned Action Approach in relation to health behaviors.

Wilding, S., Conner, M., Sandberg, T., Prestwich, A., Lawton, R., Wood, C., Miles, E., Godin, G. & Sheeran, P. (2016). The question-behavior effect: a theoretical and methodological review and meta-analysis. *European Review of Social Psychology, 27,* 196–230. An overview and meta-analysis of work on the question-behavior effect with a focus on health behaviors.

GLOSSARY

Attitude accessibility: refers to how quickly an attitude can be brought to mind.

Central or systematic route to persuasion: refers to the careful consideration of persuasive messages where strong messages with good arguments will have bigger effects on attitude change than weak messages. Attitude change by this route leads to strong attitudes that predict behavior, are stable over time and resistant to persuasion.

Health promotion behaviors: behaviors that help protect or maintain health when engaged in. These include things such as exercise, healthy eating, health screening clinic attendance, vaccination against disease, condom use in response to the threat of AIDS and compliance with medical regimens. They are normally distinguished from health risk behaviors where performance is associated with damage or risk to health.

Implementation intentions: simple if-then plans about what to do in response to a cue to further goal pursuit. For example, in pursuit of the goal of exercising more the implementation intention to go jogging on a Friday at noon may be helpful.

Peripheral or heuristic route to persuasion: refers to non-careful consideration of persuasive messages where persuasion is mainly driven by simple cues or heuristics such as longer messages are stronger. Attitude change by this route leads to weak attitudes that are less predictive of behavior, less stable over time and more open to persuasion.

Question-behavior effect: research has shown that merely asking questions about a behavior (e.g., Do you intend to eat a low fat diet?) may be sufficient to produce changes in that (e.g., eating a low fat diet) or related (e.g., eating healthily in other ways) behaviors. This has come to be known as the question-behavior effect.

Social/health cognition models: theories that specify the important thoughts and feelings (jointly referred to as social or health cognitions) that differentiate those performing and not performing a behavior.

Theory-relevant construct: a key concept or building block within a theory/model upon which the intervention is based. Example constructs in the Theory of Planned Behavior are attitudes towards the behavior, perceived behavioral control, subjective norms etc. Constructs can be further broken down into **determinants** (the predictors such as attitudes, subjective norms, PBC) or outcomes (such as behavior).

REFERENCES

Abraham, C. & Sheeran, P. (2015). The health belief model. In M. Conner & P. Norman (Eds.), *Predicting and Changing Health Behavior: Research and Practice with Social Cognition Models* (3rd edn.; pp. 30–69). Maidenhead, UK: Open University Press.

Abraham, C.S., Sheeran, P., Abrams, D. & Spears, R. (1994). Exploring teenagers' adaptive and maladaptive thinking in relation to the threat of HIV infection. *Psychology and Health, 9,* 253–272.

Ajzen, I. (1991). The theory of planned behavior. *Organizational Behavior and Human Decision Processes, 50,* 179–211.

Ajzen, I. & Fishbein, M. (1980). *Understanding Attitudes and Predicting Social Behavior.* Englewood Cliffs, NJ: Prentice-Hall.

Ar-yuwat, S., Clark, M.J., Hunter, A. & James, K.S. (2013). Determinants of physical activity in primary school students using the health belief model. *Journal of Multidisciplinary Healthcare, 6,* 119–126.

Ayres, K., Conner, M.T., Prestwich, A., Hurling, R., Cobain, M., Lawton, R. & O'Connor, D. (2013). Exploring the question-behavior effect: randomized controlled trial of motivational and question-behavior interventions. *British Journal of Health Psychology, 18,* 31–44.

Bandura, A. (1982). Self-efficacy mechanism in human agency. *American Psychologist, 37,* 122–147.

Bandura, A. (1997). *Self-Efficacy: The Exercise of Control.* New York: Freeman.

Bandura, A. (2000). Health promotion from the perspective of social cognitive theory. In P. Norman, C. Abraham & M. Conner (Eds.), *Understanding and Changing Health Behavior: From Health Beliefs to Self-Regulation* (pp. 229–242). Geneva, Switzerland: Harwood Academic.

Baranowski, T., Baranowski, J., Cullen, K.W., Marsh, T., Islam, N., Zakerei, I., Honess-Morreale, L. & deMoor, C. (2003). Squire's Quest: dietary outcome evaluation of a multimedia game. *American Journal of Preventive Medicine, 24,* 52–61.

Boer, I. & Seydel, E.R. (1996). Protection motivation theory. In M. Conner & P. Norman (Eds.), *Predicting Health Behavior* (pp. 95–120). Buckingham, UK: Open University Press.

Bogg, T. & Roberts, B.W. (2004). Conscientiousness and health-related behaviors: a meta-analysis of the leading behavioral contributors to mortality. *Psychological Bulletin, 130,* 887–919.

Chaiken, S. (1980) Heuristic versus systematic information processing and the use of source versus message cues in persuasion. *Journal of Personality and Social Psychology, 39,* 752–766.

Cohen, J. (1992). A power primer. *Psychological Bulletin, 112,* 155–159.

Conner, M. & Abraham, C. (2001). Conscientiousness and the Theory of Planned Behavior: towards a more complete model of the antecedents of intentions and behavior. *Personality and Social Psychology Bulletin, 27,* 1547–1561.

Conner, M., Abraham, C., Prestwich, A., Hutter, R.R.C., Hallam, J., Sykes-Muskett, B.J., Morris, B. & Hurling, R. (2016). Impact of goal priority and goal conflict on the intention-health behavior relationship: tests on physical activity and other health behaviors. *Health Psychology, 35,* 1017–1026.

Conner, M., Godin, G., Norman, P. & Sheeran, P. (2011a). Using the question-behavior effect to promote disease prevention behaviors: two randomized controlled trials. *Health Psychology, 30,* 300–309.

Conner, M., McEachan, R., Jackson, C., McMillan, B., Woolridge, M. & Lawton, R. (2013). Moderating effect of socioeconomic status on the relationship between health cognitions and behaviors. *Annals of Behavioral Medicine, 46,* 19–30.

Conner, M. & Norman, P. (2015). Predicting and changing health behavior: a social cognition approach. In M. Conner and P. Norman (Eds.), *Predicting and Changing Health Behavior: Research and Practice with Social Cognition Models* (3rd edn; pp. 1–29). Maidenhead, UK: Open University Press.

Conner, M., Norman, P. & Bell, R. (2002). The Theory of Planned Behavior and healthy eating. *Health Psychology, 21,* 194–201.

Conner, M., Rhodes, R., Morris, B., McEachan, R. & Lawton, R. (2011b). Changing exercise through targeting affective or cognitive attitudes. *Psychology & Health, 26*, 133–149.

Conner, M., Rodgers, W. & Murray, T. (2007). Conscientiousness and the intention-behavior relationship: predicting exercise behavior. *Journal of Sports and Exercise Psychology, 29*, 518–533.

Conner, M. & Sparks, P. (2015). The theory of planned behavior and the reasoned action approach. In M. Conner & P. Norman (Eds.), *Predicting and Changing Health Behavior: Research and Practice with Social Cognition Models* (3rd edn; pp. 142–188). Maidenhead, UK: Open University Press.

Dilorio, C., Dudley, W.N., Lehr, S. & Soet, J.E. (2000). Correlates of safer sex communication among college students. *Journal of Advanced Nursing, 32*, 658–665.

Fishbein, M. (1967). Attitude and the prediction of behavior. In M. Fishbein (Ed.), *Readings in Attitude Theory and Measurement* (pp. 477–492). New York: Wiley.

Fishbein, M. & Ajzen, I. (2010). *Predicting and Changing Behavior: The Reasoned Action Approach.* New York: Psychology Press.

Fishbein. M., Triandis, H.C., Kanfer, F.H., Becker M., Middlestadt, S.E. & Eichler, A. (2001). Factors influencing behavior and behavior change. In A. Baum, T. A. Revenson & J. E. Singer (Eds.), *Handbook of Health Psychology* (pp. 3–17). Mahwah, NJ: Lawrence Erlbaum Associates.

Friedman, H.S., Tucker, J.S., Tomlinson-Keasay, C., Schwartz, J.E., Wingard, D.L. & Criqui, M.H. (1993). Does childhood personality predict longevity? *Journal of Personality and Social Psychology, 65*, 176–185.

Friedman, H.S., Tucker, J.S., Schwartz, J.E., Martin, L.R., Tomlinson-Keasay, C., Wingard, D.L. & Criqui, M.H. (1995). Childhood conscientiousness and longevity: health behaviors and cause of death. *Journal of Personality and Social Psychology, 68*, 696–703.

Godin, G., Sheeran, P., Conner, M. & Germain, M. (2008). Asking questions changes behavior: mere measurement effects on frequency of blood donation. *Health Psychology, 27*, 179–184.

Gollwitzer, P.M. (1993). Goal achievement: the role of intentions. *European Review of Social Psychology, 4*, 142–185.

Gollwitzer, P.M. & Sheeran, P. (2006). Implementation intentions and goal achievement: a meta-analysis of effects and processes. *Advances in Experimental Social Psychology, 38*, 69–119.

Haefner, D.P. & Kirscht, J.P. (1970). Motivational and behavioral effects of modifying health beliefs. *Public Health Reports, 85*, 478–484.

Hochbaum, G.M. (1958). *Public Participation in Medical Screening Programs: A Socio-Psychological Study.* Public Health Service Publication No. 572. Washington, DC: United States Government Printing Office.

Janz, N.K. & Becker, M.H. (1984). The health belief model: a decade later. *Health Education Quarterly, 11*, 1–47.

Lawrence, J.S., Eldridge, G.D., Shelby, M.C., Little, C.E., Brasfield, T.L. & O'Bannon, R.E., III. (1997). HIV risk reduction for incarcerated women: a comparison of brief interventions based on two theoretical models. *Journal of Consulting and Clinical Psychology, 65*, 504–509.

Lawton, R., Conner, M. & McEachan, R. (2009). Desire or reason: predicting health behaviors from affective and cognitive attitudes. *Health Psychology, 28*, 56–65.

Luszczynska, A. & Schwarzer, R. (2015). Social cognitive theory. In M. Conner & P. Norman (Eds.), *Predicting and Changing Health Behavior: Research and Practice with Social Cognition Models* (3rd edn; pp. 225–251). Maidenhead, UK: Open University Press.

Maddux, J.E. & Rogers, R.W. (1983). Protection motivation and self-efficacy: a revised theory of fear appeals and attitude change. *Journal of Experimental Social Psychology, 19*, 469–479.

McCrae, R.R. & Costa, P.T. (1987). Validation of the five-factor model of personality across instruments and observers. *Journal of Personality and Social Psychology, 54*, 81–90.

McEachan, R.R.C., Conner, M., Taylor, N.J. & Lawton, R.J. (2011). Prospective prediction of health-related behaviors with the Theory of Planned Behavior: a meta-analysis. *Health Psychology Review, 5*, 97–144.

McEachan, R., Taylor, N., Harrison, R., Lawton, R., Gardner, P. & Conner, M. (2016). Meta-analysis of the Reasoned Action Approach (RAA) to understanding health behaviors. *Annals of Behavioral Medicine, 50*, 592–612.

Michie, S., Johnston, M., Abraham, C., Lawton, R., Parker, D. & Walker, A. (2005). Making psychological theory useful for implementing evidence-based practice: a consensus approach. *Quality & Safety in Health Care, 14*, 26–33.

Michie, S., Richardson, M., Johnston, M., Abraham, C., Francis, J., Hardeman, W., Eccles, M.P., Cane, J. & Wood, C.E. (2013). The behavior change technique taxonomy (v1) of 93 hierarchically-clustered techniques: building an international consensus for the reporting of behavior change interventions. *Annals of Behavioral Medicine, 46*(1), 81–95.

Milne, S., Orbell, S. & Sheeran, P. (2002). Combining motivational and volitional interventions to promote exercise participation: protection motivation theory and implementation intentions. *British Journal of Health Psychology, 7*, 163–184.

Morwitz, V.G. & Fitzsimons, G.J. (2004). The mere measurement effect: why does measuring intentions change actual behavior? *Journal of Consumer Psychology, 14*, 566–572.

Norman, P., Boer, H., Seydel, E.R. & Mulle, B. (2015). Protection motivation theory. In M. Conner & P. Norman (Eds.), *Predicting and Changing Health Behavior: Research and Practice with Social Cognition Models* (3rd edn; pp. 70–106). Maidenhead, UK: Open University Press.

Orbell, S., Hodgkins, S. & Sheeran, P. (1997). Implementation intentions and the theory of planned behavior. *Personality and Social Psychology Bulletin, 23*, 945–954.

Petty R.E. & Cacioppo, J.T. (1986). The elaboration likelihood model of persuasion. In L. Berkowitz (Ed.), *Advances in Experimental Social Psychology* (pp. 123–205). New York: Academic Press.

Plotnikoff, R.C. & Higginbotham, N. (1998). Protection motivation theory and the prediction of exercise and low-fat diet behaviors among Australian cardiac patients. *Psychology & Health, 13*, 411–429.

Prestwich, A., Conner, M., Lawton, R., Bailey, W., Litman, J. & Molyneaux, V. (2005). Individual and collaborative implementation intentions and the promotion of breast self-examination. *Psychology & Health, 20*, 743–760.

Prestwich, A., Conner, M., Lawton; R., Ward, J., Ayres, K. & McEachan, R. (2014). Partner and planning-based interventions to reduce fat consumption: randomized controlled trial. *British Journal of Health Psychology, 19*, 132–148.

Prestwich, A., Conner, M., Lawton, R., Ward, J., McEachan, R. & Ayres, K. (2012). Randomized controlled trial of collaborative implementation intentions targeting working adults' physical activity. *Health Psychology, 31*, 486–495.

Prestwich, A., Lawton, R. & Conner, M. (2003). The use of implementation intentions and a decision balance sheet in promoting exercise behavior. *Psychology & Health, 18*, 707–721.

Prestwich, A., Sheeran, P., Webb, T.L. & Gollwitzer, P.M. (2015). Implementation intentions and health behaviors. In M. Conner & P. Norman (Eds.), *Predicting and Changing Health Behavior: Research and Practice with Social Cognition Models* (3rd edn; pp. 321–357). Maidenhead, UK: Open University Press.

Sandberg, T. & Conner, M. (2009). A mere measurement effect for anticipated regret: impacts on cervical screening attendance. *British Journal of Social Psychology, 48*, 221–236.

Sandberg, T. & Conner, M. (2011). Using self-generated validity to promote exercise behavior. *British Journal of Social Psychology, 50*, 769–783.

Strauss, R.S., Rodzilsky, D., Burack, G. & Colin, M. (2001). Psychosocial correlates of physical activity in healthy children. *Archives of Pediatrics & Adolescent Medicine, 155*, 897–902.

Wilding, S., Conner, M., Sandberg, T., Prestwich, A., Lawton, R., Wood, C., Miles, E., Godin, G. & Sheeran, P. (2016). The question-behavior effect: a theoretical and methodological review and meta-analysis. *European Review of Social Psychology, 27*, 196–230.

Williams, K.E. & Bond, M.J. (2002). The roles of self-efficacy, outcome expectancies and social support in the self-care behaviors of diabetics. *Psychology, Health & Medicine, 7*, 127–41.

Wood, C., Conner, M., Sandberg, T., Godin, G. & Sheeran, P. (2014). Why does asking questions change health behaviors? The mediating role of attitude accessibility. *Psychology & Health, 29,* 390–404.

Wood, C., Conner, M., Sandberg, T., Taylor, N., Godin, G., Miles, E. & Sheeran, P. (2016). The impact of asking intention or self-prediction questions on subsequent behavior: a meta-analysis. *Personality and Social Psychology Review, 20,* 245–268.

Zhao, J., Song, F., Ren, S., Wang, Y., Wang, L., Liu, W., Wan, Y., Xu, H., Zhou, T., Hu, T., Bazzano, L. & Sun, Y. (2012). Predictors of condom use behaviors based on the health belief model (HBM) among female sex workers: a cross-sectional study in Hubei Province, China. *PLOS ONE, 7,* e49542.

8

CHAPTER 8
HEALTH RISK BEHAVIORS

OVERVIEW

Health risk behaviors, including smoking, drug use, unhealthy food consumption, being sedentary, unsafe sex, sun bathing and binge drinking, negatively influence health. Many of the approaches we discussed in Chapter 7 when discussing health promotion behaviors have also been used to examine health risk behaviors. Using a similar structure to the previous chapter we first examine how social/ health cognition models have been applied to health risk behaviors. This includes consideration of a model specifically developed in relation to health risk behaviors, the Prototype Willingness Model. We also consider important determinants of health risk behaviors that are typically not captured within social/health cognition models: affect and implicit processes. In the second half of the chapter, we explain how the key determinants of health risk behaviors can be changed.

USING SOCIAL/HEALTH COGNITION MODELS TO PREDICT HEALTH RISK BEHAVIORS

THEORY OF PLANNED BEHAVIOR

Many of the models and theories that have been used in relation to health promotion behaviors have also been used in relation to health risk behaviors. The Theory of Planned Behavior (TPB; see Chapters 2 and 7 for overviews and evaluations of the model), for example, has been used with some success to predict engagement with a range of health risk behaviors including licit (e.g., smoking, alcohol use) and illicit (e.g., cannabis, ecstasy) drug use, risky sexual behaviors and even unsafe driving behaviors (see McEachan, Conner, Taylor & Lawton, 2011; see Tables 7.1 and 7.2).

Conner and McMillan (1999) used the TPB to look at the predictors of cannabis use. Attitude and perceived behavioral control (PBC) were found to be the strongest predictors of intentions to use cannabis, while self-reported cannabis use was found to be mainly predicted by intentions. It was descriptive norms (what we perceive others to do) rather than injunctive norms (what we perceive others want us to do) that were found to also be predictive of intentions to use cannabis. Self-identity as a cannabis user also emerged as a significant additional predictor of intentions. Similar sets of predictors have emerged in large-scale surveys of the factors predicting intentions to engage in other health risk behaviors (e.g., Chorlton, Conner & Jamson, 2012, looked at motorcyclists' intentions to engage in various unsafe riding behaviors such as riding fast in a group).

Comparisons of different types of health behaviors (see Tables 7.1 and 7.2) generally indicate similar levels of predictions for applications of the TPB to both health promotion and health risk behaviors. The only obvious differences are that norms appear to be stronger predictors for both intentions and behavior among risk behaviors and that PBC may be a weaker predictor of health risk behaviors.

A number of studies using the TPB in relation to health risk behaviors have looked at how the components of the TPB might be further distinguished. For example, attitudes might split into affective versus instrumental components (see 'Affect and Health Risk Behaviors' section in this chapter), norms might be split into injunctive and descriptive norms, and PBC might be split into perceived confidence (very similar to self-efficacy) and perceived control (Conner & Sparks, 2015; Fishbein & Ajzen, 2010). This has been described as the Reasoned Action Approach (RAA; see Chapter 7 for details; Figure 7.1). Reviews of the RAA (McEachan et al., 2016) show the importance of both type of attitudes, injunctive norms and perceived confidence in predicting intentions and the importance of **affective attitudes** and descriptive norms in predicting behavior alongside intentions. In the McEachan et al. (2016) review of the RAA, intention, affective attitude, instrumental attitude, injunctive norm and descriptive norm were each significantly stronger correlates of behavior in risk compared to promotion behaviors. In addition, affective attitude and instrumental attitude were significantly stronger correlates of intention in risk compared to promotion behaviors.

An interesting question in this area is the extent to which health risk behaviors are 'planned' in the way that models such as the TPB would suggest. Let's take the example of smoking initiation in adolescents. Is it the case that the key determinant of smoking initiation in adolescents is the plan or intention to take up smoking? Alternatively is it the lack of a sufficiently strong plan not to smoke that leads to adolescents starting smoking? Although models like the TPB have typically considered doing intentions and not doing intentions as simple opposites other research has taken alternative approaches. Some research has suggested that we might usefully consider both doing and not doing cognitions as potentially independent predictors of behavior (see Burning Issue Box 8.1). Other research has suggested the need to focus on alternative predictors of these risk behaviors such as willingness or affect.

BURNING ISSUE BOX 8.1

ARE DOING AND NOT DOING HEALTH COGNITIONS OPPOSITES?

Models such as the TPB tend to focus on predicting behavior based on knowledge of the individual's cognitions (intentions, attitudes, norms, PBC) about doing that behavior. So, for example, in predicting quitting smoking we might look at intentions to quit, attitudes to quitting, norms about quitting and PBC about quitting. But what about cognitions about *not* quitting and continuing to smoke? The traditional assumption is that these two sets of cognitions (about doing and not doing) are essentially opposites and therefore we don't need to consider both. Richetin, Conner and Perugini (2011) present data from three different behaviors to suggest this is not always the case. For eating meat (a health risk behavior), doing vigorous physical activity (a health promotion behavior) and breastfeeding (a health promotion behavior) they show that cognitions about doing and not doing these behaviors both predict intentions and behavior. More importantly both types of cognition were simultaneously predictive. This research suggests the value of considering both doing and not doing cognitions in predicting why someone engages in a behavior.

Richetin et al. (2011) also suggest that doing and not doing cognitions may be based on conflicting goals. So doing vigorous physical activity might be performed to achieve goals such as staying fit and slim and eliminating stress. In contrast, not doing vigorous physical activity might serve the goals of having time for other activities, avoiding tiredness and getting rest. In terms of changing behaviors this will imply that we need to be careful about which goals we activate! For example, if we want to promote vigorous physical activity we need to be careful to promote doing cognitions and avoid promoting not doing cognitions.

PROTOTYPE WILLINGNESS MODEL: A MODEL SPECIFICALLY FOR HEALTH RISK BEHAVIORS

Gibbons and Gerrard (1995) developed the Prototype Willingness Model specifically to try and explain why many young people engage in health risk behaviors such as unprotected sex (Brooks-Gunn & Furnstenberg, 1989). They argue that young people (and presumably others) are likely to experience situations in which the opportunity to engage in different health risk behaviors presents itself. In such situations, the individual may be 'willing' to engage in the behavior given the opportunity to do so. Their behavior is assumed to reflect a reaction to the social situation rather than a premeditated intention or plan to engage in a health risk behavior. The Prototype Willingness Model (PWM; Gibbons & Gerrard, 1995; Gibbons, Gerrard, Stock & Finneran, 2015, for a review) was developed to provide an account of such health risk behavior (see Figure 8.1).

The PWM is based on three key assumptions. First, that many of the health risk behaviors performed by young people in particular are not best thought of as intentional or planned. Rather, they can be considered to be the result of reactions to 'risk-conducive situations' that many young people encounter. Second, many health risk behaviors are typically performed with, or in the presence of, others. So, Mark might be more likely to have too many alcoholic drinks when out with friends or when having dinner with his partner Sarah. The social nature of these events is key and so social comparison processes are likely to have an important impact on performance of the health risk behavior. Third, young people tend to be more concerned about their social images and, as a result, are likely to be aware and react to the social implications of their behavior (Simmons & Blyth, 1987). This is likely the case for behaviors that are performed with others in social settings and that are associated with vivid/salient images. These images might include the 'typical drinker' or the 'typical smoker' (Blanton et al., 2001). As a result, performing a health risk behavior likely has important social consequences, such as an acceptance of the image associated with the behavior.

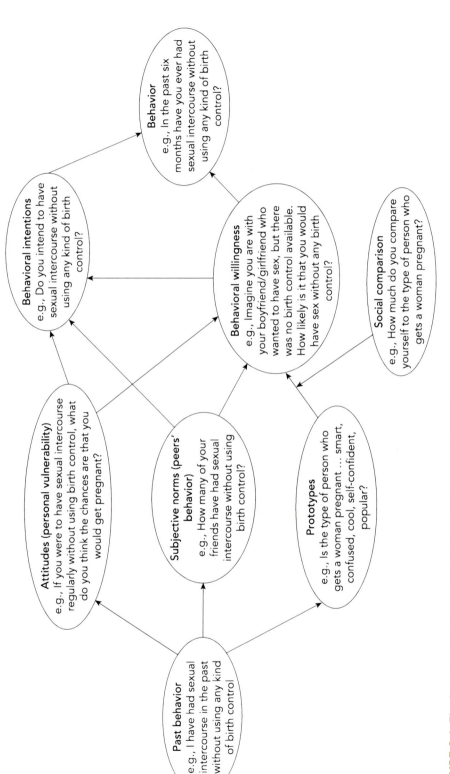

FIGURE 8.1 The Prototype Willingness Model (from Gibbons et al., 2015)

PWM describes two 'pathways' to health risk behavior among adolescents and young adults. First, a 'reasoned pathway' reflects the operation of more or less rational decision-making processes as outlined by models such as the TPB. In this pathway, health risk behavior is based on a consideration of the pros and cons of performing the behavior. Consequently, behavioral intention is seen to be the key proximal predictor of health risk behavior in this pathway (just like in the TPB). Gibbons and Gerrard (1995) used measures of behavioral expectations rather than of behavioral intentions to predict health risk behavior (see Sheppard, Hartwick & Warshaw, 1988), arguing that adolescents may be more likely to acknowledge that they are likely to perform a health risk behavior in the future than they are to admit that they intend to do so. More recently (Gibbons et al., 2015), however, they argue for using a standard behavioral intentions measure.

Second, a 'social reaction pathway' is what makes the PWM distinct from models such as the TPB. This is the pathway likely to drive behavior in risk-conducive situations and describes four factors that impact on individuals' willingness to engage in health risk behaviors when they encounter risk-conducive situations. Number one are *subjective norms* that focus on perceptions of whether important others engage in the behavior and whether they are likely to approve or disapprove of the individual performing the behavior. In this way, Gibbons and Gerrard (1995) highlight the importance of both descriptive and injunctive social norms (Cialdini, Reno & Kallgren, 1990). Number two are *attitudes* that are primarily concerned with the perceived likelihood of negative outcomes (e.g., perceived vulnerability). In particular, a willingness to perform a health risk behavior in a risk-conducive situation may be associated with a downplaying of the risks associated with the behavior. Number three is *past behavior*. Given that many health risk behaviors attract social approval and are enjoyable, having performed a health risk behavior in the past may be associated with more positive subjective norms (Gerrard, Gibbons, Bentin & Hessling, 1996), more positive attitudes (Bentler & Speckart, 1979) and a greater willingness to perform the behavior again in the future (Gibbons, Gerrard, Blanton & Russell, 1998a). Number four is the *prototype* associated with the health risk behavior, i.e., the image that people have of the type of person who engages in a certain behavior (e.g., the 'typical ecstasy user'). According to the PWM, prototype favorability (i.e., the extent to which the image is positively evaluated) and prototype similarity (i.e., the perceived similarity between that image and how you view yourself) interact to impact on individuals' willingness to engage in a health risk behavior. The four factors identified in the 'social reaction pathway' have their influence on behaviors through **behavioral willingness**. Gibbons and Gerrard (1995) argue that the willingness to engage in a health risk behavior in a risk conducive situation, compared to behavioral expectations, provides a better prediction of subsequent behavior as it reflects the social reactive nature of many of the health risk behaviors performed by young people.

The PWM has been applied to a variety of health risk behaviors including smoking (e.g., Blanton, Gibbons, Gerrard, Conger & Smith, 1997), unprotected sex (e.g., Thornton, Gibbons & Gerrard, 2002), alcohol use (e.g., Gerrard et al., 2002) and drink driving (e.g., Gibbons, Gerrard, Ouellette & Burzette, 1998b). These studies provide reasonable support for various key aspects of the PWM. For example, studies have shown behavioral willingness to be predictive of subsequent health risk behavior, independent of behavioral expectations (e.g., Gerrard et al., 2002). In addition, prototype perceptions have been found to predict both behavioral willingness (e.g., Thornton et al., 2002) and health risk behavior (e.g., Blanton et al., 1997).

A good example of a PWM application is provided by the Gibbons et al. (1998a) study on unprotected sexual intercourse among college students (see Figure 8.1). The PWM was found to provide a good level (explaining 66% of the variance) of prediction of sexual behavior (i.e., sexual intercourse without using any form of birth control) with past behavior, behavioral expectation and behavioral willingness each having direct, significant effects. In turn, behavioral expectation was predicted by subjective norms, attitudes and past behavior. These same three variables were also predictive of behavioral willingness along with prototype perceptions. It is noteworthy that prototype perceptions only had an effect on behavioral willingness, in line with PWM predictions.

Overall, there is good empirical support for the PWM in relation to the prediction of health risk behavior among young people (see Gibbons et al., 2015, for a review). The PWM adds to our understanding of health risk behaviors in two important ways. First, the PWM highlights that many health risk behaviors are not intentional or planned. Instead, people may be reacting to risk-conducive situations in which they are willing to perform the behavior. Second, the PWM highlights the importance of prototype perceptions as an additional source of normative influence on health behavior.

EXPECTANCIES AND REASONS

Models like the TPB and Social Cognitive Theory considered in Chapters 2 and 7 emphasize the importance of expectancies as determining individuals' decisions about how to act. They suggested that behavior and decisions are based upon an elaborate, but subjective, cost/benefit analysis of the likely outcomes of differing courses of action. As such they have roots going back to Expectancy-Value Theory (Peak, 1955) and Subjective Expected Utility Theory (SEU; Edwards, 1954). It is assumed that individuals generally aim to maximize utility and so prefer behaviors which are associated with the highest expected utility (i.e., lots of benefits and few costs). The overall utility or desirability of a behavior is assumed to be based upon the summed products of the probability (expectancy) and utility (value) of specific, salient outcomes or consequences. Each behavior may have differing subjective expected utilities because of the value of the different outcomes associated with each behavior and the probability of each behavior being associated with each outcome. Whilst such a model allows for subjective assessments of both probability and utility, it is assumed that these assessments are combined in a rational and consistent way.

As an example, imagine that David and Sarah both perceive the key outcomes of taking up smoking to be effects on their health and whether smoking will make them look cool. We can assess the utility of taking up smoking to David and Sarah by getting them to rate each outcome in terms of likelihood (e.g., Taking up smoking will damage my health, very unlikely -2 -1 0 $+1$ $+2$ very likely) and value (e.g., Damaging my health is . . . very bad -2 -1 0 $+1$ $+2$ very good). David thinks taking up smoking is slightly likely to damage his health (rated $+1$) and slightly likely to look cool (rated $+1$) but rates damaging his health as very bad (rated -2) and being cool as slightly good (rated $+1$). His overall utility for taking up smoking will be -1 ($[+1 \times -2] + [+1 \times +1]$). Sarah is not sure taking up smoking will really damage her health (rated 0) but will definitely look cool (rated +2) and rates damaging her health as slightly bad (rated −1) and being cool as really good (rated +2). Her overall utility for taking up smoking will be +4 ([0 × −1] + [+2 × +2]). In this case we might expect Sarah to be more likely to take up smoking than David because she rates the behavior more positively (i.e., her utility for smoking is higher).

Whilst such considerations may well provide good predictions of which behaviors are selected, it has been noted by several authors that they do not provide an adequate description of the way in which individuals make decisions (e.g., Frisch & Clemen, 1994; Jonas, 1993). For example, except for the most important decisions it is unlikely that individuals integrate information in this way (van der Pligt, de Vries, Manstead & van Harreveld, 2000) because it requires a lot of mental energy to achieve this. Nevertheless considerable research emphasizes the power of outcome expectancies to predict intentions and behavior. They provide an important insight into why individuals perform behaviors and also useful targets for interventions to change behaviors.

Research in recent years has looked at different dimensions on which such beliefs might fall. For example, Rhodes, Fiala and Conner (2010) suggested three dimensions along which outcome expectancies might be placed. First, beliefs may be distinguished along positive (e.g., physical activity makes me feel good) and negative (e.g., physical activity is painful) valences. This approach is central to assessment of attitudinal ambivalence (e.g., Armitage & Conner, 2000; Conner, Povey, Sparks, James & Shepherd, 2003), and a focus of belief structure in models like the transtheoretical model (Prochaska & DiClemente, 1984) and health belief model (Rosenstock, 1974). It has also been argued that it is the positive-negative dimension that value judgments tap in traditional applications of the TPB/TRA (Conner & Sparks, 2015). Second, beliefs may be distinguished across an affective (e.g., physical activity is fun) and instrumental (physical activity prevents disease) continuum (Lawton, Conner & McEachan, 2009). This distinction has been made with considerable success in attitude constructs in the exercise domain (e.g., French et al., 2005; Lowe, Eves & Carroll, 2002). Third, beliefs may be distinguished by the temporal proximity of the expected outcome. That is, physical activity has proximal (e.g., stress management) and distal (e.g., weight control, disease prevention) temporal outcomes.

Rhodes et al.'s (2010) 2 × 2 × 2 model of beliefs suggests eight different types of beliefs that might be distinguished (Figure 8.2). Future research might usefully assess whether particular types of beliefs are key for particular behaviors. For example, Rhodes et al. (2010) present data suggesting that interventions targeting proximal positive affective beliefs (fun, accomplishment, stress relief) may yield higher intentions to be physically active, and a secondary focus on overcoming proximal negative affective beliefs (muscle soreness, pain) may also have merit. This would be in contrast to typical health promotion messages that might target distal negative instrumental beliefs (physical activity will help you live longer). Studies support the focus on affective compared to instrumental beliefs when changing behaviors such as physical activity (Conner, Prestwich & Ayres, 2011) or fruit and vegetable consumption (Carfora, Caso & Conner, 2016). Whether changing affective beliefs has an even greater effect on changing risk behaviors is an interesting question for future research.

	Positive outcomes		Negative outcomes	
	Proximal outcomes	Distal outcomes	Proximal outcomes	Distal outcomes
Affective outcomes	Feeling good about self for stopping smoking	Feeling pride in being a non-smoker	Missing the pleasure of smoking	Regretting never being able to have a cigarette
Instrumental outcomes	Saving money by not buying cigarettes	Being healthier as a non-smoker	Not knowing what to do with your hands	Not wanting to be around people smoking

FIGURE 8.2 A 2 × 2 × 2 structure for behavioral beliefs as applied to smoking cessation

Health risk behaviors like binge drinking may also be particularly influenced by proximal positive affective beliefs (fun, stress relief). A number of studies have begun to use parts of this classification of beliefs or outcomes in relation to understanding health risk behaviors. For example, Goldberg, Halpern-Felsher and Millstein (2002) noted the importance of positive beliefs (e.g., There is an x% chance that I'll have a better time at the party if I drink alcohol than if I don't drink) in relation to predicting drinking in young people, while Grogan, Conner, Fry, Gough and Higgins (2009) reported that for boys, negative instrumental beliefs (e.g., Smoking makes you have more coughs) predicted later smoking, while for girls positive instrumental beliefs (e.g., Smoking helps you relax) predicted later smoking in adolescents. Research also suggests that people tend, in general, to emphasize proximal over distal outcomes. For example, Hall and Fong's (2007) temporal self-regulation theory emphasizes the importance of proximal over distal outcomes in determining behavior (see Burning Issue Box 8.2 on discounting).

BURNING ISSUE BOX 8.2

DISCOUNTING OF OUTCOMES

Another bias in our use of information in outcomes refers to temporal discounting. This refers to the idea that temporally proximal outcomes influence behavior more strongly than do distal consequences. For example, Madon, Guyll, Scherr, Greathouse and Wells (2012) showed that individuals were more prepared to admit to criminal and unethical behaviors to avoid a proximal consequence even though doing so increased their risk of incurring a distal penalty.

Temporal Self-Regulation Theory (TST; Hall & Fong, 2007) provides one account of why maladaptive behaviors (e.g., excessive drinking) are adopted even though the long-term negative consequences seem to vastly outweigh the short-term positive consequences. TST, like models such as the TPB, suggests that intentions are key determinants of behavior. However, TST also suggests that self-regulatory capacity and behavioral prepotency are additional key determinants of behavior. Behavioral prepotency refers to the frequency of past performance of the behavior and the presence of cues to action in the environment (i.e., the fact that we tend to act in similar ways to which we have in the past, especially when in similar environments). Self-regulatory capacity refers to the individual's capacity to effortfully regulate their own behavior (this may be determined by executive function, energy levels or conscientiousness).

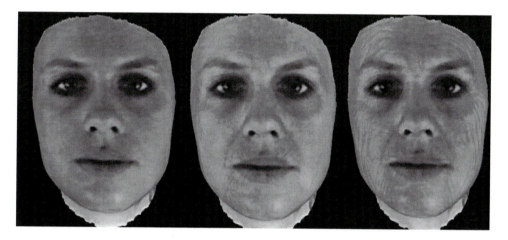

FIGURE 8.3 Effects of smoking on aging – baseline photo; photo aged to 50 years without smoking; photo aged to 50 years with smoking (from Grogan et al., 2011)

Grogan et al. (2011) used an interesting intervention focusing on the proximity of the outcome to reduce smoking in a sample of young women. In this research a computerized facial age-progression technique was used to show how the individual's face 'aged' differently if they continued to smoke or not (Figure 8.3). This technique made the distal negative outcome of smoking on how the face looks more immediate and proximal and reduced self-reported smoking. Research has shown this technique to also be effective in reducing sun exposure (Williams, Grogan, Clark-Carter & Buckley, 2013).

AFFECT AND HEALTH RISK BEHAVIORS

Models like the PWM or the TPB have been criticized for focusing on cognitive influences at the expense of affective influences (i.e., feelings) on behavior. This criticism seems particularly pertinent to health risk behaviors that may be driven by affect. Two related but distinct types of affect have been considered as important influences on health behavior. One is affective attitudes and the other is **anticipated affect**. The two types of affect can be distinguished in three important ways. First, work on anticipated affect tends to focus on the affect that is expected to follow after performance or non-performance of a behavior rather than that expected to occur while the behavior is being performed. Second, anticipated affect measures tend to focus on what Giner-Sorolla (2001) describes as self-conscious emotions (e.g., regret, guilt), whereas affective attitudes tend to focus on hedonic emotions (e.g., enjoyment, excitement). Third, research on anticipated affect has tended to examine the negative affect (particularly associated with non-performance of the behavior; e.g., regret, guilt) while affective attitudes tend to focus on positive affect (e.g., enjoyment, excitement).

AFFECTIVE ATTITUDES

There has been a long established distinction between, for example, cognitive and affective attitudes (e.g., Abelson, Kinder, Peters & Fiske, 1982; Trafimow & Sheeran, 1998) and such distinctions have been incorporated into the RAA (Conner & Sparks, 2015; Fishbein & Ajzen, 2010; see Chapter 7 for description of the RAA). **Cognitive attitudes** tend to be tapped by semantic differentials such as harmful-beneficial or negative-positive (e.g., My smoking would be . . . harmful-beneficial). In contrast affective attitudes tend to be tapped by semantic differentials such as unpleasant-pleasant or not enjoyable-enjoyable.

The relative importance of affective and cognitive attitudes in predicting the performance of health behavior is nicely illustrated in a study by Lawton et al. (2009). In this study, members of the general public completed measures of both affective and cognitive attitudes. Comparisons of the simple correlations showed that compared to cognitive attitudes, affective attitudes were stronger predictors of intentions (towards 10 out of 14 behaviors) and behavior (13 out of 14 behaviors). Importantly, when both types of attitude were simultaneously entered, the predictive power (beta weight) of affective attitudes were significantly stronger than the predictive power of cognitive attitudes when looking at intentions (7 out of 14 behaviors; Table 8.1) and behavior (9 out of 14 behaviors; Table 8.2). For health risk behaviors the pattern was even stronger with affective attitudes significantly stronger predictors of intentions and behavior in 4 out of 5 comparisons (Tables 8.1 and 8.2).

ANTICIPATED AFFECT

Anticipated affect – particularly anticipated regret (the extent to which an individual feels they would regret doing a behavior) – has also received attention as a determinant of intentions and behavior. Sandberg and Conner's (2008) meta-analysis suggests that anticipated regret has a strong effect on intentions ($r_+ = .47, k = 25; 95\%CI .19$ to .74) and a small to medium effect on behavior ($r_+ = .28, k = 8; 95\%CI .06$ to .50). Regressions indicated anticipated regret was a significant predictor of both intentions and behavior when controlling for TPB variables suggesting that this variable would represent a useful addition to the TPB.

The research presented above supports a small but significant role for both affective attitudes and anticipated affect on intentions and action for health behaviors. However, it leaves open the question of their simultaneous effects. Perhaps both tap the same affective influence on intentions and behavior or perhaps the two represent independent influences on intentions and behavior.

Meta-analytic reviews of the limited number of studies (Conner, McEachan, Taylor, O'Hara & Lawton, 2015; $k = 13$) that have measured both affective attitudes and anticipated affect suggest the latter. There is only a small to medium sized relationship between affective attitudes and anticipated regret ($r_+ = .23$, $k = 13$), although, compared to anticipated regret, affective attitudes tend to be more strongly correlated with both intentions ($r_+ = .45$ vs. .29, $k = 13$) and behavior ($r_+ = .29$ vs. .19, $k = 13$). Interestingly this meta-analysis did not indicate affective attitude or anticipated affect to be stronger predictors for health risk behaviors compared to health promotion behaviors.

TABLE 8.1 Predicting intention to perform different health behaviors from cognitive and affective attitudes (Lawton et al., 2009). Table shows correlation and beta weight of cognitive (judgment of how harmful to beneficial the behaviour is) and affective (judgment of how not enjoyable to enjoyable the behavior is) attitude in predicting *intention* to perform the behavior. R^2 is the amount of variance explained in each intention by the cognitive and affective attitudes

Behavior	Harmful-beneficial		Not enjoyable-enjoyable			β for affective > β for cognitive
	r	β	r	β	R^2	
Health risk						
Binge drinking	.37***	.14**	.61***	.55***	.38**	***
Daily alcohol use	.36***	.23***	.46***	.39***	.26***	*
Illegal drugs	.38***	.21***	.47***	.38***	.26***	*
Smoking	.17***	.01	.73***	.73***	.53***	***
Speeding	.44***	.31***	.41***	.24***	.24***	
Health promotion						
Brushing teeth	.27***	.23***	.20***	.14**	.09***	
Exercising	.25***	.15**	.37***	.32***	.16***	*
Flossing teeth	.18***	.21***	.27***	.30***	.20***	
Fruit and vegetable consumption	.24***	.04	.45***	.43***	.20***	*
Low fat diet	.37***	.28***	.39**	.31***	.22***	
Physical activity	.18**	.03	.41***	.40***	.17***	***
Self-examination	.03	.05	.12*	.13*	.02	
Sunscreen use	.30***	.27***	.29***	.25***	.15***	
Vitamin use	.40***	.34***	.29***	.16**	.19***	

* p<0.05; ** p<0.01; *** p<0.001.

TABLE 8.2 Predicting performance of different health behaviors from cognitive and affective attitudes (Lawton et al., 2009). Table shows correlation and beta weight of cognitive (judgment of how harmful to beneficial the behaviour is) and affective (judgment of how not enjoyable to enjoyable the behavior is) attitude in predicting self-reported *frequency of performance of the behavior*. R^2 is the amount of variance explained in each behavior by the cognitive and affective attitudes

Behavior	Harmful-beneficial		Not enjoyable-enjoyable			
	r	β	r	β	R^2	β for affective > β for cognitive
Health risk						
Binge drinking	.24***	.07	.49***	.42***	.20**	***
Daily alcohol use	.21***	.06	.47***	.49***	.22***	***
Illegal drugs	.30***	.16**	.37***	.29***	.16***	
Smoking	.17*	.03	.63***	.62***	.39***	***
Speeding	.39***	.17**	.51***	.41***	.28***	*
Health promotion						
Brushing teeth	.21***	.16**	.24***	.20***	.08***	
Exercising	.18***	.07	.36***	.34***	.14***	**
Flossing teeth	.10*	.13*	.26***	.28***	.09***	*
Fruit and vegetable consumption	.17*	−.04	.46***	.48***	.21***	***
Low fat diet	.30***	.21***	.38***	.32***	.19***	
Physical activity	.12*	.01	.30***	.30***	.09***	**
Self-examination	−.06	−.04	.21***	.20***	.04***	***
Sunscreen use	.21**	.17*	.24***	.21**	.09***	
Vitamin use	.37**	.31***	.27***	.16**	.16***	

* $p<0.05$; ** $p<0.01$; *** $p<0.001$.

STRESS

Another important influence on health risk behaviors is stress. In general too much stress is thought to be bad for us in terms of morbidity and mortality. Part of the reason for this may be that individuals are more likely to engage in health risk behaviors when they are stressed. Individuals often report that when they feel stressed they are more likely to smoke or drink alcohol or snack on unhealthy foods. In this section we take a look at research that has focused on stress as a determinant of engaging in health risk behaviors and focus on unhealthy snacking in particular.

The concept of stress has been difficult to define and operationalize. However, most researchers agree that stress is an aversive state in which the well-being of the organism is threatened and is commonly assumed to be the result of the individual's perception that the demands of the environment exceed, or threaten to exceed, the available resources to cope (Lazarus & Folkman, 1984). Stress has been examined in both experimental and correlational research. In experimental research, stressors include mood manipulations (e.g., videos of unpleasant accidents), cognitive tasks (e.g., counting backward by sevens) and physical stressors (e.g., partial immersion in very cold water) presented in the laboratory. Such manipulations have the clear advantage of ensuring each participant is exposed to the same stressor. However, such stressors are generally weaker and of shorter duration than those experienced in naturalistic settings (e.g., death of a close relative). In correlational research, an important issue has been one of how to define and measure stressors. Early approaches focused on stressful major life events such as bereavement, divorce or job loss (e.g., Holmes & Rahe, 1967), while later work has emphasized the stressful nature of many minor life events, often referred to as hassles (DeLongis, Coyne, Dakof, Folkman & Lazarus, 1982). These include irritating, but minor, events such as losing one's keys.

Although much research on stress and eating has focused on the question of whether stress makes us eat more or less (Greeno & Wing, 1994) more recent research has focused on whether stress makes us eat more or less healthily and what types of individuals are most affected. For example, Mark finds he is much more likely to eat sweet snacks when he has a work deadline to complete. He is not alone. Oliver, Wardle and Gibson (2000) found changes in consumption of sweet high fat foods and more energy dense foods in individuals when stressed. In addition, Steptoe, Lipsey and Wardle (1998) demonstrated that 'fast food' was eaten more frequently when respondents reported experiencing greater number of hassles. In one of the larger studies in this area, O'Connor, Jones, Conner, McMillan and Ferguson (2008) investigated the types of daily hassles associated with changes in between-meal snacking. The results showed that more daily hassles were associated with increased consumption of high fat/sugar snacks and with a reduction in main meals and vegetable consumption. Ego-threatening (e.g., stressors linked to a fear of failure), interpersonal (e.g., an argument with a friend) and work-related (e.g., a large and approaching deadline for completing a piece of work) hassles were significantly associated with increased snacking, whereas physical stressors (e.g., a fight) were significantly associated with decreased snacking. These results suggest that when encountering various stressors, individuals may shift their preference to more palatable and energy dense snack foods, which are less healthy and higher in fat, thus potentially increasing their risk of cardiovascular disease and cancer.

IMPLICIT INFLUENCES

In Chapter 2 we noted that other than the influences described in models like the TPB, more implicit or impulsive influences may drive health behavior and this may be particularly the case for risk behaviors. The Reflective-Impulsive Model (RIM; covered also in Chapter 2) developed by Strack and Deutsch (2004) distinguishes two separate but interacting systems that together guide behavior: the reflective and the impulsive. The **reflective system** is seen as reasoned, conscious and intentional and covers many of the models described in this chapter and elsewhere (e.g., Chapters 2 and 7). In contrast, an **impulsive system** consists of associative clusters that have been learned through experience. These learned associations can then trigger a behavior in response to a simple stimuli. For example, for Mark the smell of coffee can be enough to automatically direct attention to cake (attentional bias), thoughts of cake (implicit attitudes: automatic positive or negative evaluations) and to his buying and eating cake if available.

Attentional bias and implicit attitudes have been associated with health behaviors. For example, Calitri, Pothos, Tapper, Brunstrom and Rogers (2010) reported that greater attentional bias for health foods and less attentional bias for non-food words both predicted reductions in body mass index over a period of a year. Implicit attitudes have been found to be associated with condom use (Stacy, Ames, Ullman, Zogg & Leigh, 2006), smoking (Payne, McClernon & Dobbins, 2007), snack consumption (Conner, Perugini, O'Gorman, Ayres & Prestwich, 2007) and physical activity (Calitri, Lowe, Eves & Bennett, 2009). Various reviews also suggest that implicit attitudes are predictive of behavior even after taking account of explicit attitude measures (Hofmann, Friese & Wiers, 2008; Rooke, Hine & Thorsteinsson, 2008) or other explicit cognitions such as outcomes expectancies, self-efficacy and intention (Conroy, Hyde, Doerksen & Ribiero, 2010). However, there is continuing debate about the power of implicit attitudes to predict behavior after controlling for affective attitudes (Ayres, Conner, Prestwich & Smith, 2012; Conner et al., 2011), suggesting that some explicit measures like affective attitudes may also tap these impulsive influences.

CHANGING HEALTH RISK BEHAVIORS

In this section we look at research that has attempted to change health risk behaviors focusing in part on the determinants of these behaviors identified in the previous section. We first look at how persuasive messages are presented or framed can change health risk behaviors such as sun bathing and the role of self-affirmation in making individuals fully consider such messages. We then look at the potential for interventions focusing on affect. Finally, we overview different techniques that can be used to change implicit processes including attentional bias and implicit attitudes. Identifying strategies that can change reflective and automatic processes can give rise to exciting new interventions that combine different types of techniques to achieve more substantial and sustained health behavior change in the future.

PERSUASIVE MESSAGES

In this section we look at two important research areas in relation to using persuasive messages to change health risk behaviors. First, we consider **message framing** research that tests whether equivalent information presented as a potential loss or potential gain leads to different behavioral effects. Second, we consider self-affirmation which is a useful strategy to ensure individuals do not dismiss messages regarding health risks.

Message framing

Prospect theory states that presenting the same information about an outcome or risk in different ways alters people's perspectives, preferences and actions (Kahneman & Tversky, 1979; see Burning Issue Box 2.9). People tend to avoid risks when they are considering gains (e.g., how many people saved) and prefer risks when considering losses (e.g., how many people died). Rothman and Salovey built on prospect theory and reasoned that within the health domain, the influence of gain and loss framed messages is contingent on the perceived function of the health behavior and its associated risk (Rothman, Martino, Bedell, Detweiler & Salovey, 1999; Rothman & Salovey, 1997). Health detection behaviors (such as screening) carry the risk that a disease or abnormality will be found and therefore are perceived as risky, whereas health promotion behaviors (such as eating healthily) or health risk behaviors (such as quitting smoking) are perceived as being relatively risk free as they are performed to avoid future health problems. They suggest that detection behaviors will be encouraged when health information is framed in terms of losses (i.e., if you do not do X you will not achieve Y; failing to attend for screening will mean you miss out on the chance to get treatment for any problems), and promotion/risk behaviors will be encouraged when gain framed messages are employed (i.e., if you do X you will achieve Y; quitting smoking can lead to improved health and living a longer life). However, while meta-analytic evidence supports the gain framed advantage for illness prevention behaviors (doing more health promoting behaviors and fewer health risk behaviors), it does not support the loss framed advantage for detection behaviors (see Gallagher & Updegraff, 2012).

Self-affirmation

Self-affirming involves reflecting on one's cherished values, actions or attributes. The result of this self-reflection is to restore or reinforce the person's sense of who they are and what they stand for in the face of perceived threats to their identity. Self-affirmation theory calls this sense of who they are 'self-integrity' which is defined as the experience of the self as 'adaptively and morally adequate' (Steele, 1988, p. 262). The theory suggests that people are strongly motivated to maintain self-integrity. As health messages are often perceived as threatening to self-integrity, individuals may be motivated to denigrate such messages. So, for example, a smoker exposed to a health message about the risks of smoking may protect their self-integrity in one of two ways, either denigrate the potential risks of smoking set out in the message or make renewed efforts to quit smoking. Unfortunately from the point of view of the originator of the message it is often the former response that is adopted. Self-affirmation theory offers a useful way round this problem. It is suggested that self-integrity can be restored or reinforced by affirming sources of self-worth that are important to the person's identity but unrelated to the threat. For example, a smoker may remind herself of her strengths as a mother leading to the self-concept of being a smoker becoming less threatening to her self-integrity. The key consequence from the point of view of the intervention is that salient, self-affirming thoughts can reduce the pressure to diminish the threat in other self-threatening information and thereby promote the ability to think objectively (Steele, 1988). Someone who self-affirms in this way then has available to them the perspective and resources to better confront a self-threat (Sherman & Cohen, 2006).

The idea that self-affirming can promote more objective appraisal of threatening material is appealing to researchers interested in using health messages to change behavior. This is because such messages typically contain important yet unwelcome information and resistance to them is common, particularly among high risk groups (Freeman, Hennessy & Marzullo, 2001; Kunda, 1990; Liberman & Chaiken, 1992).

Epton, Harris, Kane, van Koningsbruggen and Sheeran (2015) reviewed 144 studies testing the effects of self-affirming on health-related cognition, affect and behavior. Overall there appeared to be good evidence that self-affirming promotes greater general and personal acceptance of health risk information, and less message derogation. For example, Armitage, Harris, Napper and Hepton (2008) reported self-affirmation to promote acceptance of information about the health risks of smoking among a sample of smokers while Jessop, Simmonds and Sparks (2009) reported that self-affirmation led to sunbathing women rating a leaflet about skin cancer and sun safety as less overblown, exaggerated, manipulative and straining the truth. Napper, Harris and Epton (2009) showed that self-affirmation in heavier drinking female students led to them being more likely to rate a message about breast cancer and alcohol as being just as relevant to them personally as to the average student. Several studies also show that self-affirmation led to stronger intentions to change health risk behaviors (Armitage et al., 2008; Harris, Mayle, Mabbott & Napper, 2007; Harris & Napper, 2005) and even health relevant behaviors (Armitage et al., 2008; Sherman, Nelson & Steele, 2000). For example, Sherman et al., (2000, study 2) showed that compared to non-self-affirmed the self-affirmed took more leaflets about HIV/AIDS and purchased more condoms. Future research could usefully address whether self-affirmation can have effects on behavior change that is sustained over time.

Social norms

A further intervention technique used with risk behaviors is entitled the Social Norms Approach (SNA; Perkins, 2003; Berkowitz, 2004). The SNA suggests that the correction of misperceptions about social norms is an important mechanism for changing behavior. For example, believing that most other people like you regularly drink alcohol can promote alcohol use. The SNA provides accurate feedback about what other people think and do in relation to a behavior as a means to change behaviors such as alcohol intake (Bewick et al., 2013) and smoking (Phua, 2013). However, a recent review has suggested that even when large changes in normative beliefs are achieved, there is only a small reduction in alcohol intake (Prestwich et al., 2016).

CHANGING AFFECT

Earlier we discussed the idea of two types of affect influencing health risk behaviors (i.e., affective attitudes and anticipated affect). Here we consider studies that have looked at changing these affect-related variables and tested their subsequent impact on behavior. To date many of these studies have looked at health promoting behaviors rather than health risk behaviors, although we might expect such interventions to be equally or even more effective in health risk behaviors given the evidence that affect may be a more important determinant of such behaviors (Lawton et al., 2009). Meta-analyses of experimental studies would also appear to support the idea that changing *affective attitudes* can be a useful way to change health behavior, although the reported effect sizes tend to be small. For example, Sheeran, Harris and Epton (2014) in a review across a broad range of health behaviors suggest similar sized effects; they did not report any differences between health risk and health promoting behaviors.

Experimental studies targeting changing anticipated affect have been less commonly reported. In part this may be attributable to the difficulty of changing how much regret or guilt individuals anticipate experiencing. One way round this problem is to manipulate how much the individual's attention is drawn to potential anticipated affect. For example, we can compare groups who receive and complete versus are not exposed to anticipated affect questions (see Wood et al., 2016, for a review). Sandberg and Conner (2009) used this approach in a sample of women invited for cervical screening. Women were randomly allocated to simply receive a normal invitation for screening, to receive a normal invitation plus complete a TPB questionnaire about screening, or to receive a normal invitation plus complete a TPB questionnaire about screening that included an anticipated regret question. Screening attendance as measured by medical records showed higher attendance in the two TPB conditions (26%) compared to the no questionnaire condition (21%). Among those who completed and returned the questionnaire (and were therefore definitely exposed to the regret questions) attendance was considerably higher in the TPB plus regret condition (65%) compared to the TPB only condition (44%). Further analyses showed this was mainly due to changes in attendance among those with strong intentions to attend screening. Meta-analytic reviews of the limited number of experimental studies available suggest a small-to-medium-sized effect of anticipated affect on health behavior (Conner, 2013: $d_+ = .29$, $k = 6$; 95%CI .12 to .46; see also Sheeran et al., 2014). Testing these effects in health risk behaviors would be a useful development in this area.

IMPLICIT INFLUENCES

Implicit influences on health behaviors may be more difficult to change given they are often based on prolonged periods of learning. However, learning approaches have been used to try to reduce risk behaviors via changes in implicit cognition (attentional biases, automatic approach tendencies, implicit attitudes) and priming has been used to change health behaviors more directly.

Attentional bias

Training to reduce attentional bias has been shown to promote reduction in alcohol consumption and delayed relapse over a three-month period among those with alcohol dependence (Schoenmakers et al., 2010). The formation of implementation intentions (see Chapter 3) has also been shown to reduce attentional bias and impact on habitual behaviors like high fat food consumption (Achtziger, Gollwitzer & Sheeran, 2008).

Automatic approach tendencies

Using the 'go-no-go' paradigm, pictures of unhealthy foods may be paired with cues that the recipient is asked to respond to, for example, by touching a screen ('go'), or refrain from responding to, for example, by not touching a screen ('no-go'). If recipients are conditioned not to touch the unhealthy but desirable food images over many pairings this may help inhibit automatic approach responses in the real world (Lawrence, Verbruggen, Morrison, Adams & Chambers, 2015; Veling, Aarts & Stroebe, 2013). For example, being trained not to respond to pictures of doughnuts or chocolate may make it easier to ignore or refuse these foods subsequently. A meta-analysis of 19 experimental studies, conducted mainly with undergraduate students, suggested that inhibition training of this kind may be effective in changing health behavior patterns (Allom, Mullen & Hagger, 2016). The effect size was small ($d = 0.38$) and varied depending on how long the training lasted (longer training worked better). With an alternative approach, Wiers, Eberl, Rinck, Becker and Lindenmeyer (2011) used a computer task to train alcohol-dependent patients to make an avoidance movement (i.e., push) to pictures of alcohol and an approach movement (i.e., pull) to non-alcoholic drinks. They showed this reduced alcohol relapse rates compared to a control condition from 59% to 43% over a one-year period.

Implicit attitudes

Interventions to change implicit attitudes have used evaluative conditioning (EC) which attempts to change the valence of an evaluation of a target by pairing the target with another positive or negative stimulus. In one of the few studies on health behaviors, Hollands, Prestwich and Marteau (2011) measured implicit and explicit attitudes to snacks and then paired images of snacks with aversive images of obesity and heart disease. The EC procedure reduced the favorability of implicit attitudes to snacks without changing explicit attitudes and also reduced the likelihood of choosing a snack as a reward. Mediation analyses showed the change in implicit attitude partially explained the impact of EC on behavior.

Priming

Research on goal-priming has shown that mental representations of goals can be activated without the individual knowing about or intending it. This can be achieved through subliminal presentation of goal-relevant stimuli or through subtle and unobtrusive supraliminal presentation. Stroebe, Mensink, Aarts, Schut and Kruglanski (2008) showed that subliminally priming the goal of eating enjoyment inhibited the goal of controlling one's weight in restrained eaters. Albarracin, Leeper and Wang (2009) reported that participants primed with exercise words consumed more food in a taste test compared to controls. Fishbach, Friedman and Kruglanski (2003) found that participants exposed to magazines about food or slimming in a room while they waited to participate in an experiment were more likely to activate a slimming goal and to subsequently choose an apple over a chocolate bar compared to controls. In a field study, Papies and Hamstra (2010) showed that priming the goal of dieting via a subtle exposure to a poster led to a reduced number of snacks being consumed by restrained eaters.

BURNING ISSUE BOX 8.3

QUESTIONS AND ANSWERS ON CHANGING HEALTH RISK BEHAVIORS

Question 1: Are health risk behaviors more difficult to *predict* than health promotion behaviors?

There is no definitive answer to this question. The data from McEachan et al. (2011) presented in Chapter 7 (Table 7.2) suggest that the key predictors of behavior in the Theory of Planned Behavior (TPB) do similarly well in predicting health promotion and health risk behaviors. When we examine the overall amount of variance explained together by intentions and perceived behavioral control from the TPB then less variance in risk behaviors is explained compared to that explained for physical activity and dietary behaviors. However, the amounts of variance explained for risk behaviors is similar to that explained for detection, safer sex and abstinence behaviors.

Question 2: Are health risk behaviors more difficult to *change* than health promotion behaviors?

The simple answer is yes. Health risk behaviors tend to be more ingrained and based on past behavior or the formation of bad habits. For example, McEachan et al. (2011) showed that past behavior was considerably more important in predicting risk behaviors than physical activity, dietary or abstinence behaviors. This may mean we need to do more to change health risk behaviors particularly where there is an addictive element such as in smoking. Nevertheless interventions like implementation intentions can be effective in changing even health risk behaviors.

Question 3: What's the best model of health risk behavior?

There is no simple answer to this question. Very few studies have attempted to directly compare models for the same sample of individuals either for health promotion or health risk behaviors. Models like the TPB appear to do quite well although models such as the Prototype Willingness Model (Gibbons & Gerrard, 1995) that were specifically developed for such behaviors might be expected to work best.

Question 4: What's the single biggest determinant of engaging in risky behavior?

Aside from past behavior, intentions are probably the strongest determinant of health risk behaviors as they are for health promotion behaviors.

SCIENCE OF HEALTH BEHAVIOR CHANGE: IN ACTION

In the previous chapter, we illustrated how the scientific approach to health behavior change can be applied in relation to a study testing the effects of an intervention to promote a healthy behavior. In this chapter, we consider the framework in relation to a study by Carels et al. (2007) who tested the impact of motivational interviewing as an addition to usual obesity treatment in improving weight loss in a sample of obese individuals. Weight loss is an outcome rather than a behavior but is closely related to changes in diet and physical activity. With this in mind the study also examined effects on physical activity and diet as potential mediators of the effect of the intervention on weight loss (see Science of Health Behavior Change: In Action Box 8.1).

SCIENCE OF HEALTH BEHAVIOR CHANGE

In Action Box 8.1

Study: Carels et al. (2007). *Using motivational interviewing as a supplement to obesity treatment: A stepped care approach*	
Aim: To increase weight loss in obese individuals who were failing to meet weight loss goals on a behavioral weight loss program.	
Method: Participants were randomized to one of two conditions: behavioral weight loss program and a behavioral weight loss program with stepped care. The stepped care component involved a motivational interviewing intervention for those failing to meet weight loss goals.	
Results: Both groups significantly decreased their weight, increased physical activity/ fitness and improved dietary intake from before to after the intervention (within-subject differences). Those in the combined group lost significantly more weight and engaged in more physical activity compared to the behavioral weight loss only group (between-subject differences).	
Authors' conclusion: For individuals experiencing weight loss difficulties during a behavioral weight loss program, motivational interviewing may have considerable promise.	
THEORY AND TECHNIQUES OF HEALTH BEHAVIOR CHANGE	
BCTs	INTERVENTION: Based on Michie et al.'s (2013) taxonomy:
	Behavioral weight loss program plus motivational interviewing (combined) intervention: 1.1 Goal setting (outcome); 3.3 Social support (emotional); 6.0 Social comparison; 8.7 Graded tasks.
	Behavioral weight loss program only: 1.1 Goal setting (outcome); 6.2 Social comparison.
	CONTROL: N/A
Critical Skills Toolkit	

3.1	Does the design enable the identification of which BCTs are effective?	Yes – the addition of motivational interviewing to the behavioral weight loss program in the combined condition allowed the authors to assess the unique impact of motivational interviewing on weight loss. Including conditions where participants received no intervention and just a motivational interviewing intervention would allow the authors to more fully test the independent and combined effects of the behavioral weight loss program and motivational interviewing.
4.1	Is the intervention based on one theory or a combination of theories (if any at all)?	On the basis that motivational interviewing is a behavior change technique rather than a theory, the intervention was not based on a theory.
	Are all constructs specified within a theory targeted by the intervention?	Not applicable.
	Are all behavior change techniques explicitly targeting at least one theory-relevant construct?	Not applicable.
	Do the authors test why the intervention was effective or ineffective (consistent with the underlying theory)?	Not applicable given there was no theory base but the authors did assess the effects of the combined intervention compared to the behavioral weight loss program only condition on physical activity/fitness, and dietary intake. Only effects on physical activity were significant (i.e., only potential mediator). No formal test of whether the changes in physical activity mediated the effects on weight loss.
4.2	Does the study tailor the intervention based on the underlying theory?	Not applicable.
2.1, 2.2	What are the strengths/limitations of the underlying theory?	Not applicable but see Chapter 3 for strengths and limitations of motivational interviewing.
THE METHODOLOGY OF HEALTH BEHAVIOR CHANGE		
5.1, 5.3, 5.4, 5.6	Methodological approach	The study adopted an experimental design (see Critical Skills Toolkit 5.4).
6.1	For experimental designs: is the study between-subjects, within-subjects or mixed?	Mixed design because participants were allocated to one of two conditions (between-subjects) and completed measures at multiple time-points (within-subjects). For advantages and disadvantages of this design, see Critical Skills Toolkit 6.1.

5.2, 5.5	Are the measures reliable and valid?	The main outcome variable – body weight – was measured objectively. Fitness was also measured objectively. Physical activity duration and food intake were assessed by diary (no known reliability or validity).
5.5	May other variables have been manipulated other than the independent variable?	Low risk of bias. The manipulations appeared appropriate. Thus, the internal validity of the experiment was not threatened by the risk of confounds.
	Non-random allocation of participants to condition	Low risk. Participants were randomized to condition and an appropriate method of randomization was used (computerized random number generator). There were no reported differences across the groups at baseline (suggesting randomization was successful). The focus on participants who failed to meet initial weight loss goals was not based on randomization.
	Blinding and allocation concealment	Unclear risk. There was no evidence of blinding or allocation concealment, this may be less problematic given weight loss was objectively measured.
ANALYZING HEALTH BEHAVIOR CHANGE DATA		
6.2	Was the sample size calculated a-priori?	The sample size was not calculated a-priori.
Fig. 6.1	Was the hypothesis tested with an appropriate statistical test?	Yes.
5.5, 6.4	Incomplete outcome data	Attrition rates were similar across the two conditions but relatively large (4 out of 28 in the combined condition; 5 out of 27 in the behavioral weight loss only condition). However, given the effects of the combined intervention were large, it is unlikely that the results would suggest different conclusions if they were analyzed on an intention-to-treat basis.
5.5	Selective outcome reporting	Unclear given the trial protocol was not pre-published – however, all of the measures reported in the Method section were analyzed and reported in the Results section.
4.2	Lack of variability (non-sig. effects only)	Not applicable – the participants in the combined intervention lost more weight than those in the behavioral weight loss only condition.
6.3	Non-linear relationship (non-sig. effects only)	Not applicable – effects significant.

SUMMARY

This chapter examined health risk behaviors. We first reviewed the application of the Theory of Planned Behavior to health risk behaviors and then overviewed a development of this model specifically designed to predict adolescent risk behaviors, the Prototype Willingness Model. The importance of affective influences and affective attitudes and anticipated affect in particular were then examined. The role of stress and implicit influences on health risk behaviors were also considered. Approaches to changing health risk behaviors were examined in the second part of the chapter. These included the use of persuasive messages to change these behaviors and the contributions of work on message framing and self-affirmation. We then examined ways of changing affective attitudes and anticipated affect as ways to change health risk behaviors. Finally, we explored how targeting implicit influences on behavior could be used to change health risk behaviors.

FURTHER READING

Lawton, R., Conner, M. & McEachan, R. (2009). Desire or reason: predicting health behaviors from affective and cognitive attitudes. *Health Psychology*, *28*, 56–65. This paper examines the power of affective and instrumental attitudes to predict intentions and behavior in 20 different health behaviors.

McEachan, R.R.C., Conner, M., Taylor, N.J. & Lawton, R.J. (2011). Prospective prediction of health-related behaviors with the Theory of Planned Behavior: a meta-analysis. *Health Psychology Review*, *5*, 97–144. A comprehensive review of the application of prospective tests of the TPB to health behaviors that draws attention to differences across behaviors.

O'Connor, D.B., Jones, F., Conner, M., McMillan, B. & Ferguson, E. (2008). Effects of daily hassles and eating style on eating behavior. *Health Psychology*, *27*, S20–S31. Reports a large-scale test of the impact of stress on eating behaviors and shows how effects change for different measures of stress and eating and explores potential moderating factors.

Sheeran, P., Bosch, J.A., Crombez, G., Hall, P.A., Harris, J.L., Papies, E.K. & Wiers, R.W. (2016). Implicit processes in health psychology: diversity and promise. *Health Psychology*, *35*, 761–766. This introduction to a special issue of the journal on implicit processes and health behaviors overviews and summarizes the range of approaches taken in recent research.

GLOSSARY

Affective attitudes: attitudes tapped by semantic differentials such as unpleasant-pleasant or not enjoyable-enjoyable (e.g., My using ecstasy would be ... boring-exciting).

Anticipated affect: attitudes tapped by semantic differentials such as no regret-regret or not guilty-guilty and referring to how one might feel after performing the behavior (e.g., If I used ecstasy I would feel regret, strongly disagree-strongly agree).

Behavioral willingness: distinct from behavioral intention or expectation, behavioral willingness refers to perceived likelihood of engaging in a behavior in a specified context (see example item in Figure 8.1)

Cognitive attitudes: attitudes tapped by semantic differentials such as harmful-beneficial or negative-positive (e.g., My using ecstasy would be . . . harmful-beneficial).

Health risk behaviors: behaviors that damage or risk health. These include behaviors such as smoking, alcohol consumption, eating high fat diets and drug use. They are normally distinguished from health promotion behaviors where performance is associated with increasing health.

Impulsive system: part of the reflective-impulsive model. Refers to the way in which a variety of less reasoned influences can impact on behavior. Many of these influences are based on earlier learning processes.

Message framing: whether the persuasive message focuses on losses or gains. For example, in relation to quitting smoking messages could focus on the losses associated with continuing (e.g., Smoking can lead to worse health and dying younger) or the gains associated with quitting (e.g., Quitting smoking can lead to improved health and living a longer life).

Reflective system: part of the reflective-impulsive model. Refers to the way in which a variety of more reasoned influences can impact on behavior.

REFERENCES

Abelson, R.P., Kinder, D.R., Peters, M.D. & Fiske, S.T. (1982). Affective and semantic components in political person perception. *Journal of Personality and Social Psychology, 42*, 619–630.

Achtziger, A., Gollwitzer, P.M. & Sheeran, P. (2008). Implementation intentions and shielding goal striving from unwanted thoughts and feelings. *Personality and Social Psychology Bulletin, 34*, 381–393.

Albarracin, D., Leeper, J. & Wang, W. (2009). Immediate increases in eating after exercise promotion messages. *Obesity, 17*, 1451–1452.

Allom, V., Mullen, B. & Hagger, M. (2016). Does inhibitory control training improve health behaviour? A meta-analysis. *Health Psychology Review, 10*, 168–186.

Armitage, C. J. & Conner, M. (2000). Attitudinal ambivalence: a test of three key hypotheses. *Personality and Social Psychology Bulletin, 26*, 1421–1432.

Armitage, C. J., Harris, P. R., Napper, L. & Hepton, G. (2008). Efficacy of a brief intervention to increase acceptance of health risk information among adult smokers with low socioeconomic status. *The Psychology of Addictive Behaviors, 22*, 88–95.

Ayres, K., Conner, M.T., Prestwich, A. & Smith, P. (2012). Do implicit measures of attitudes incrementally predict snacking behaviour over explicit affect-related measures? *Appetite, 58*, 835–841.

Bentler, P.M. & Speckart, G. (1979). Model of attitude-behavior relations. *Psychological Review, 86*, 452–464.

Berkowitz, A. (2004). *The Social Norms Approach: Theory, Research and Annotated Bibliography.* Retrieved on July 3, 2017 from: www.alanberkowitz.com/articles/social_norms.pdf.

Bewick, B.M., West, R.M., Barkham, M., Mulhern, B., Marlow, R., Traviss, G. & Hill, A.J. (2013). The effectiveness of a web-based personalized feedback and social norms alcohol intervention on United Kingdom university students: randomized controlled trial. *Journal of Medical Internet Research, 15*, e137.

Blanton, H., Gibbons, F.X., Gerrard, M., Conger, K.J. & Smith, G.E. (1997). Development of health risk prototypes during adolescence: family and peer influence. *Journal of Family Psychology*, *11*, 271–288.

Blanton, H., Van den Eijnden, R.J.J.M., Buunk, B.P., Gibbons, F.X., Gerrard, M. & Bakker, A. (2001). Accentuate the negative: social images in the prediction and promotion of condom use. *Journal of Applied Social Psychology*, *31*, 274–295.

Brooks-Gunn, J. & Furnstenberg, F.F. (1989). Adolescent sexual behaviour. *American Psychologist*, *44*, 249–257.

Calitri, R., Lowe, R., Eves, F.F. & Bennett, P. (2009). Associations between visual attention, implicit and explicit attitude and behaviour for physical activity. *Psychology & Health*, *24*, 1105–1123.

Calitri, R., Pothos, E.M., Tapper, K., Brunstrom, J.M. & Rogers, P.J. (2010). Cognitive biases to healthy and unhealthy foods words predict change in BMI. *Obesity*, *18*, 2282–2287.

Carels, R.A., Darby, L., Cacciopaglia, H.M., Konrad, K., Coit, C., Harper, J., Kaplar, M.E., Young, K., Baylen, C.A. & Versland, A. (2007). Using motivational interviewing as a supplement to obesity treatment: a stepped care approach. *Health Psychology*, *26*, 369–374.

Carfora, V., Caso, D. & Conner, M. (2016). Randomized controlled trial of 'messaging intervention' to increase fruit and vegetable intake in adolescents: affective versus instrumental messages. *British Journal of Health Psychology*, *21*, 937–955.

Chorlton, K., Conner, M. & Jamson, S. (2012). Identifying the psychological determinants of risky riding: an application of an extended Theory of Planned Behaviour. *Accident Analysis & Prevention*, *49*(SI), 142–154.

Cialdini, R.B., Reno, R.R. & Kallgren, C.A. (1990). A focus theory of normative conduct: recycling the concept of norms to reduce littering in public places. *Journal of Personality and Social Psychology*, *58*, 1015–1026.

Conner, M. (2013). *Health Cognitions, Affect and Health Behaviors*. Keynote speaker at European Health Psychology Society Annual Conference, Bordeaux, France, July 17–20.

Conner, M., McEachan, R., Taylor, N., O'Hara, J. & Lawton, J. (2015). Role of affective attitudes and anticipated affective reactions in predicting health behaviors. *Health Psychology*, *34*, 642–652.

Conner, M. & McMillan, B. (1999). Interaction effects in the theory of planned behaviour: studying cannabis use. *British Journal of Social Psychology*, *38*, 195–222.

Conner, M., Perugini, M., O'Gorman, R., Ayres, K. & Prestwich, A. (2007). Relations between implicit and explicit measures of attitudes and measures of behavior: evidence of moderation by individual difference variables. *Personality and Social Psychology Bulletin*, *33*, 1727–1740.

Conner, M., Povey, R., Sparks, P., James, R. & Shepherd, R. (2003). Moderating role of attitudinal ambivalence within the Theory of Planned Behaviour. *British Journal of Social Psychology*, *42*, 75–94.

Conner, M., Prestwich, A. & Ayres, K. (2011). Using explicit affective attitudes to tap impulsive influences on health behaviour: a commentary on Hofmann et al. (2008). *Health Psychology Review*, *5*, 145–149.

Conner, M. & Sparks, P. (2015). The theory of planned behaviour and the reasoned action approach. In M. Conner & P. Norman (Eds.), *Predicting and Changing Health Behaviour: Research and Practice with Social Cognition Models* (3rd edn; pp. 142–188). Maidenhead, UK: Open University Press.

Conroy, D.E., Hyde, A.L., Doerksen, S.E. & Ribiero, N.F. (2010). Implicit attitudes and explicit motivation prospectively predict physical activity. *Annals of Behavioral Medicine*, *39*, 112–118.

DeLongis, A., Coyne, J.C., Dakof, G., Folkman, S. & Lazarus, R.S. (1982). Relationships of daily hassles, uplifts, and major life events to health status. *Health Psychology*, *1*, 119–136.

Edwards, W. (1954). The theory of decision making. *Psychological Bulletin*, *51*, 380–417.

Epton, T., Harris, P.R., Kane, R., van Koningsbruggen, G.M. & Sheeran, P. (2015). The impact of self-affirmation on health-behavior change: a meta-analysis. *Health Psychology*, *34*, 187–196.

Fishbach, A., Friedman, R.S. & Kruglanski, A.W. (2003). Leading us not unto temptation: momentary allurements elicit overriding goal activation. *Journal of Personality and Social Psychology, 84,* 296–309.

Fishbein, M. & Ajzen, I. (2010). *Predicting and Changing Behavior: The Reasoned Action Approach.* New York: Psychology Press.

Freeman, M.A., Hennessy, E.V. & Marzullo, D.M. (2001). Defensive evaluation of antismoking messages among college-age smokers: the role of possible selves. *Health Psychology, 20,* 424–433.

French, D.P., Sutton, S., Hennings, S.J., Mitchell, J., Wareham, N.J., Griffin, S., et al. (2005). The importance of affective beliefs and attitudes in the theory of planned behavior: predicting intention to increase physical activity. *Journal of Applied Social Psychology, 35,* 1824–1848.

Frisch, D. & Clemen, R.T. (1994). Beyond expected utility: rethinking behavioral decision making. *Psychological Bulletin, 116,* 46–54.

Gallagher, K. & Updegraff, J.A. (2012). Health message framing effects on attitudes, intentions, and behaviour: a meta-analytic review. *Annals of Behavioral Medicine, 43,* 101–116.

Gerrard, M., Gibbons, F.X., Bentin, A.C. & Hessling, R.M. (1996). The reciprocal nature of risk behaviors and cognitions: what you think shapes what you do and vice versa. *Health Psychology, 15,* 344–354.

Gerrard, M., Gibbons, F.X., Reis-Bergan, M., Trudeau, L., Vande Lune, L.S. & Buunk, B.P. (2002). Inhibitory effects of drinker and non-drinker prototypes on adolescent alcohol consumption. *Health Psychology, 21,* 601–609.

Gibbons, F.X. & Gerrard, M. (1995). Predicting young adults' health risk behaviour. *Journal of Personality and Social Psychology, 69,* 505–517.

Gibbons, F.X., Gerrard, M., Blanton, H. & Russell, D.W. (1998a). Reasoned action and social reaction: willingness and intention as independent predictors of health risk. *Journal of Personality and Social Psychology, 74,* 1164–1181.

Gibbons, F.X., Gerrard, M., Ouellette, J.A. & Burzette, R. (1998b). Cognitive antecedents to adolescent health risk: discriminating between behavioural intention and behaviour willingness. *Psychology and Health, 13,* 319–339.

Gibbons, F.X., Gerrard, M., Stock, M.L. & Finneran, S.D. (2015). The prototype/willingness model. In M. Conner & P. Norman (Eds.), *Predicting and Changing Health Behaviour: Research and Practice with Social Cognition Models* (3rd edn; pp. 189–224). Maidenhead, UK: Open University Press.

Giner-Sorolla, R. (2001). Guilty pleasures and grim necessities: affective attitudes in dilemmas of self-control. *Journal of Personality and Social Psychology, 80,* 206–221.

Goldberg, J.H., Halpern-Felsher, B.L. & Millstein, S.G. (2002). Beyond invulnerability: the importance of benefits in adolescents' decision to drink alcohol. *Health Psychology, 21,* 477–484.

Greeno, C.G. & Wing, R.R. (1994). Stress-induced eating. *Psychological Bulletin, 115,* 444–464.

Grogan, S., Conner, M., Fry, G., Gough, B. & Higgins, A. (2009). Gender differences in smoking: a longitudinal study of beliefs predicting smoking in 11–15 year olds. *Psychology & Health, 24,* 301–316.

Grogan, S., Flett, K., Clark-Carter, D., Conner, M., Davey, R., Richardson, D. & Rajaratnam, G. (2011). Brief report: a randomized controlled trial of an appearance-related smoking intervention. *Health Psychology, 30,* 805–809.

Hall, P.A. & Fong, G.T. (2007). Temporal self-regulation theory: a model for individual health behaviour. *Health Psychology Review, 1,* 6–52.

Harris, P.R., Mayle, K., Mabbott, L. & Napper, L. (2007). Self-affirmation reduces smokers' defensiveness to graphic on-pack cigarette warning labels. *Health Psychology, 26,* 434–446.

Harris, P.R. & Napper, L. (2005). Self-affirmation and the biased processing of health-risk information. *Personality and Social Psychology Bulletin, 31,* 1250–1263.

Hofmann, W., Friese, M. & Wiers, R.W. (2008). Impulsive versus reflective influences on health behavior: a theoretical framework and empirical review. *Health Psychology Review, 2,* 111–137.

Hollands, G.J., Prestwich, A. & Marteau, T.M. (2011). Using aversive images to enhance healthy eating food choices and implicit attitudes: an experimental test of evaluative conditioning. *Health Psychology, 30,* 195–203.

Holmes, T.H. & Rahe, R.H. (1967). The social readjustment rating scale. *Journal of Psychosomatic Research, 11,* 213–218.

Jessop, D.C., Simmonds, L.V. & Sparks, P. (2009). Motivational and behavioural consequences of self-affirmation interventions: a study of sunscreen use among women. *Psychology and Health, 24,* 529–544.

Jonas, K. (1993). Expectancy-value models of health behaviour: an analysis by conjoint measurement. *European Journal of Social Psychology, 23,* 167–183.

Kahneman, D. & Tversky, A. (1979). Prospect theory: an analysis of decision under risk. *Econometrica, 47,* 263–291.

Kunda, Z. (1990). The case for motivated reasoning. *Psychological Bulletin, 108,* 480–498.

Lawton, R., Conner, M. & McEachan, R. (2009). Desire or reason: predicting health behaviors from affective and cognitive attitudes. *Health Psychology, 28,* 56–65.

Lawrence, N.S., Verbruggen, F., Morrison, S., Adams, R.C. & Chambers, C.D. (2015). Stopping to food can reduce intake. Effects of stimulus-specificity and individual differences in dietary restraint. *Appetite, 85,* 91–103.

Lazarus, R.S. & Folkman, S. (1984). *Stress, Appraisal and Coping.* New York: Springer.

Liberman, A. & Chaiken, S. (1992). Defensive processing of personally relevant health messages. *Personality and Social Psychology Bulletin, 18,* 669–679.

Lowe, R., Eves, F. & Carroll, D. (2002). The influence of affective and instrumental beliefs on exercise intentions and behavior: a longitudinal analysis. *Journal of Applied Social Psychology, 32,* 1241–1252.

Madon, S., Guyll, M., Scherr, K.C., Greathouse, S. & Wells, G.L. (2012). Temporal discounting: the differential effect of proximal and distal consequences on confession decisions. *Law and Human Behavior, 36,* 13–20.

McEachan, R.R.C., Conner, M., Taylor, N.J. & Lawton, R.J. (2011). Prospective prediction of health-related behaviors with the Theory of Planned Behavior: a meta-analysis. *Health Psychology Review, 5,* 97–144.

McEachan, R., Taylor, N., Harrison, R., Lawton, R., Gardner, P. & Conner, M. (2016). Meta-analysis of the Reasoned Action Approach (RAA) to understanding health behaviors. *Annals of Behavioral Medicine, 50,* 592–612.

Michie, S., Richardson, M., Johnston, M., Abraham, C., Francis, J., Hardeman, W., Eccles, M.P., Cane, J. & Wood, C.E. (2013). The behavior change technique taxonomy (v1) of 93 hierarchically-clustered techniques: building an international consensus for the reporting of behavior change interventions. *Annals of Behavioral Medicine, 46*(1), 81–95.

Napper, L., Harris, P.R. & Epton, T. (2009). Developing and testing a self-affirmation manipulation. *Self and Identity, 8,* 45–62.

O'Connor, D.B., Jones, F., Conner, M., McMillan, B. & Ferguson, E. (2008). Effects of daily hassles and eating style on eating behavior. *Health Psychology, 27,* S20–S31.

Oliver, G., Wardle, J. & Gibson, E.L. (2000). Stress and food choice: a laboratory study. *Psychosomatic Medicine, 62,* 853–865.

Papies, E.K. & Hamstra, P. (2010). Goal priming and eating behavior: enhancing self-regulation by environmental cues. *Health Psychology, 29,* 38384–38388.

Payne, B.K., McClernon, F.J. & Dobbins, I.G. (2007). Automatic affective responses to smoking cues. *Experimental and Clinical Psychopharmacology, 15,* 400–409.

Peak, H. (1955). Attitude and motivation. In M.R. Jones (Ed.), *Nebraska Symposium on Motivation* (Vol. 3, pp. 149–188). Lincoln: University of Nebraska Press.

Perkins, H.W. (2003). *The Social Norms Approach to Preventing School and College Age Substance Abuse: A Handbook for Educators, Counsellors, and Clinicians*. San Francisco: Jossey-Bass.

Phua, J.J. (2013). The reference group perspective for smoking cessation: an examination of the influence of social norms and social identification with reference groups on smoking cessation self-efficacy. *Psychology of Addictive Behaviors, 27*, 102–112.

Prestwich, A., Kellar, I., Conner, M., Lawton, R., Gardner, P. & Turgut, L. (2016). Does changing social influence engender changes in alcohol intake? A meta-analysis. *Journal of Consulting and Clinical Psychology, 84*, 845–860.

Prochaska, J.O., and DiClemente, C.C. (1984). *The Transtheoretical Approach: Crossing Traditional Boundaries of Therapy*. Homewood, IL: Dow Jones Irwin.

Rhodes, R., Fiala, B. & Conner, M. (2010). A review and meta-analysis of affective judgments and physical activity in adult populations. *Annals of Behavioral Medicine, 38*, 180–204.

Richetin, J., Conner, M. & Perugini, M. (2011). Not doing is not the opposite of doing: implications for attitudinal models of behavioral prediction. *Personality and Social Psychology Bulletin, 37*, 40–54.

Rooke, S.E., Hine, D.W. & Thorsteinsson, E.B. (2008). Implicit cognition and substance use: a meta analysis. *Addictive Behaviors, 33*, 1314–1328.

Rosenstock, I.M. (1974). Historical origins of the health belief model. *Health Education Monographs, 2*, 1–8.

Rothman, A.J., Martino, S.C., Bedell, B., Detweiler, J. & Salovey, P. (1999). The systematic influence of gain- and loss-framed messages on interest in different types of health behaviour. *Personality and Social Psychology Bulletin, 25*, 1357–1371.

Rothman, A.J. & Salovey, P. (1997). Shaping perceptions to motivate healthy behaviour: the role of message framing. *Psychological Bulletin, 121*, 3–19.

Sandberg, T. & Conner, M. (2008). Anticipated regret as an additional predictor in the theory of planned behaviour: a meta-analysis. *British Journal of Social Psychology, 47*, 589–606.

Sandberg, T. & Conner, M. (2009). A mere measurement effect for anticipated regret: impacts on cervical screening attendance. *British Journal of Social Psychology, 48*, 221–236.

Schoenmakers, T.M., de Bruin, M., Lux, I.F.M., Goertz, A.G., van Kerkhof, D.H.A.T. & Wiers, R.W. (2010). Clinical effectiveness of attentional bias modification in abstinent alcoholic patients. *Drug and Alcohol Dependence, 109*, 30–36.

Sheeran, P., Harris, P.R. & Epton, T. (2014). Does heightening risk appraisals change people's intentions and behavior? A meta-analysis of experimental studies. *Psychological Bulletin, 140*, 511–543.

Sheppard, B.H., Hartwick, J. & Warshaw, P.R. (1988). The theory of reasoned action: a meta-analysis of past research with recommendations for modifications and future research. *Journal of Consumer Research, 15*, 325–339.

Sherman, D.K. & Cohen, G.L. (2006). The psychology of self-defense: self affirmation theory. *Advances in Experimental Social Psychology, 38*, 183–242.

Sherman, D.A.K., Nelson, L.D. & Steele, C.M. (2000). Do messages about health risks threaten the self? Increasing the acceptance of threatening health messages via self-affirmation. *Personality and Social Psychology Bulletin, 26*, 1046–1058.

Simmons, R.G. & Blyth, D.A. (1987). *Moving into Adolescence: The Impact of Pubertal Change and School Context*. Hawthorne, NJ: Aldine.

Stacy, A.W., Ames, S.L., Ullman, J.B., Zogg, J.B. & Leigh, B.C. (2006). Spontaneous cognition and HIV risk behavior. *Psychology of Addictive Behaviors, 20*, 196–206.

Steele, C.M. (1988). The psychology of self-affirmation: sustaining the integrity of the self. *Advances in Experimental Social Psychology, 21*, 261–302.

Steptoe, A., Lipsey, Z. & Wardle, J. (1998). Stress, hassles and variations in alcohol consumption, food choice and physical exercise: a diary study. *British Journal of Health Psychology, 3*, 51–63.

Strack, F. & Deutsch, R. (2004). Reflective and impulsive determinants of social behaviour. *Personality and Social Psychology Review, 8*, 220–247.

Stroebe, W., Mensink, W., Aarts, H., Schut, H. & Kruglanski, A. W. (2008). Why dieters fail: testing the goal conflict model of eating. *Journal of Experimental Social Psychology, 44*, 26–36.

Thornton, B., Gibbons, F.X. & Gerrard, M. (2002). Risk perceptions and prototype perception: independent processes predicting risk behavior. *Personality and Social Psychology Bulletin, 28*, 986–999.

Trafimow, D. & Sheeran, P. (1998). Some tests of the distinction between cognitive and affective beliefs. *Journal of Experimental Social Psychology, 34*, 378–397.

van der Pligt, J., de Vries, N.K., Manstead, A.S.R. & van Harreveld, F. (2000). The importance of being selective: weighing the role of attribute importance in attitudinal judgment. *Advances in Experimental Social Psychology, 32*, 135–200.

Veling, H., Aarts, H. & Stroebe, W. (2013). Using stop signals to reduce impulsive choices for palatable unhealthy foods. *British Journal of Health Psychology, 18*, 354–368.

Wiers, R.W., Eberl, C., Rinck, M., Becker, E. & Lindenmeyer, J. (2011). Retraining automatic action tendencies changes alcoholic patients' approach bias for alcohol and improves treatment outcome. *Psychological Science, 22*, 290–297.

Williams, A.L., Grogan, S., Clark-Carter, D. & Buckley, E. (2013). Impact of a facial-aging intervention versus a health literature intervention on women's sun protection attitudes and intentions. *Psychology & Health, 28*, 993–1008.

Wood, C., Conner, M., Sandberg, T., Taylor, N., Godin, G., Miles, E. & Sheeran, P. (2016). The impact of asking intention or self-prediction questions on subsequent behavior: a meta-analysis. *Personality and Social Psychology Review, 20*, 245–268.

9

CHAPTER 9
ENVIRONMENT- AND POLICY-BASED APPROACHES TO HEALTH BEHAVIOR CHANGE

OVERVIEW

In this chapter we examine the role of environmental factors and policies that influence health behaviors. Various aspects of the environment might be expected to influence our behavior. For example, a lack of suitable exercise facilities in the local area can impact on even the most fervent exerciser. Similarly, a lack of financial resources can prevent individuals from buying healthier but more expensive foods and consumer products. However, these influences of the environment can have effects on behavior either directly (where a mediating variable is not proposed, is automatic/unconscious, or there is no evidence of a mediating variable), indirectly (mediated effects) or by interacting with cognitions (moderation effects). In this chapter we consider these direct, mediated and moderated effects by which environmental factors may influence our behavior. Under direct paths we explore and examine nudge theory and choice architecture as a research area that has examined how making changes to our environment (broadly defined) might change our behavior. Under mediated paths we look at research on how changes in the environment may produce changes in cognitions, such as social norms or intentions, which in turn produce changes in behavior. Under moderated paths we look at how aspects of the environment may interact with cognitions to produce behavior. We then consider the effects of public policy-based solutions and social marketing approaches in changing behavior.

USING CLASSIC AND SOCIAL/HEALTH COGNITION MODELS

The behaviorist approach considered in Chapter 2 has always focused on external, environmental reinforcement contingencies as primary explanations for behavior and behavior change. The simple formula is: change the reinforcement schedule or behavioral cost, and you will see a change in the behavior. This approach is direct in nature and is similar to nudging behavior (which we overview later in this chapter) which impacts behavior via non-conscious processes, because deliberative or reflective cognitive processes need not be invoked or involved in changing behavior. By changing the accessibility, availability, desirability or cost of performing certain behavioral alternatives, corresponding changes in the behaviors should be observed.

In support of this behavioral approach, Faith, Rose, Matz, Pietrobelli and Epstein (2006) randomly assigned sets of 5-year-old twins to a treatment or control condition, one twin in each condition. In the contingent rewards condition, children were told that, for each serving of fruits or vegetables that they selected in their lunch, they would receive a voucher that could be exchanged for prizes at a later time. In the non-contingent rewards (control) condition, the children were told that they would receive a set of vouchers for prizes during lunch, but were not told that they were based on selecting certain types of food. Compared to their baseline eating behavior, twins in the contingent rewards group significantly increased their consumption of vegetables and fruits, and decreased their consumption of total energy and fat. Children in the control condition did not change their eating behavior compared to baseline levels. Findings such as these illustrate the power of positive reinforcement as an environmental variable that can increase healthier eating behaviors and other positive health behaviors.

The environment has also played a prominent role in some social/health cognition models, albeit in different ways. For instance, in the major theorist model (Fishbein et al., 2001; see Chapter 2), the environment is assumed to have a **direct effect** on behavior, facilitating behavior or preventing action even when the individual has the necessary skills and intentions. In contrast, in the Social Cognitive Theory (see Chapter 2), environmental factors are assumed to only influence behavior indirectly through changing goals or intentions, which in turn influence behavior (i.e., an **indirect/ mediated effect**).

Many social/health cognition models have been used to inform environment-based interventions. For example, in the area of social marketing (discussed in detail later in this chapter), Luca and Suggs (2013) reported that the most common theories used to develop social marketing interventions were the Stages of Change/Transtheoretical model (e.g., Prochaska & DiClemente, 1986; see also Gallivan, Lising, Ammary & Greenberg, 2007; Richert, Webb, Morse, O'Toole & Brownson, 2007) and the Theory of Reasoned Action/Theory of Planned Behavior (e.g., Ajzen, 1991; Fishbein & Ajzen, 1975; see also Long, Taubenheim, Wayman, Temple & Ruoff, 2008; Peterson, Abraham & Waterfield, 2005). However, they report that the majority of interventions in their review were not clearly designed according to any theoretical framework. Several studies did discuss theoretical models or frameworks, but did not discuss clearly or at all *how* the theory was used in designing their intervention. As we discussed in Chapter 4, this has important implications for how the results can and should be interpreted and used in future research.

———————————

DIRECT ENVIRONMENTAL IMPACTS ON BEHAVIOR

NUDGE THEORY AND CHOICE ARCHITECTURE

Thaler and Sunstein (2008) are behavioral economists whose book *Nudge: Improving Decisions about Health, Wealth, and Happiness* has been influential in attempts to change behavior based on changing aspects of the environment. They focus on the impact of the environment on decisions and behaviors. They suggest that we do not make choices in a vacuum but in an environment where many features of that environment influence our decisions. It is assumed that many of these environmental features are designed to influence behavior directly, outside of conscious awareness. Others are more transparent and require more cognitive and behavioral effort to have their effect.

Thaler and Sunstein use the term **choice architecture** to describe the creation or modification of aspects of the environment that influence choices. *Nudge* attempts to show how choice architecture can be used to help influence people into making certain choices using a variety of tools. The authors have created a website (www.nudges.org) where they describe various strategies under headings such as defaults, expecting error, giving feedback and creating incentives. For example, the idea of changing defaults from an 'opt in' default to an 'opt out' default has been shown to be successful in changing different types of behavior for quite some time now. One famous example by Johnson and Goldstein (2003) shows that by making organ donation consent the default option (compared to the requirement that potential donors exert the effort to opt in to the donation program), donation rates increase dramatically. To cite some specific cases, *opt-out* countries such as Sweden and Austria reported significantly higher numbers of donors (85.9% and 99.98%, respectively), compared to *opt-in* countries such as Denmark, the Netherlands and the UK (4.25%, 27.5% and 17.17%, respectively).

Since the publication of *Nudge* and related work, there have been several attempts to test the ideas scientifically in socially important contexts. For example, a team of researchers (see Levy, Riis, Sonnenberg, Barraclough & Thorndike, 2012; Thorndike, Sonnenberg, Riis, Barraclough & Levy, 2012; Thorndike, Riis, Sonnenberg & Levy, 2014) tested some relevant nudges and choice architecture interventions to decrease the likelihood of employees purchasing high-calorie foods and to increase the likelihood of their purchasing healthier foods. In one of their studies, they created a nine-month longitudinal design with interventions introduced sequentially. First, after a baseline period, they introduced food labels with a traffic light signal theme. Foods were labeled as 'green' (healthy), 'yellow/amber' (neutral) or 'red' (unhealthy/high calorie). Three months after the traffic light scheme had been introduced, they then used choice architecture to make 'green' choices more available and accessible, and to make the 'red' choices less available and accessible. Following their interventions they found significant reductions in 'red' choices, especially for 'red' (high calorie) beverages, which were reduced by 39%. In addition, most of their changes were sustained over two years post-intervention. In another study, Hanks, Just, Smith and Wansink, (2012) tested the idea of a 'convenience line' in addition to standard cafeteria lines in a school. In the convenience line students could only purchase healthy items (e.g., salads, sandwiches, fruits, and vegetables). This additional convenience line resulted in a significant reduction in the purchase of unhealthy foods. These studies illustrate the power of choice architecture in influencing healthier eating behaviors.

FIGURE 9.1 Images such as this one are used to nudge people in the direction of healthy food choices
Note: Red shown as black, yellow shown as gray and green shown as white.

A related intervention was undertaken in a Florida public school lunch program (see Miller, Gupta, Kropp, Grogan & Mathews, 2016). In this study, two interventions were compared to a control condition. The first intervention required that students use an online pre-ordering system for their lunches, whereas the second intervention used the same pre-ordering system along with behavioral nudges, which helped students to order a balanced and healthy meal. Specifically, students were prompted to order one element of each from among fruits, vegetables, whole grains, dairy and a main entrée. The second intervention yielded the best outcomes overall, compared to both other conditions. Specifically, students using the program with behavioral nudges for ordering more balanced meals did in fact select more fruits, vegetables and low fat milk with their lunches.

A variety of other interventions that target small but effective changes in the environment as a means to nudge or change behavior directly have been attempted. For example, Grant and Hofmann (2011) used a very simple manipulation of a sign about hand hygiene to change behavior among health professionals in a hospital. In study 1, one of three messages was randomly assigned to be displayed next to hand-sanitizing gel dispensers around the hospital. The control sign read, 'Gel in, wash out'; the personal consequences sign read, 'Hand hygiene prevents you from catching diseases'; the patient-consequences sign read, 'Hand hygiene prevents patients from catching diseases.' Based on measuring the amount of gel used, the rates of dispenser use were 40.1%, 34.0% and 54.2% respectively for the three groups showing that the message emphasizing patient consequences and presumably cueing professional behavior was most effective. In a second study, the personal consequences and patient consequences signs were compared using covert, independent observation. The rates of hand-hygiene adherence in the two groups were almost identical at baseline but 9.5% higher in the patient compared to personal consequences condition (89.2% vs. 79.7% adherence) at follow-up. These findings are a striking demonstration of how a simple manipulation (in this case changing one word) can produce significant changes in behavior.

How do people feel about nudges?

As we noted above, some of the environmental cues or nudges that influence behavior are largely outside of our awareness, whereas others are more visible and require more conscious, deliberate decision-making. Some researchers (e.g., Jung & Mellers, 2016; Kahneman, 2011) have used the terms **System 1 thinking** and **System 2 thinking** to refer to these types of nudges, respectively (see also Strack & Deutsch, 2004, for a discussion of a similar model, called the Reflective-Impulsive Model also covered in Chapters 2 and 8). That is, System 1 nudges tend to have more of an automatic or impulsive influence on behavior. Examples of this type of nudge include automatic enrollment into an organ donation program, smaller portions of food and changes in the visibility and accessibility of food items in shops or cafeterias. System 2 nudges, by comparison, require more effort, deliberation and reflection. For example, System 2 nudges might include food labels, nutritional information charts and overt prompts to make different food selections. These types of nudges can provide education and information enabling individuals to make more informed choices. So, when consumers are made aware of these different types of nudges influencing their behavior, how do they feel about them? One hypothesis is that people may feel that nudges are an attempt to control or manipulate their behavior, reacting negatively and resisting the nudge attempt, especially if those nudges are of the System 1 type.

In a US sample of adults, Jung and Mellers (2016) explored the role of individual differences in support for different types of nudges, and found some interesting patterns. First, there was general support for nudges to increase the likelihood of positive behaviors, but stronger support was obtained for System 2 (informational) nudges than for System 1 (automatic/default) nudges. Concerning individual differences, or preferences based on dispositional variables, empathetic people showed support for both types of nudges, especially when they were framed as have societal benefits. People scoring high on individualism and politically conservative respondents were unfavorable towards both types of nudges. Participants with high scores on a scale of reactance (e.g.,'I become frustrated when I am unable to make free and independent decisions' and 'When someone forces me to do something, I feel like doing the opposite'; see Hong & Page, 1989) and who reported a strong desire for control were primarily against System 1 nudges, and mediation models showed that the key determining factors in their resistance to such nudges were feelings that their autonomy was threatened by such nudges, and that such nudges were too paternalistic.

In samples of adults in both the UK and the US, Petrescu, Hollands, Couturier, Ng and Marteau (2016) asked respondents about the acceptability of a variety of interventions, based on nudging or choice architecture, to reduce obesity. These interventions, such as reducing portion sizes, changing the size and shape of containers, and making foods differentially accessible to consumers, included both System 1 and System 2 type nudges. In both the UK and US samples, respondents showed a preference for educational interventions (System 2 nudges) to policy-based interventions, such as taxation on sugary beverages. Attitudes towards interventions based on choice architecture were also assessed in their study. In this case, respondents preferred interventions that were presented as effective in solving the problem, even when told about the automatic or 'System 1' nature of them. That is, generally speaking, as long as an intervention works, respondents rated them as acceptable even knowing that it works largely non-consciously.

BURNING ISSUE BOX 9.1

ARE NUDGES ETHICAL?

Some people might be uncomfortable with or even explicitly oppose nudges and choice architecture, especially if they are perceived as reducing personal autonomy and freedom, or if they are seen as 'sneaky' and being used outside of our awareness or consent. This issue is something that several researchers and economists (e.g., Fischer & Lotz, 2014) have discussed, under the broader consideration of the ethical implications of applying these principles, even if it is presumably for the 'greater good' of society.

One ethical concern with nudges is that nudging programs may actually exacerbate or contribute to health inequalities and disparities. Some communities simply have limited or no access to more optimal choices, like adequate health care and healthy food choices. This latter point is a concern in many parts of the world, including even in the US, where many rural regions are referred to as 'food deserts' because people in such regions (numbering about 23 million Americans) have no transportation and no supermarkets with fresh, healthy food within a mile. In the UK, food deserts (defined in the UK as being more than 500 meters from adequate food provisions) tend to be concentrated instead in urban areas (Wrigley, 2002). Choice architecture interventions are moot for such communities because the healthier options are not available in the first place. From this perspective, nudges and choice architecture can be seen as partially instrumental in perpetuating inequalities, such that those with privilege and access benefit from such interventions, and those without privilege and access cannot benefit from them in the first place.

Another ethical concern is that if nudging and choice architecture techniques are assumed to be effective and low-cost interventions, then other strategies (like economic and policy-based solutions, discussed below) might be abandoned. For example, instead of raising the price of tobacco or alcohol (economic policies which are known to be effective), there could be sole reliance on nudges to change behavior, which would be a mistake even if such nudges are perceived as being less paternalistic.

Sunstein (2015), one of the original co-authors of *Nudge*, has discussed the ethics of nudges in the light of several critiques, some of which are discussed above. Ethical arguments against nudges (see reviews in Kosters & Van der Heijden, 2015; see also Rachlin, 2015) are typically captured by the sentiment that our tendency to behave in certain default ways should not be used against us, such as increasing organ donation rates. This is especially true if such techniques are outside of our awareness or threaten our autonomy or our freedom to choose. Sunstein argues that nudges and choice architecture are everywhere already, and that they do not necessarily constrain human agency, but instead promote or facilitate it.

SOCIAL NORMS AS ENVIRONMENTAL GUIDES TO BEHAVIOR

There are two general types of social norms that guide behavior: descriptive and injunctive social norms. Descriptive norms refer simply to who is doing what, or to how many others are engaged in a certain behavior. For example, a perceived descriptive norm might include the percentage of university students that a particular person believes drinks lots of alcohol on regular occasions. These kinds of norms signal to us what is generally typical of those around us. Injunctive norms, on the other hand, refer to what others consider to be acceptable or unacceptable behavior. Perceived injunctive norms guide behavior by signaling what is acceptable, appropriate or valid behavior (Cialdini, Reno & Kallgren, 1990). They may also include sanctions or consequences for engaging in or refraining from certain behaviors. Descriptive and injunctive norms sometimes pull us in different directions. Jared may see many of his peers smoking cigarettes (descriptive norm), but he knows that his family and close friends would strongly disapprove (injunctive norm) if they were to discover him smoking.

In the UK in the last few years, there has been an embracing of these ideas by government in an attempt to address various public health behaviors that have social consequences. A Behavioral Insights Team was set up by the government in 2010 with the aim of using influence techniques like social norms and related concepts (discussed further below) to design simple interventions to change important behaviors. Concerning social norms, the Behavioral Insights Team has focused on the ways that healthy behaviors can spread contagiously through social networks. They cite a large study of American smokers and their families over three generations beginning in the late 1940s (Christakis & Fowler, 2008). In this study, people in close social networks exerted influence on each other, and it was observed that spouses and friends tended to quit smoking together. This is an example of how the behavior of other people can impact our own behavior.

INDIRECT IMPACTS ON BEHAVIOR: HOW CHANGING THE ENVIRONMENT MAY CHANGE COGNITIONS

While the social norms-type approach has features of direct environmental effects on behavior (i.e., that the effects are likely to work to a large extent relatively automatically), it is probable that this approach changes norms which in turn explains subsequent changes in behavior (i.e., a mediated approach).

The *social norms* approach has been used in attempts to change various behaviors, such as the misuse of alcohol and smoking initiation in young people (Haines, Barker & Rice, 2003). The key feature of this approach as a research tool is that individuals first provide information about their own behavior and attitudes. Later, the same individuals make estimates of the numbers of others in their local environment who perform the behavior or approve of the behavior. Feedback is then provided on the actual behaviors and attitudes of others based on the earlier survey. So, for example, an individual might estimate that about half the members of their school would approve of smoking and that about one quarter are actual smokers. Based on the survey they can then be provided with information to debunk these ideas by showing the actual numbers are quite a lot lower (e.g., showing that only 1 in 5 approve of smoking and only 1 in 10 actually smoke). The assumption is that this more accurate information concerning prevalent social norms will prompt the individuals to decide not to smoke and to be less likely to take up smoking in the future. There is some evidence for the success of this approach, particularly in relation to reducing drinking (Bewick et al., 2013; Moreira, Smith & Foxcroft, 2009). However, a recent review suggests that even medium-to-large changes in norms engender only small changes in drinking behavior and no change in alcohol-related problems (Prestwich et al., 2016). Other researchers (e.g., Chung, Christopoulos, King-Casas, Ball & Chiu, 2015; see also Smith & Delgado, 2015) have shown that exposure to others making either risky or safer decisions in domains like gambling or food choices influence the degree to which we make similar risky or safe decisions.

Burger and Shelton (2011) used a similar technique to change the use of stairs over the lift in order to promote physical activity. They found that a sign emphasizing the benefits of using the stairs only produced a modest increase in use of the stairs, while a sign emphasizing that most people used the stairs showed a significant increase in stair use (from 85% to 92% comparing before and after the sign).

In a meta-analytic review of several experimental tests of the effect of social norms on eating behavior, Robinson, Thomas, Aveyard and Higgs (2014) found clear evidence that informational social norms have an impact. When study participants were given a 'high intake norm,' or information about others consuming a lot of food, it increased the amount of food consumed, compared to control conditions. Likewise, the studies that manipulated a 'low intake norm' also found a significant effect such that, compared to controls, low intake norms reduced food consumption in study participants. In addition to impacting the quantity of food consumed, social norms can also impact the type of food chosen (healthy snacks versus junk food). It is worth nothing that in most of these studies (e.g., Cruwys et al., 2012; Robinson, Benwell & Higgs, 2013), participants are given free access to food such as popcorn, pizza or fruits and vegetables, so the dependent variables are objective, observable behaviors.

One caveat to the social norms approach, especially when considering *perceived* social norms, is that people often display a heuristic thinking pattern known as the False Consensus Effect, which means that they generally overestimate the prevalence of support for their attitudes, traits or behaviors (see Kenworthy & Miller, 2001; Krueger & Clement, 1994). In addition, there is evidence for a selective exposure effect in estimating agreement for our behavioral and attitudinal positions (e.g., Bosveld, Koomen & Pligt, 1994). This means that, when estimating the number of people who behave like us or share our opinions, we typically refer cognitively to those who are already similar to us to begin with. We might therefore believe that our unhealthy behaviors are more acceptable because of a perceived social norm that is artificially inflated due to heuristic thinking.

BURNING ISSUE BOX 9.2

HOW CAN INDIVIDUALS FOREGO PERSONAL GAINS FOR THE GREATER GOOD?

In 1968, Garrett Hardin published a paper in *Science* titled 'The Tragedy of the Commons.' This describes the story of how herdsmen add extra cows to their own herds for personal gains. Unfortunately, this ultimately destroys the communal land that the cows graze leading to hardship for all. Many environmental and health problems have a similar profile. In the short term, each individual wanting to travel in the city may gain by taking their car rather than using the bus (more convenience, comfort etc.). However, if everyone uses a car to travel, then in the longer term everyone will suffer due to poor air quality and increased traffic. In terms of public health, widespread immunization can help to break the chain of infection. However, in a population where a lot of people are immune there is a relatively low risk of infection anyway and there are drawbacks to the individual of being immunized (e.g., some people perceive certain immunizations to contain harmful ingredients, they have side effects etc.). By deciding to not vaccinate based on these assumptions, individuals risk the status of public immunity (as well as increasing their own risk for contracting harmful, infectious diseases); as the proportion of non-immune individuals increases in a population, the likelihood of disease outbreaks also increases (see Fu, Rosenbloom, Wang & Nowak, 2011).

Such a discussion is not just an academic exercise. In 2014, the Philippines had a severe outbreak of measles, and this disease was subsequently introduced to the US population. In that year, the US experienced 23 different measles outbreaks, infecting hundreds of people. The vast majority of those infected during these measles outbreaks were unvaccinated (Centers for Disease Control and Prevention, 2016). Mandatory immunization would help to protect the status of public immunity and solve the social dilemma, but there are some obvious ethical concerns with forced immunization. The good news is that general vaccination programs do work. Recently, the Americas were declared free of measles by the Pan American Health Organization, meaning that transmission of measles does not occur for local strains of the disease. The bad news is that strains from other countries can still be introduced to the Americas and infect non-vaccinated or susceptible people, and that decisions to not vaccinate are potentially a threat to public health.

Commons dilemmas can be difficult to resolve because the problem is not strongly influenced one way or another by a single individual taking action. One more person using the car rather than the bus will not markedly affect air pollution or congestion. Similarly, one person switching from using the car to the bus will have little impact in general. Indeed, for that individual, switching to traveling by bus in the city may not be in their interest (i.e., less comfort and flexibility). However, across a range of individual health behaviors, many individuals do choose to act in ways that might benefit the good of all to the potential detriment of their own perceived self-interests because individuals often consider the *right* or *moral* thing to do. According to the Norm Activation Model (NAM; Schwartz, 1977; Schwartz & Howard, 1984), a given behavior is adopted not because of the expected outcomes of performance, but for more internalized feelings that can be captured by the concept of moral or personal norm. Personal norms are activated when individuals are aware of the potential adverse consequences of their actions on others or on the environment, and when they believe they can reverse or prevent those consequences. Both sets of beliefs need to be made salient or applied for behavior consistent with the moral norm to occur and to actively influence behavior.

Returning to our example of car use contributing to air pollution, an individual needs to believe their car use is contributing to air pollution and that their reducing car use will help reduce air pollution before the moral norm will be activated (i.e., for the individual to decide it is the right thing to do to reduce use of their car and to take action). Schwartz (1977) proposed that these personal norms are not experienced as intentions, but as feelings of moral obligation and so can directly influence behavior rather than indirectly through changing intentions. A number of studies have shown the NAM to provide good levels of prediction of low-cost environmental behaviors like using public transport over personal cars. Others have argued that moral norms may also moderate the relationship between intentions and behavior by strengthening the relationship between intentions and behaviors perceived to have moral consequences (e.g., Godin, Conner & Sheeran, 2005).

One other aspect of the environment that has received quite a lot of research attention in terms of how its effects on behavior are mediated by other variables is *level of deprivation*. Deprivation can be measured in a number of ways including income, education and material deprivation (e.g., the extent to which the area you live in is materially deprived). Analyses of neighborhood-level indices of deprivation show that increasing deprivation is associated with lower levels of physical activity (see Cubbin et al., 2006; Sundquist, Malmstrom & Johansson, 1999).

In a sample of nearly 1,500 Canadian adults, Godin et al. (2010) examined level of education, family income, material deprivation and social deprivation as predictors of physical activity. Importantly, they also measured intention and perceived behavioral control (PBC) over physical activity in the same sample. This was done to allow for tests of mediation effects on subsequent physical activity. In their data, simple correlations showed education, income and material deprivation to be significantly associated with physical activity levels (social deprivation was not significantly associated with physical activity levels). As you might guess, physical activity was higher among those who were better educated, had higher income and were less deprived. However, these effects were modest compared to the effects for intention and PBC. Specifically, the effect sizes for the environmental variables were small, but the effect sizes for intentions and PBC were of medium magnitude. Interestingly, the effects of both education and income were partially mediated by intention and PBC (there were no significant effects for material deprivation). These findings suggest that part, but not all, of the effect of education and income on physical activity is explained by differences in intentions and PBC for physical activity. In other words, having less education and/or less income results in lower levels of engaging in physical activity partly *because* education and income also yield lower levels of intention and PBC over physical activity. The fact that mediation is partial in this case suggests there are likely other mechanisms by which education and income impact on physical activity levels. For example, it may be the case that such people have fewer opportunities to be physically active in sports centers.

Getting a better understanding of when cognitions do not mediate, partially mediate or completely mediate the effects of changes in the environment on behavior might help us design more effective interventions. For example, where the effects of the environment are mediated by cognitions, it may be useful to consider combining interventions that target environmental changes (e.g., providing more sports centers) with ones that target different cognition changes (e.g., strengthening intentions to be physically active).

HOW THE ENVIRONMENT INTERACTS WITH COGNITIONS IN DETERMINING BEHAVIOR

In addition to mediated effects, we may also find **moderated effects**, or interaction effects, between aspects of the environment and cognitions about the behavior itself, in determining behavior. In general, an interaction effect means that the direct effect of one variable, such as the environment, is different for different groups of people. These groups may be based on experimental conditions, created by random assignment, or they may be formed by self-selection, such as when people prefer to live in one neighborhood over another because of factors such as income, ethnicity or religion. Comparisons of differential effects can also use groups based on individual differences or personality factors. For example, the influence of intentions to engage in healthy behaviors on actual behavior might be strongest for people who score high on personality-level conscientiousness.

The study by Godin et al. (2010) that we considered above contains one example of such an interactive, or moderated, effect. Godin et al. showed that, in addition to the mediation of intentions and PBC on behavior, education level *moderated* the effect of intentions to engage in physical activity on subsequent physical activity levels: intentions were weaker predictors of physical activity among the less educated participants than among the more educated. This is quite important because it suggests that interventions designed to increase intentions to engage in physical activity in a sample or population (as is common in many health promotion messages) will be less effective for those with less education compared to those with more education. It could be the case that among those with less education an intervention targeting intentions to engage in physical activity needs to also target some of the tangible barriers to physical activity.

Concerning health behaviors generally, a key environmental variable has been **socio-economic status (SES)**. SES refers to the social standing of an individual or group in the social hierarchy, and is measured by factors such as relative material deprivation, income, education and occupational classification. Low SES is consistently associated with both increased morbidity and mortality rates (Adler et al., 1994; Centers for Disease Control and Prevention, 2011). In addition, research has demonstrated parallel differences in engagement with a variety of health behaviors as a function of SES (Blaxter, 1990; Ford et al., 1991). For example, health risk behaviors such as smoking and alcohol dependency tend to be higher for low SES groups compared to high SES groups, and health protective behaviors such as physical activity and healthy eating tend to be lower. In fact, recent research has suggested the link between SES and mortality is attributable to differences in engagement with various health behaviors (Nandi, Glymour & Subramanian, 2014; Stringhini et al., 2010).

One pertinent question is whether SES also moderates the effects of *cognitions* on health behaviors. Findings from Conner et al. (2013) suggest this to be the case. They found that the relationship between intentions to engage in a specific health behavior and subsequent performance was moderated by participants' level of SES: lower SES weakened the intention–behavior relationship.

Other types of moderation effects have been detected. For example, O'Brien (2012), using a longitudinal design of US adults over 10 years, found that SES (operationalized as the number of years of education) was (as expected) a strong predictor of changes in chronic illness (including diabetes, lupus, cancer etc.) over time, such that less educated respondents reported significantly greater increases in chronic illnesses. However, control beliefs (including both personal mastery and personal constraints/obstacles) interacted with SES in predicting changes in reported chronic illness. When control beliefs were weak, there was a significant difference between low SES and high SES respondents. However, when control beliefs were strong, no differences were found between low and high SES groups. Another way to look at their findings is to consider that the greatest increases in chronic illness were reported among respondents with both low SES and weak control beliefs.

POLICY-BASED APPROACHES TO BEHAVIOR CHANGE

In relation to policy-based approaches to behavior change we will now examine how making behaviors illegal (e.g., seat belt wearing), changing pricing (e.g., for alcohol and tobacco, high sugar drinks) and requiring health warnings (e.g., fat consumption, texting and driving, smoking) have been shown to be effective means of changing a range of health behaviors. In this section we will discuss findings based on examining the direct behavioral outcomes of public policies, and we will also discuss a subset or corollary of the policy-based approach, which is typically referred to as the *social marketing* approach to behavior change.

The approaches that fall under the category of policy-based interventions are generally of two types. They will either be based on an informational strategy, or be based on changing the market environment itself. Informational approaches are focused on getting people to think more about their choices, or to be aware of the benefits of certain choices or the dangers of other choices (see also the 'empowerment' approach; Feufel et al., 2011). One drawback to these approaches is that they may not reliably result in behavior change even though people may be more knowledgeable, aware or persuaded about the consequences of certain behaviors. The other type of strategy involves changing the market environment directly. These may be seen as more difficult, expensive and intrusive (see Brambila-Macias et al., 2011), but tend to be quite effective in producing changes to behavior and other desired psychological outcomes. In this section, we will review some important areas of health behavior where changes to policies have had measureable impacts.

SEAT BELTS

Over the past few decades the mandatory use of seat belts in motor vehicles has increased to the point where most developed countries now have compulsory seat belt laws. There are variations to these laws, both across countries as well as within them. In the US, for example, each state has its own seat belt laws. Currently, the only US state without compulsory seat belts for adults is New Hampshire, whose state motto is, appropriately, 'Live Free or Die.'

The introduction of seat belt laws has reduced fatalities and related outcomes in the UK (Rutherford, 1985) and the US (Cohen & Einav, 2003). It is unclear, however, what psychological mechanisms might be at work generally in producing greater compliance with seat belt laws. It could be the case that seat belt laws have a direct effect on behavior. Alternatively, such laws may change cognitive processes, which in turn affect behavior. For example, Stasson and Fishbein (1990) reported that perceived risk (of injury/death) does not have a direct effect on seat belt usage. Instead, that behavior is predicted proximally by intentions to use a seat belt. In their study, intentions were best predicted by perceived risk and social norms. Sutton and Eiser (1990) also showed that fear arousal and perceived risk predicted seat belt use intentions, but that over time intentions became less important and past behavior (i.e., automatic tendencies, or habits)

FIGURE 9.2 This Norwegian advertisement emphasizes important social connections to remind people to wear their seat belts while driving

emerged as the main predictor of seat belt use. Regardless of the exact mechanisms, policies and laws requiring the use of seat belts increase seat belt usage and ultimately prevent injuries and save lives.

TEXTING AND DRIVING

In the UK, using a handheld device while driving has been illegal since 2003, but of the UK vehicle fatalities caused by distractions in 2012, nearly 20% of those were due to mobile phone usage. Although there are not (yet) many long-term studies examining the effectiveness of mobile phone restrictions, there are some recently published articles that shed some light on the issue. One such study (Ehsani, Bingham, Ionides & Childers, 2014; see also Highway Loss Data Institute, 2010) reported an increase in crashes following the introduction of a 2010 texting restriction law put into place in the US state of Michigan. Ehsani et al. speculate that this result may be due to an unintended consequence of the law, which is that people will likely deliberately conceal their mobile phone use behavior while driving so as to avoid being seen by others, especially by police officers/law enforcement. Thus, by keeping their mobile phones out of sight, their driving vision impairments and distractions are exacerbated.

However, larger-scale studies tell a different story. Ferdinand et al. (2014; see also Abouk & Adams, 2013) used a specialized vehicle fatality reporting system to examine the rate of fatal vehicle accidents across 10 years in the US, comparing states with and without texting restrictions or bans. They found a difference overall in fatalities between states with primary bans on texting (drivers can be stopped and fined because they are using their mobile phones), compared to states with secondary bans (drivers must be stopped for some other infraction first, then may be issued a fine for mobile phone usage). Specifically, secondary bans on texting had no effect on traffic fatalities, whereas primary bans did have an effect on reducing fatalities. In fact, the primary bans were found to have the strongest life-saving impact on the sector of the population most at-risk for texting-related accidents and deaths: young people.

Thus, generally speaking, although mobile phone use bans may produce a shift in behavior from overt to covert in some cases, such laws do have a positive effect on reducing accidents and on saving lives. However, researchers should examine the social and cognitive mechanisms by which better, less distracted driving behavior can be encouraged.

DRINK DRIVING

There are various policies, laws and blood alcohol content (BAC) limits in countries around the world, some of which are much more stringent than others. These limits range from an upper limit of around 0.08% (e.g., Mexico, US, Canada) down to 0% (e.g., Brazil, Czech Republic, United Arab Emirates). There are also variations in these laws within countries, such as more stringent restrictions on younger drivers or on commercial operators. The penalties for drink driving offenses also vary widely. In the state of California, for example, a new law will go into effect in 2019, requiring that all first-time offenders install an ignition-lock breathalyzer in their vehicle or else be restricted to driving only to and from work or on other necessary trips.

Because drink driving has been a serious public health problem for a long time, a variety of policy- and law-based solutions have been tested and implemented over the years. For example, Fell and Voas (2006) examined the outcomes of 14 different studies on the effectiveness of BAC-limit laws, around the US and in Europe and Australia, and concluded that having lower BAC limits (e.g., from 0.08% to 0.05% or lower) does serve to reduce the number of vehicle accidents, injuries and deaths. Some of the more effective laws, apart from BAC laws described above, include license bans/suspension, publicized sobriety checkpoints, alcohol ignition locks (for repeat offenders), minimum drinking age laws and zero tolerance laws (see Goodwin et al., 2015).

WARNING LABELS AND PRICE HIKES

Over the years, there have been many tests of the question of whether price or tax increases on certain products have their desired effects. Bader, Boisclair and Ferrence (2011) reviewed many such studies in relation to smoking and found that the majority of studies reviewed did find that increasing the price of tobacco products reduced both the prevalence of youth smoking behavior as well as the amount of tobacco that they consumed. The evidence is more mixed concerning the initiation or uptake of smoking behavior, however; some studies found some impact on preventing smoking, whereas others found no effect at all. One concern with raising prices or taxes on certain products is that such a policy risks being socially regressive, or more punishing to the finances of poorer people. That is, they must spend a greater proportion of their total income on raised prices, compared to wealthier people. Thus, Bader et al. examined whether price increases on tobacco products had differential effects on low SES versus higher SES groups of consumers. Although a minority of studies reviewed showed that increasing tobacco prices is good for all socioeconomic groups approximately equally as far as the reduction in smoking participation and consumption are concerned, the majority of studies reviewed showed an equal or better impact of price increases on low SES groups compared to the general population. Specifically, increasing tobacco prices is good for all socioeconomic groups approximately equally as far as the reduction in smoking participation and consumption are concerned. However, one of the unintended consequences of price increases is that lower SES groups tend to show more demand for smuggled cigarettes when prices go up (e.g., Thomas et al., 2008; Wiltshire, Bancroft, Amos & Parry, 2001).

TOBACCO AND SUGARY DRINKS

With taxes and price hikes on sugared products being implemented in both the UK and in the US, the key question of course is whether and how they work in favor of public health. Researchers in both countries (e.g., Brownell & Frieden, 2009; Michie, 2016) argue for a tax on sugar-sweetened beverages because such a policy would almost certainly improve health and reduce obesity. Such beverages are seen as a leading cause of obesity, and reductions in sugar beverage intake are clearly associated with improved health over time (see Vartanian, Schwartz & Brownell, 2007). One point of uncertainty in this research so far concerns which alternative foods people would buy instead of sugary drinks. Cartwright (2014) argues that warning label policies are good for academics and people who think rationally about the relationships among consumption of calories, weight gain and associated diseases. However, warning labels are perhaps unlikely to have much of an impact on people who struggle with weight gain for a variety of reasons. One of the ethical considerations for warning labels about obesity is that such labels may lead to further stigmatization and moral judgment of people who choose to consume such products.

Concerning the issue of the effectiveness of warning labels on behavioral choice, VanEpps and Roberto (2016) conducted a representative online study to test whether warning labels for sugar-sweetened beverages can influence beverage choices. They gathered responses from over 2,200 adolescents aged 12–18 years. The key independent variable was the type of label accompanying different drinks. They compared a condition with no warning label to a condition with just a calorie indicator label, and to four different types of health warnings telling the prospective consumer that sugary drinks were linked to weight gain, obesity, diabetes and tooth decay. The main outcome in this study was a hypothetical choice of beverage from a vending machine. Warning labels, compared to control and calorie-only labels, generally and significantly reduced the percentage of participants choosing sugar-sweetened beverages.

Because increasing taxes on sugary drinks is such a recent phenomenon, there is relatively little data so far concerning the actual behavioral purchasing habits of consumers, not to mention the longer-term health effects of such policies. Some recent findings are encouraging, however. In California, voters in two neighboring cities (San Francisco and Berkeley) voted in 2014 on proposals to add a sugar tax to beverages sold in those cities (see Charles, 2016). Voters in Berkeley approved the tax, whereas voters in San Francisco rejected the proposal. This 'natural experiment' yielded some important, if preliminary data. Compared to baseline data, in which residents in both cities reported drinking about 1.5 sugary, fizzy drinks per day, the sugar tax seems to have had its intended effects. Residents in Berkeley reported about 20% lower consumption

FIGURE 9.3 Most 12-ounce sugary drinks contain about 10 teaspoons of sugar!

of sugary drinks (and an increase in reported water consumption) following the introduction of the tax, whereas reported consumption of sugary drinks in San Francisco did not change over time. Of course, it remains to be seen whether such taxes in the UK and the US have their desired effects on behavior and health over the long term, not just on raising money for government programs. One recent meta-analysis provides some information on this issue. Cabrera Escobar, Veerman, Tollman, Bertram and Hofman (2013) gathered studies from around the world (e.g., Brazil, France, Mexico, USA) in which the authors examined the effects of price hikes or taxes on sugar-sweetened beverages, and found that such policies do tend to reduce obesity and BMI, and that they may be effective policies generally, despite their 'regressive' nature. There is no doubt that many researchers will continue to collect data on this issue in order to understand not just what the patterns of behavior are, but why and under what conditions they occur.

SOCIAL MARKETING APPROACH TO BEHAVIOR CHANGE

As an increasingly popular method of health promotion, social marketing tries to influence behavior by offering people tangible and social benefits, by reducing barriers and constraints that may block them physically or emotionally, and by using persuasion in targeted or personalized ways to create behavior change. It is a model that differs from traditional health promotion programs, which tend to simply instruct people on how to behave. Instead, social marketing is about getting people to 'buy' the better behavior because it is desirable and worth their time, energy or resources (Grier & Bryant, 2005).

The core of the social marketing approach is applying known and proven techniques of influence in consumer behavior to encourage or promote change in health behaviors (see Andreasen, 2002). The ideal outcome is that individuals make more healthy choices for their own benefit as well for the benefit of society as a whole (Luca & Suggs, 2013; Spotswood, French, Tapp & Stead, 2012). According to this approach, researchers and practitioners should examine and understand the values and beliefs that motivate and underlie a variety of health behaviors, so that those values and beliefs can be targeted in creating messages or interventions that have the greatest likelihood of effecting change. Although you will undoubtedly recognize this as similar to other models and theories discussed in this book so far, proponents of the social marketing approach argue that it is distinct in some key ways.

According to Andreasen (2002), there are six criteria that should be met in order for an intervention to qualify as social marketing. First, the intervention must focus on behavior change (rather than intentions or attitudes) in its design and evaluation. Second, social marketing should focus on the motives and needs of the target audience, including both pretesting ideas and monitoring them as they are implemented. Third, interventions should be tailored to specific segments of the population (e.g., based on ethnicity, sex, language etc.), without assuming that a general intervention can be implemented for all members of a population. Fourth, the intervention should be based on exchange theory, emphasizing the rewards of behavior change and lowering the costs of compliance. Fifth, the intervention should utilize the four Ps of traditional marketing: *Product* (rewards, benefits), *Price* (cost, effort), *Place* (ease of access) and *Promotion* (relevance to the target audience). Finally, the intervention should be designed around an understanding of the competition for an individual's behavior change choices. That is, the behavior change strategy should focus on minimizing the likelihood of other possible behaviors, including current behaviors.

Social marketing strategies and interventions have been developed and used in a variety of countries and cultures, and for an array of health behaviors. One innovative program utilizing this approach was designed to increase the use of insecticide-treated mosquito nets in Tanzania (Kikumbih, Hanson, Mills, Mponda & Schellenberg, 2005) through social promotion of this behavior using stickers, flags, shirts and billboards. The campaign increased the usage of mosquito nets in the intervention area, compared to a control area of the country.

In a social marketing campaign involving nearly 3,000 Canadian university students, Scarapicchia et al. (2015) aimed to increase self-efficacy, outcome expectancies, behavioral intentions to exercise and, ultimately, changes in moderate to vigorous physical activity. You probably recognize these constructs from the theories discussed in earlier chapters. Their campaign contained social marketing elements emphasizing the benefits of exercise, including stress reduction, enjoyment and academic achievement. These messages were disseminated in postcards, posters, online social media, in classrooms and via face-to-face interactions with peer 'ambassadors' from the campaign. Overall, their findings supported the model that they proposed based on the social marketing principles as well as the theoretical framework guiding the choice of measured variables. Specifically, awareness of the campaign predicted greater outcome expectancies (e.g., 'Regular physical activity helps me manage stress'), which were associated with greater perceived self-efficacy (e.g., 'I am confident that I can regularly do 30 minutes or more of moderate physical activity per day most days of the week'). In turn self-efficacy predicted both stronger intentions to be physically active as well as higher self-reported participation in moderate and vigorous physical activity.

In addition to a focus on increasing healthy behaviors, several studies aim to reduce or prevent harmful behaviors. Glider, Midyett, Mills-Novoa, Johannessen and Collins (2001), using a social marketing intervention that included school newspaper advertisements, awareness activities and interviews in the local radio and television media, reduced alcohol-related behaviors within the university population. They also saw changes in perceived campus norms, including a significant decrease in the percentage of students who believe that most students have five or more drinks at parties, and that drinking alcohol makes sexual opportunities more likely. However, the study was limited as it did not employ a control group.

Rather than the mediated-type effect demonstrated by Glider et al., a similar intervention conducted in Australia found a moderated effect. In this study, Dietrich et al. (2015) randomly assigned 20 high schools to an alcohol social marketing intervention and another 20 schools to serve as no-exposure controls and found differential effects of social marketing across different segments of the population studied: abstainers, bingers and moderate drinkers. For example, participation in the intervention resulted in a significant reduction in intentions to binge drink, but only among the bingers. For them, their changed knowledge about, and attitudes towards drinking impacted their subsequent intentions to binge drink. The same pattern was not observed for the abstainers and moderate drinkers, but their baseline intentions to binge drink were already quite low to begin with.

In an early review of social marketing interventions, Gordon, McDermott, Stead and Angus (2006) found the approach to be effective in increasing consumption of fruits and vegetables, reducing fat intake and improving people's attitudes towards healthy eating; the findings were more heterogeneous for physical activity, with several studies showing a positive effect on exercise and several showing no effects (but was seemingly effective for changing people's awareness, knowledge or attitudes about exercise); and reasonably successful for substance misuse such as smoking and illicit drug use (although social marketing was less effective in smoking cessation than in preventing or reducing smoking behavior). Gordon et al. also report that social marketing interventions can be effective across a range of different target groups and in different settings, such as in schools, churches, workplaces and even in supermarkets.

Limitations to the social marketing approach

There are a number of limitations to this approach. First, Kubacki, Rundle-Thiele, Pang and Buyucek (2015) noted that, despite a focus in the literature on six key, benchmark criteria (discussed above; see Andreasen, 2002) of a social marketing intervention, few studies employ all six criteria.

Second, some critics (e.g., Langford & Panter-Brick, 2013) argue that social marketing focuses too much on individual agency and individual behavior, without taking into account the very real structural constraints of many populations, especially disadvantaged populations that are often the most in need of health interventions. For example, when individuals in disadvantaged populations or areas become motivated to change via social marketing campaigns, they often cannot because of resource constraints. In the end, they may have even worse outcomes because they can feel powerless to act, and ashamed or stigmatized for not changing their behavior.

Third, and as a related point, because many of the principal factors influencing health behavior are social and political, public health campaigns (including those using social marketing) should include attempts to change public policy so that the barriers and constraints on opportunities can be reduced or removed for everyone. Such a sentiment is not inconsistent with the major theorist, integrated model of behavior change presented elsewhere in this book, in which constraints are a major factor in determining behavior change.

Fourth, although the studies testing social marketing can possess good external validity, they tend to suffer from a lack of internal validity. Such studies employ their methods in the real world, outside of the laboratory, so they cannot typically randomly assign their participants to conditions or get representative, random samples of their populations. Caution is warranted because these approaches tend to combine several variables or interventions together, and they lack strong theoretical frameworks. This makes it difficult for scientists and consumers to have a clear sense of which factors are responsible for any observed effects, or of why they occurred in the first place. On the other hand, applying techniques in a problem-focused way is often done with the goal of solving some social problem – in this case improving individual and public health. Thus, we may see a sacrificing of strict internal validity to research when lives are at stake.

Finally, if these strategies are seen to be effective, then they will likely require long-term investments by communities and their respective governments. This is because such interventions must compete against a constant array of countervailing forces encouraging us to engage in unhealthy behaviors.

SCIENCE OF HEALTH BEHAVIOR CHANGE: IN ACTION

In Action Box 9.1 considers an experiment by Robinson et al. (2013). In this study, the authors examined the impact of different social norms on eating behavior. They manipulated a low intake norm, a high intake norm and a no norm control condition, and measured how many cookies participants ate following the presentation of those norms. The theory suggests that such norms will act as direct modeling influences on eating behavior, so the authors expected that participants would eat more cookies than controls in the high intake norm condition, and fewer cookies than controls in the low intake norm condition.

SCIENCE OF HEALTH BEHAVIOR CHANGE

In Action Box 9.1

Study: Robinson et al. (2013). *Food intake norms increase and decrease snack food intake in a remote confederate study*	
Aim: To examine the effects of social norms on snack food intake.	
Method: Participants were randomized to one of three conditions: a low intake norm, a high intake norm and no norm (control). Under the cover story of a taste test, they were presented with a well-stocked bowl of cookies, and were left alone to eat for 15 minutes. Empathy levels were also measured; this variable was expected to predict the outcomes as well.	
Results: The intake norms affected behavior as expected, such that participants consumed the fewest number of cookies in the low intake norm condition, the highest number of cookies in the high intake norm condition and an intermediate number in the control condition. Empathy had no direct or interactive effect on eating behavior.	
Authors' conclusion: Participants given intake norms from (fictitious) prior participants matched those norms in their own eating behavior. Social norms for eating can have a strong influence on eating behavior.	

THEORY AND TECHNIQUES OF HEALTH BEHAVIOR CHANGE		
BCTs	INTERVENTION: Based on Michie et al.'s (2013) taxonomy:	
	Low intake and high intake norm conditions: 6.2 Social comparison.	
	CONTROL: None	
Critical Skills Toolkit		
3.1	Does the design enable the identification of which BCTs are effective?	*Yes – the intervention manipulates norms only (which in the Michie et al., 2013, taxonomy is labeled social comparison).*
4.1	Is the intervention based on one theory or a combination of theories (if any at all)?	*The intervention is based on the findings of previous studies but no formal theory is explicitly noted as providing the basis for the intervention.*
	Are all constructs specified within a theory targeted by the intervention?	*Not applicable – no formal theory stated.*
	Are all behavior change techniques explicitly targeting at least one theory-relevant construct?	*Not applicable – no formal theory stated.*
	Do the authors test why the intervention was effective or ineffective (consistent with the underlying theory)?	*No; mediation analyses were not conducted.*
4.2	Does the study tailor the intervention based on the underlying theory?	*Not applicable – no formal theory stated.*

GLOSSARY

Choice architecture: part of Nudge Theory, suggesting that we can alter the environment in which decisions are made to make certain choices more or less likely.

Direct effect: simple case where changes in behavior are explained by changes in the environment.

Indirect/mediated effect: where changes in behavior are explained by changes in the ways that individuals view the behavior, such as cognitions about the environment, which in turn are caused by changes in the environment.

Moderated effect: where the relationship between cognitions and behavior is explained by changes in the environment

(e.g., living in a deprived area reducing the impact of your intentions to not smoke on your subsequent smoking behavior).

Socio-economic status (SES): refers to the social standing of an individual or group in a social hierarchy and is measured by factors such as relative material deprivation, income, education and occupational classification.

System 1 thinking: refers to non-reflective, automatic or impulsive influences on behavior.

System 2 thinking: refers to more effortful, conscious, deliberative and reflective thought processes impacting behavior.

REFERENCES

Abouk, R. & Adams, S. (2013). Texting bans and fatal accidents on roadways: do they work? Or do drivers just react to announcements of bans? *American Economic Journal: Applied Economics, 5*(2), 179–199.

Adler, N.E., Boyce, T., Chesney, M.A., Cohen, S., Folkman, S., Kahn, R.L. et al. (1994). Socioeconomic status and health. The challenge of the gradient. *American Psychologist, 49,* 15–24.

Ajzen, I. (1991). The theory of planned behavior. *Organizational Behavior and Human Decision Processes, 50,* 179–211.

Andreasen, A.R. (2002). Marketing social marketing in the social change marketplace. *Journal of Public Policy & Marketing, 21*(1), 3–13.

Bader, P., Boisclair, D. & Ferrence, R. (2011). Effects of tobacco taxation and pricing on smoking behavior in high-risk populations: a knowledge synthesis. *International Journal of Environmental Research and Public Health, 8*(11), 4118–4139.

Bewick, B.M., Bell, D., Crosby, S., Edlin, B., Keenan, S., Marshall, K. & Savva, G. (2013). Promoting improvements in public health: using a Social Norms Approach to reduce use of alcohol, tobacco and other drugs. *Drugs: Education, Prevention and Policy, 20*(4), 322–330. doi: 10.3109/09687637.2013.766150.

Blaxter, M. (1990). *Health and Lifestyles.* London: Tavistock.

Bosveld, W., Koomen, W. & Pligt, J. (1994). Selective exposure and the false consensus effect: the availability of similar and dissimilar others. *British Journal of Social Psychology, 33*(4), 457–466.

Brambila-Macias, J., Shankar, B., Capacci, S., Mazzocchi, M., Perez-Cueto, F.J., Verbeke, W. & Traill, W.B. (2011). Policy interventions to promote healthy eating: a review of what works, what does not, and what is promising. *Food and Nutrition Bulletin, 32*(4), 365–375.

Brownell, K.D. & Frieden, T.R. (2009). Ounces of prevention – the public policy case for taxes on sugared beverages. *New England Journal of Medicine, 360*(18), 1805–1808.

Burger, J.M. & Shelton, M. (2011). Changing everyday health behaviours through descriptive norm manipulations. *Social Influence, 6*, 69–77.

Cabrera Escobar, M.A., Veerman, J.L., Tollman, S.M., Bertram, M.Y. & Hofman, K.J. (2013). Evidence that a tax on sugar sweetened beverages reduces the obesity rate: a meta-analysis. *BMC Public Health, 13*, 1072. doi.org/10.1186/1471–2458–13–1072.

Cartwright, M.M. (2014). *Soda Warning Labels: Rated 'F' for Futility: Why Warning Labels on Sugary Beverages Will Not Impact Obesity.* Retrieved on June 30, 2017 from: www.psychologytoday.com/blog/food-thought/201406/soda-warning-labels-rated-f-futility-0

Centers for Diseases Control and Prevention. (2011). CDC health disparities and inequalities report – United States, 2011. *Morbidity and Mortality Weekly Reports, 60*, 1–113.

Centers for Diseases Control and Prevention. (2016). *Measles Cases and Outbreaks.* Retrieved on September 30, 2016 from: www.cdc.gov/measles/cases-outbreaks.html.

Charles, D. (2016). *Berkeley's Soda Tax Appears To Cut Consumption Of Sugary Drinks.* Retrieved on June 30, 2017 from: www.npr.org/sections/thesalt/2016/08/23/491104093/berkeleys-soda-tax-appears-to-cut-consumption-of-sugary-drinks.

Christakis, N.A. & Fowler, J.H. (2008) The collective dynamics of smoking in a large social network. *New England Journal of Medicine, 358*(21), 2249–2258.

Chung, D., Christopoulos, G.I., King-Casas, B., Ball, S.B. & Chiu, P.H. (2015). Social signals of safety and risk confer utility and have asymmetric effects on observers' choices. *Nature Neuroscience, 18*(6), 912–916.

Cialdini, R.B., Reno, R.R. & Kallgren, C.A. (1990). A focus theory of normative conduct: recycling the concept of norms to reduce littering in public places. *Journal of Personality and Social Psychology, 58*, 1015–1026.

Cohen, A. & Einav, L. (2003). The effects of mandatory seat belt laws on driving behavior and traffic fatalities. *Review of Economics and Statistics, 85*(4), 828–843.

Conner, M., McEachan, R., Jackson, C., McMillan, B., Woolridge, M. & Lawton, R. (2013). Moderating effect of socioeconomic status on the relationship between health cognitions and behaviors. *Annals of Behavioral Medicine, 46*(1), 19–30.

Cruwys, T., Platow, M.J., Angullia, S.A., Chang, J.M., Diler, S.E. Kirchner, J.L., ... & Wadley, A.L. (2012). Modeling of food intake is moderated by salient psychological group membership. *Appetite, 58*(2), 754–757.

Cubbin, C., Sundquist, K., Ahlen, H., Johansson, S.E., Winkleby, M.A. & Sundquist, J. (2006). Neighborhood deprivation and cardiovascular disease risk factors: protective and harmful effects. *Scandinavian Journal of Public Health, 34*, 228–237.

Dietrich, T., Rundle-Thiele, S., Schuster, L., Drennan, J., Russell-Bennett, R., Leo, C., ... & Connor, J.P. (2015). Differential segmentation responses to an alcohol social marketing program. *Addictive Behaviors, 49*, 68–77.

Ehsani, J.P., Bingham, C.R., Ionides, E. & Childers, D. (2014). The impact of Michigan's text messaging restriction on motor vehicle crashes. *Journal of Adolescent Health, 54*(5), S68–S74.

Faith, M.S., Rose, E., Matz, P.E., Pietrobelli, A. & Epstein, L.H. (2006). Co-twin control designs for testing behavioral economic theories of child nutrition: methodological note. *International Journal of Obesity, 30*(10), 1501–1505.

Fell, J.C. & Voas, R.B. (2006). The effectiveness of reducing illegal blood alcohol concentration (BAC) limits for driving: evidence for lowering the limit to .05 BAC. *Journal of Safety Research, 37*(3), 233–243.

Ferdinand, A.O., Menachemi, N., Sen, B., Blackburn, J.L., Morrisey, M. & Nelson, L. (2014). Impact of texting laws on motor vehicular fatalities in the United States. *American Journal of Public Health, 104*(8), 1370–1377.

Feufel, M.A., Antes, G., Steurer, J., Gigerenzer, G., Muir Gray, J.A., Mäkelä, M., ... & Wennberg, J.E. (2011). How to achieve better health care: better systems, better patients, or both? In G. Gigerenzer & J.A.M. Gray (Eds.), *Better Doctors, Better Patients, Better Decisions: Envisioning Healthcare 2020* (pp. 117–134). Cambridge, MA: MIT Press.

Fischer, M. & Lotz, S. (2014). Is soft paternalism ethically legitimate? – The relevance of psychological processes for the assessment of nudge-based policies. *Cologne Graduate School Working Paper Series (05–02)*. Retrieved on May 30, 2014 from: https://ideas.repec.org/p/cgr/cgsser/05-02.html.

Fishbein, M. & Ajzen, I. (1975). *Belief, Attitude, Intention, and Behavior.* Reading, MA: Addison-Wesley.

Fishbein, M., Triandis, H.C., Kanfer, F.H., Becker, M., Middlestadt, S.E. & Eichler, A. (2001). Factors influencing behaviour and behaviour change. In A. Baum, T.A. Revenson & J.E. Singer (Eds.), *Handbook of Health Psychology* (pp. 3–17). Mahwah, NJ: Lawrence Erlbaum Associates.

Ford, E.S., Merritt, R.K., Heath, G.W., Powell, K.E., Washburn, R.A., Kriska, A. & Haile, G. (1991). Physical activity behaviors in lower and higher socioeconomic status populations. *American Journal of Epidemiology, 133*(12), 1246–1256.

Fu, F., Rosenbloom, D.I., Wang, L. & Nowak, M.A. (2011). Imitation dynamics of vaccination behaviour on social networks. *Proceedings of the Royal Society of London B: Biological Sciences, 278*(1702), 42–49.

Gallivan, J., Lising, M., Ammary, N.J. & Greenberg, R. (2007). The National Diabetes Education Program's 'Control Your Diabetes. For Life.' campaign: design, implementation, and lessons learned. *Social Marketing Quarterly, 13,* 65–82.

Glider, P., Midyett, S.J., Mills-Novoa, B., Johannessen, K. & Collins, C. (2001). Challenging the collegiate rite of passage: a campus-wide social marketing media campaign to reduce binge drinking. *Journal of Drug Education, 31*(2), 207–220.

Godin, G., Conner, M. & Sheeran, P. (2005). Bridging the intention-behavior 'gap': the role of moral norm. *British Journal of Social Psychology, 44,* 497–512.

Godin, G., Conner, M., Sheeran, P., Bélanger-Gravel, A., Nolin, B. & Gallani, M.C. (2010). Social structure, social cognition, and physical activity: a test of four models. *British Journal of Health Psychology, 15,* 79–95. doi: 10.1348/135910709X429901.

Goodwin, A., Thomas, L., Kirley, B., Hall, W., O'Brien, N. & Hill, K. (2015). *Countermeasures that Work: A Highway Safety Countermeasure Guide for State Highway Safety Offices* (8th edn). Report No. DOT HS 812 202. Washington, DC: National Highway Traffic Safety Administration.

Gordon, R., McDermott, L., Stead, M. & Angus, K. (2006). The effectiveness of social marketing interventions for health improvement: what's the evidence? *Public Health, 120*(12), 1133–1139.

Grant, A.M. & Hofmann, D.A. (2011). It's not all about me: motivating hand hygiene among health care professionals by focusing on patients. *Psychological Science, 22,* 1494–1499.

Grier, S. & Bryant, C. (2005). Social marketing in public health. *Annual Review of Public Health, 26,* 319–339.

Haines, M.P., Barker, G. & Rice, R. (2003). Using social norms to reduce alcohol and tobacco use in two midwestern high schools. In H.W. Perkins (Ed.), *The Social Norms Approach to Preventing School and College Age Substance Abuse: A Handbook for Educators, Counselors, and Clinicians* (pp. 235–244). San Francisco: Jossey-Bass.

Hanks, A.S., Just, D.R., Smith, L.E. & Wansink, B. (2012). Healthy convenience: nudging students toward healthier choices in the lunchroom. *Journal of Public Health, 34*(3), 370–376.

Hardin, G. (1968). The tragedy of the commons. *Science, 162,* 1243–1248.

Highway Loss Data Institute. (2010). Texting laws and collision claim frequencies. *Highway Loss Data Institute Bulletin.* Retrieved on June 30, 2017 from: www.iihs.org/media/fc495300-6f8c-419d-c3b94d178e5a/enPLrA/HLDI%20Research/Bulletins/hldi_bulletin_27.11.pdf.

Hong, S.M. & Page, S. (1989). A psychological reactance scale: development, factor structure and reliability. *Psychological Reports, 64*(3 suppl), 1323–1326.

Johnson, E.J. & Goldstein, D. (2003). Do defaults save lives? *Science, 302*(5649), 1338–1339.

Jung, J.Y. & Mellers, B.A. (2016). American attitudes toward nudges. *Judgment And Decision Making, 11*(1), 62–74.

Kahneman, D. (2011). *Thinking, Fast and Slow.* New York: Farrar, Straus, and Giroux.

Kenworthy, J.B. & Miller, N. (2001). Perceptual asymmetry in consensus estimates of majority and minority members. *Journal of Personality and Social Psychology, 80*(4), 597–610.

Kikumbih, N., Hanson, K., Mills, A., Mponda, H. & Schellenberg, J.A. (2005). The economics of social marketing: the case of mosquito nets in Tanzania. *Social Science & Medicine, 60*(2), 369–381.

Kosters, M. & Van der Heijden, J. (2015). From mechanism to virtue: evaluating Nudge theory. *Evaluation: The International Journal of Theory, Research and Practice, 21*(3), 276–291. doi: 10.1177/1356389015590218.

Krueger, J. & Clement, R.W. (1994). The truly false consensus effect: an ineradicable and egocentric bias in social perception. *Journal of Personality and Social Psychology, 67*(4), 596–610.

Kubacki, K., Rundle-Thiele, S., Pang, B. & Buyucek, N. (2015). Minimizing alcohol harm: a systematic social marketing review (2000–2014). *Journal of Business Research, 68*(10), 2214–2222.

Langford, R. & Panter-Brick, C. (2013). A health equity critique of social marketing: where interventions have impact but insufficient reach. *Social Science & Medicine, 83*, 133–141.

Levy, D.E., Riis, J., Sonnenberg, L.M., Barraclough, S.J. & Thorndike, A.N. (2012). Food choices of minority and low-income employees: a cafeteria intervention. *American Journal of Preventive Medicine, 43*(3), 240–248. doi: 10.1016/j.amepre.2012.05.004.

Long, T., Taubenheim, A.M., Wayman, J., Temple, S. & Ruoff, B.A. (2008). The heart truth: using the power of branding and social marketing to increase awareness of heart disease in women. *Social Marketing Quarterly, 14*(3), 3–29.

Luca, N.R. & Suggs, L.S. (2013). Theory and model use in social marketing health interventions. *Journal of Health Communication, 18*(1), 20–40.

Michie, C. (2016). Childhood obesity: enough discussion, time for action. *British Journal of Diabetes, 16*(1), 4–5.

Michie, S., Richardson, M., Johnston, M., Abraham, C., Francis, J., Hardeman, W., Eccles, M.P., Cane, J. & Wood, C.E. (2013). The behavior change technique taxonomy (v1) of 93 hierarchically clustered techniques: building an international consensus for the reporting of behavior change interventions. *Annals of Behavioral Medicine, 46*, 81–95.

Miller, G.F., Gupta, S., Kropp, J.D., Grogan, K.A. & Mathews, A. (2016). The effects of pre-ordering and behavioral nudges on national school lunch program participants' food item selection. *Journal of Economic Psychology, 55*, 4–16. doi: 10.1016/j.joep.2016.02.010.

Moreira, M.T., Smith, L.A. & Foxcroft, D. (2009). Social norms interventions to reduce alcohol misuse in university or college students. *Cochrane Database of Systematic Reviews*, Issue 3. Art. No.: CD006748. doi: 10.1002/14651858.CD006748.pub2.

Nandi, A., Glymour, M.M. & Subramanian, S.V. (2014). Association among socioeconomic status, health behaviors, and all-cause mortality in the United States. *Epidemiology, 25*(2), 170–177.

O'Brien, K.M. (2012). Healthy, wealthy, wise? Psychosocial factors influencing the socioeconomic status–health gradient. *Journal of Health Psychology, 17*(8), 1142–1151.

Peterson, M., Abraham, A. & Waterfield, A. (2005). Marketing physical activity: lessons learned from a statewide media campaign. *Health Promotion Practice, 6*, 437–446.

Petrescu, D.C., Hollands, G.J., Couturier, D.L., Ng, Y.L. & Marteau, T.M. (2016). Public acceptability in the UK and USA of nudging to reduce obesity: the example of reducing sugar-sweetened beverages consumption. *PLOS ONE, 11*(6), e0155995.

Prestwich, A., Kellar, I., Conner, M., Lawton, R., Gardner, P. & Turgut, L. (2016). Does changing social influence engender changes in alcohol intake? A meta-analysis. *Journal of Consulting and Clinical Psychology, 84*, 845–860.

Prochaska, J.O. & DiClemente, C.C. (1986). Toward a comprehensive model of change. In W.R. Miller & N. Heather (Eds.), *Treating Addictive Behaviors* (pp. 3–27). New York: Plenum Press.

Rachlin, H. (2015). Choice architecture: a review of *Why Nudge: The Politics of Libertarian Paternalism*. *Journal of the Experimental Analysis of Behavior, 104*(2), 198–203. doi: 10.1002/jeab.163.

Richert, M.L., Webb, A.J., Morse, N.A., O'Toole, M.L. & Brownson, C.A. (2007). Move more diabetes: using lay health educators to support physical activity in a community based chronic disease self-management program. *The Diabetes Educator, 33*(Suppl 16), 179S–184S.

Robinson, E., Benwell, H. & Higgs, S. (2013). Food intake norms increase and decrease snack food intake in a remote confederate stud. *Appetite, 65*(1), 20–24.

Robinson, E., Thomas, J., Aveyard, P. & Higgs, S. (2014). What everyone else is eating: a systematic review and meta-analysis of the effect of informational eating norms on eating behavior. *Journal of the Academy of Nutrition and Dietetics*, *114*(3), 414–429.

Rutherford, W.H. (1985). The medical effects of seat-belt legislation in the United Kingdom: a critical review of the findings. *Archives of Emergency Medicine*, *2*(4), 221–223.

Scarapicchia, T.M., Sabiston, C.M., Brownrigg, M., Blackburn-Evans, A., Cressy, J., Robb, J. & Faulkner, G.E. (2015). MoveU? Assessing a social marketing campaign to promote physical activity. *Journal of American College Health*, *63*(5), 299–306.

Schwartz, S.H. (1977). Normative influence on altruism. In L. Berkowitz (Ed.), *Advances in Experimental Social Psychology, Vol. 10* (pp. 221–279). New York: Academic Press.

Schwartz, S.H. & Howard, J.A. (1984). Internalized values as moderators of altruism. In E. Staub, D. Bar-Tal, J. Karylowski & J. Reykowski (Eds.), *Development and Maintenance of Prosocial Behavior* (pp. 229–255). New York: Plenum.

Smith, D.V. & Delgado, M.R. (2015). Social nudges: utility conferred from others. *Nature Neuroscience*, *18*(6), 791–792.

Spotswood, F., French, J., Tapp, A. & Stead, M. (2012). Some reasonable but uncomfortable questions about social marketing. *Journal of Social Marketing*, *2*(3), 163–175.

Stasson, M. & Fishbein, M. (1990). The relation between perceived risk and preventive action: a within subject analysis of perceived driving risk and intentions to wear seatbelts. *Journal of Applied Social Psychology*, *20*(19), 1541–1557.

Strack, F. & Deutsch, R. (2004). Reflective and impulsive determinants of social behavior. *Personality and Social Psychology Review*, *8*(3), 220–247.

Stringhini, S., Sabia, S., Shipley, M., Brunner, E., Nabi, H., Kivimaki, M. & Singh-Manoux, A. (2010). Association of socioeconomic position with health behaviors and mortality. *Journal of the American Medical Association*, *303*, 1159–1166.

Sundquist, J., Malmstrom, M. & Johansson, S.E. (1999). Cardiovascular risk factors and the neighbourhood environment: a multilevel analysis. *International Journal of Epidemiology*, *28*, 841–845.

Sunstein, C.R. (2015). Nudges, agency, and abstraction: a reply to critics. *Review of Philosophy and Psychology*, *6*(3), 511–529. doi: 10.1007/s13164–015–0266–z.

Sutton, S.R. & Eiser, J.R. (1990). The decision to wear a seat belt: the role of cognitive factors, fear and prior behaviour. *Psychology and Health*, *4*(2), 111–123.

Thaler, R. & Sunstein, C. (2008). *Nudge: Improving Decisions about Health, Wealth, and Happiness*. London: Penguin.

Thomas, S., Fayter, D., Misso, K., Ogilvie, D., Petticrew, M., Sowden, A., ... & Worthy, G. (2008). Population tobacco control interventions and their effects on social inequalities in smoking: systematic review. *Tobacco Control*, *17*(4), 230–237.

Thorndike, A.N., Riis, J., Sonnenberg, L.M. & Levy, D.E. (2014). Traffic-light labels and choice architecture: promoting healthy food choices. *American Journal of Preventive Medicine*, *46*(2), 143–149. doi: 10.1016/j.amepre.2013.10.002.

Thorndike, A.N., Sonnenberg, L., Riis, J., Barraclough, S. & Levy, D.E. (2012). A 2-phase labeling and choice architecture intervention to improve healthy food and beverage choices. *American Journal of Public Health*, *102*(3), 527–533. doi: 10.2105/AJPH.2011.300391.

VanEpps, E.M. & Roberto, C.A. (2016). The influence of sugar-sweetened beverage warnings: a randomized trial of adolescents' choices and beliefs. *American Journal of Preventive Medicine*, *51*(5), 664–672.

Vartanian, L.R., Schwartz, M.B. & Brownell, K.D. (2007). Effects of soft drink consumption on nutrition and health: a systematic review and meta-analysis. *American Journal of Public Health*, *97*(4), 667–675.

Wiltshire, S., Bancroft, A., Amos, A. & Parry, O. (2001). 'They're doing people a service' – qualitative study of smoking, smuggling, and social deprivation. *BMJ*, *323*, 203–207.

Wrigley, N. (2002). 'Food deserts' in British cities: policy context and research priorities. *Urban Studies*, *39*(11), 2029–2040.

10

CHAPTER 10
TECHNOLOGY-BASED APPROACHES TO HEALTH BEHAVIOR CHANGE

OVERVIEW

In this chapter we consider an array of technological advances that have been employed in the service of behavior change. Technological advances, including the development of smartphones, provide a platform through which to change the health behaviors of individuals and groups at any point on any given day. In this chapter we examine the use of computers, the internet, smartphone applications (or apps) and other modern technologies in the context of health behavior change.

USING CLASSIC AND SOCIAL/ HEALTH COGNITION MODELS

In their review of internet-based interventions for health behavior change, Webb, Joseph, Yardley and Michie (2010) concluded that interventions that made greater use of theory were more likely to be effective. The trouble is that many of these types of interventions do not employ theory (e.g., Azar et al., 2013) and those that do typically do not target all constructs within the chosen theory (e.g., Hale, Capra & Bauer, 2015). However, there is vast potential for theory to contribute to informing what should be incorporated within these types of interventions (e.g., which behavior change techniques to use) and many technology-based interventions are, or could be, at least theory-inspired.

In a recent review of how theory has been applied to digital health interventions, Morrison (2015) highlights the role of many theories covered elsewhere in this book. For instance, the Elaboration Likelihood Model (see Chapter 7) proposes that more personally relevant messages are more likely to be centrally processed by recipients. Thus, message tailoring is a potentially useful element of technology-driven health behavior change. Similarly, stage-type models such as the Transtheoretical Model (see Chapter 2) lend themselves nicely to tailoring within information technology-based, electronic health (**eHealth**) and mobile health (**mHealth**) interventions. Indeed, this theory has been applied widely to inform technology-based interventions for behaviors such as physical activity (see LaPlante & Peng, 2011).

Self-Determination Theory (SDT; Ryan & Deci, 2000; see also Chapter 2) posits that increasing autonomous motivation, for example by providing choice rather than external pressure, maximizes the likelihood that behavior change is initiated and maintained in the future. Thus, employing strategies to promote a sense of choice within the architecture of technology-based interventions should maximize effectiveness. Choi, Noh and Park (2014) conducted a content analysis of smartphone smoking apps, in which they searched for elements that were conceptually related to SDT. The important concepts from this theory are autonomy, competence and relatedness to others. Of the more than 300 apps identified as being designed for smoking cessation, only about 10% of randomly selected apps had all three theoretical components.

Gamification, which involves the application of game-like features such as incentives, prizes, points, rewards and competitions to non-game contexts, has been increasingly utilized within web-based platforms (see Lister, West, Cannon, Sax & Brodegard, 2014). For example, mobile apps like *Fitocracy* provide points for workouts and badges for special physical activity achievements, while apps such as *Strava* encourage competition to promote physical activity, performance and fitness. The many aspects of gamification employed to make the behavior targeted in the intervention more fun is also consistent with SDT given its tenet that intrinsically rewarding behaviors are more likely to be maintained in the long term. And, of course, the use of incentives and rewards is very much in keeping with classic behaviorist models/operant conditioning (see Chapter 2) – rewarding behavior contingent on its performance should help to promote future, regular performance of the target behavior.

FIGURE 10.1 Wearable, mobile devices like smartwatches help to promote achievements in physical activity

A BRIEF HISTORY OF TECHNOLOGICAL AIDS TO HEALTH BEHAVIOR

In the early days of health and lifestyle apps (beginning around 2009), the majority of interventions and studies were concerned primarily with using the new technology to track and monitor behaviors, which as you know by now is an important part of self-regulation and behavior change (see, for example, Chapter 3). Even in those early days, researchers (e.g., Cummiskey, 2011) noted that the Apple App store already had many thousands of apps designed for health and fitness. It took a few more years before interventions were designed to help people make changes, such as eating healthier, quitting smoking or reducing alcohol intake. Many of these interventions were not grounded in any behavior change theory, but some were. For example, some attempted to leverage the power of social norms, or other forms of social influence (e.g., Gasser et al., 2006). Others focused on making health information and encouragement more available or cognitively accessible to users (e.g., Consolvo et al., 2008).

One early review of smartphone apps designed for behavioral health (see Luxton, McCann, Bush, Mishkind & Reger, 2011) provided an overview of the different kinds of targeted behaviors, which ranged from developmental, cognitive and mood disorders to substance use, eating and sleep disorders. Luxton et al. concluded that although such technology has emerged as an important component of behavioral health care, much work is still needed to ensure that healthcare policies and evidence-based practices keep up with the rapid acceleration of the technology. In their review of experimental studies testing internet-based interventions to improve health by promoting physical activity, healthy eating or reductions in smoking or drinking, Webb et al. (2010) reported that the benefits of internet-based interventions, on average, were small. However, studies that also incorporated text messages within their internet-based interventions yielded larger effects, highlighting the utility of this approach. In any case, one of the advantages of internet and mobile health apps is that they fit nicely within person-centered models of healthcare. These models emphasize individual involvement, autonomy and self-management in the direction and practice of health behaviors (see Handel, 2011). For example, mobile apps are especially useful for making users aware of their physical activity levels (Winter et al., 2012), and for giving support and encouragement in engaging in specific behavioral changes.

In the medical field, smartphone apps are typically found within three categories: clinical decision-making tools, patient education/support and enabling peripheral devices (Mertz, 2012). Clinical decision-making tools provide information and in doing so act, essentially, as a modern-day library. The supercomputer named 'Watson,' developed and built by IBM, made headlines when it won the $1 million first prize on the television show *Jeopardy!* in 2011. IBM has indicated that one of the primary future applications of the Watson project is to facilitate medical decision-making. One can imagine a future smartphone app that is connected, via the internet, to the vast databases that are becoming available to medical practitioners.

The second category of apps focuses on educating, encouraging and helping people to change their behaviors to become healthier. For example, Ahlers-Schmidt et al. (2010)

noted that the majority of parents would like to receive text message reminders about immunizations for their children, and are likely to have mobile phones (see also Peck, Stanton & Reynolds, 2014). We will discuss several of these interventions throughout this chapter. The final category involves using smartphones as a hub for peripheral devices that include heart rate monitors, blood glucose monitors and even blood alcohol concentration calculators. There is even an app and connecting device for using a smartphone as a personal, low-cost ultrasonic monitoring device. This can accompany some of the rising number of pregnancy and maternity-relevant apps (see Tripp et al., 2014).

TECHNOLOGICAL SOLUTIONS FOR PHYSICAL HEALTH AND BEHAVIOR CHANGE

The following sections explore the various technology-based solutions and interventions for some important categories of behavior change concerning physical health. These include alcohol consumption, smoking and general physical activity and diet.

CURBING ALCOHOL CONSUMPTION

There are many new (and not so new) internet and smartphone tools for helping people who want to cut back on alcohol. Websites such as www.CheckYourDrinking. net can be used to help curb drinking by providing feedback to users about how their drinking compares to their peers (to promote awareness of potentially high levels of drinking), whether their drinking is likely to be causing them harm (to motivate people to reduce their drinking to reduce their risk of alcohol-related harm) and how much their drinking is costing them (to promote awareness of the tangible costs of drinking). Smartphone apps have many of the same functions. *Drinkcontrol* is one such app that tracks how much a user drinks, how many calories those drinks represent and how much money has been spent on drinks.

There is some scientific evidence to support the use of websites and smartphone apps to change this behavior. For example, the Check Your Drinking (CYD) screener has been tested in a handful of experiments. Cunningham, Wild, Cordingley, van Mierlo and Humphreys (2009) conducted a randomized controlled trial comparing the use of CYD to a no-intervention control group. Those in the CYD condition reduced their problem drinking by around six drinks per week at the 6-month follow-up, compared to approximately a one drink per week reduction in the control group. Cunningham (2012) randomly assigned problem drinkers to the CYD website or to an extensive online help website for drinking (www.alcoholhelpcenter.net). Those in the CYD group reduced their problem drinking over time, but the effects were even stronger for those who used the AlcoholHelpCenter website (see also Hester, Lenberg, Campbell & Delaney, 2013, who examined the efficacy of another web-based intervention: www.overcomingaddictions.net).

With the advent of smartphone apps to help control alcohol and drinking behavior, research has now focused on comparing the effectiveness of web- versus app-based tools. In one such investigation, Gonzalez and Dulin (2015) compared a smartphone app monitoring intervention to an internet-based motivational intervention. Although their study was limited in sample size, they found that those in the self-administered smartphone app conditions did have a significant increase in the percentage of days abstinent from alcohol over six weeks, compared to the internet-based intervention.

As noted above, several more recent app-based interventions have been designed with behavior change theories in mind. Garnett, Crane, West, Brown and Michie (2015) noted that there is great potential for smartphone apps to engage users with evidence-based techniques, but that there is little research examining which behavior change techniques can be effective in such a medium. They argue that the behavior change techniques with the greatest likelihood of helping smartphone users reduce their alcohol intake were goal setting, self-monitoring, planning deliberate action and giving goal-relevant feedback. Dulin, Gonzalez and Campbell (2014) found that when drinkers used apps with a variety of theory-based features, they reported that the most useful features were those that helped them to monitor consumption, manage their cravings and identify the cues or triggers that made them most likely to drink. Participants in their study also showed a significant decrease in dangerous alcohol consumption during the study period.

Despite the benefits of such alcohol-related smartphone apps, caution is warranted with their use. For example, as Weaver, Horyniak, Jenkinson, Dietze and Lim (2013) noted, apps that track consumption and BAC levels are not very accurate for a variety of reasons, and many apps that can be found in the app stores actually encourage drinking behavior. There is a good chance that if you were to open your smartphone's app store right now and search for alcohol, you would find that a majority of them will facilitate drinking behavior (e.g., get wine delivery, how to mix any drink, learn drinking games etc.) rather than help to discourage or control it. On the other hand, there is evidence to support the idea that people who are committed to monitoring and controlling their drinking behavior can be helped in some ways by smartphone apps. Monk, Heim, Qureshi and Price (2015) showed that alcohol consumption recorded into a smartphone app by users during their drinking sessions was quite different from their retrospective reports of drinking, such as during the day after. Such apps could be useful for more accurate self-monitoring of alcohol consumption.

BURNING ISSUE BOX 10.1

HOW GOOD ARE INTERNET-BASED INTERVENTIONS FOR PROBLEM DRINKING? (CUNNINGHAM & VAN MIERLO, 2009)

1. *Is it fair to assume that they are effective?* Many internet-based interventions are based on brief face-to-face interventions. How well these internet-based interventions work compared to face-to-face interventions needs to be tested; you cannot assume that the internet-based intervention will work as well. Using face-to-face delivery, the healthcare professional can pick up on body language, tone of voice and hesitation in speech that can help inform delivery of the intervention. Such verbal or non-verbal cues can be difficult to integrate within online systems and this may reduce how effective they are.

2. *Temptation.* When you're receiving an intervention face-to-face, it's hard to get away! When using an online intervention, escape is possible with just one click. As a result, people may not complete all of the elements of the intervention and this may make the online intervention less effective (especially when used in the real world, outside the lab).

3. *Where should the intervention be tested?* The researcher could get people into the lab to test out the online intervention. The advantage of this approach is that participants are more likely to do what they're supposed to do (e.g., less likely to click away from the online intervention to check the latest football scores) and any technical issues can be resolved face-to-face – but this is problematic as testing the online intervention in the lab is moving away from the beauty of it being used outside of the lab. If you evaluate the intervention outside of the lab then you run the risk of temptation, technical issues putting the user off visiting the site and people generally not using the online intervention as intended. Delivering the intervention in the lab increases internal validity (the strength of control and being used as intended) but reduces external validity (how the results can be generalized to users in real-world settings outside of the lab).

4. *How should the participants be recruited?* Trials that recruit people online, while more closely mirroring the real world, typically use pre-post designs without control groups. As a consequence, the people entering the trial and using the online intervention may be people who would have reduced their drinking anyway. This is particularly true given the high motivation required to complete the online intervention and avoid the other temptations on offer through the internet. Recruiting people online to complete measures twice (before and after the intervention) can be extremely difficult leading to high risk of participants dropping out of the study and thus not returning to complete the follow-up measures to see how their drinking behavior (or other behaviors) have changed.

5. *More evidence is needed to support online interventions.* This is particularly true of studies conducted outside the lab, which mirror more closely how the intervention might be delivered outside the context of an experiment.

6. *Do online interventions work for everybody?* They may work for everybody but they may not. For example, they may work only for people experienced in using computers and the internet; they may work only for volunteers than for problem drinkers directly requested to use the site.

7. *Which parts of the online intervention work?* Online interventions are often complex and involve many different types of behavior change techniques. Without full factorial designs the use of each specific behavior change technique cannot be determined.

8. *How does the intervention work?* By identifying the psychological determinants of drinking (such as motivation and self-efficacy, confidence in being able to reduce drinking) and testing whether these determinants change or not can help to inform how the online intervention can be modified to make it more effective. For example, if the intervention only changes motivation and not self-efficacy then the addition of behavior change techniques most likely

to boost self-efficacy (such as modeling, Bandura, 1998) could make the intervention more effective in reducing problem drinking. There is a need for studies to evaluate whether the intervention changes psychological determinants of behavior. This can help explain why an intervention was effective or ineffective and suggest ways in which the intervention can be improved.

CURBING TOBACCO USE

For those who want to cut back on or give up cigarettes, there are also several websites, such as www.quitnet.com or www.quit4good.com, which provide both expert advice on quitting as well as social support networks. There are also now dozens of smartphone apps (including one connected to www.quitnet.com) to help users stop smoking.

Several technology-based interventions have been developed to help smokers quit cigarettes (see Muñoz et al., 2006). Free et al. (2011) randomly assigned nearly 6,000 British smokers to either an intervention or a control condition. In the intervention condition (called the text2stop intervention), they received five texts per day for the first five weeks, then three texts per week for another 26 weeks. These texts were personalized and emphasized the damages of smoking and the benefits of quitting. For example, on 'quit day', they received a text saying, 'This is it! – QUIT DAY, throw away all your fags. TODAY is the start of being QUIT forever, you can do it!' If participants ever felt a craving, they could send a 'crave' text and receive a text saying, 'Cravings last less than 5 minutes on average. To help distract yourself, try sipping a drink slowly until the craving is over.' In the control condition, participants received one text every two weeks with a simple thanks for their participation in the study. Those in the text2stop condition had a significantly higher rate of abstinence from smoking at 6 months, compared to the control condition.

In examining the effectiveness of a smartphone app, Ubhi, Michie, Kotz, Wong and West (2015) evaluated the abstinence rates in over 1,100 quitting smokers who used a smartphone app to quit, compared to a comparable national British sample of those who attempted to quit unaided. The app-based intervention employed gamification-type features such as rewarding users with 'stars' and 'hearts' on their phone for abstinent days, as well as information about how much money had been saved thus far during the period of abstinence. They found a small but significant effect, such that users of the app reported better abstinence rates than unaided controls. This research design was not experimental, however, so there is a need for randomized controlled trials (RCT; see Chapter 5).

As with apps for reducing alcohol intake, in more recent years the research designs for testing the effectiveness of quit-smoking apps tend to compare text messaging or internet-based interventions to those employing smartphone app usage. Buller, Borland, Bettinghaus, Shane and Zimmerman (2014) randomly assigned their smokers to a smartphone app condition or to a text messaging service condition to aid them in quitting tobacco. They found no strong differences between the conditions; using either service increased abstinence at 12 weeks, as long as participants actually used the service. Those who used the mobile services had a 47% rate of abstinence, compared to 20% for those who didn't follow through on their use. Buller et al. noted that the smartphone app, while theoretically grounded, was more complicated and difficult to use. By contrast, the text messages came to their normal text messaging inbox, requiring less effort or complication. Although these authors did not report differential rates of abstinence for those who fully complied with the smartphone app versus the text messaging service, there are theoretical reasons to suspect that the greater level of effort required by the smartphone app might yield better outcomes. Cognitive Dissonance Theory (Festinger, 1957; Harmon-Jones & Mills, 1999; Kenworthy, Miller, Collins, Read & Earleywine, 2011) proposes that when greater effort is required to achieve something, we cognitively justify that time and effort spent, resulting in a greater commitment to the decision. For example, Axsom and Cooper (1985) randomly assigned women at a weight loss clinic to a high effort or a low effort condition while undertaking weight loss counseling. Those in the high effort condition were asked to complete a series of cognitively demanding tasks whenever they came to the clinic. In the low effort condition, they completed much easier versions of the same tasks during their clinic visits. Those in the high effort condition lost significantly more weight, which was apparent at 3 months, 6 months and one year following initial treatment. The argument for why such findings were obtained is that the participants became more committed to the decision to lose weight after exerting greater amounts of effort to obtain the goal, compared to those who exerted less effort. Perhaps this principle of **effort justification** could be incorporated into smoking cessation programs as well.

Sometimes the development of technology can outpace evidence-based practice and awareness. For example, in Van Agteren, Carson, Jayasinghe and Smith's (2016) focus groups of Australian smokers and health professionals, both groups of participants showed enthusiasm for technology-based apps to quit smoking because they emphasize personal agency in quitting over pharmacology and counseling-based approaches. However, both groups also showed low experience and awareness of such interventions. Recent app-based interventions share a common theme in focusing on individual agency and self-determining their own choices and behavior.

Mindfulness and technology-aided smoking cessation

You have no doubt encountered the concept of *mindfulness* emerging as part of modern applied philosophy and meditation practices. There are several forms of Cognitive Behavior Therapy (CBT) for behavior change that involve the notion of mindfulness. Some of these CBT techniques are now being incorporated into technology-based solutions for behavior change. With respect to smoking cessation, the general formula for an intervention is to get mobile-based mindfulness training. In this context, mindfulness means developing a non-judgmental awareness of your discomfort and cravings for tobacco, accepting those affective states and drives. You are also taught to practice creating psychological distance between yourself and your cravings. Then, the focus is on behaving according to your values and specific plans. Thus, for research purposes abstinence is the primary outcome, but reductions in cravings and other negative emotions are of secondary importance to the mindfulness training.

In an early examination of these ideas, Jonathan Bricker and colleagues (2014) tested a smartphone app for smoking cessation using techniques from their model, called

Acceptance and Commitment Therapy (ACT). This work was important because it used a double-blind, randomized controlled trial design. The techniques from ACT involve training users to be willing to accept smoking cravings, and to be aware of and accept negative feelings and thoughts, while at the same time committing to values-based behavior change. The app based on ACT was compared to a comparison app using an existing technique used by the US National Cancer Institute. The app employing ACT techniques had better quit rates than the comparison group. Because this was a small-sample pilot test, there was not enough power for firm conclusions. However, there have been other tests of these ideas.

Heffner, Vilardaga, Mercer, Kientz and Bricker (2015), for instance, tested an ACT-based app called *SmartQuit*. In their study, they found that the features that best predicted smoking cessation were a) practicing the skill of letting urges and cravings pass and b) concretely planning to deal constructively with having urges or experiencing lapses. In this sense, the approach overlaps in many ways with the Relapse Prevention Model (see Chapter 2). In a similar exploration of these techniques, Zeng, Heffner, Copeland, Mull and Bricker (2016) tested a smartphone app-based intervention that is similar to mindfulness in that it also encourages awareness and acceptance of aversive internal states (craving) without using smoking to reduce those feelings. In their study, those who fully adhered to the app training components on a regular basis were four times more likely to quit smoking than those who did not adhere fully. The training components were having a quit plan, competing eight daily training modules, practicing the skill of letting 10 smoking urges pass and visiting the online coach (which provided social support and other practical exercises).

CHANGING PHYSICAL ACTIVITY AND DIET

Most developed or developing countries in the modern era are experiencing an epidemic of obesity. Obesity can generally be traced to the disruption of a simple formula of behavioral energy balance, or behaving in such a way as to disrupt the equilibrium between the energy taken in from food and the energy expended on daily activities. Although there are some other contributing factors (genetics, environmental conditions etc.), poor diet and inactivity – things that are largely within our personal control – are the primary causes of people becoming overweight or obese (see Popkin, Adair & Ng, 2012).

In addition to traditional means of self-regulation in diet and exercise, smartphone apps can also be useful for creating and maintaining exercise regimens and for monitoring the intake of calories. Fitness or activity apps take advantage of the built-in GPS capabilities and accelerometers of smartphones and allow users to track the number of steps taken, their speed, distance and progress towards other goals. Apps like *Runkeeper* or *Nike+ Running* also interface with social media websites, so you can share your workouts with friends and get feedback and encouragement from them as well. Apps are now capable of communicating with each other to integrate data about a person's physical activity, sleep patterns and diet. For example, the app *Myfitnesspal* can be used to track calories consumed, and it can also accept exercise data from the *Runkeeper* app, weight data from a Bluetooth-enabled scale and steps taken from a *Fitbit* device. Jared has been using

Myfitnesspal in conjunction with *Runkeeper* for several months now. The calories that he burns by cycling and jogging are synced up automatically from his *Runkeeper* app to his *Myfitnesspal* app, increasing his daily number of allowable food calories consumed. By staying at or below the daily limit of calories consumed (referred to as energy balance earlier), he was able to lose more than 20 pounds in about 100 days, and maintain it ever since by regular monitoring and balancing of calories consumed and calories burned!

In a recent RCT of smartphone-facilitated control of obesity, Allen et al. (2013) investigated the differences in weight loss for participants using counseling, self-monitoring of food intake via a smartphone app, and combinations of traditional counseling and smartphone app usage. In this study, those who had counseling and used the smartphone app were most likely to reduce their caloric intake and lose weight. Receiving only counseling without the smartphone app or using the smartphone app without counseling resulted in less favorable outcomes.

Given the relatively recent development of smartphone apps for tracking food intake, it is a reasonable question to ask how well they do in helping people to monitor and control their calorie consumption. Semper, Povey and Clark-Carter (2016) reviewed some studies that had examined this question, with a focus on studies with good research designs. For the majority of the studies that they reviewed, the apps were shown to be effective in their intended purpose, which was to facilitate efforts to lose weight. However, it is important to note here that although the apps were shown to be effective tools, they often did not produce a significant difference in weight loss from their respective control groups, which were either websites or traditional paper diaries of food intake. But the apps did tend to result in greater adherence to a self-monitoring program, compared to other methods, signaling their convenience. So, since participants using the smartphone apps dropped out of their regimens at a lower rate compared to other methods, this is encouraging for the future of apps in personal healthcare, especially given the growing ubiquity of smartphones.

Concerning the prevalence and use of physical activity apps, Bort-Roig, Gilson, Puig-Ribera, Contreras and Trost (2014) reviewed the evidence for the effectiveness of mobile devices to track and change behavior and noted that few employed RCT designs and large samples. They also found that the strategies employed generally tended not to be theory-based. However, there were some elements identified that were deemed to be useful in encouraging more physical activity. These elements included user-created physical activity profiles, the setting of concrete goals, getting social support and building social networks, receiving feedback in real time about one's activities and having online consultation with experts. However, many of these techniques are typically delivered in combination with other techniques and thus it is not always easy to identify effective behavior change techniques.

In a recent study, however, through a carefully crafted design, we managed to isolate the effect of manipulating competition on physical activity within a web-based intervention (Prestwich et al., 2017). In this study, physically inactive adults were randomized to one of three web-based conditions: a group encouraged to self-monitor their steps and who received basic feedback (self-monitoring group); a second, identical group who were additionally exposed to additional feedback to instigate competition (competition group); or a control group. Participants in the competition group increased their step counts over the 4-week intervention period significantly more than those in the control group and those in the self-monitoring group. Making people feel like they were in a competition, by showing participants a continually updated 'leaderboard' with those achieving the most daily steps appearing near the top and those with the least appearing towards the bottom, boosted steps via improvements in various types of motivation.

BURNING ISSUE BOX 10.2

ADVANTAGES AND DISADVANTAGES OF INTERNET- AND APP-BASED APPROACHES TO HEALTH BEHAVIOR CHANGE

Advantages

1. Reach. a) They can change health behaviors in a wide range of people given many people have access to the internet; b) they can be used by people who are reluctant to access local services involving face-to-face contact; c) based on these points, they could be used as a means of potentially reducing health inequalities (but see related disadvantage on smartphones).
2. Can be used to change health behaviors at any time.
3. They are a useful means of encouraging people to actively engage with their behavior change.
4. Generally low cost (e.g., compared to interventions delivered face-to-face).
5. Internet and mobile app approaches are potentially effective – at least in the short term (Afshin et al., 2016).
6. Potentially cost-effective given relatively low cost and potential to effectively change behavior.
7. Behavior change techniques and other features can be tailored to the needs of the individual.
8. Well-positioned to provide ongoing support over the longer term – especially if the content is engaging and easy to use.
9. It can be a more convenient and easy means to screen people for different illnesses (including those related to mental health). Linked to this, it can also reduce human data entry errors.
10. People tend to be more honest, especially about issues of a personal or sensitive nature, when disclosing online compared to face-to-face settings.
11. Reliability and validity of measures comparable to non-online methods (e.g., Donker, van Straten, Marks & Cuijpers, 2010).
12. With the growing ubiquity of smartphone-based health app usage, there is a corresponding potential for data aggregation, meaning that companies and governments can look for broader population patterns (for things like foods consumed, calories burned, physical activity levels, BMI etc.) as a function of different demographic categories and locations. This could make it easier and more efficient to create targeted interventions for certain groups (but see related disadvantage regarding ethics and privacy).

Disadvantages

1. Many (if not most) health apps have not yet been peer-reviewed by health professionals, so the theoretical and practical value of such apps can be questionable.
2. Most apps are not developed based on evidence-based models or on tested and validated theories of behavior change.
3. There are few tests of internet- and mobile app-based interventions over the longer term (e.g., past one year; see Afshin et al., 2016), although this is a broader problem applicable to non-technology focused health behavior change research.
4. The majority of these studies are done in high-income countries (Afshin et al., 2016), sometimes referred to as *WEIRD* countries (Henrich, Heine & Norenzayan, 2010), an abbreviation for Western, Educated, Industrialized, Rich and Democratic. It remains to be seen how well internet and smartphone tools can generalize to non-WEIRD countries and cultures.
5. Higgins (2016) notes that individuals must own a smartphone and have reliable and adequate cellular or wi-fi data plans, limiting access to those who can afford it.
6. Need to be well-designed and user-friendly.
7. Certain populations are still largely left out of the targeted client base, including the elderly who may not use a smartphone, and people with certain physical or intellectual disabilities that prevent them from engaging with standard smartphone apps.
8. There are complex ethical issues linked to issues such as maintaining privacy (see Clarke & Steele, 2015). In addition, some individuals may become upset after completing an online behavior change intervention or screening questionnaire (e.g., upon realizing that they may have symptoms) and their subsequent behaviors are out of researchers' control.
9. Relatedly, there is a risk that app developers, most of which are unregulated, may misuse personal data without users' knowledge or consent, such as selling it to third parties (see Jiya, 2015). Users also risk identity theft when collected data are not safeguarded properly.
10. Risk of **false positives/false negatives**. Deciding whether the cut-off scores for app-based screenings are the same as for traditional measures is not straightforward (Houston et al., 2001). Taking action on a screening score that is too low indicates a false positive and potentially wasted resources. Setting the cut-off scores too high, by contrast, can result in false negatives, or not acting on patients who may be in life-threatening situations.
11. Inaccurate app information may be relatively harmless in some cases (e.g., when a step counter slightly overestimates the number of steps a user takes) but could be dangerous (e.g., a food nutrient estimation tool underestimates the sugar, sodium or cholesterol content of foods, leading users to consume potentially harmful levels).
12. Encouraging even greater use of technological solutions – especially increased use of the internet – does little to curb the risk of problematic internet usage.

SCIENCE OF HEALTH BEHAVIOR CHANGE: IN ACTION

In Action Box 10.1 considers a randomized clinical trial by Gustafson et al. (2014) in which patients being treated for alcohol use disorders were randomly assigned to a treatment as usual condition or to treatment as usual supplemented by a smartphone app focusing on constructs from Self-Determination Theory (SDT; see Deci & Ryan, 2002). Their aim was to reduce the number of risky drinking days in their participants, who were patients leaving a treatment facility for alcohol use disorder. In the intervention condition, the smartphone app that participants used was designed to encourage the SDT constructs of autonomy, competence and relatedness to others. This was done via a variety of smartphone features. Proponents of the theory suggest that if individuals can gain competence, leverage intrinsic and autonomous motivation for behavior change and foster social support and encouragement from others, their behavior should change and be more long lasting.

SCIENCE OF HEALTH BEHAVIOR CHANGE

In Action Box 10.1

Study: Gustafson et al. (2014). *A Smartphone Application to Support Recovery From Alcoholism: A Randomized Clinical Trial*
Aim: To reduce the number of risky drinking days in patients leaving a residential alcohol use disorder treatment facility.
Method: Participants were randomly assigned to treatment as usual, or treatment as usual with a smartphone app focusing on Self-Determination Theory (SDT) constructs.
Results: At 4 months, 8 months and 12 months following discharge from the facility, participants in the smartphone-aided condition reported significantly fewer average risky drinking days than did those in the treatment as usual condition. The SDT construct of competence mediated the effects.
Authors' conclusion: Usual treatment for alcohol use disorders can be supplemented with SDT-based smartphone features.

THEORY AND TECHNIQUES OF HEALTH BEHAVIOR CHANGE	
BCTs	INTERVENTION: Treatment as usual, plus a smartphone app with features based on SDT. Based on Michie et al.'s (2013) taxonomy: 1.2 Problem solving; 2.2 Feedback on behavior; 2.3 Self-monitoring of behavior; 3.1 General social support; 3.2 Practical social support; 3.3 Emotional social support; 4.1 Instruction on how to perform a behavior; 5.4 Monitoring of emotional consequences of behavior; 6.2 Social comparison; 6.3 Information about others' approval; 7.1 Prompts/cues; 8.2 Behavior substitution; 11.2 Reduce negative emotions; 12.3 Avoidance/reducing exposure to cues for the behavior; 12.4 Distraction; 12.6 Body changes.
	CONTROL: Treatment as usual

Critical Skills Toolkit		
3.1	Does the design enable the identification of which BCTs are effective?	*No – the smartphone app condition contained several BCTs, and smartphone features were voluntary. Also, there was no indication that SDT components were provided to control (i.e., non-smartphone) participants. It is thus unclear which components are sufficient for behavior change.*
4.1	Is the intervention based on one theory or a combination of theories (if any at all)?	*The intervention was based on a single theory (SDT).*
	Are all constructs specified within a theory targeted by the intervention?	*Although the authors specify that the intervention would target autonomy, competence and relatedness (key constructs within SDT) and they specify a range of BCTs, the authors were not explicit about which specific constructs were targeted by which specific BCTs.*
	Are all behavior change techniques explicitly targeting at least one theory-relevant construct?	*No – the BCTs were not explicitly linked to a theory-relevant construct.*
	Do the authors test why the intervention was effective or ineffective (consistent with the underlying theory)?	*Yes – the authors tested mediation and showed that perceived competence at 4 months mediated the relationship between the intervention and risky drinking days at 8 months. Other theory-relevant constructs did not show evidence of mediating the outcomes.*
4.2	Does the study tailor the intervention based on the underlying theory?	*The authors note in the trial registry that the intervention would be tailored to the needs of the participants but it is not clear how this was done on the basis of the underlying theory.*
2.1, 2.2	What are the strengths/limitations of the underlying theory?	*SDT proposes three basic motivations for behavior, which overlap conceptually with other needs and motivations, such as the Need to Belong and Self-Efficacy. SDT perhaps undervalues the role of external influences on behavior and is rather complex relative to many other theories.*
THE METHODOLOGY OF HEALTH BEHAVIOR CHANGE		
5.1, 5.3, 5.4, 5.6	Methodological approach	*The study adopted an unblinded clinical trial with randomization. This means that both patients and physicians were aware of the condition into which participants were randomized.*

6.1	For experimental designs: is the study between-subjects, within-subjects or mixed?	*Mixed design because participants were allocated to one of two conditions (between-subjects) and then completed measures at multiple time-points (within-subjects). For advantages and disadvantages of this design, see Critical Skills Toolkit 6.1.*
5.2, 5.5	Are the measures reliable and valid?	*The authors did not cite any evidence that the primary outcome measure had been previously shown to be reliable or valid.*
5.5	May other variables have been manipulated other than the independent variable?	*Moderate to high risk. Although participants were randomly assigned to conditions, the smartphone intervention condition contained several features, which were voluntary. It is thus unclear which features of the intervention condition were responsible for the outcomes.*
	Non-random allocation of participants to condition	*Low risk. Participants were randomized to conditions on a 1:1 ratio using a computer program, in blocks of 8. The study design was registered at clinicaltrials.gov.*
	Blinding and allocation concealment	*Both participants and physicians were aware of allocation to conditions. Given the nature of the intervention, this was probably unavoidable. This may be problematic, however, given that drinking behaviors were measured by self-report rather than objectively.*
ANALYZING HEALTH BEHAVIOR CHANGE DATA		
6.2	Was the sample size calculated a-priori?	*Yes, the sample size was calculated a-priori, based on an estimated effect size.*
Fig. 6.1	Was the hypothesis tested with an appropriate statistical test?	*Yes.*
5.5, 6.4	Incomplete outcome data	*Low risk. The analysis accounted for missing data.*
5.5	Selective outcome reporting	*Low risk. The study's design and measures were registered at clinicaltrials.gov, and all of the measures reported in the Method section were analyzed and reported in the Results section.*
4.2	Lack of variability (non-sig. effects only)	*Not applicable – the participants in the intervention condition reported fewer risky drinking days compared to the control condition.*
6.3	Non-linear relationship (non-sig. effects only)	*Not applicable – effects significant.*

SUMMARY

This chapter examined emerging technological aids in the service of health behavior change, with a focus on the internet, smartphones and other modern technologies. We reviewed how a range of theories of behavior change can and should be incorporated into technological advances in health interventions. We covered the technological tools that have been developed for helping people to curb alcohol consumption, to quit smoking, to change their diets and physical activity levels. At the same time, we examined some relevant research evaluating the effectiveness of those approaches. We noted that many internet and smartphone apps lack a strong theoretical basis, and that in the future program developers and behavior change professionals should spend more time and energy collaborating for the benefit of users.

FURTHER READING

Bort-Roig, J., Gilson, N.D., Puig-Ribera, A., Contreras, R.S. & Trost, S.G. (2014). Measuring and influencing physical activity with smartphone technology: a systematic review. *Sports Medicine, 44*(5), 671–686. This paper reviews several studies examining the effectiveness of smartphone interventions to promote physical activity. Discusses the limitations and potential of such applications.

Deci, E. & Ryan, R. (Eds.) (2002). *Handbook of Self-Determination Research.* Rochester, NY: University of Rochester Press. This book gives an overview of Self-Determination Theory, discusses classic and contemporary research on the topic, and explores the general issue of motivation for human behavior.

Hekler, E.B., Michie, S., Pavel, M., Rivera, D.E., Collins, L.M., Jimison, H.B., Garnett, C., Parral, S. & Spruijt-Metz, D. (2016). Advancing models and theories for digital behavior change interventions. *American Journal of Preventive Medicine, 51*(5), 825–832. Attempts to guide the use of theory in building digital interventions for health behavior. Focuses on variations between individuals and on changes to behavior over time.

Higgins, J.P. (2016). Smartphone applications for patients' health and fitness. *The American Journal of Medicine, 129*(1), 11–19. Written from a physician's perspective, this paper gives an overview of smartphone apps that can be useful in helping patients to reach their goals, including those for diet, exercise and stress management.

Lathia, N., Pejovic, V., Rachuri, K.K., Mascolo, C., Musolesi, M. & Rentfrow, P. J. (2013). Smartphones for large-scale behavior change interventions. *IEEE Pervasive Computing, 12*(3), 66–73. Describes the multidisciplinary project called UBhave (www.ubhave.org), which explores the use of mobile phones and social networking in Digital Behavior Change Interventions (DBCIs).

GLOSSARY

Effort justification: a concept from Cognitive Dissonance Theory describing a change in attitudes, commitment or loyalty towards something, which comes about due to increased time, energy and effort spent towards it.

eHealth: refers to using information technology (e.g., internet, gaming, robotics, virtual reality etc.) to promote health behaviors.

Gamification: refers to the use of game-like features such as incentives, prizes, points, rewards, status, connectedness and competitions to promote non-game behaviors, such as health behaviors.

False negative: when a test result indicates that some condition has not been met or fulfilled, when in actuality it has. This is also referred to as a *Type 2 error.*

False positive: when a test result indicates that some condition has been met or

fulfilled, when in actuality it has not. This is also referred to as a *Type 1 error.*

mHealth: refers to wireless or mobile apps and devices, including the use of social media, to promote and deliver health-related information and services.

Self-Determination Theory: this theory concerns the degree to which our actions are intrinsically- or self-motivated. Proponents argue that there are three general, intrinsic, psychological motivations, namely autonomy, competence and relatedness to others.

REFERENCES

Afshin, A., Babalola, D., Mclean, M., Yu, Z., Ma, W., Chen, C.Y., ... & Mozaffarian, D. (2016). Information technology and lifestyle: a systematic evaluation of internet and mobile interventions for improving diet, physical activity, obesity, tobacco, and alcohol use. *Journal of the American Heart Association, 5*(9), e003058.

Ahlers-Schmidt, C.R., Chesser, A., Hart, T., Paschal, A., Nguyen, T. & Wittler, R.R. (2010). Text messaging immunization reminders: feasibility of implementation with low-income parents. *Preventive Medicine, 50*(5), 306–307.

Allen, J.K., Stephens, J., Dennison Himmelfarb, C.R., Stewart, K.J. & Hauck, S. (2013). Randomized controlled pilot study testing use of smartphone technology for obesity treatment. *Journal of Obesity, 2013,* art.151597, 7pp. doi: 10.1155/2013/151597.

Axsom, D. & Cooper, J. (1985). Cognitive dissonance and psychotherapy: the role of effort justification in inducing weight loss. *Journal of Experimental Social Psychology, 21,* 149–160.

Azar, K.M., Lesser, L.I., Laing, B.Y., Stephens, J., Aurora, M.S., Burke, L.E. & Palaniappan, L.P. (2013). Mobile applications for weight management: theory-based content analysis. *American Journal of Preventive Medicine, 45,* 583–589.

Bandura, A. (1998). Health promotion from the perspective of social cognitive theory. *Psychology & Health, 13,* 623–649.

Bort-Roig, J., Gilson, N.D., Puig-Ribera, A., Contreras, R.S. & Trost, S.G. (2014). Measuring and influencing physical activity with smartphone technology: a systematic review. *Sports Medicine, 44*(5), 671–686.

Bricker, J.B., Mull, K.E., Kientz, J.A., Vilardaga, R., Mercer, L.D., Akioka, K.J. & Heffner, J.L. (2014). Randomized, controlled pilot trial of a smartphone app for smoking cessation using acceptance and commitment therapy. *Drug and Alcohol Dependence, 143,* 87–94.

Buller, D.B., Borland, R., Bettinghaus, E.P., Shane, J.H. & Zimmerman, D.E. (2014). Randomized trial of a smartphone mobile application compared to text messaging to support smoking cessation. *Telemedicine and e-Health, 20*(3), 206–214.

Choi, J., Noh, G.Y. & Park, D.J. (2014). Smoking cessation apps for smartphones: content analysis with the self-determination theory. *Journal of Medical Internet Research*, *16*(2), e44.

Clarke, A. & Steele, R. (2015). Smartphone based public health information systems: anonymity, privacy and intervention. *Journal of the Association for Information Science and Technology*, *66*(12), 2596–2608.

Consolvo, S., McDonald, D.W., Toscos, T., Chen, M.Y., Froehlich, J., Harrison, B. ... & Smith, I. (2008). Activity sensing in the wild: a field trial of ubifit garden. In *Proceedings of the SIGCHI Conference on Human Factors in Computing Systems* (CHI '08) (pp. 1797–1806). New York: ACM. doi.org/10.1145/1357054.1357335.

Cummiskey, M. (2011). There's an app for that smartphone use in health and physical education. *Journal of Physical Education, Recreation & Dance*, *82*(8), 24–30.

Cunningham, J.A. (2012). Comparison of two internet-based interventions for problem drinkers: randomized controlled trial. *Journal of Medical Internet Research*, *14*(4), e107.

Cunningham, J.A. & van Mierlo, T. (2009). Methodological issues in the evaluation of internet-based interventions for problem drinking. *Drug and Alcohol Review*, *28*, 12–17.

Cunningham, J.A., Wild, T.C., Cordingley, J., van Mierlo, T. & Humphreys, K. (2009). A randomized controlled trial of an internet-based intervention for alcohol abusers. *Addiction*, *104*, 2023–2032.

Deci, E. & Ryan, R. (Eds.). (2002). *Handbook of Self-Determination Research*. Rochester, NY: University of Rochester Press.

Donker, T., van Straten, A., Marks, I. & Cuijpers, P. (2010). Brief self-rated screening for depression on the internet. *Journal of Affective Disorders*, *122*(3), 253–259.

Dulin, P.L., Gonzalez, V.M. & Campbell, K. (2014). Results of a pilot test of a self-administered smartphone-based treatment system for alcohol use disorders: usability and early outcomes. *Substance Abuse*, *35*(2), 168–175.

Festinger, L. (1957). *A Theory of Cognitive Dissonance*. Evanston, IL: Row, Peterson.

Free, C., Knight, R., Robertson, S., Whittaker, R., Edwards, P., Zhou, W. & ... Roberts, I. (2011). Smoking cessation support delivered via mobile phone text messaging (txt2stop): a single-blind, randomised trial. *The Lancet*, *378*(9785), 49–55.

Garnett, C., Crane, D., West, R., Brown, J. & Michie, S. (2015). Identification of behavior change techniques and engagement strategies to design a smartphone app to reduce alcohol consumption using a formal consensus method. *JMIR mHealth and uHealth*, *3*(2), e73.

Gasser, R., Brodbeck, D., Degen, M., Luthiger, J., Wyss, R. & Reichlin, S. (2006). Persuasiveness of a mobile lifestyle coaching application using social facilitation. In W.A. IJsselsteijn, Y.A.W. de Kort, C. Midden, B. Eggen & E. van den Hoven (Eds.), *Persuasive Technology. PERSUASIVE 2006. Lecture Notes in Computer Science*, Vol. 3962. Berlin and Heidelberg: Springer. doi: 10/1007/11755494_5.

Gonzalez, V.M. & Dulin, P.L. (2015). Comparison of a smartphone app for alcohol use disorders with an internet-based intervention plus bibliotherapy: a pilot study. *Journal of Consulting and Clinical Psychology*, *83*(2), 335–345.

Gustafson, D.H., McTavish, F.M., Chih, M.Y., Atwood, A.K., Johnson, R.A., Boyle, M.G., ... & Shah, D. (2014). A smartphone application to support recovery from alcoholism: a randomized clinical trial. *JAMA Psychiatry*, *71*(5), 566–572.

Hale, K., Capra, S. & Bauer, J. (2015). A framework to assist health professionals in recommending high-quality apps for supporting chronic disease self-management: illustrative assessment of type 2 diabetes apps. *JMIR mHealth and uHealth*, *3*(3), e87.

Handel, M.J. (2011). mHealth (mobile health) – using apps for health and wellness. *EXPLORE: The Journal of Science and Healing*, *7*(4), 256–261.

Harmon-Jones, E. & Mills, J. (Eds.). (1999). *Cognitive Dissonance: Progress on a Pivotal Theory in Social Psychology*. Washington, DC: American Psychological Association.

Heffner, J.L., Vilardaga, R., Mercer, L.D., Kientz, J.A. & Bricker, J.B. (2015). Feature-level analysis of a novel smartphone application for smoking cessation. *The American Journal of Drug and Alcohol Abuse*, *41*(1), 68–73.

Henrich, J., Heine, S.J. & Norenzayan, A. (2010). The weirdest people in the world? *Behavioral and Brain Sciences, 33*(2–3), 61–83.

Hester, R.K., Lenberg, K.L., Campbell, W. & Delaney, H.D. (2013). Overcoming addictions, a web-based application, and SMART recovery, an online and in-person mutual help group for problem drinkers, Part 1: three-month outcomes of a randomized controlled trial. *Journal of Medical Internet Research, 15*(7), 11–25. doi: 10.2196/jmir.2565.

Higgins, J.P. (2016). Smartphone applications for patients' health and fitness. *The American Journal of Medicine, 129*(1), 11–19.

Houston, T.K., Cooper, L.A., Vu, H.T., Kahn, J., Toser, J. & Ford, D.E. (2001). Screening the public for depression through the internet. *Psychiatric Services, 52*(3), 362–367.

Jiya, T. (2015). A realisation of ethical concerns with smartphone personal health monitoring apps. *ACM SIGCAS Computers and Society, 45*(3), 313–317.

Kenworthy, J.B., Miller, N., Collins, B.E., Read, S.J. & Earleywine, M. (2011). A trans-paradigm theoretical synthesis of cognitive dissonance theory: illuminating the nature of discomfort. *European Review of Social Psychology, 22*, 36–113.

LaPlante, C. & Peng, W. (2011). A systematic review of e-Health interventions for physical activity: an analysis of study design, intervention characteristics, and outcomes. *Telemedicine and e-Health, 17*(7), 1–15.

Lister, C., West, J.H., Cannon, B., Sax, T. & Brodegard, D. (2014). Just a fad? Gamification in health and fitness apps. *JMIR Serious Games, 2*(2), e9.

Luxton, D.D., McCann, R.A., Bush, N.E., Mishkind, M.C. & Reger, G.M. (2011). mHealth for mental health: integrating smartphone technology in behavioral healthcare. *Professional Psychology: Research and Practice, 42*(6), 505–512.

Mertz, L. (2012). Ultrasound? Fetal monitoring? Spectrometer? There's an app for that! *IEEE Pulse, 3*, 16–21.

Michie, S., Richardson, M., Johnston, M., Abraham, C., Francis, J., Hardeman, W., Eccles, M.P., Cane, J. & Wood, C.E. (2013). The behavior change technique taxonomy (v1) of 93 hierarchically clustered techniques: building an international consensus for the reporting of behavior change interventions. *Annals of Behavioral Medicine, 46*, 81–95.

Monk, R.L., Heim, D., Qureshi, A. & Price, A. (2015). 'I have no clue what I drunk last night': using smartphone technology to compare in-vivo and retrospective self-reports of alcohol consumption. *PLOS ONE, 10*(5), e0126209.

Morrison, L.G. (2015). Theory-based strategies for enhancing the impact and usage of digital health behavior change interventions: a review. *Digital Health, 1*, 2055207615595335.

Muñoz, R.F., Lenert, L.L., Delucchi, K., Stoddard, J., Perez, J.E., Penilla, C. & Pérez-Stable, E.J. (2006). Toward evidence-based internet interventions: a Spanish/English web site for international smoking cessation trials. *Nicotine & Tobacco Research, 8*, 77–87.

Peck, J.L., Stanton, M. & Reynolds, G.E. (2014). Smartphone preventive health care: parental use of an immunization reminder system. *Journal of Pediatric Health Care, 28*(1), 35–42.

Popkin, B.M., Adair, L.S. & Ng, S.W. (2012). Global nutrition transition and the pandemic of obesity in developing countries. *Nutrition Reviews, 70*(1), 3–21.

Prestwich, A., Conner, M., Morris, B., Finlayson, G., Sykes-Muskett, B. & Hurling, R. (2017). Do web-based competitions promote physical activity? Randomized controlled trial. *Psychology of Sport & Exercise, 29*, 1–9.

Ryan, R.M. & Deci, E.L. (2000). Self-determination theory and the facilitation of intrinsic motivation, social development, and well-being. *American Psychologist, 55*(1), 68–78.

Semper, H.M., Povey, R. & Clark-Carter, D. (2016). A systematic review of the effectiveness of smartphone applications that encourage dietary self-regulatory strategies for weight loss in overweight and obese adults. *Obesity Reviews, 17*(9), 895–906.

Tripp, N., Hainey, K., Liu, A., Poulton, A., Peek, M., Kim, J. & Nanan, R. (2014). An emerging model of maternity care: smartphone, midwife, doctor? *Women and Birth, 27*(1), 64–67.

Ubhi, H.K., Michie, S., Kotz, D., Wong, W.C. & West, R. (2015). A mobile app to aid smoking cessation: preliminary evaluation of SmokeFree28. *Journal of Medical Internet Research, 17*(1), e17.

Van Agteren, J., Carson, K., Jayasinghe, H. & Smith, B. (2016). The barriers and facilitators to effective use of a smartphone application for smoking cessation by health professionals and smokers. *Respirology*, *21*(Suppl. 2), 42. doi: 10.1111/resp.12754_11.

Weaver, E.R., Horyniak, D.R., Jenkinson, R., Dietze, P. & Lim, M.S. (2013). 'Let's get wasted!' and other apps: characteristics, acceptability, and use of alcohol-related smartphone applications. *JMIR mHealth and uHealth*, *1*(1), e9.

Webb, T.L., Joseph, J., Yardley, L. & Michie, S. (2010). Using the internet to promote health behavior change: a meta-analysis of the impact of theoretical basis, use of behavior change techniques, and mode of delivery on efficacy. *Journal of Medical Internet Research*, *12*(1), e4.

Winter, S.J., Hekler, E.B., Grieco, L.A., Chen, F., Pollitt, S., Youngman, K. & King, A.C. (2012). Teaching old dogs new tricks: perceptions of SmartPhone-naïve midlife and older adults about using SmartPhones and SmartPhone applications to improve health behaviors. *Annals of Behavioral Medicine*, *43*(1), s41.

Zeng, E.Y., Heffner, J.L., Copeland, W.K., Mull, K.E. & Bricker, J.B. (2016). Get with the program: adherence to a smartphone app for smoking cessation. *Addictive Behaviors*, *63*, 120–124.

11

CHAPTER 11
FUTURE DIRECTIONS

OVERVIEW

The science underpinning health behavior change is clearly at a relatively early stage of development. Much more remains to be learned. Highlighting all possible future directions in the area of health behavior change, therefore, is a challenging task. So, in this chapter, we focus our attention on three broad themes: 1. What factors influence intervention success and how should these be characterized? 2. How can health behavior change be achieved on a widespread, global stage to tackle current and emergent health issues? 3. Given the need to address critical questions well enough and quickly enough, how can the science of behavior change develop more quickly?

IDENTIFYING AND CHARACTERIZING FACTORS THAT INFLUENCE INTERVENTION SUCCESS

In this book, we have covered a range of factors that can influence how successful an intervention is for health behavior change. An obvious component of this is the content of the intervention (see, for example, Chapter 3) and possibly the underlying theory (see, in particular, Chapters 2 and 4), how the intervention is tailored to individuals or groups (see, for example, Chapter 3) and the characteristics of individuals receiving the intervention such as their socio-economic status (see Burning Issue Box 7.1). In addition, intervention effectiveness could be improved by delivering it with greater intensity or for more time, or via interventionists with specific characteristics such as high credibility or expertise (see, for example, the Elaboration Likelihood Model covered in Chapter 7).

There are other factors that are likely to be important in achieving health behavior change but have been covered comparatively less within the existing literature. For instance, in a recent review, Prestwich et al. (2017) demonstrated that interventions to reduce smoking in patients awaiting elective surgery were more effective when delivered by nurses. The mode of delivery, setting and characteristics of the target behavior itself are other examples of factors that could modify the success of a behavioral intervention and represent important areas for future research (see Burning Issue Box 11.1 and also Dombrowski, O'Carroll & Williams, 2016). Taxonomies – like the ones used for behavior change techniques (BCTs) – do not currently exist for many other intervention elements.

BURNING ISSUE BOX 11.1

WHICH FACTORS INFLUENCE THE SUCCESS OF A BEHAVIORAL INTERVENTION?

Factor	Examples
Content	Behavior change techniques
Theory	Whether the behavior change techniques are consistent with the underlying theory; are all appropriate theoretical constructs targeted? Which theory was applied?
Mode of delivery	Is the intervention delivered directly to participants face-to-face or through a mediated form (e.g., computer; post)? Delivered by a group vs. an individual; delivered to a group vs. to an individual
Intensity/ duration	How many sessions were delivered over what time frame? How long was each session? What was the total amount of contact? Over what period of time did participants have access to intervention content? Did the intervention intensity increase, decrease or remain stable over time?
Interventionist	Sex; age; years of experience; level of training; profession; whether they are part of the research team or whether they have been trained by the research team; credibility
Participants	Behavior levels before intervention; their underlying cognitions and feelings; their level of support (from other people and/or aspects of the environment); demographics such as socio-economic status, age, sex
Tailoring	What features of the intervention (e.g., content, mode of delivery, intensity/duration) were tailored, and on what basis (e.g., characteristics of the participants, setting etc.)? How was the underlying theory used to tailor the intervention?
Setting	Is the setting familiar vs. unfamiliar to the participants and/or interventionist? Medical vs. non-medical? Educational vs. non-educational? Home-based or not?
Cost	Financial cost; time cost; do the benefits outweigh the costs?
Acceptability	Is the intervention acceptable to those delivering it (interventionists), those receiving it (target population) and those endorsing it (e.g., policymakers)? Are there ethical issues and can these be adequately resolved?
Scalability	Are the resources (e.g., financial, people) required to deliver the intervention on a larger scale available and sufficient? To how many people, groups, countries, conditions etc. can the intervention be applied and at what cost?

Sustainability	How will the target population continue to receive intervention content over the long term? Is this achievable? Are there any barriers (e.g., cost, materials, other resources, desire to sustain the intervention)?
Behavior	One-off behavior (e.g., immunization) vs. repeated behavior (e.g., exercise; diet); health promoting vs. health risk vs. detection; level of ease/difficulty; habitual vs. non-habitual; whether the behavior generates short-term vs. long-term costs/benefits
Fidelity	Were the other important characteristics (e.g., content, theory, mode of delivery, intensity/duration) utilized as intended? If not, how did they differ? What proportion of participants was affected?
Measurement	Is the behavior assessed while the intervention is still being delivered or after the intervention has stopped? Does the measure capture behavior throughout the assessment period or just at specific stages? Is the measure reliable? Is the measure valid?
Comparison group	On which features (e.g., content, mode, intensity/duration) does the comparison group differ from the intervention and how do they differ? Over what period of time did the intervention and comparison groups differ?
Risk of bias	Can specific risks of bias (e.g., lack of randomization; lack of blinding) account for the intervention effects? Is the intervention effective when risk of bias is low?

To characterize the different elements of health behavior interventions in a way that has been achieved for BCTs, however, is likely to be challenging. For example, producing a taxonomy that can be used reliably by a wide range of users is no mean feat. Rather disappointingly, results from Wood et al. (2015) suggest that the most comprehensive taxonomy of BCTs produced to date (by Michie et al., 2013) is generally not used reliably before – or even after – training. Moreover, in these evaluations, only some of the BCTs were used rather than all 93 BCTs. If the studies were repeated using the full 93-item taxonomy, it seems likely that the reliability may drop further. For taxonomies that comprise fewer techniques, reliability may be better. However, direct comparisons of these different taxonomies are needed to establish the most reliable option. Given the least reliable option could be the taxonomy with the most techniques, there may need to be some trade-off between reliability and comprehensiveness (number of BCTs) in identifying the most appropriate taxonomy. The most appropriate taxonomy may also differ for different behaviors with taxonomies designed for smoking (Michie, Hyder, Walia & West, 2011), for instance, more likely to be suitable for smoking research than more general taxonomies that were designed for use across different behaviors (e.g., Michie et al., 2013). Taxonomies for mode of delivery, setting, types of behavior or other factors outlined in Burning Issue Box 11.1 would face similar challenges and would do so from a 'standing start' given the lack of work in these areas.

Characterizing specific features of interventions can be useful when attempting to synthesize the available evidence through systematic review and/or meta-analysis (see Chapters 5 and 6) as it can be used as a way to identify features in which certain studies are sufficiently similar and other studies that differ. These studies can then be grouped and compared to identify whether the presence or absence of a particular feature influences the success of an intervention.

However, Ogden (2016) has argued that taking this approach is overly simplistic as well as problematic if the evidence that is being synthesized is weak, reported badly (an issue that we consider later in this chapter) and/or based on what was intended to be done within the intervention rather than what was actually done (i.e., the fidelity of the intervention). Thus, Ogden argues that the time to use approaches such as the BCTTv1 taxonomy of behavior change techniques (Michie et al., 2013) may be in the future rather than now.

There is no doubt that interventions are very complex and that intervention content is only one component that can influence the success of an intervention (see Burning Issue Box 11.1). In addition, when synthesizing evidence using taxonomies such as BCTTv1, there are risks that certain BCTs will be confounded with other BCTs (i.e., a specific BCT may *appear* to be effective – but not actually be – simply because it is typically delivered alongside a different BCT that is effective) and other intervention features. Taking account of the potential risk of confounds is possible though, for example through relatively advanced statistical techniques such as multivariate meta-regressions (e.g., see Prestwich et al., 2014a, and Prestwich et al., 2016). We agree with Ogden (2016), however, that the task of synthesizing evidence through taxonomies will be easier and more fruitful in the future when there are more studies conducted that are well-reported and of higher quality. So, hopefully, the scientific evidence will continue to grow at a rapid rate in the future and the benefits of synthesizing evidence through taxonomies will become even more useful.

ACHIEVING HEALTH BEHAVIOR CHANGE ON A GLOBAL STAGE

Scalability (how well an intervention can be delivered on a larger, mass scale), acceptability (the extent to which people are willing to try the intervention, use the intervention, endorse or tolerate it) and sustainability (how well an intervention can achieve success in the longer term) represent vital factors (in addition to intervention effectiveness) that influence the potential wider impact that an intervention can achieve at the level of the wider population. Such factors are crucial the world over but are particularly important in lower-income countries which face issues such as environmental hazards (e.g., droughts, land degradation) and increases in chronic, non-communicable disease such as cardiovascular disease and cancer with relatively few resources. Achieving widespread behavior change to facilitate better health across large populations is a global, grand challenge for now and in the future.

An important area of focus is the most effective means to change health behaviors and maintain any change. Maintenance of change is important because for many health promotion behaviors such as physical activity or healthy eating the health benefits only accrue after long-term performance of these behaviors. Increasingly studies focus on impacts on behavior change over longer time intervals with 6-month and 12-month follow-up periods now quite common. Further research might usefully look at the ways in which current interventions might be supplemented to promote long-term change. Strategies that are likely to be low-cost, scalable, acceptable and sustainable, like implementation intentions (e.g., see Chapter 3), may be particularly helpful. There are many issues to be addressed in relation to these techniques. For instance, the long-term effects of implementation intentions may be enhanced if they are repeated at regular intervals (e.g., Conner & Higgins, 2010). However, one factor that is likely to be key is maintaining the motivation to engage in the behavior because we know that implementation intentions are more effective for those with strong motivation to perform the behavior.

Another efficient way to achieve greater changes in health behaviors is to consider how change on one health promotion behavior (e.g., exercise) is independent or related to changes in other health behaviors (e.g., drinking alcohol). If change in one health promoting behavior diffuses to other related behaviors this may allow synergy among interventions. However, if individuals compensate for improvements in one health promoting health behavior by doing less of another or more of the health risking behaviors (e.g., rewarding yourself for going running by having a few more alcoholic drinks) then we may need to think more carefully about the impact on overall health of specific health behavior interventions. A recent review highlights the issue that while attempting to change a small number of behaviors together may be beneficial, trying to tackle many health behaviors simultaneously can lead less change overall (Wilson et al., 2015).

So, impact on a global stage could be achieved by delivering interventions with the right qualities linked to characteristics such as scalability and acceptability. We also highlight that tackling multiple health behaviors simultaneously may be an efficient approach, albeit complex. Critically, however, in the face of a number of known and current unknown health challenges across low- and middle-income countries, in particular, but also in high-income countries, there is a need for the science of health behavior change to continue its momentum and preferably to speed up its development. We turn to this issue next.

ACCELERATING THE RATE OF SCIENTIFIC PROGRESS

WITH BETTER THEORIES AND TECHNIQUES

Evidence regarding the effect of using theory on intervention success is rather mixed (Prestwich, Webb & Conner, 2015). While some reviews suggest that using theory increases intervention success (e.g., Webb, Joseph, Yardley & Michie, 2010) other reviews suggest little or no benefit in terms of intervention success (e.g., Prestwich et al., 2014b). Part of the reason for this may be the quality of theories upon which the interventions are based. Many theories are built on correlational data. This approach has a number of inherent weaknesses (e.g., see Chapter 5) and hinder attempts to establish which theories are useful. In addition, theories are not often directly compared to help determine which theories work best in different situations. In the future, there will need to be more experimental tests of theories to provide a stronger basis for establishing which theories work best, for whom and in which situations. For some theories there are few, if any, experimental tests. For example, tests of integrated theories, such as Fishbein et al. (2001), are needed (see Chapter 2) to identify whether these combined theories are superior to (and as usable as) individual theories. In relation to dual process models (e.g., Strack & Deutsch, 2004; see Chapter 2), more studies are needed that attempt to manipulate both reflective and impulsive systems to create more sustained change than merely targeting either reflective or impulsive systems.

In addition, Sheeran, Klein and Rothman (2017) highlight the issue that few studies attempt to identify the situations under which aspects of theories *fail*. For example, highlighting situations when self-efficacy does not influence behavior could be a means to improve the precision and specificity of models/theories that highlight the role of self-efficacy in influencing behavior. This type of mindset may represent an important approach for future research.

WITH BETTER REPORTING AND MEASURES

In the future, methodological statements such as the **CONSORT** and **PRISMA** guidelines will be adopted more widely across the field of health behavior change, encouraging the standard reporting of key methodological and statistical information for randomized controlled trials and systematic reviews respectively. Similarly, use of BCT taxonomies, as well as similar approaches to help ensure use of theory is clearly reported (Prestwich et al., 2015), will also improve the reporting of techniques and theories. Clear reporting makes it easier to identify what has and what has not been tested and thus gaps in knowledge can be more easily detected.

Furthermore, as Sheeran et al. (2017) note, there are several issues with measurement of constructs within theories. These include: relying on self-reports which are subject to a range of biases; measuring constructs at a single moment in time when the construct is more dynamic and variable over time (i.e., an individual may strongly intend to exercise at one point in the day but if assessed at a different time in the day, may not intend to exercise at all); lack of standardization such that different researchers use different measures to assess the same construct (see also Spruijt-Metz et al., 2015).

Just as there have been attempts to standardize the use of BCTs, there have been steps taken to encourage researchers to use standard, reliable measures of constructs including those highlighted in health behavior models/theories such as the Patient-Reported Outcomes Measurement Information System (PROMIS; Carle, Riley, Hays & Cella, 2015) and the Grid-Enabled Measures (GEM) project (Moser et al., 2011). As well as improving reliability and validity, the standardization of measures would help in comparing the efficacy of different interventions across studies in the future. There have also been recent advances in measures that do not rely on self-report such as the neurological measures that we highlight later in this chapter, and mobile technologies that permit continuous assessment of constructs in real time. These constructs are not just limited to behavior (e.g., physical activity assessed through accelerometers, diet choices through purchase transactions) but also individuals' thoughts and feelings (via social media, self-reports via apps, physiological measures etc.) and their environment (e.g., via **mobile sensing**).

WITH COMPUTER SCIENCE

With the ability to assess so many important influences on behaviors, as well as behavior itself, researchers have access to a vast amount of data that can be used to understand the dynamic processes underlying an individual's behavior. These data can then be used to develop new forms of personalized interventions. Moreover, by aggregating data across individuals, computational models of human behavior can be developed and later tested across large samples of individuals and across many complex environments (Spruijt-Metz et al., 2015). Such models require significant volumes of data that are difficult to aggregate across studies given issues with reporting and measures (see the previous section). However, with enhanced data sharing and development of common languages via, for example, taxonomies of BCTs, data across hundreds of studies – at the level of the individual – could be shared and combined to overcome issues regarding limited data.

Systematic reviews (see Chapter 5) represent a useful way of combining data at study level but as the number of publications escalates rapidly, conducting systematic reviews is becoming more burdensome. Fortunately, **text mining** is a technique in which computers can be used to identify automatically the studies most likely to be eligible for a particular review. Different text mining techniques are currently being developed so this area of research methodology remains relatively new but current estimates are that using text mining as opposed to humans can lead to a time-saving of up to 70% (O'Mara-Eves, Thomas, McNaught, Miwa & Ananiadou, 2015).

An ongoing project – called the Human Behaviour Change Project – led by Susan Michie at University College London (UCL) will also make use of computer science by building an artificial intelligence system that will continually scan the behavior change literature and extract relevant information. The aim of this work is to identify which behavior change interventions work and relevant modifying factors such as how personal characteristics, settings and behavior type influence this success. By making use of computer science, the project has the ability to synthesize and analyze volumes of data that are beyond the capabilities and time resources of even the most efficient and best systematic review teams (see also Larsen et al., 2017).

WITH ADAPTIVE DESIGNS

More advanced methodological designs such as Sequential Multiple Assignment Randomized Trials (SMART; Lei, Nahum-Shani, Lynch, Oslin & Murphy, 2012) offer a flexible and more efficient way to test the individual and combined effects of specific techniques relative to using full factorial designs (see Critical Skills Toolkit 3.1). In a SMART design, participants are randomized to different interventions at multiple stages. In the first stage, participants are typically randomized to one of two conditions. At the next stage (e.g., a week later), participants are classified as responders (e.g., their behavior changes) and non-responders (e.g., their behavior does not change and/or they have missed intervention sessions). The responders and non-responders are then separated and randomized again to different interventions or the same intervention. This process is repeated at multiple stages. Consequently, the approach maximizes the likelihood of behavior change (i.e., it should be a more efficacious approach) and it permits the examination of different combinations of techniques. Such adaptive designs offer interesting insights into which intervention techniques should be most effective for whom and in what doses. These insights however should be further tested in standard RCTs.

WITH MORE SOPHISTICATED USE OF STATISTICS

Newer statistical approaches are being developed and used by behavioral scientists to address important questions. For example, rather than simply look at pools of studies collated through systematic review and then via meta-analysis or meta-regression techniques (see Chapters 5 and 6) to infer which individual, specific BCTs are effective, Dusseldorp, van Genugten, van Buuren, Verheijden and van Empelen (2014) used an approach called 'meta-CART' (classification and regression trees) to identify which combinations of BCTs are effective. On the basis of their review, Dusseldorp et al. concluded that combining providing information about the health behavior link and prompt intention formation was the most effective approach while combining feedback on performance without providing instructions was the least effective. Other statistical developments within meta-analyses include the use of meta-analytic path analyses to test specific paths stipulated by theories of health and social behavior using data across multiple studies. This approach has been applied, for example, to validate aspects of the Theory of Planned Behavior (Hagger, Chan, Protogerou & Chatzisarantis, 2016). Outside of meta-analysis, other statistical approaches will continue to evolve too – especially in the area of multilevel modeling. Recent developments include structural equation methods to assess moderation in multilevel models (Preacher, Zhang & Zyphur, 2016).

On a broader level, researchers will be more likely to be required to publish their planned statistical methods within a study protocol in advance of actually conducting the study and to publish datasets alongside their scientific publication. Given that datasets can be analyzed using various statistical methods (e.g., ANOVA, ANCOVA, regression), publishing the protocol in advance minimizes the likelihood of selecting the statistical test that is most likely to produce a significant effect while publishing the dataset allows for the possibility of re-analysis by other research groups. On a related matter, there is a need to standardize approaches to identifying and removing statistical **outliers**, as well as how information relating to these is reported within health behavior change articles.

The trend of behavioral scientists working more and more within multidisciplinary teams will continue. A consequence of this will be that behavioral scientists will become acquainted with, and use, more sophisticated (and complex!) statistical procedures. The Human Behaviour Change Project noted earlier in this chapter, which involves behavioral scientists, provides a good illustration of multidisciplinary working relevant to behavior change that makes use of emerging technology and complex data systems.

WITH CONSIDERATION OF BIOLOGICAL AND NEUROLOGICAL INFLUENCES

There are many kinds of interaction effects that researchers should explore, and undoubtedly will in the years to come. For example, some researchers have examined how environmental influences interact with genetic influences to predict a variety of behaviors. Griffin, Cleveland, Schlomer, Vandenbergh and Feinberg (2015) studied the moderating effect of one such genetic factor: the dopamine receptor D4 gene (DRD4). This gene is a good candidate gene because it is assumed to influence individuals' (especially adolescents') susceptibility to social influence because of the role that dopamine plays in reward sensation. Griffin and colleagues found that although peer pressure for antisocial behaviors (such as cheating or petty theft) had a significant influence on alcohol use, this effect was even stronger in those participants who had the DRD4 genotype, compared to those who did not (for a similar discussion concerning sexual behavior, see Kogan et al., 2014).

BURNING ISSUE BOX 11.2

WHAT DOES SOCIAL NEUROSCIENCE BRING TO HEALTH BEHAVIOR CHANGE?

1. It helps assess processes that are difficult to assess otherwise

At its core, social neuroscience attempts to identify individual differences in social behaviors (including those related to health) by identifying biological differences (typically brain activity or genetic) across individuals. Moreover, the tools of social neuroscience that provide metabolic and electrophysiological images of activity in the brain can provide detailed information, as it emerges, regarding when and where social cognition is occurring.

2. It can provide unique answers to behavioral problems

. . . such as that people who have difficulty in self-regulating their behavior – including levels of physical activity – have a different neurobiology than those who are more successful (Hall et al., 2008).

3. It helps develop more comprehensive theories of social and health behavior and this helps behavioral scientists better predict behavior

By identifying that activity in specific brain regions correlate with behavior, over and above self-report measures (e.g., Falk, Berkman, Whalen & Lieberman, 2011; Reuter, Frenzel, Walter, Markett & Montag, 2011), social neuroscience can help develop more comprehensive models and theories of behavior. These models would incorporate constructs reflecting neural activity alongside constructs available to introspection such as an individual's intentions to perform a particular behavior. As measures of neural activity in specific regions of the brain can explain unique variance in behavior, theories that incorporate neural activity should lead to better, more reliable predictions of how individuals or groups are likely to behave.

4. It helps develop effective behavior change interventions

By identifying that activity in specific regions of the brain are linked to changes in health behavior, work by researchers such as Falk (Falk, Berkman, Harrison, Mann & Lieberman, 2010; Falk et al., 2011) could help lead to the development of more effective behavior change interventions. Specifically, by identifying health-based messages, or other types of interventions, that are more likely to increase activity in regions of the brain linked to positive changes in health behavior (e.g., regions of the medial prefrontal cortex) one could be more confident that these interventions are likely to lead to actual health behavior change.

SUMMARY

In this chapter we highlighted some key issues for further research to tackle. We are at a stage at which health behavior change research is rapidly accelerating in an attempt to catch up with more traditional sciences, as well as to address important health-related challenges. However, getting the discipline 'in-shape' through better reporting, methods, analyses and ultimately theories and techniques is critical – as is the need to consider broader aspects of the intervention that could influence success such as who delivered it and how. We have noted that by working with computer scientists, as well as those with expertise in relation to methods, statistics, the environment, genetics and neuroscience, behavioral scientists are well positioned to address these issues and to make even more important contributions to health- and social-related challenges. Time will tell which directions bear most fruit but undeniably, the future is exciting.

FURTHER READING

Collins, L.M., Baker, T.B., Mermelstein, R.J., Piper, M.E., Jorenby, D.E., Smith, S.S., Christiansen, B.A., Schlam, T.R., Cook, J.W. & Fiore, M.C. (2011). The multiphase optimization strategy for engineering effective tobacco use interventions. *Annals of Behavioral Medicine, 41*, 208–226. This paper introduces another adaptive design with some overlap with SMART designs.

Dombrowski, S.U., O'Carroll, R.E. & Williams, B. (2016). Form of delivery as a key 'active ingredient' in behaviour change interventions. *British Journal of Health Psychology, 21*, 733–740. Argues for the importance of form of delivery (defined as how the intervention is delivered) within behavior change interventions.

Dusseldorp, E., van Genugten, L., van Buuren, S., Verheijden, M.W. & van Empelen, P. (2014). Combinations of techniques that effectively change health behavior: evidence from Meta-CART analysis. *Health Psychology, 33*, 1530–1540. Differs from similar reviews that focus on identifying single effective behavior change techniques, by applying a different statistical approach to detect effective *combinations* of behavior change techniques for healthy eating and physical activity.

Ogden, J. (2016). Theories, timing and choice of audience: some key tensions in health psychology and a response to commentaries on Ogden (2016). *Health Psychology Review, 10*, 274–276. Offers an interesting counter-position to the movement towards standardized approaches such as behavior change techniques and taxonomies.

GLOSSARY

CONSORT (Consolidated Standards of Reporting Trials): a set of reporting guidelines for those wishing to transparently report key methodological details from randomized controlled trials. These guidelines have since been extended for other types of studies such as pilot trials.

Mobile sensing: an approach to gathering and presenting data from sensors internal to smartphones such as accelerometers (that could be used to track physical activity) and GPS (to track location).

Outliers: data points that differ substantially from other data points within the dataset and can unduly influence the results from a study.

PRISMA (Preferred Reporting Items for Systematic Reviews and Meta-Analyses): a set of reporting guidelines for those wishing to transparently report key methodological details from systematic reviews and meta-analyses of randomized controlled trials or other studies testing interventions.

Text mining: a form of computer science used to identify patterns in text, extract key information and support decision-making (e.g., whether to include or exclude a particular study for a systematic review).

REFERENCES

Carle, A.C., Riley, W., Hays, R.D. & Cella, D. (2015). Confirmatory factor analysis of the Patient Reported Outcomes Measurement Information System (PROMIS) adult domain framework using item response theory scores. *Medical Care, 53,* 894–900.

Conner, M. & Higgins, A.R. (2010). Long-term effects of implementation intentions on prevention of smoking uptake among adolescents: a cluster randomized controlled trial. *Health Psychology, 29,* 529–538.

Dombrowski, S.U., O'Carroll, R.E. & Williams, B. (2016). Form of delivery as a key 'active ingredient' in behaviour change interventions. *British Journal of Health Psychology, 21,* 733–740.

Dusseldorp, E., van Genugten, L., van Buuren, S., Verheijden, M.W. & van Empelen, P. (2014). Combinations of techniques that effectively change health behavior: evidence from Meta-CART analysis. *Health Psychology, 33,* 1530–1540.

Falk, E.B., Berkman, E.T., Harrison, B., Mann, T. & Lieberman, M.D. (2010). Predicting persuasion-induced behavior change from the brain. *Journal of Neuroscience, 30,* 8421–8424.

Falk, E.B., Berkman, E.T., Whalen, D. & Lieberman, M.D. (2011). Neural activity during health messaging predicts reductions in smoking above and beyond self-report. *Health Psychology, 30,* 177–185.

Fishbein, M., Triandis, H.C., Kanfer, F.H., Becker, M., Middlestadt, S.E. & Eichler, A. (2001). Factors influencing behaviour and behaviour change. In A. Baum, T.A. Revenson & J.E. Singer (Eds.), *Handbook of Health Psychology* (pp. 3–17). Mahwah, NJ: Lawrence Erlbaum Associates.

Griffin, A.M., Cleveland, H.H., Schlomer, G.L., Vandenbergh, D.J. & Feinberg, M.E. (2015). Differential susceptibility: the genetic moderation of peer pressure on alcohol use. *Journal of Youth and Adolescence, 44*(10), 1841–1853.

Hagger, M.S., Chan, D.K.C., Protogerou, C. & Chatzisarantis, N.L.D. (2016). Using meta-analytic path analysis to test theoretical predictions in health behavior: an illustration based on meta-analyses of the theory of planned behavior. *Preventive Medicine, 89,* 154–161.

Hall, P.A., Elias, L.J., Fong, G.T., Harrison, A.H., Borowsky, R. & Sarty, G.E. (2008). A social neuroscience perspective on physical activity. *Journal of Sport & Exercise Psychology, 30,* 432–449.

Kogan, S.M., Lei, M.K., Beach, S.R., Brody, G.H., Windle, M., Lee, S., MacKillop, J. & Chen, Y.F. (2014). Dopamine receptor gene D4 polymorphisms and early sexual onset: gender and environmental moderation in a sample of African-American youth. *Journal of Adolescent Health, 55*(2), 235–240.

Larsen, K.R., Michie, S., Hekler, E.B., Gibson, B., Spruijt-Metz, D., Ahern, D., Cole-Lewis, H., Ellis, R.J., Hesse, B., Moser, R.P. & Yi, J. (2017). Behavior change interventions: the potential of ontologies for advancing science and practice. *Journal of Behavioral Medicine, 40,* 6–22.

Lei, H., Nahum-Shani, I., Lynch, K., Oslin, D. & Murphy, S.A. (2012). A 'SMART' design for building individualized treatment sequences. *Annual Review of Clinical Psychology, 8,* 21–48.

Michie, S., Hyder, N., Walia, A. & West, R. (2011). Development of a taxonomy of behaviour change techniques used in individual behavioural support for smoking cessation. *Addictive Behaviors, 36,* 315–319.

Michie, S., Richardson, M., Johnston, M., Abraham, C., Francis, J., Hardeman, W., Eccles, M.P., Cane, J. & Wood, C.E. (2013). The behavior change technique taxonomy (v1) of 93 hierarchically clustered techniques: building an international consensus for the reporting of behavior change interventions. *Annals of Behavioral Medicine, 46,* 81–95.

Moser, R.P., Hesse, B.W., Shaikh, A.R., Courtney, P., Morgan, G. et al. (2011). Grid-enabled measures: using Science 2.0 to standardize measures and share data. *American Journal of Preventive Medicine, 40*(5), S134–143.

Ogden, J. (2016). Theories, timing and choice of audience: some key tensions in health psychology and a response to commentaries on Ogden (2016). *Health Psychology Review, 10,* 274–276.

O'Mara-Eves, A., Thomas, J., McNaught, J., Miwa, M. & Ananiadou, S. (2015). Using text mining for study identification in systematic reviews: a systematic review of current approaches. *Systematic Reviews*, 4, 5.

Preacher, K.J., Zhang, Z. & Zyphur, M.J. (2016). Multilevel structural equation models for assessing moderation within and across levels of analysis. *Psychological Methods*, 21, 189–205.

Prestwich, A., Kellar, I., Conner, M., Lawton, R., Gardner, P. & Turgut, L. (2016). Does changing social influence engender changes in alcohol intake? A meta-analysis. *Journal of Consulting and Clinical Psychology*, 84, 845–860.

Prestwich, A., Kellar, I., Parker, R., MacRae, S., Learmonth, M., Sykes, B., Taylor, N. & Castle, H. (2014a). How can self-efficacy be increased? Meta-analysis of dietary interventions. *Health Psychology Review*, 8, 270–285.

Prestwich, A., Moore, S., Kotze, A., Budworth, L., Lawton, R. & Kellar, I. (2017). How can smoking cessation be induced before surgery? A systematic review and meta-analysis of behaviour change techniques and other intervention characteristics. *Frontiers in Psychology*, 8, 915.

Prestwich, A., Sniehotta, F.F., Whittington, C., Dombrowski, S.U., Rogers, L. & Michie, S. (2014b). Does theory influence the effectiveness of health behavior interventions? Meta-analysis. *Health Psychology*, 33, 465–474.

Prestwich, A., Webb, T.L. & Conner, M. (2015). Using theory to develop and test interventions to promote changes in health behaviour: evidence, issues and recommendations. *Current Opinion in Psychology*, 5, 1–5.

Reuter, M., Frenzel, C., Walter, N.T., Markett, S. & Montag, C. (2011). Investigating the genetic basis of altruism: the role of the COMT Val158Met polymorphism. *Social Cognitive and Affective Neuroscience*, 6, 662–668.

Sheeran, P., Klein, W.M. & Rothman, A.J. (2017). Health behavior change: moving from observation to intervention. *Annual Review of Psychology*, 68, 573–600.

Spruijt-Metz, D., Hekler, E., Saranummi, N., Intille, S., Korhonen, I., Nilsen, W., Rivera, D.E., Spring, B., Michie, S., Asch, D.A., Sanna, A., Salcedo, V.T., Kukafka, R. & Pavel, M. (2015). Building new computational models to support health behaviour change and maintenance: new opportunities in behavioral research. *Translational Behavioral Medicine*, 5, 335–346.

Strack, F. & Deutsch, R. (2004). Reflective and impulsive determinants of social behavior. *Personality and Social Psychology Review*, 8, 220–247.

Webb, T.L., Joseph, J., Yardley, L. & Michie, S. (2010) Using the internet to promote health behavior change: a systematic review and meta-analysis of the impact of theoretical basis, use of behavior change techniques, and mode of delivery on efficacy. *Journal of Medical Internet Research*, 12, e4.

Wilson, K., Senay, I., Durantini, M., Sánchez, F., Hennessy, M., Spring, B. & Albarracín, D. (2015). When it comes to lifestyle recommendations, more is sometimes less: a meta-analysis of theoretical assumptions underlying the effectiveness of interventions promoting multiple behavior domain change. *Psychological Bulletin*, 141, 474–509.

Wood, C.E., Richardson, M., Johnston, M., Abraham, C., Francis, J., Hardeman, W. & Michie, S. (2015). Applying the behaviour change technique (BCT) taxonomy v1: a study of coder training. *Translational Behavioral Medicine*, 5, 134–148.

INDEX

Bold indicates table references; italic indicates figure references.